# Italic Calligraphy

## From Learning the Fundamentals to Dancing with Your Pen

FIREFLY BOOKS

A FIREFLY BOOK

Published by Firefly Books Ltd. 2026

First printing

**Library of Congress Control Number:** 2026942054

**Library and Archives Canada Cataloguing in Publication**
Title: Italic calligraphy : from learning the fundamentals to dancing with your pen / Kathie McIlvride.
Names: McIlvride, Kathie, author.
Identifiers: Canadiana 20260187623 | ISBN 9780228105961 (softcover)
Subjects: LCSH: Calligraphy—Technique. | LCSH: Writing, Italic—Handbooks, manuals, etc.
Classification: LCC Z43 .M35 2026 | DDC 744.4/2—dc23

Published in the United States by
Firefly Books (U.S.) Inc.
P.O. Box 1338, Ellicott Station
Buffalo, New York 14205

Published in Canada by
Firefly Books Ltd.
50 Staples Avenue, Unit 1
Richmond Hill, Ontario L4B 0A7

Cover and interior design: Hartley Millson

Printed in China | E

We gratefully acknowledge the financial support of the Government of Canada for our publishing program.

THIS BOOK IS
DEDICATED TO BRIAN WHO
LOVES ME EVEN THOUGH
HE CAN'T READ MY

writing

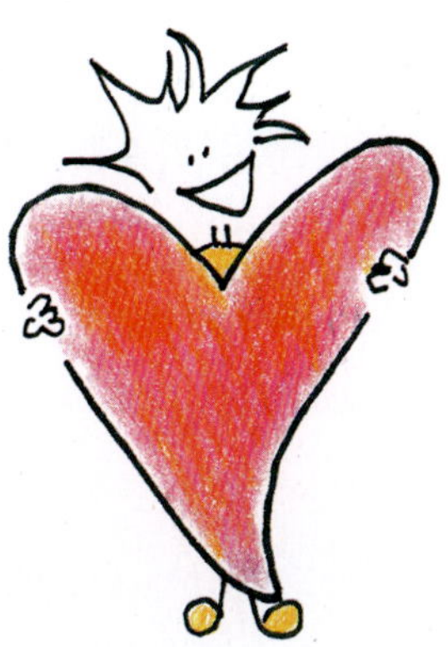

it is fun to have fun but you have to know how

Dr. Seuss

# *Italic*
# Calligraphy

# Table of Contents



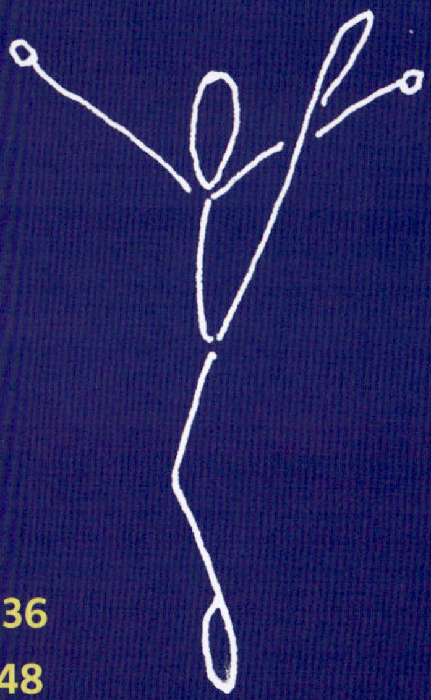

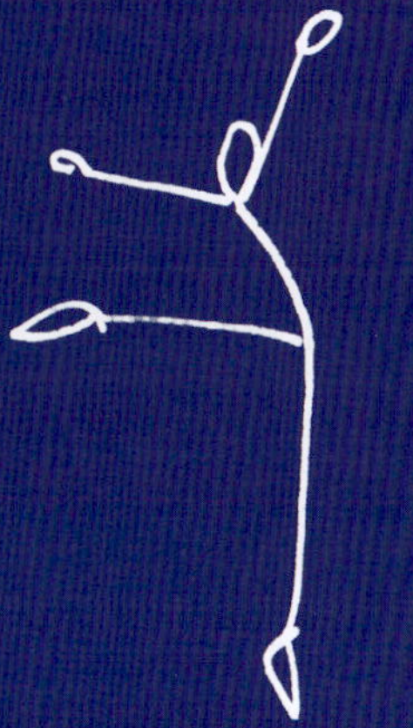

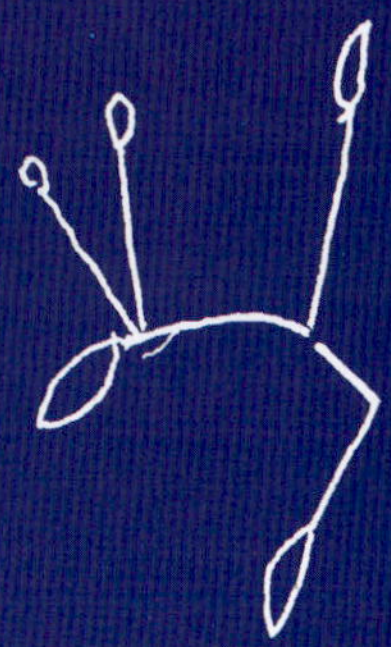

# Preface

**THIS BOOK IS ABOUT THE CRAFT AND THE ART OF** Italic calligraphy.

The *Oxford English Dictionary* defines "craft" as "an activity involving a special skill at making things with your hands." As a verb it is "to make or produce with care, skill or ingenuity." From the same dictionary, the word "art" is defined as "the expression or application of human creative skill and imagination typically in a visual form to be appreciated for its beauty and/or emotional power."

My objective in writing this book is to teach you how to develop the skill of Italic calligraphy to be enjoyed in itself, but also to show you how you can use it to create art.

Now a few words on how I got here. When I was a little girl, I received a large hardcover book as a gift. It was magical to me. I suppose I could read by then, but my focus was not the story (as I was not much of a reader) but rather the letters that filled the first page. I was enthralled and immediately began copying from the book letter-for-letter and word-for-word, never questioning what I was writing. I was intrigued and intent, taking delight in the simple activity of copying the letters. What they said was irrelevant.

Years later, when I took out my first fountain pen, holding it poised over my paper as I sat in a classroom awaiting instruction, I felt giddy with anticipation. I remember little else of that very first calligraphic experience other than the brown corduroys my teacher wore as she stood beside me making far superior versions of the scratches that crossed my page. Yet with this limited exposure (having already missed a few sessions), I went on, puffed up with ambition, to design my own wedding invitations! Oh boy ...

This was in the early '80s, when Italic calligraphy had a surge in popularity in North America. I loved its elegant look and the appeal of calligraphy, and so I wanted to be able to do it. What better place to start than with my own wedding invitations?

I felt confident in this endeavor and proceeded to produce the ugliest wedding invitations imaginable, complete with a spelling mistake, which my future mother-in-law pointed out to my future husband, but only after they had all been printed and sent out!

Yet surprisingly my desire to letter continued. I threw out those humiliating miscreants (invitations, not in-laws), carried on seeking direction and finally found my way through books, teachers and guilds. My path has taken me across Canada, from city to city and province to province, with a foray here and there across country borders to learn from expert calligraphers at various conferences and workshops.

From the time my daughter was born I began teaching Italic calligraphy. She is now in her 40s (which is hard to believe), and over these many years I have learned more about Italic, and what you can do with it — as well as what you should not do.

When I say Italic calligraphy, I am referring to a specific script created during the Italian Renaissance to accommodate the need for faster and more graceful writing and that uses thick and thin strokes that imitate the look of twisted ribbon. The word "calligraphy" comes from the Greek words *kallos* (meaning "beauty") and *graphein* (meaning "to write") — in other words, "beautiful writing."

In addition to teaching courses and workshops on Italic and other calligraphy styles, I've taken on many of the traditional types of commissions throughout my career. Over the years I have designed cards for card companies in Canada and the U.S., lettered many certificates and created wedding invitations and custom logos. I've also had the honor of making a memorial book for Kelvin High School in Winnipeg, which listed all the students who had served during World War II, and I was even commissioned to create a prop for a movie called *A Haunting in Connecticut*. My task for that project was to write and draw scratches and symbols akin to what a truly mad scientist might make in his journal!

From my own experience, I know that calligraphy can be learned. Anyone can create wonderful letters. You need only the desire to learn, a few supplies and good instruction. Calligraphy combines proficiency with your tools and an intimate knowledge of the form and flow of letters. With careful practice you will achieve this skill, but it is important to realize that there are no shortcuts. Practice is key.

One of my favorite things to do is to create workshops where I can teach others my love of calligraphy in the hopes that they can discover theirs. I am delighted to have written this book as it brings together the various workshops I have created over many years. I look forward to guiding you on how to create the traditional Italic script and then how to make it dance with more and more freedom. Here's how we'll approach it in this book:

**Section One** covers every detail I have gathered up during my many years of teaching Italic calligraphy. I have broken down the details with the hope that it all is very easy to understand. Once you begin, each step will build on the previous one. We will cover basic strokes and shapes, turning these into letters and, with practice, gaining the skills to create well-lettered sentences with proper spacing. You will also learn how to make your own template to copy from based on the nib width of your writing tools.

**Section Two** will expand on what you learned in the first section, teaching you additional skills to add character and style to your Italic calligraphy, such as flourishes, pen manipulation, cursive elements and much more.

**Section Three** will help you break down the boundaries of traditional calligraphy, creating letters and words that push the limits and become vibrant dancing partners in play. This section will guide you on gestural strokes, composition and different tools and how they can all come together to create something beautiful and uniquely yours.

Throughout, you will find exercises to practice and fun projects that will inspire your journey with Italic calligraphy. Let's begin!

# A (very) Brief History of Italic: How the Italic Script Emerged

## FROM ROMAN TO ITALIC LETTERING

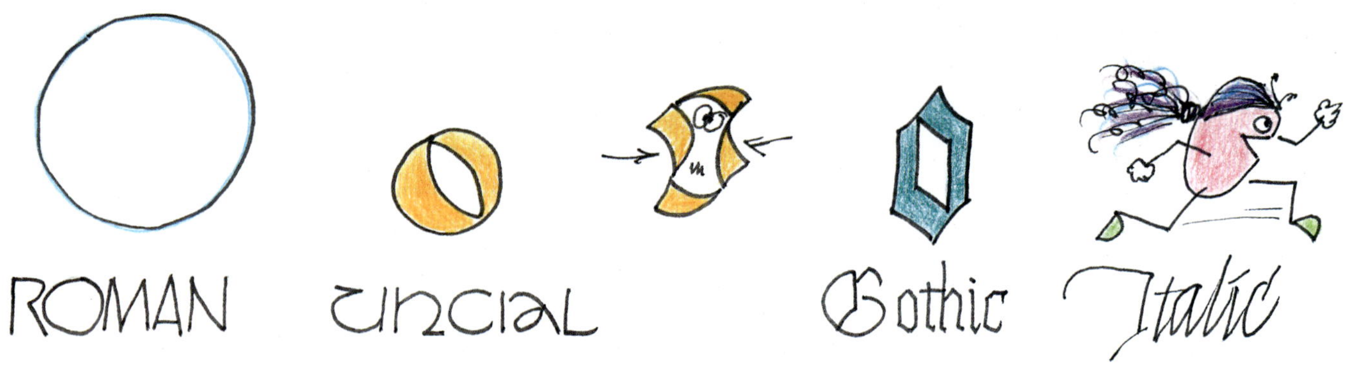


### ROMAN

The capital letters that we learned as children are based on the Roman alphabet of the 6th century BCE. Those stately letters were painted first and then chiseled. I can't imagine making a spelling mistake!

The Roman alphabet featured only capital letters and just 23 of them (no *J*, *U* or *W*).

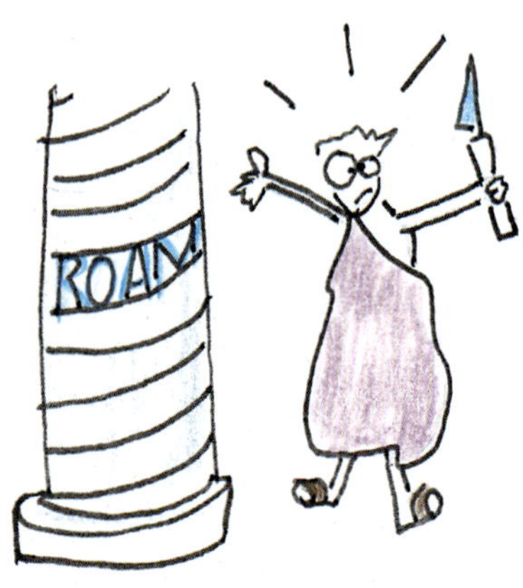

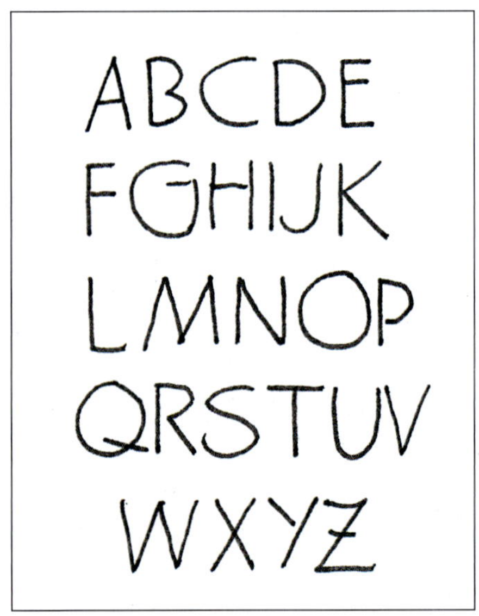


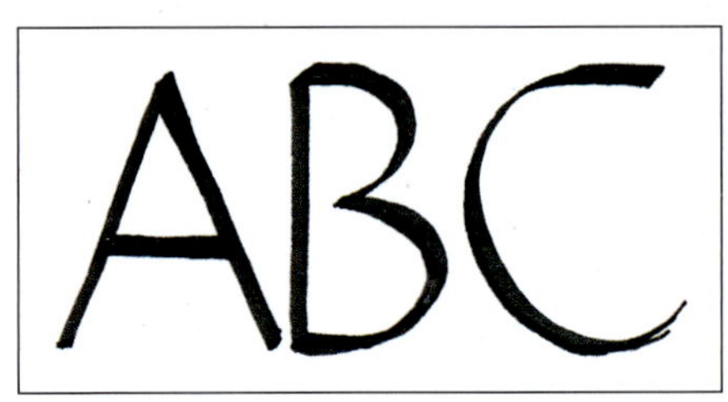

## UNCIAL

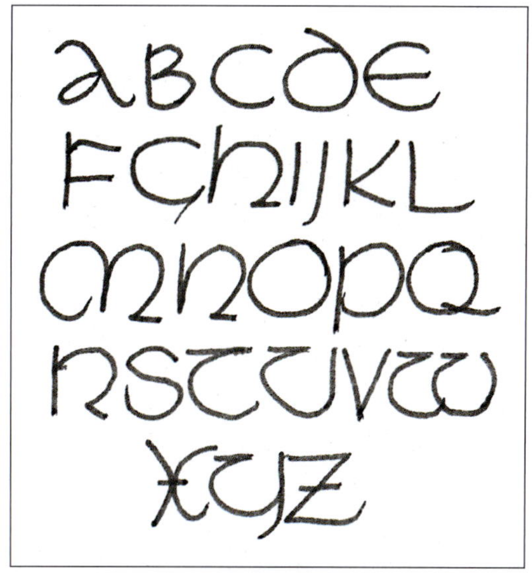


Pronounced "un'see-ul" or "un'-shul," this short, round style emerged from the Roman letters. It was still made of only capitals. The letters were originally created using a reed or quill (metal nibs replaced quills and reeds by the 1700s). Though this style of calligraphy is still in use today, it was most prominent from the 3rd to 8th centuries CE.

Originally manuscripts were written on vellum (calf's skin) or parchment (goat's or sheep's skin). However, one of the earliest writing surfaces was papyrus, which was made from the papyrus plant found in northern Africa. (The earliest known roll of papyrus was discovered in a tomb in Saqqara, Egypt, and dated from 2900 BCE.)

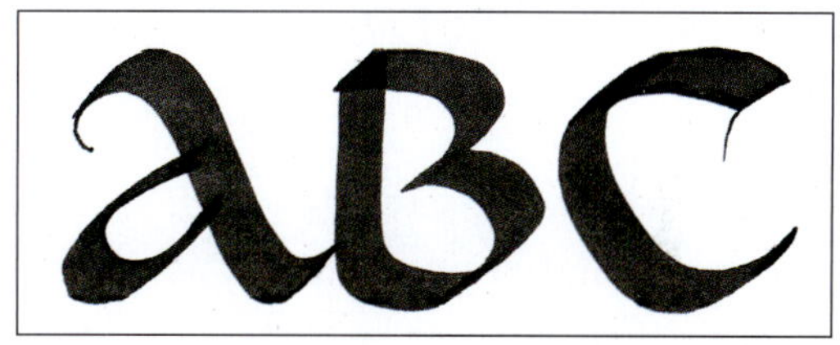


## GOTHIC SCRIPT OR BLACKLETTER

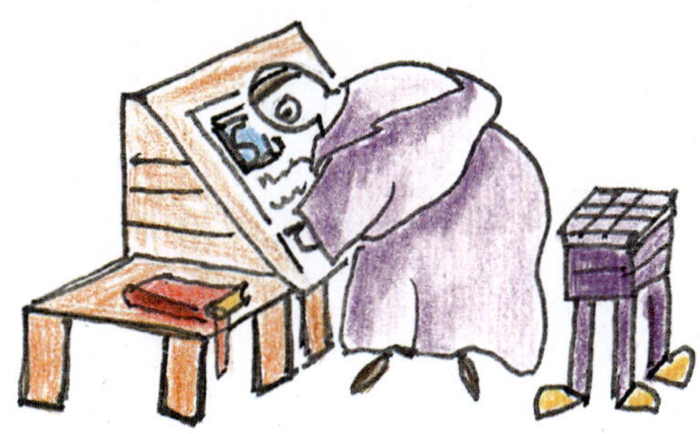

Gothic script, which was a derogatory way of describing the pointy architecture of its day, took less space than Uncial but borrowed Uncial letters for its capitals. Gothic was dominant between the 12th and 15th centuries CE. It's also known as Blackletter, Old English and Textura. There are a few variations of this script.

Even though Gothic letters take up less space than Uncial, this type of calligraphy requires many pen lifts to create the letters, so whatever money was made up for in saving space on expensive vellum was lost in time.

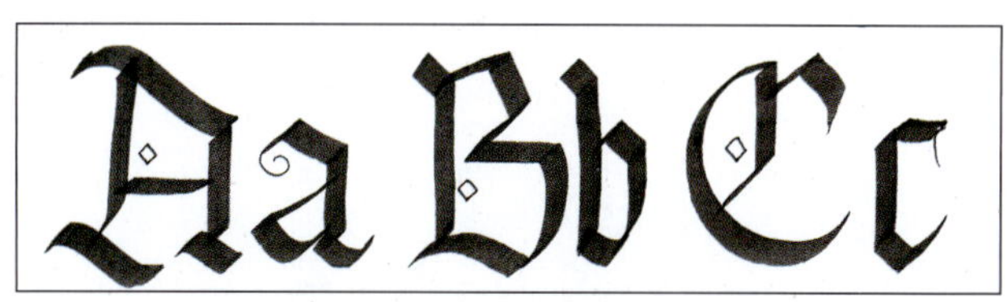


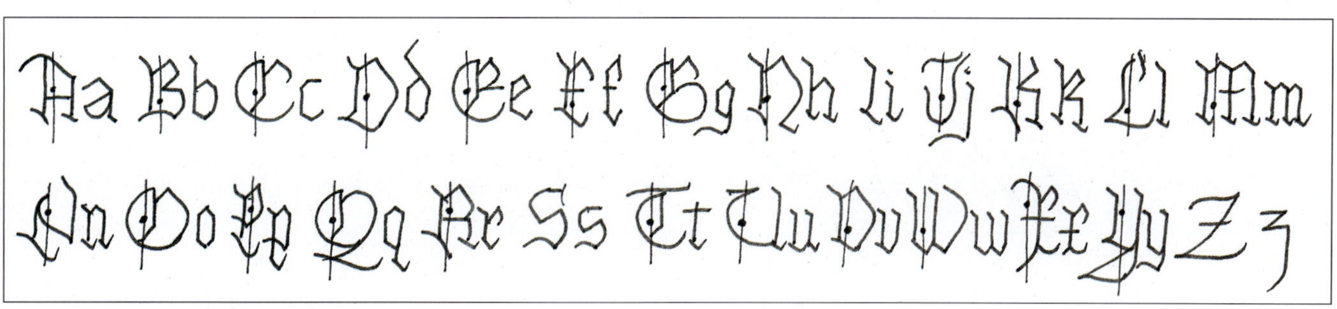

## ITALIC

Italic developed during the Italian Renaissance, about 1500 CE. Compared to Gothic script, which many found laborious and difficult to read, Italic required fewer pen lifts, and with the forward-leaning angle of the letters, it allowed for speedier writing.

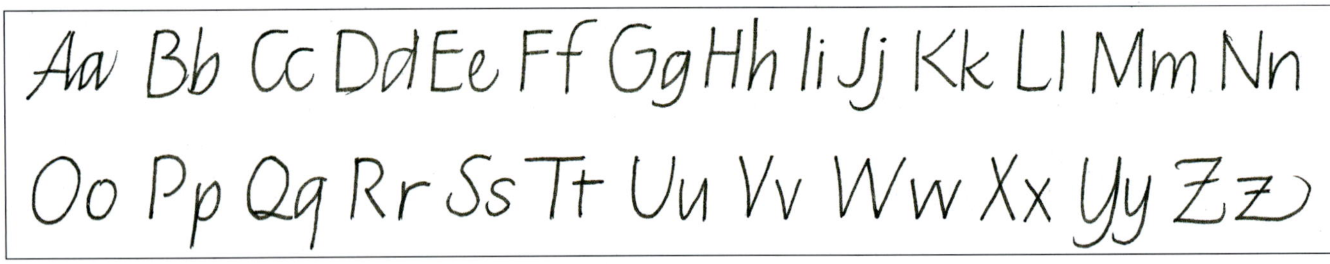


The enticement of rhythm when it comes to calligraphy is best seen in the Italic script. The movement of the upstrokes and downstrokes feels comparable to a dance with the pen, with upbeats and downbeats, leaps and landings.

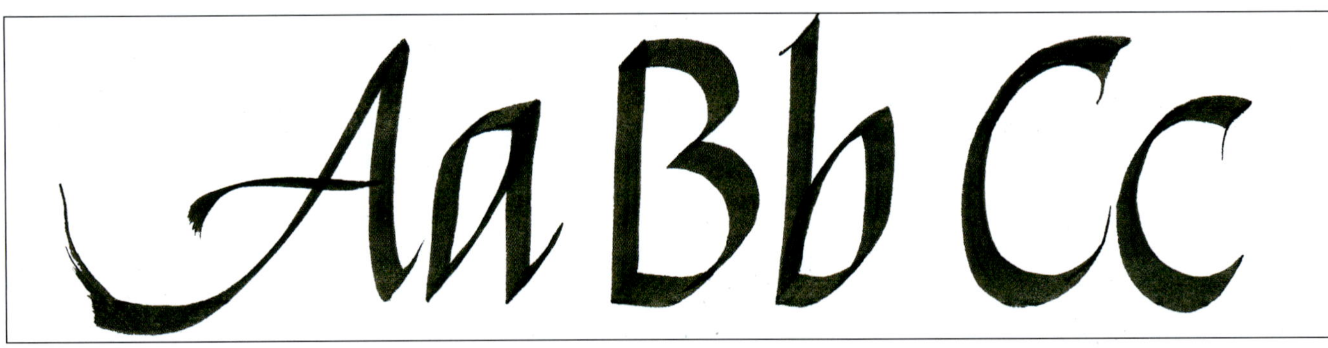


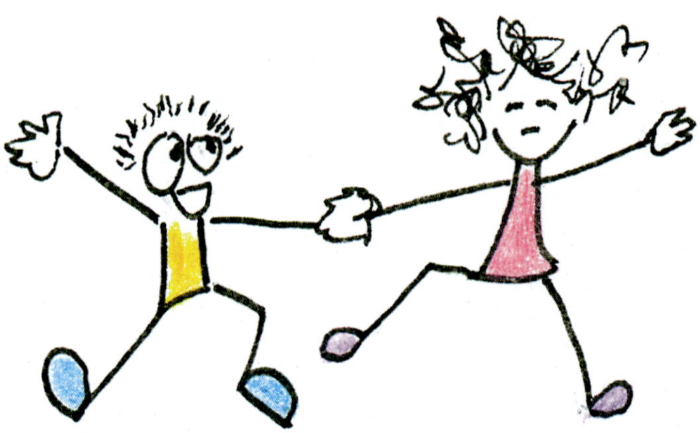

# Section 1

In Section One, the focus is on learning the traditional Italic script, which is foundational to exploring the vast potential of the world of Italic calligraphy. You will learn about what tools and paper to use, how to set up your work area, how to hold a pen and how the letters are created. This will include the study of the order of strokes in creating letters, pen angle, letter heights and many other key components to create this elegant script.

# Getting Started

## Tools & Supplies

For Section One we require just a few supplies (note: the projects at the end of the chapter will require a few more and each section will cover new tools as we go along):

- **Pen (no smaller than ⅛" or 3.8 mm)**
- **Paper**
- **Pencil**
- **Black fine-liner marker (I use a Sakura Pigma Micron, size 05)**
- **Eraser**
- **Ruler**
- **Scissors**
- **Colored pencils**

### PENS AND CALLIGRAPHY MARKERS

When I used to teach beginners in an Italic calligraphy class, I always included calligraphy markers on the supply list. This was for several reasons: they are inexpensive, they work on most paper and they are easy to use.

However, lately I have found the markers I once suggested are now less than satisfactory. The ones I once found reliable will often not touch down on the paper with both sides of the nib. This is frustrating for anyone but especially for the beginner, who will blame themselves for any faults. The nibs of markers will also get mushy over time, or they will dry up and become useless.

So I now recommend the Pilot Parallel Pen. It is a calligraphy pen with a strong metal nib that will not get mushy, like markers. It does not require dipping as it is designed to use an ink cartridge, like a fountain pen. When the cartridges run out you can buy more to replace them. However, when this happens to me, I continue to use them by dipping them into ink rather than purchasing more cartridges. They work well as dip pens.

With better paper, I feel it is the ideal tool for beginners and more advanced calligraphers alike. The pens are more expensive but will last forever. There are eight sizes plus left-handed pens to choose from. I recommend the green cap (⅛-inch/3.8 mm) nib size. Most of the exercises throughout this book will use a ⅛-inch nib size.

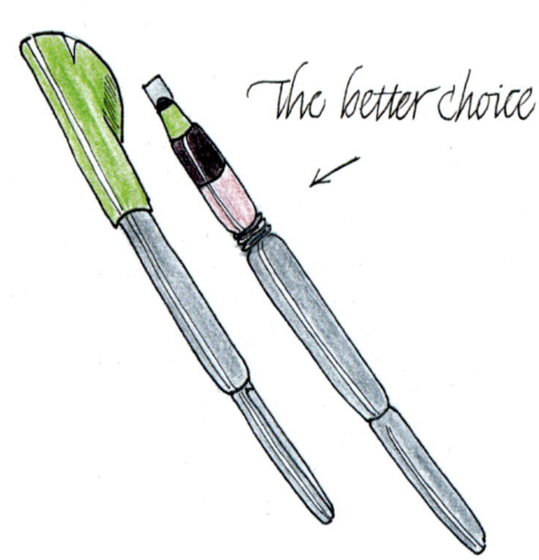

## PAPER

Decent paper is imperative for happy results. An all-purpose sketchbook or a pen and ink pad both work well and hold ink nicely if you're using a Pilot Parallel Pen. Aim for 9 inches by 12 inches (22.86 cm by 30.48 cm) or so. Ideally the sketchbook should lie open flat.

Rhodia is a good brand for practice paper. They offer a wide variety of pads that I find hold ink nicely. I have to order these online, but they are readily available from a variety of online retailers. Your local art store may carry them, too. We will discuss other papers in the later sections as well as other recommended supplies at the back of the book.

## DIFFERENT QUALITY, DIFFERENT RESULTS

The quality of the writing tools and the paper can make a huge difference. For example, cheap calligraphy markers can get mushy (as I mentioned), leaving a mark that can be very discouraging for the one using them, especially the beginner just getting into calligraphy. Cheap paper may bleed, leaving the letters with feathering ink that might not be the look you were hoping for.

To the right, I've created samples to show how the quality of the materials can affect the results. I've chosen three different writing tools and three different papers:

1. Cheap calligraphy marker
2. More-expensive calligraphy marker
3. Pilot Parallel Pen (with a metal nib)

- **A.** Printer paper
- **B.** Rhodia paper
- **C.** Arches 140 lb. hot-pressed watercolor paper

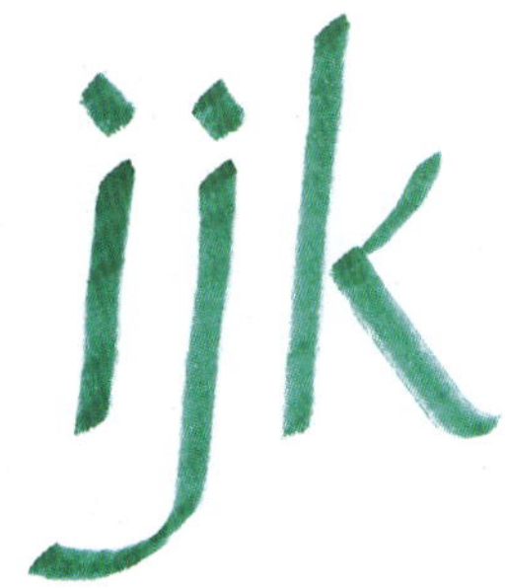


**1A:** Cheap calligraphy marker on printer paper

*Comments:* There are no sharp lines

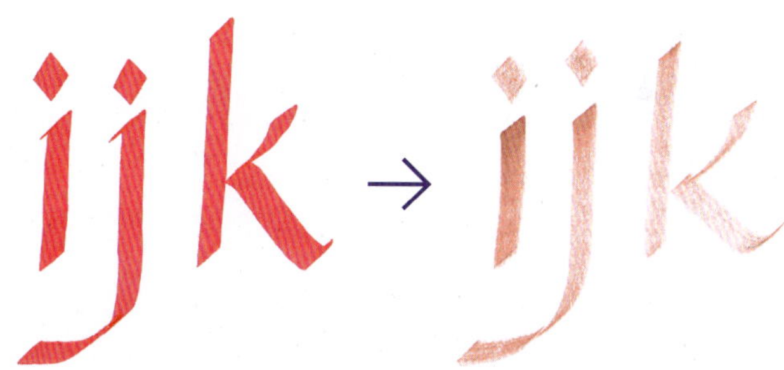


**2A:** More-expensive calligraphy marker on printer paper

*Comments:* You get sharper lines, but they will lose their ink, resulting in more faded letters

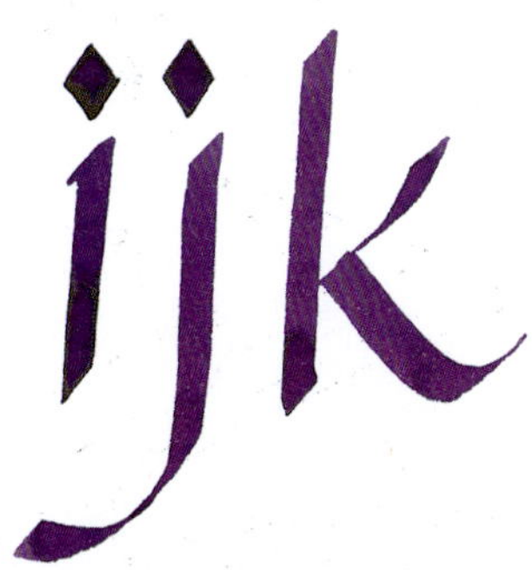


**3B:** Pilot Parallel Pen on Rhodia paper

*Comments:* You get crisper lines because of the metal nib and decent-quality paper

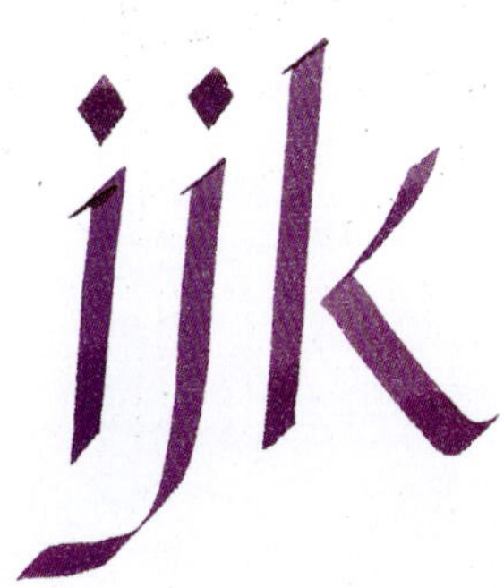


**3C:** Pilot Parallel Pen on Arches 140 lb. hot-pressed watercolor paper

*Comments:* These are the crispest lines because of the metal nib and the good-quality watercolor paper

# *Setting Up*

One of the great things about calligraphy is that it can be practiced wherever you have access to paper and writing tools, but if you're going to be writing for long stretches, you want to take care of your neck, shoulders and back. There are a few elements to keep in mind as you build your ideal setup.

> **A Note on Posture**
>
> **The key to being able to practice calligraphy as long as you would like is strong posture. When you're seated, be sure to have your feet on the floor facing forward, your back straight and your writing surface raised at an angle to avoid neck strain. Always listen to your body — your neck, shoulders, upper and lower back, hips and legs. Muscle fatigue is not to be ignored. Be sure to stretch and take a break. Perhaps take it a bit at a time, building up to the amount of time you'd like to work.**

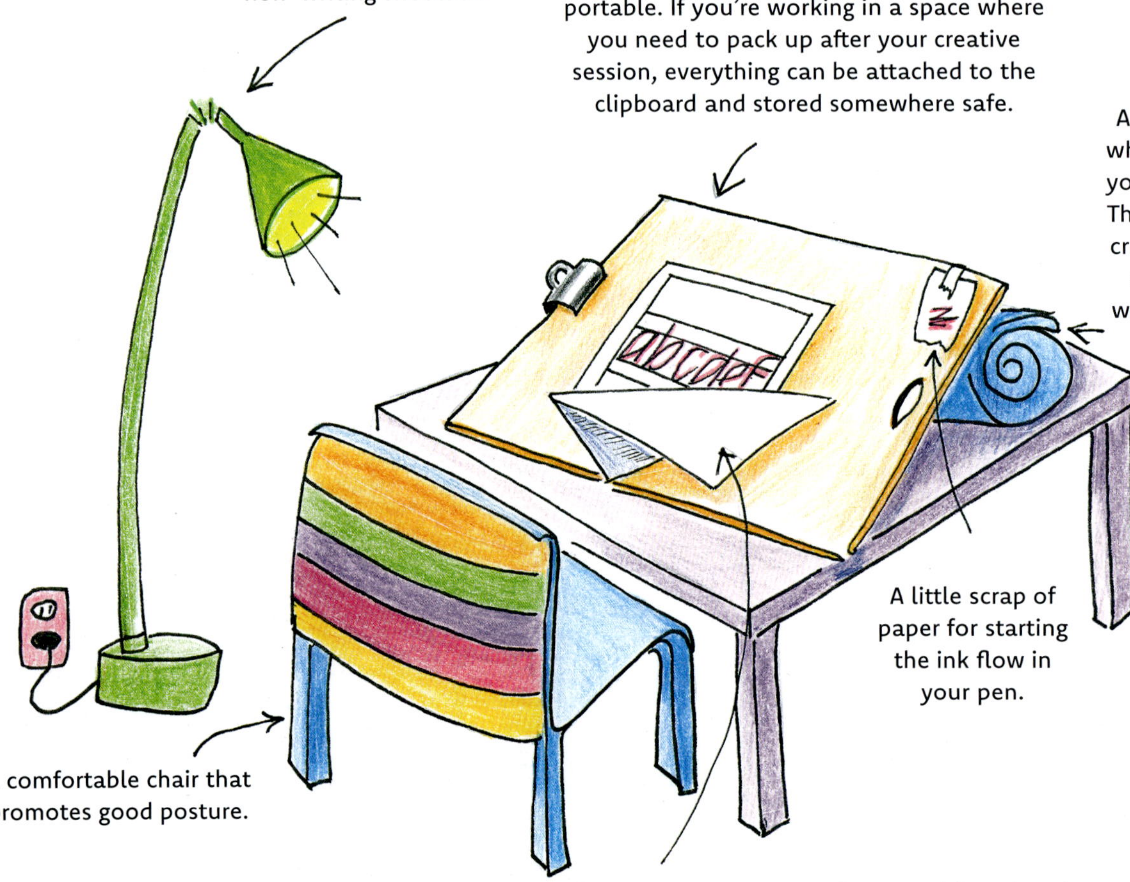

# Chapter 1

# Understanding Letter Spacing

The key to making letters that appear attractive and proportional is to use templates that determine the size of the letters, including their ascenders (the upward vertical strokes or stems) and descenders (downward vertical strokes). Spacing between letters and strokes is also an important skill to learn, one that will come with diligent practice and training your eyes.

## The Crucial Nib Width

The nib width is so named because it is the width of your nib. The nib width (or NW) allows you to find the proper proportions of the letters you wish to create by using ratios. The Italic script (or "hand") is a tall, elegant script requiring more height than others.

Let's find your nib width:

1. On a blank piece of paper, measure down 4 inches from the top edge on the far left and mark with a pencil. Repeat on the far right. Draw a line with your pencil connecting the two marks. You have just created your baseline, the line on which small letter bodies will sit.

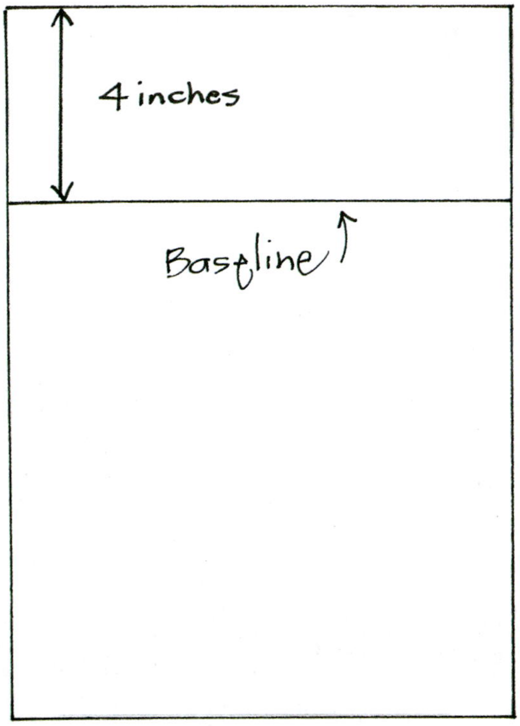

2. With your calligraphy pen held perpendicular to the baseline, draw the nib to the right to create a square, making sure the left side of the pen's nib never leaves the baseline you have drawn. The box you have created is a nib width. Go along the same line and slowly, carefully create a few more for practice. It will look like boxes on a line.

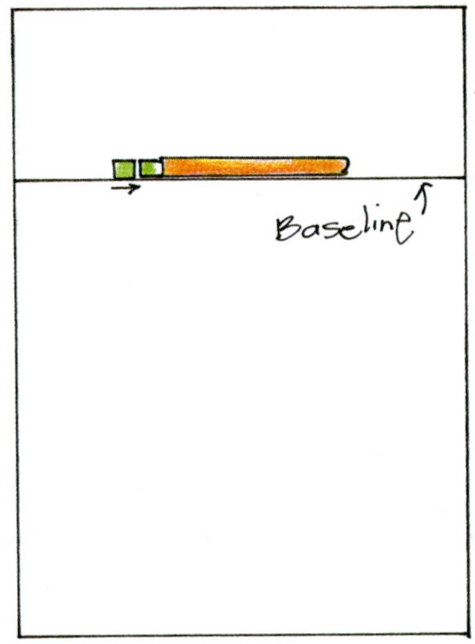


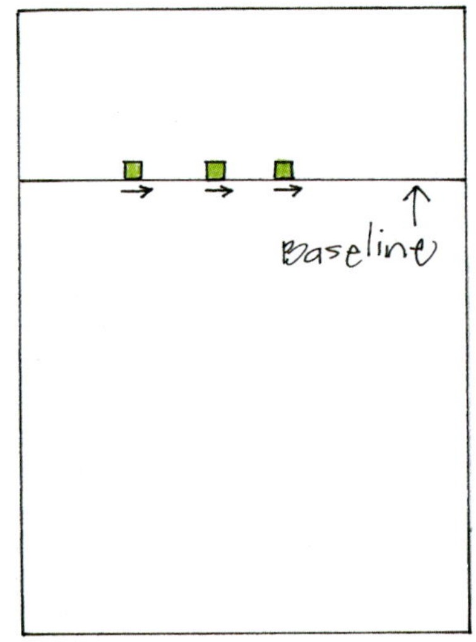


3. Now that you understand how to make a nib width, try to imagine that each of these boxes is filled with very fragile glasses. With that in mind, carefully "pile" one box on top of the box on the baseline. Make sure it's not overlapping or there's no space between the boxes — we don't want that glass to break. Continue to add boxes until the pile is five nib widths high.

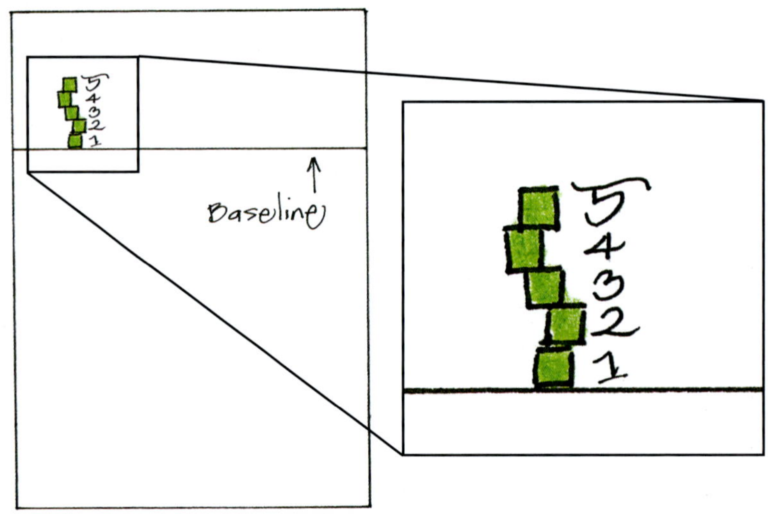


4. After stacking the five boxes of glasses ever so carefully, make a mark with your pencil at the top of the pile. Measure from the top of the paper down to the top of your pile. Use that measurement for the right side and mark it with a pencil. Draw a line across. You have just created the waistline, the line under which most small letter bodies will sit.

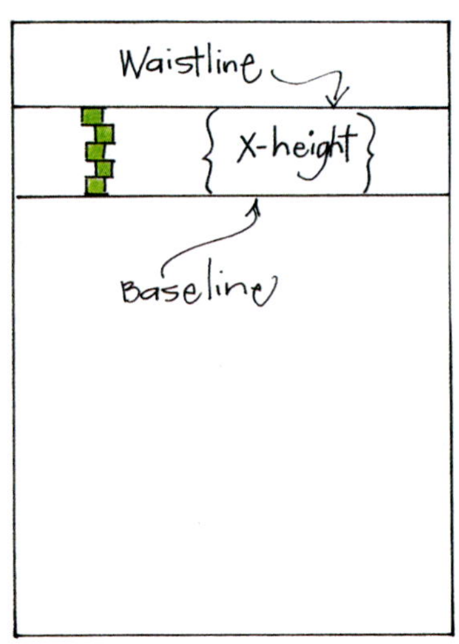


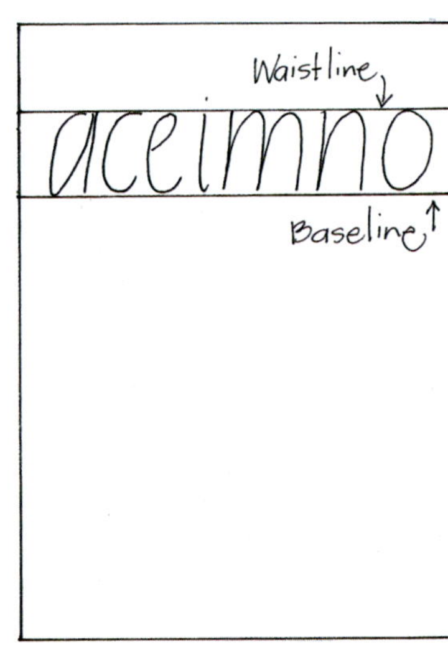


The X-height encases all small letters that don't require ascenders or descenders.

The area/space between the waistline and baseline is called the "X-height," which is the height of the letter *x* and the bodies of many of the small letters (also called "minuscules"). The ascenders and descenders extend above and below the X-height.

# Accommodating Ascenders & Descenders

In order to create space for ascenders and descenders there is the need for more careful box piling. On top of the five boxes that you have already gently placed, stack three more nib widths with your calligraphy pen. Measure from the top of the page down to the topmost box and mark with your pencil. Make a mark of equal distance from the top on the far right and draw a line to connect the marks with your pencil. Stack an additional three nib widths below the baseline and with your pencil draw a line for the bottom of the descenders.

The nib width ratio for the X-height is 1:5. The nib width ratio for the letter ascenders and descenders is 1:3.

These ratios allow you to use any size of nib and retain the elegance of the Italic script. The ratio 1:3 is what I prefer to use for my ascenders and descenders, but some may prefer longer or shorter ones. That's fine! The key is to be consistent with whatever ratios you choose.

The four lines that you have drawn will house all the small (lowercase or minuscule) letters. Now that you know your letter dimensions based on your nib width, you can proceed to lining your first practice page.

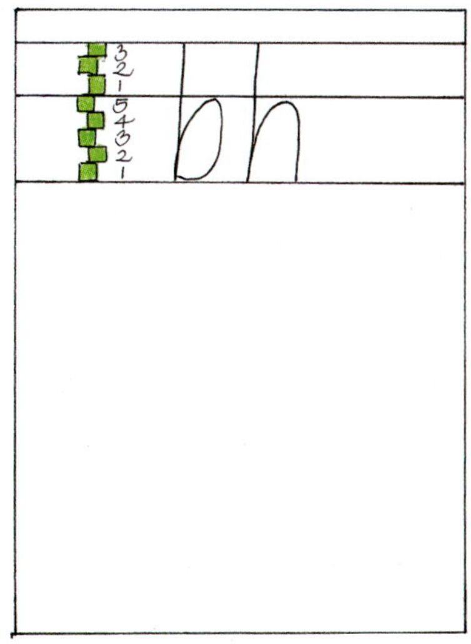


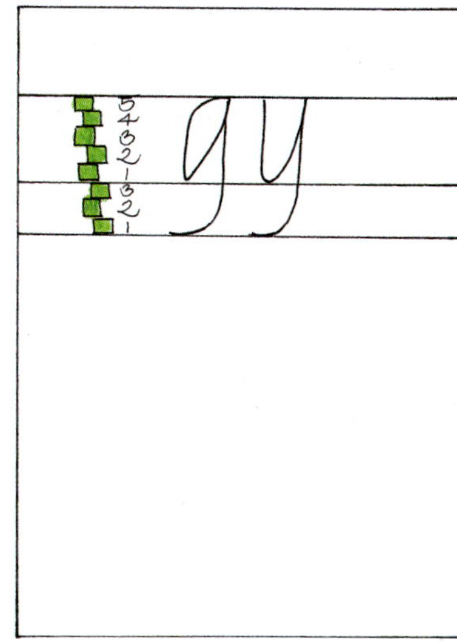


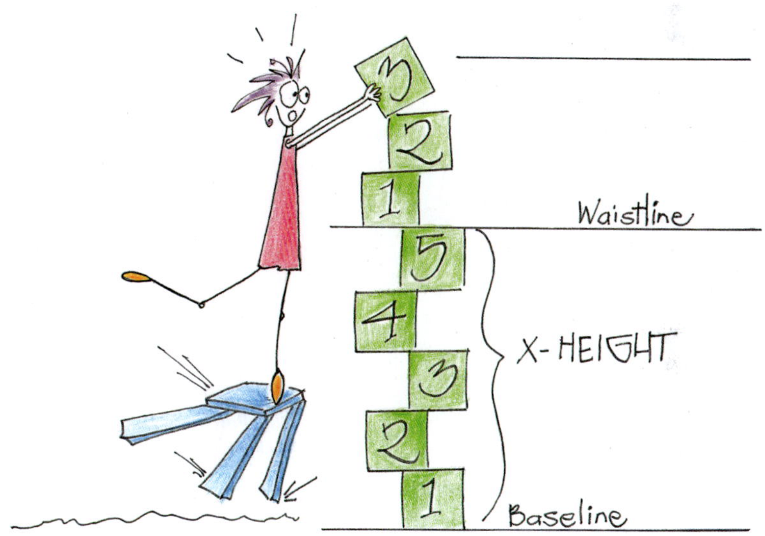


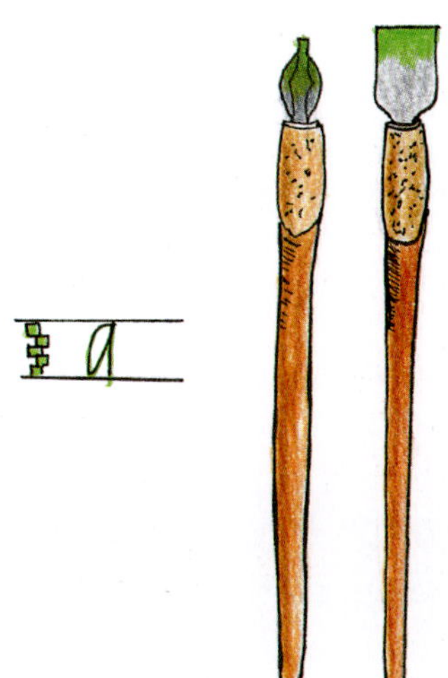

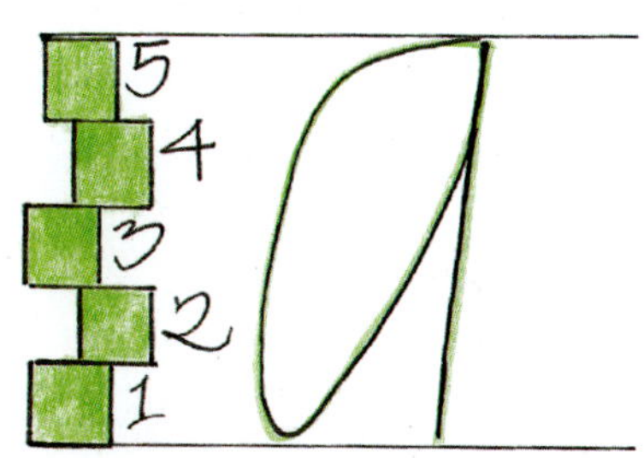


Compare the X-height of a very narrow nib width with the X-height of a very wide nib width. Quite the difference!

# Lining Your Page

Once you have the dimensions for your lowercase letters as determined by the nib width of your pen, you can now line a whole page to begin your practice on. Here's how:

1. With a spare piece of paper, cut a 1-inch by 6-inch strip. Line up the short edge of the strip (i.e., the 1-inch side) with the top of your new practice sheet, which will become your template. With a ruler and pencil, measure and mark ¾ of an inch down from the top of your page on both the strip of paper and the left side and right side of your practice sheet template. Draw a line across. This is your top margin and the top of your ascender line.

2. Three nib widths below that line will mark your waistline. Five nib widths below that will mark your baseline, and three more nib widths below the baseline is the bottom of your descenders. Mark these on both your strip of paper and practice sheet template.

3. To make additional lines on your practice sheet template, move the strip of paper down the left side of the practice sheet template so the mark for the top of the ascenders on the paper strip lines up with the bottom of the descenders on the template. Transfer the marks from the strip to the template. Continue doing this until you get down to the bottom margin, which will be around 1¼ inches above the bottom of the practice sheet template. This is the bottom margin for your template.

4. After marking along the left side of your sheet, shift your slip of paper over to the right side. Transfer the marks on the strip of paper to the practice sheet template in the same way as you did on the left. Mark all the way down to the bottom margin.

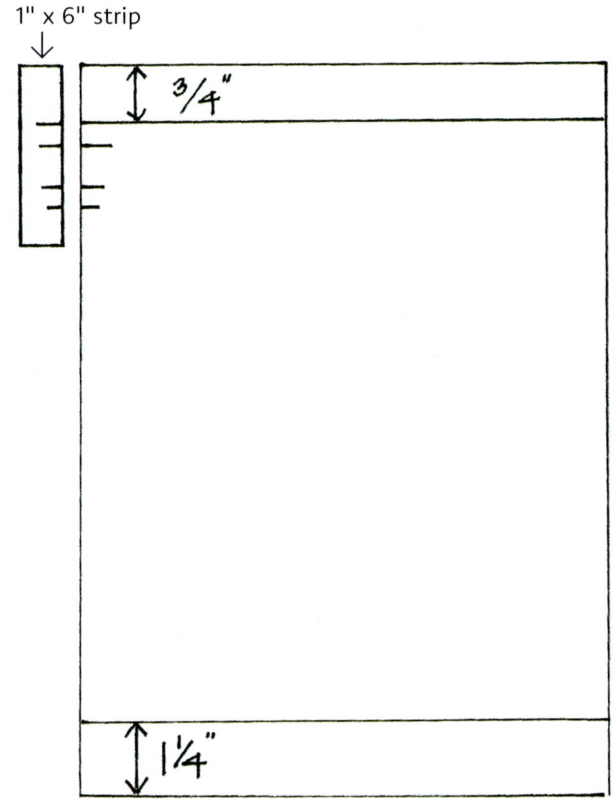


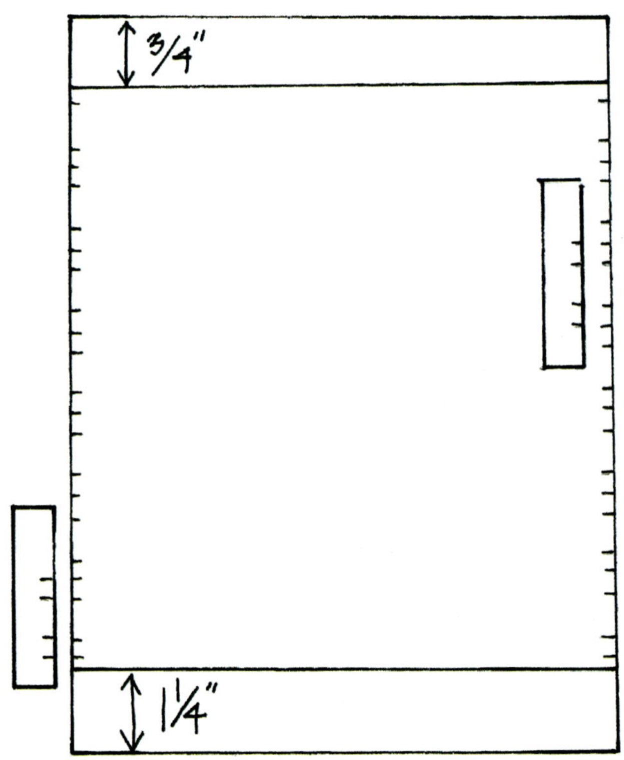

5. Connect the marks on opposite sides of the practice sheet template by drawing lines across the template. Add side margins last, making them ¾ of an inch from the left and right sides of the template (or equal to the margin at the top). Erase the lines that appear in the margins.

6. Once you have your template penciled in, go over all the lines with a ruler and a black fine-liner marker. After you're done, take a break to let the ink dry. Go for a little stroll, roll your shoulders, rub your neck and then carefully erase all the pencil marks. Now your practice sheet template is ready to use under a blank practice sheet or to make photocopies. You are ready to start!

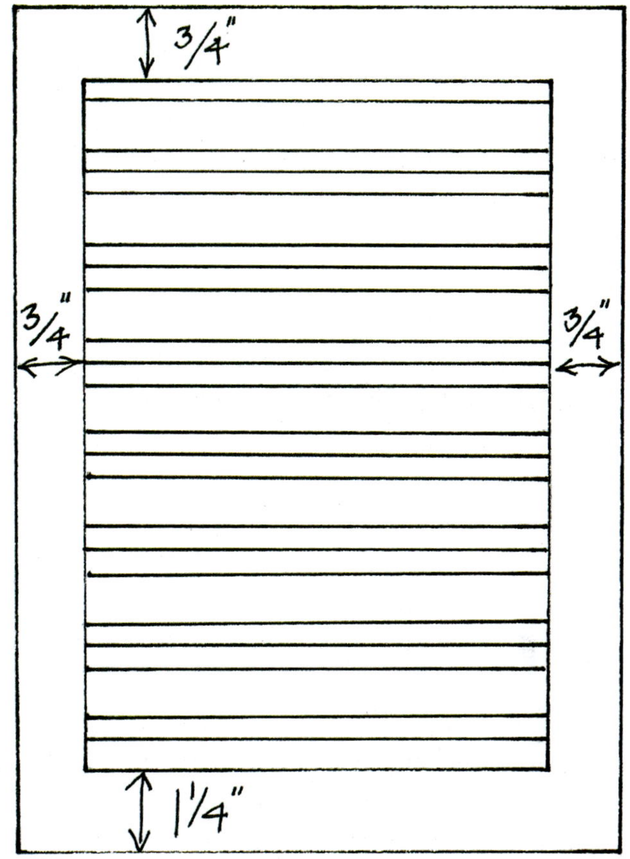


**Note:** As you progress through your learning, you will be making modifications to your practice sheets, such as adding slope lines and lines for capital letters. If you're photocopying your practice sheet, be mindful not to make too many copies, as your sheet may be modified later (and then you would need to make even more copies of the modified sheet!). An effective way around this is making a master practice sheet template that you use under your blank practice sheets. As the modifications come along, you'll need to modify only the master practice sheet.

## A Few Tips on Erasing

**When erasing pencil lines of any kind — whether on your practice templates or penciled-in guides for drawing your letters — there are a few things to keep in mind (which, of course, I learned the hard way!):**

1. **Always let your inked work dry longer than you think necessary before erasing the pencil lines.**
2. **Don't use dirty or ridiculously cheap erasers. The white ones work well.**
3. **Always experiment first with a scrap of the type of paper you are using to make sure the pencil does erase.**
4. **While erasing, try not to frantically erase back and forth. Hold down your work with one hand and carefully, lightly, gently erase in only one direction. This will prevent your works from crinkling beyond repair, which could result in a plethora of expletives.**

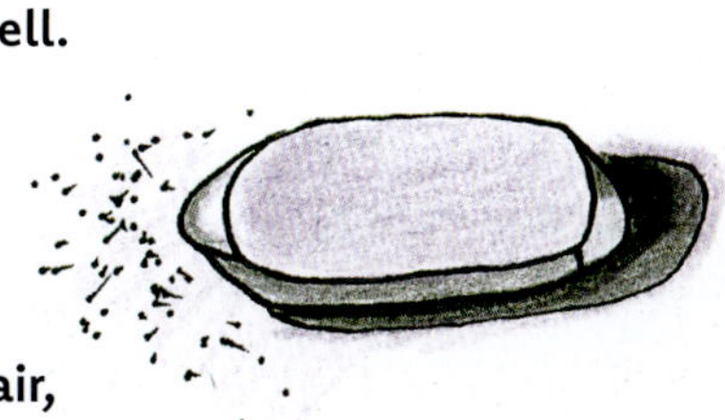

# Finding the Pen Angle

In Italic calligraphy, the nib of the pen is angled at 45 degrees. This might sound daunting, but this angle is easily found through a simple exercise. Draw a small square box and divide it in half diagonally by drawing a line from the upper-right corner of the box to the lower left. This line indicates the angle that the nib should be kept when creating strokes for the Italic script. As you start practicing, if you find you are not happy with some of your letters, go back to this box and check that your angle is correct. You could even draw a little box with the 45-degree angle at the top of each practice sheet as a reference.

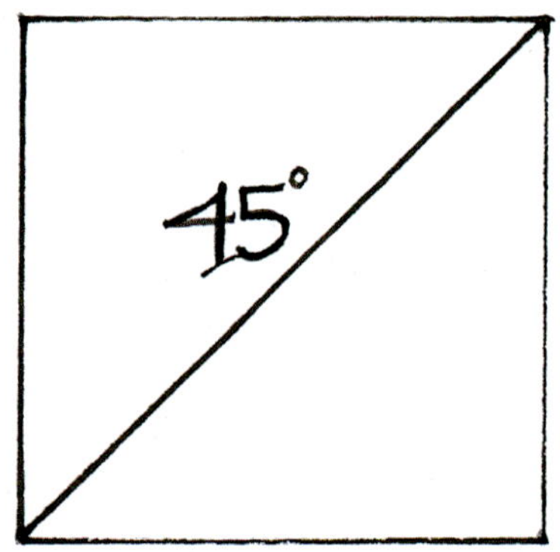


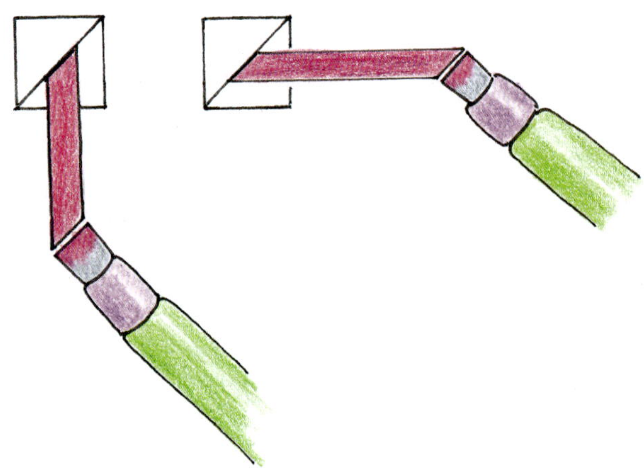

This 45-degree angle means that both ends of the stroke remain equally pointy. The points allow for much more energy and movement in this script. Think of dancers on pointe rather than flat-footed — much easier to fly!

Try practicing some downward strokes within the X-height of the first row on a practice page (with your template underneath or using a photocopy of your template). When making downward strokes, start with the right tip of the nib at the waistline. Draw straight down until the left tip of the nib just touches the baseline. In doing this, your stroke will begin with a point and end with a point.

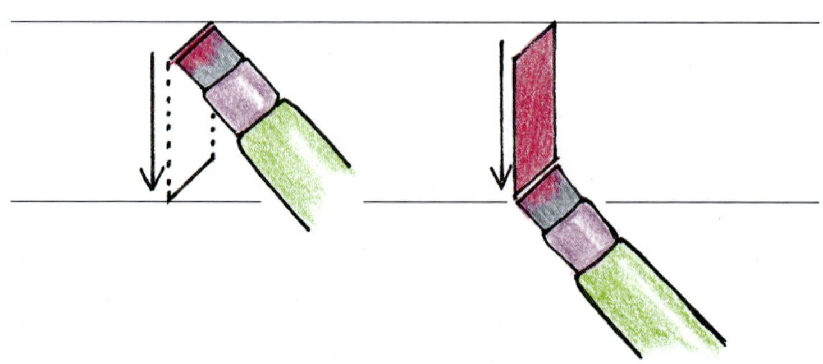

Now try some horizontal strokes in the space below the baseline (i.e., where the descenders of letters will eventually go). Be sure to maintain your 45-degree angle as you move your pen from left to right.

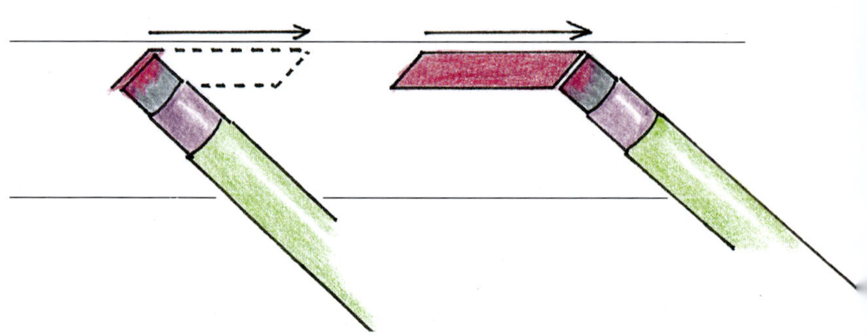

And lastly, try to draw some diamonds in the space above the waistline, where the ascenders will eventually go. With your pen nib still angled at 45 degrees, pull the pen down and to the right so that you're creating diamonds.

Repeat these strokes and fill a whole practice page. Diamonds above the waistline, vertical strokes within the X-height and horizontal strokes below the baseline.

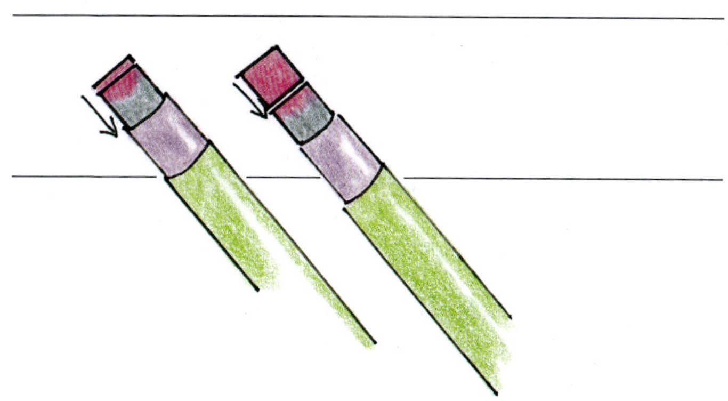

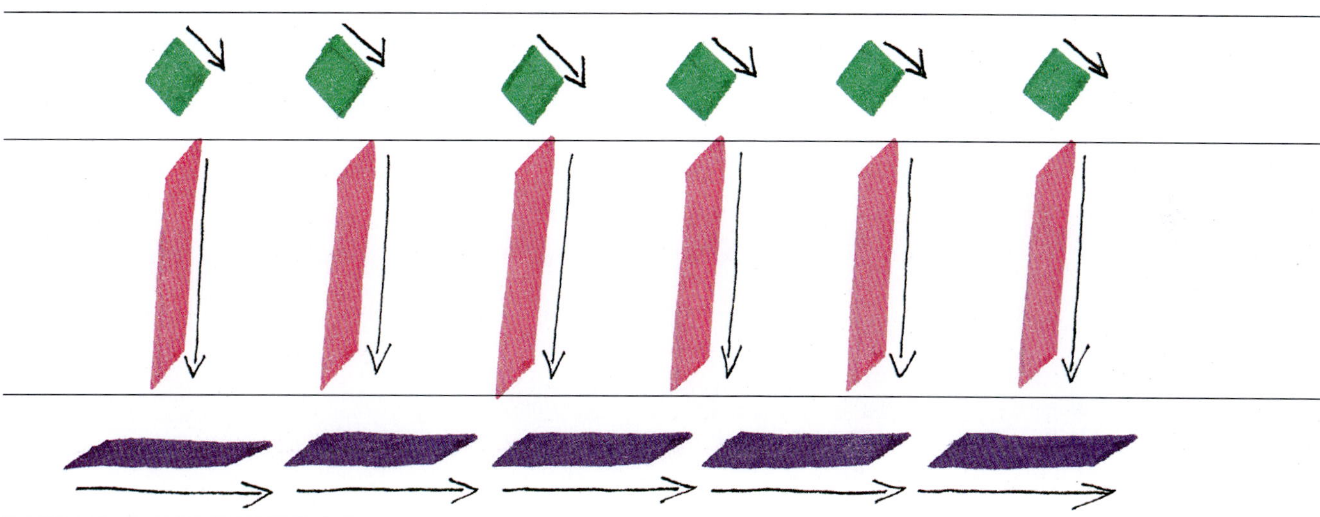

## A Look at How You Should Hold Your Pen

**The illustrations throughout this book often focus solely on pen angle and creating strokes. These can be misleading because the pen appears to be lying flat. This is, of course, not the case when you start writing!**

**How you comfortably hold a pencil is how you should hold your calligraphy pen. This will allow you to practice with less muscle fatigue while also allowing for cleaner, crisper strokes. Experiment to discover what feels best for you!**

**If you're left-handed, refer to pages 26–27 for some tips on how to hold your pen and create strokes.**

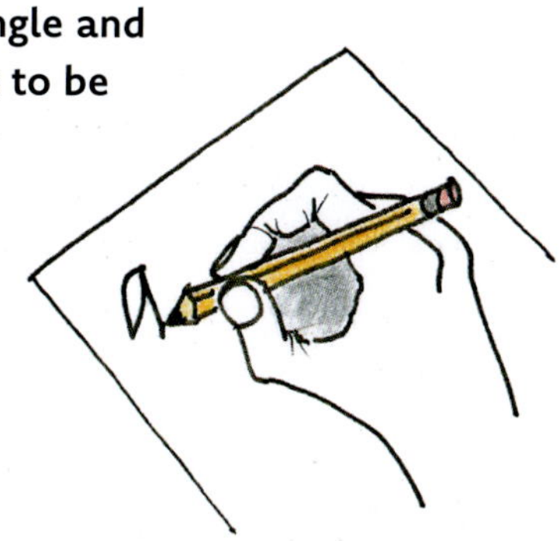

# Spacing & Noticing

While learning the variety of strokes and letters of the Italic hand, you are training not only your arm, wrist and fingers but also your precious eyes.

You will begin to notice when you make one letter better than another. You will also begin to appreciate well-placed and well-spaced letters and pick out those that are neither. This is a wonderful thing. The more your eyes become attuned to these important details, the better your calligraphy becomes.

Wonderful letters can be destroyed with poor spacing, yet excellent spacing can help one overlook less confident letters. When I first began calligraphy, I had no concept of spacing. As a result, I struggled with getting my letters to look just right.

The first two strokes you make determine the space between all the strokes of the line. So as you create new strokes, constantly glance back at your earlier strokes to determine the spacing you should aim for.

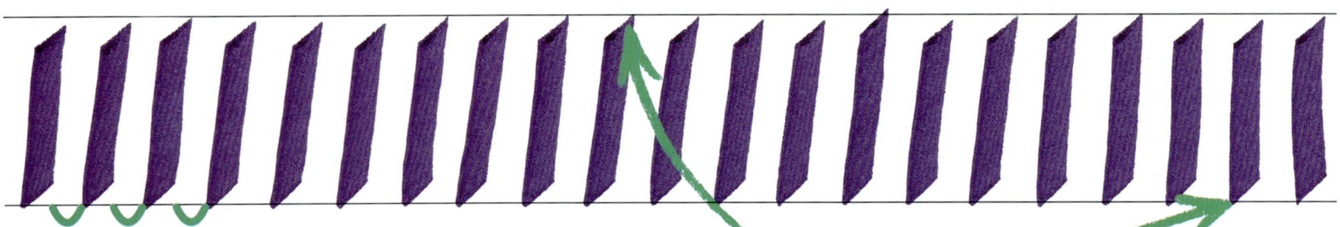

*Aim for the same spacing between strokes for the rest of your line.*

*And remember, make sure there are points on the beginnings and ends of all your strokes.*

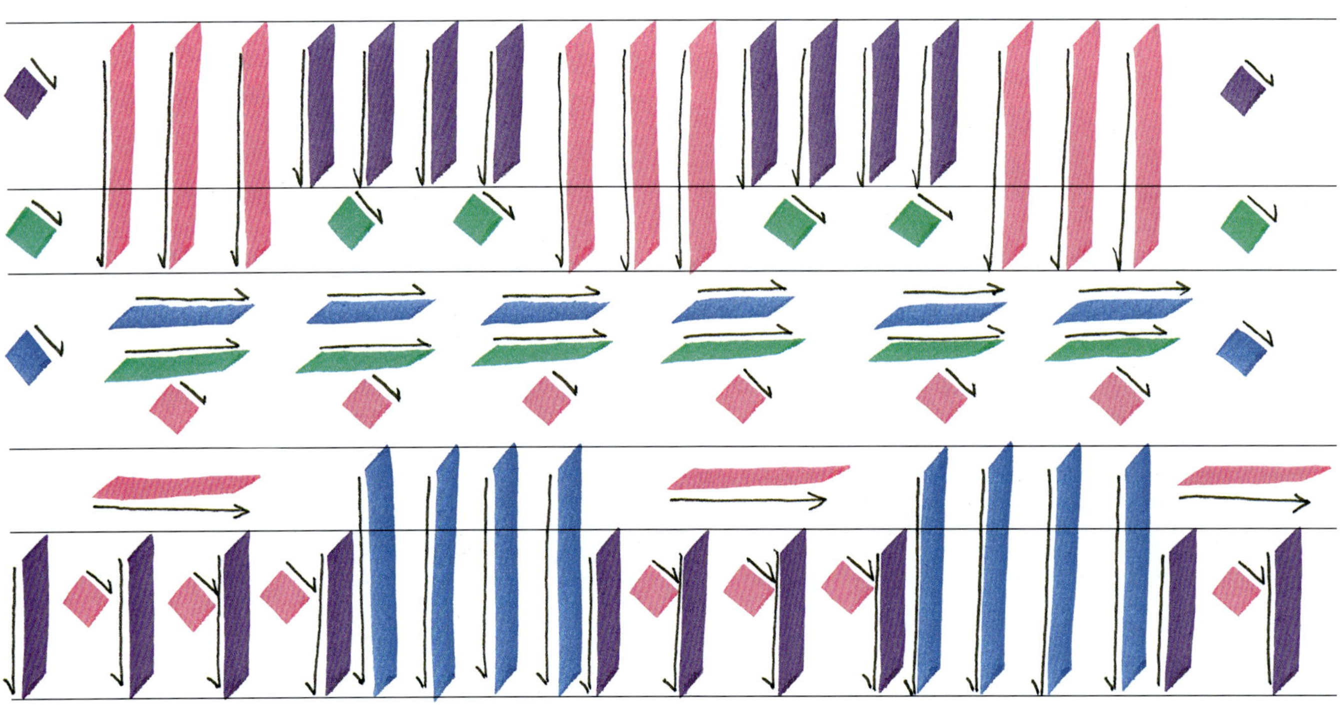

# Practicing Angles & Spacing

Now let's put what we've learned about angles and spacing to the test. Take one of your practice sheets and put it on a raised surface (see "Setting Up" on page 16). Make sure before you start, you have a protective sheet of paper under your writing hand and arm so that you don't smear your strokes.

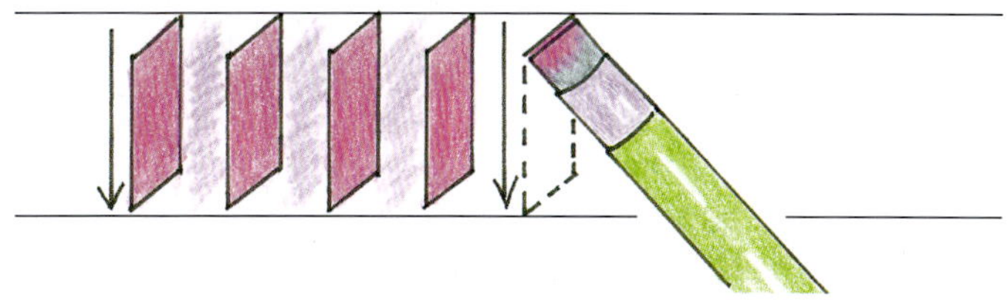

On the first line of your practice sheet, make your first downward strokes within the X-height, and try to achieve equal spacing between each stroke. Breathe out as you make your downstrokes, breathe in to begin again. As you continue to create these strokes, keep your spacing in mind.

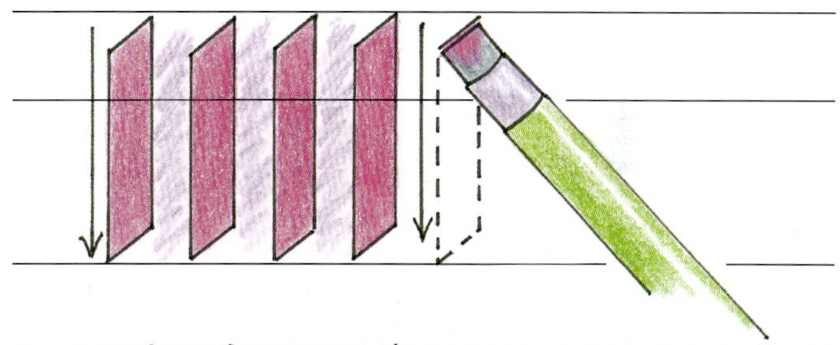

Next, try making longer downward strokes, with some strokes starting at the top where the ascenders begin and ending at the baseline. Try other long strokes that start at the waistline and end below the baseline, where the descenders end. Remember to maintain your spacing. This is the most important thing right now!

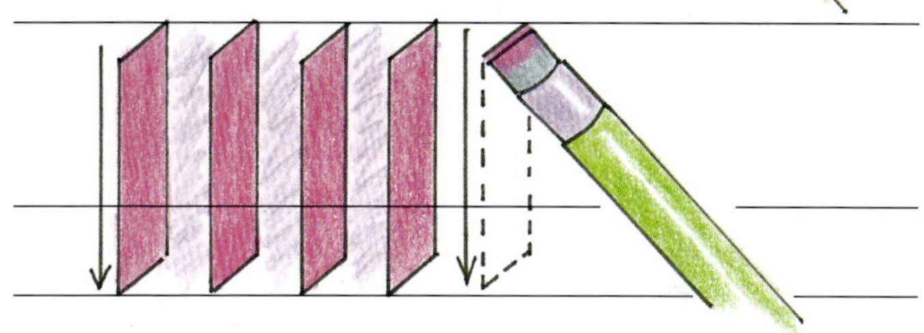

Next, create a line of diamonds, being mindful of the space between each one.

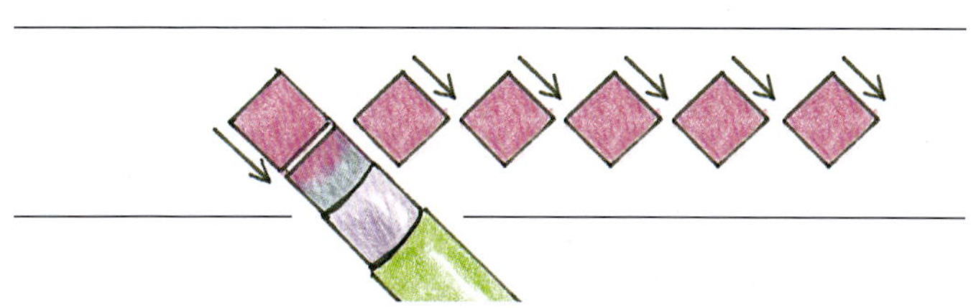

And lastly, create some horizontal strokes, or crossbars. Make one stroke at the top of the X-height, below the waistline, and make a second stroke of equal length at the bottom of the X-height, above the baseline. Complete a line of these horizontal strokes, maintaining equal spacing between sets of crossbars as well.

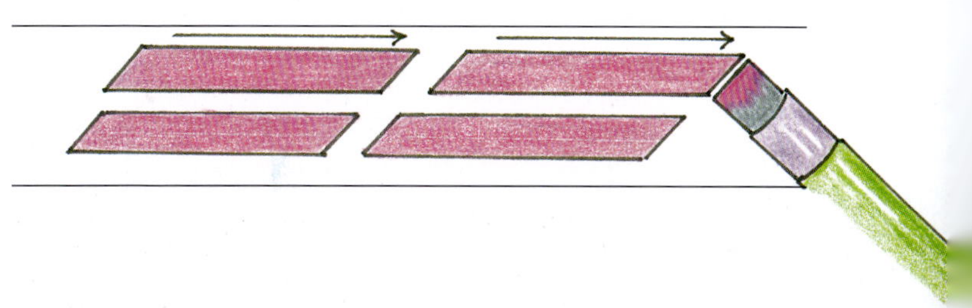

**TIP**

**Don't rush through this exercise! Take an inordinate amount of purposeful time for each stroke!**

# Let's Talk Left-Handed

My heart broke when a woman in one of my adult classes expressed her last experience in a calligraphy class. She had been told that she would never be able to do calligraphy because she was left-handed. I admired her tremendously for trying again! I felt determined to help her realize how utterly untrue that statement was.

The left-handed writer lives in a right-handed world and is challenged from the start. A large proportion of society is right-handed, and as a result the most common flow of letters in the majority of countries is from left to right. This is the biggest challenge for left-handed calligraphers.

When right-handed calligraphers letter, they see what they are writing because their hand and tool are ahead of what they are writing. The left-handed calligrapher follows behind the letters with their hand and tool, blocking their view and often smudging the ink as their hand brushes the letters. Fortunately, being left-handed is now significantly more recognized in the calligraphic world, allowing left-handers to move forward confidently using tools designed for them.

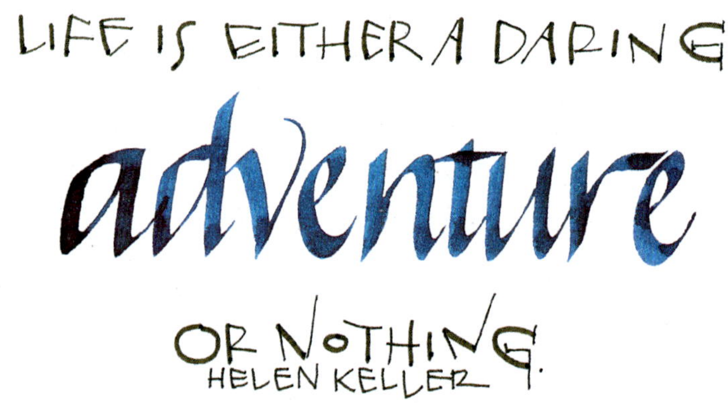


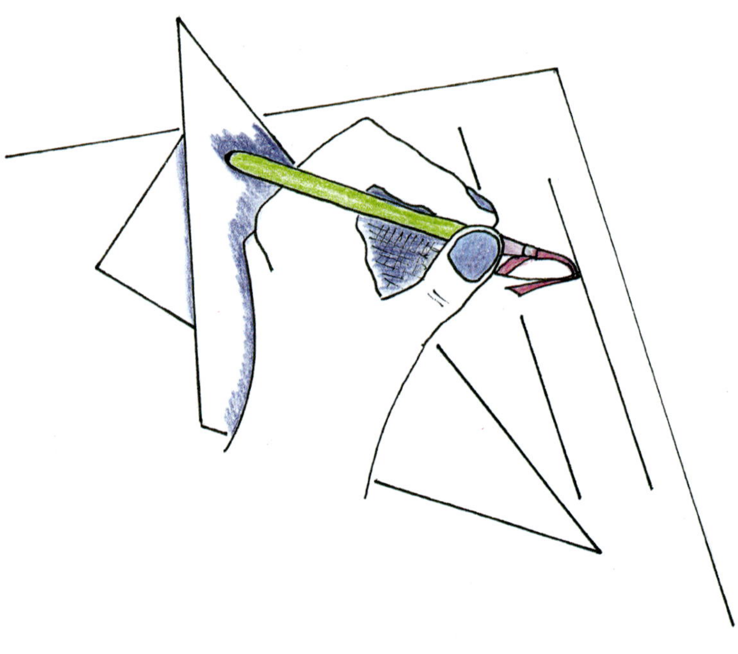

As I am a right-handed calligrapher, the following tips and suggestions are based on my own observations working with left-handed calligraphers who have learned how to create wonderful calligraphy.

You may have heard suggestions about hooking your arm and turning pages nearly upside down. Unless this already works very well for you, I strongly suggest taking less drastic measures. These writing positions can be very uncomfortable, thereby lessening the time and ease with which you can letter due to muscle strain and fatigue.

Try these tips instead:

1. The knuckle of your baby finger (also known as the pinky finger) balances the hand on the paper while you are holding the pen.

2. Your page should be tilted up to the left — perhaps almost perpendicular to your body. Go for comfort and whatever allows you to make the strokes most successfully. Remember to keep your nib at a 45-degree angle.

3. Make sure that you are working on a slanted board or surface to help prevent too much strain for your neck and shoulders.

4. With the paper tilted as it is, you will be pulling your downstrokes to the left, the upstrokes to the right and crossbars toward you. To help, you can take a sample letter you are working on and turn it to the same angle you are working at as a visual guide to copy.

5. The position of your pen can help tremendously. If you hold your pen angled in a slightly more upright way (but not completely upright), while still paying attention to your comfort, you will decrease the tendency to smudge while being able to clearly see the strokes and letters you are creating. This is depicted in the illustration on page 26.

6. The light that shines over your shoulder should be placed on your right side. This will literally shed light on the strokes you are making rather than casting a shadow if the light is on your left side.

7. Remember, always use a protective sheet under your hand to protect the paper you are writing on.

## A Final Word for Left-Handers

**The most important thing I would like you to take away from this is that**

**YES,**
**you absolutely can create wonderful, beautiful, creative calligraphy with your left hand. Please don't let anyone tell you otherwise!**

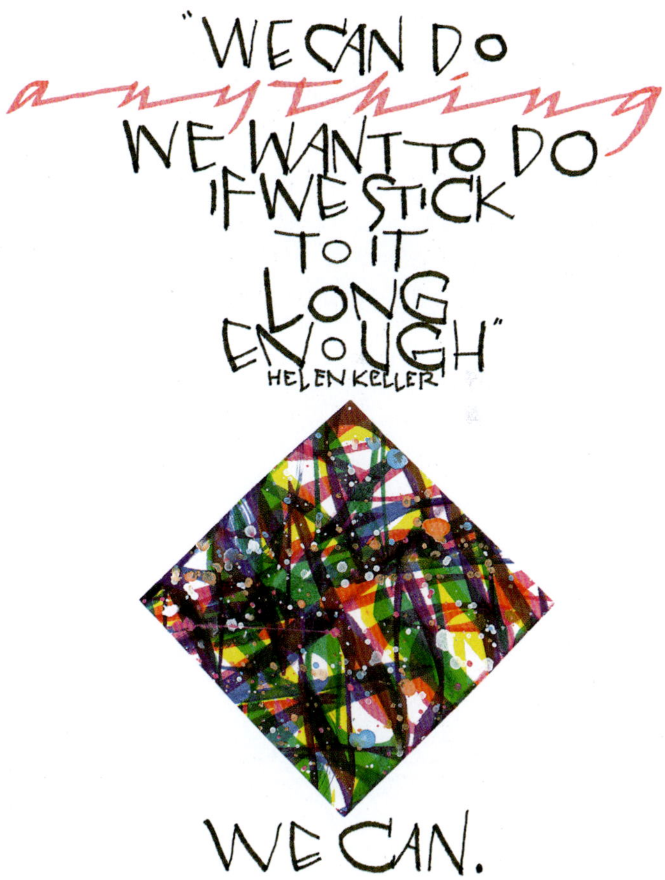

# Chapter 2

# Learning the Strokes & Joins

This chapter is all about learning the different strokes that will form the basis of your letters. Beyond basic strokes, you'll learn about letter widths and how to join parts of a letter with ease, giving you the skills you need to complete the entire alphabet. By the end, you will have tried your hand at creating all the lowercase letters in the alphabet.

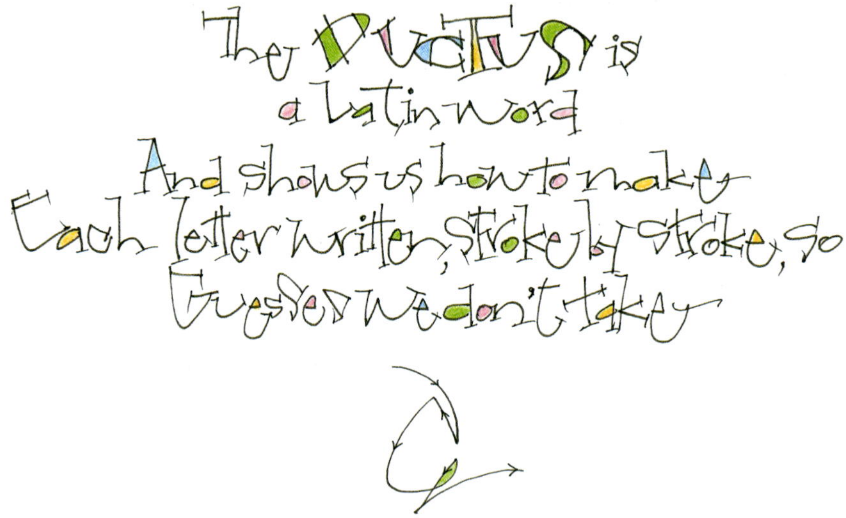


### Discover Ductus

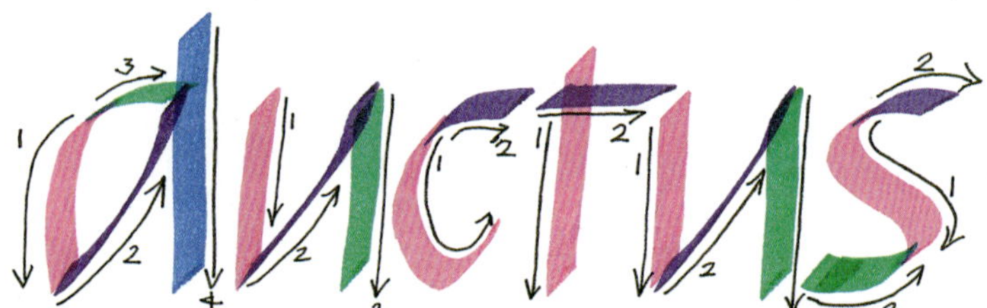


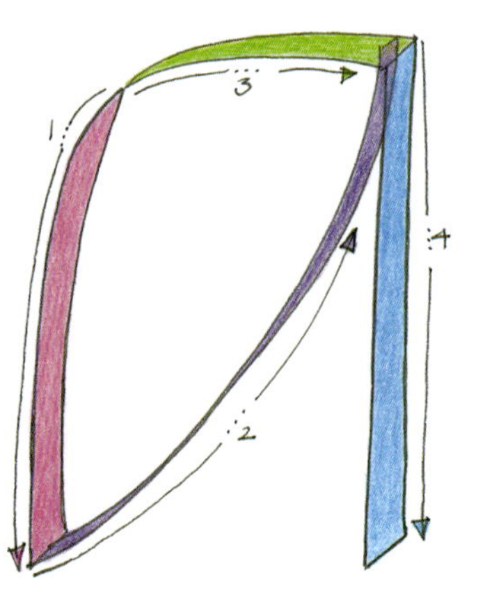

Ductus means the direction and order of strokes for each letter. Knowing a letter's ductus is key to making smooth, attractive and consistent letters. As you can see throughout the rest of the book, I've used a different color for each stroke to show you the ductus. When you're practicing, you only need to use one color but still follow the order and direction of the ductus as shown.

# Straight Strokes - i, l, t

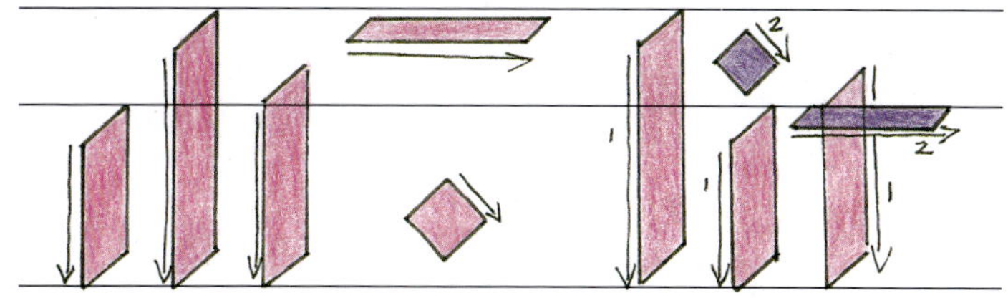

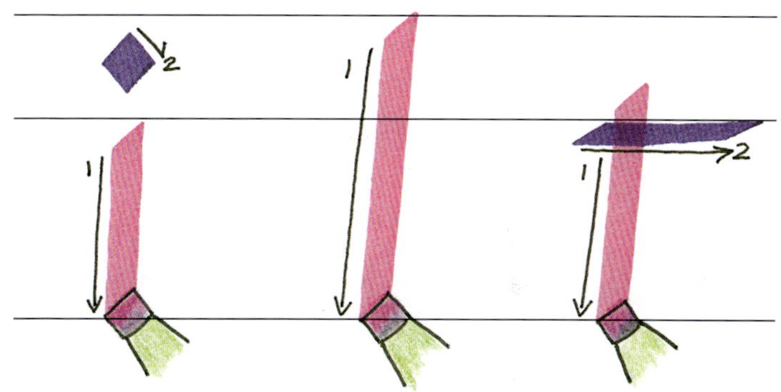

The first type of stroke we're going to learn should look familiar. The downward, horizontal and diamond-shaped strokes that you practiced in Chapter 1 form the basis of lowercase letters (minuscules) like *i*, *l* and *t*, and these straight strokes are used in a good proportion of the rest of the alphabet.

Let's start with the lowercase *i*. The downward stroke for the *i* should begin at the waistline and end at the baseline. The diamond of the *i* should point down to the middle of the body of the *i*, like it's a candle. Practice a row of this letter on your practice sheet.

Now practice the straight strokes of the lowercase letter *l* on your practice sheet. The top of the *l*'s straight downward stroke should start at the ascender line and end at the baseline. Try to synchronize your breathing to the downstroke, like we did in Chapter 1. Breathe out for the downstroke and breathe in when you lift your pen. Do a line of *l*'s across your sheet.

Next, try a row of the lowercase letter *t*. The top of the *t*'s straight downward stroke should begin just above the waistline and end at the baseline. The second stroke, the horizontal crossbar, should be thinner than the first stroke. This is done by changing the angle of the nib to a flatter angle by turning the nib clockwise (i.e., approximately 30 degrees instead of 45 degrees). It starts under the waistline and just to the left of the downstroke: the right side of the nib should meet the downstroke's body. Pull your pen horizontally across to the right so that the length of the stroke on the right side of the downstroke is roughly twice the length of the stroke on the left side.

To finish our review of these strokes, let's form little groups of letters, spelling *lit*. Be sure to keep the spaces between the letters in a group the same. Also keep the spaces between the groups the same, though they should be bigger than the spaces between the letters. I suggest practicing two rows of the word *lit*.

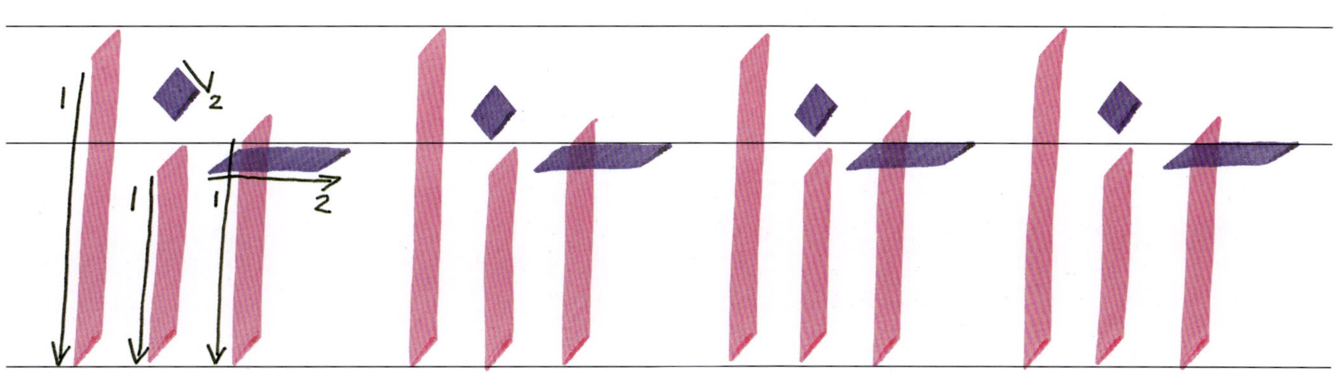

# Diagonal Strokes-v,w,x,z,k

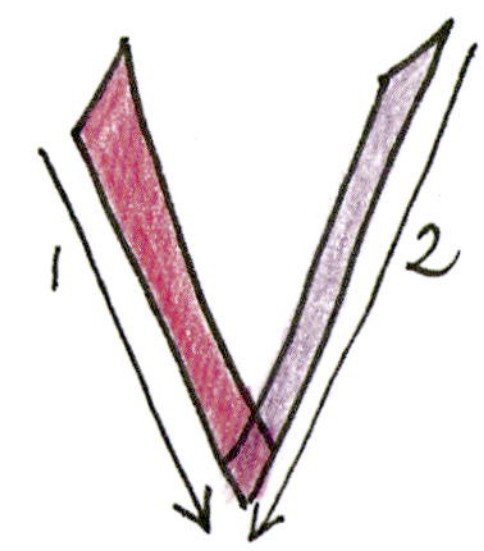


When creating diagonal strokes, we must steepen the angle of our pen. Instead of 45 degrees, we use an angle closer to 50 degrees but only for the diagonal downstrokes moving from right to left. We use this steepened angle for lowercase letters like *v*, *w*, *x*, *z* and *k*.

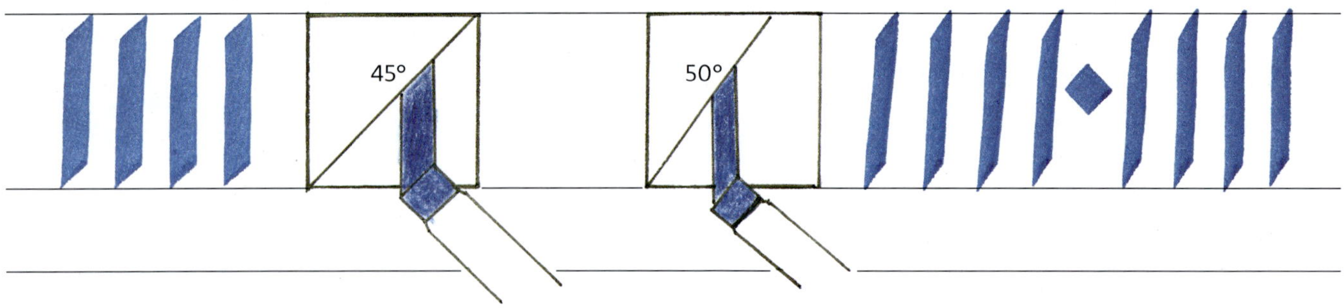


If these letters used diagonal strokes at 45 degrees, rather than the narrower 50 degrees, both the strokes and the spacing would look too wide compared to other letters that don't use diagonal strokes. Look at the spacing contrast between these two sets of letters:

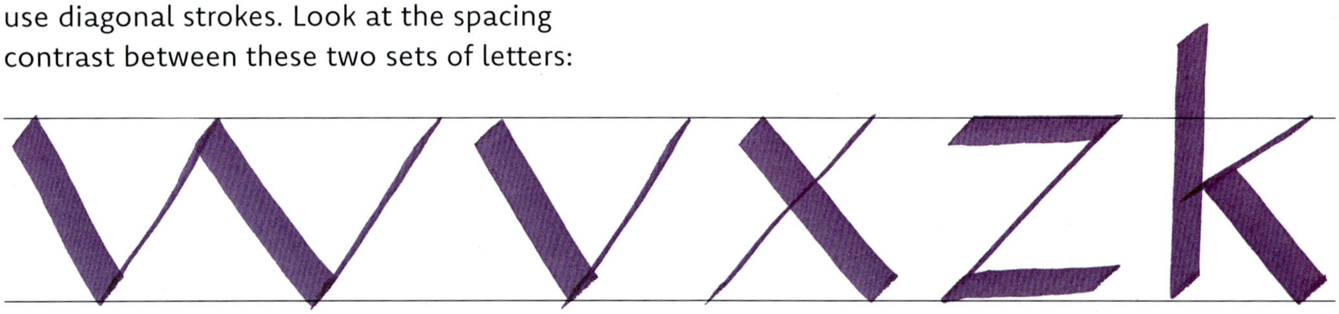

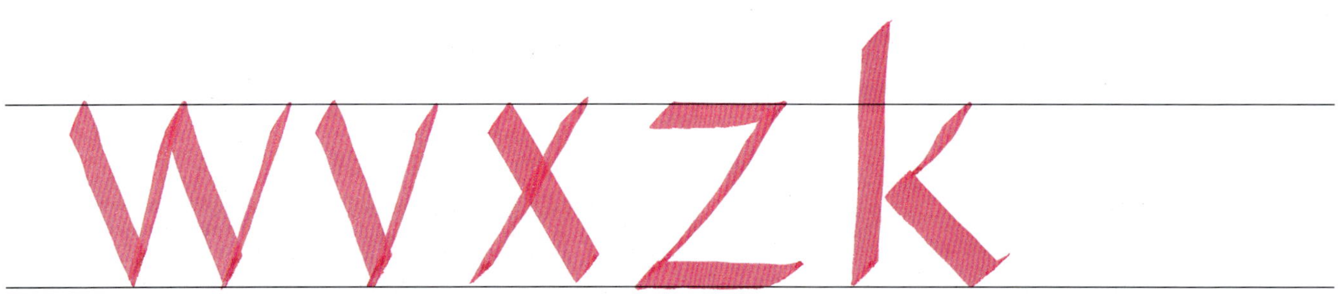

The steepened angle on the diagonal stroke helps to slim down heavy strokes and also beef up the skinny ones.

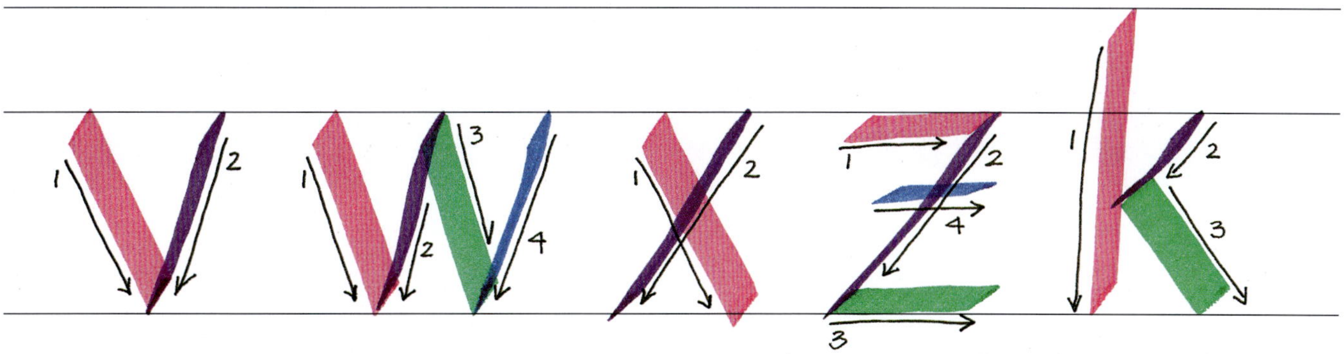


Let's practice a row of the lowercase *v*. With your pen at a 45-degree angle, make your first diagonal stroke on your practice sheet. The top of the stroke should start at the waistline and end at the baseline. Similarly, the second stroke should start at the waistline and connect to the first stroke at the baseline. However, this second diagonal downstroke needs to be at a steeper angle, making it thinner than the first stroke.

The lowercase *w* uses the same strokes as the *v*, but the spacing between the strokes is slightly narrower. All the strokes are downward, and, as you'll see, strokes 1 and 3 are parallel and strokes 2 and 4 are also parallel and at a steeper angle.

Next, let's try the diagonal strokes of the lowercase *x*, which cross each other. The top triangle of the *x* should be smaller than the bottom (otherwise the *x* might look a bit top-heavy), and the arms should line up vertically. Your first diagonal stroke should begin at the waistline and end at the baseline. Your second, thinner diagonal stroke should do the same while crossing the first stroke just above the middle.

For the lowercase *z*, the diagonal stroke is sandwiched between two horizontal strokes. This means you'll have to be conscious of adjusting your nib angle from 45 degrees for the first horizontal stroke, to the steeper angle for the diagonal stroke, then, at last, back to 45 degrees for the third horizontal stroke. Visually you want the diagonal stroke to line up with the beginning of the first stroke. And the end of the final horizontal stroke should line up with the end of the first stroke. The crossbar is optional and is created with a flatter angle (like the letter *t*) and crosses just above the middle.

At last, we come to the lowercase *k*, which uses a vertical stroke and two diagonal strokes. The first vertical stroke starts at the ascender line and ends at the baseline. The first diagonal stroke (which needs to be thinner than the second diagonal stroke) starts at the waistline, and the second diagonal stroke ends at the baseline. Visually, these strokes should line up vertically, or with the bottom stroke slightly further to the right. As well, the top triangle of the *k* ought to be smaller than the bottom triangle. Even if they're the same size, the letter will look unbalanced and top-heavy. As you do your practice row, you can try variations of the final diagonal stroke to the baseline.

These letters require added effort because we're needing to alter the steepness of our pen angle. After working on these, take a break and stretch your arms, hands, neck and back. Go for a walk, have some tea and then continue on.

# More Practice with Straight & Diagonal Strokes: n, m, h, r

Now that you have a better sense of straight and diagonal strokes, you can begin to construct more letters, like the lowercase letters *n*, *m*, *h* and *r* — although these letters use upward diagonal strokes to connect the vertical strokes at a steeper angle to keep the letter narrower.

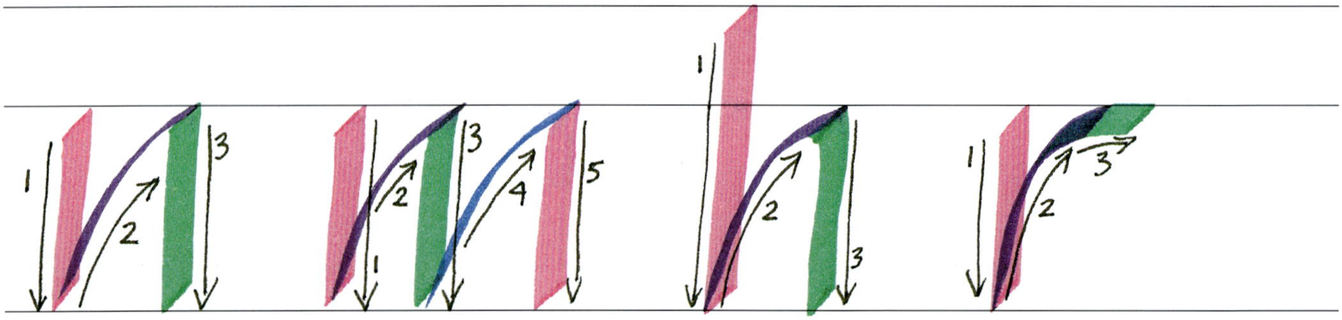


The *n* starts with a straight downstroke from the waistline to the baseline. The second stroke is a thinner stroke that arches up and out to the waistline. The third stroke comes down to the baseline, parallel to the first stroke.

The *m* is two slightly narrower versions of the letter *n*.

The *h* starts at the ascender line and descends to the baseline. The second stroke is an arch up to the waistline (exactly like the *n*) and the final stroke is a straight downstroke from the waistline to the baseline.

The *r* starts with a straight downstroke from the waistline to the baseline. The second stroke comes up in a thinner arched line but runs up the middle of the stem before arching out to touch the waistline. Before it touches the waistline, the pen angle becomes less steep, which allows for the stroke to thicken as it runs along the waistline. Alternatively, you can have the thin arch reach the waistline and then finish with a very short, widened downward stroke as though you were starting the last stroke of the letter *n* (as shown in the words *rim* and *trim* on the ensuing page).

Use your practice sheets to create rows of these letters.

Then create words with all the letters you've learned so far: *h*, *i*, *k*, *l*, *m*, *n*, *r*, *t*, *v*, *w*, *x* and *z*. You could try words like *him*, *rim*, *tin*, *trim*, *zit*, *vim*, *kit* and *nix*. Remember to keep the spacing consistent between each letter of a word. Put a diamond between each word.

him · rim · tin

trim · zit · lit

vim · kit · nix

### More Words to Practice

- hint
- kiln
- knit
- milk
- mint
- mirth
- rink
- think
- twill
- twin
- whirl
- whiz
- wilt
- wink

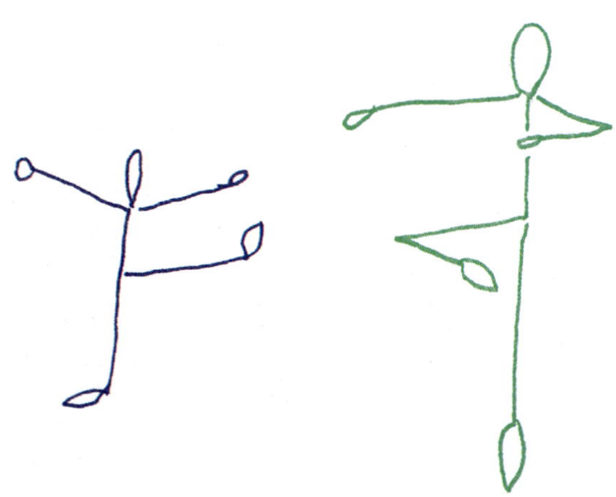

# Whisper and Snuggle Joins

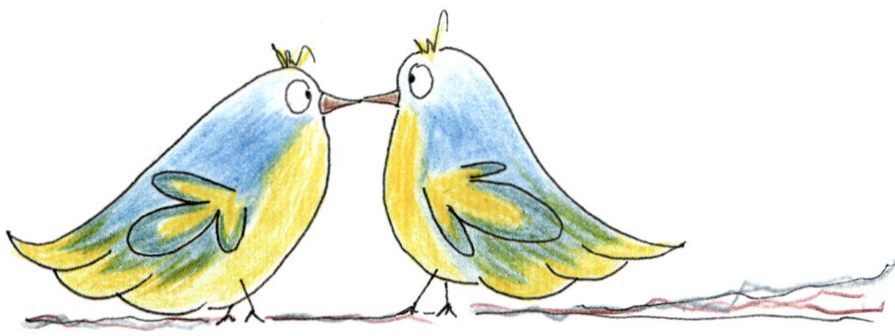

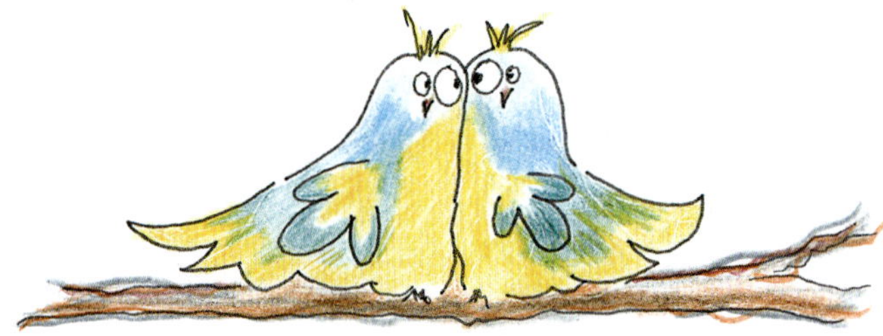

What I call "joins" here are features of a stroke that connect two strokes — for example, a vertical stroke and a horizontal stroke — together. As you'll see, a "whisper join" is when two strokes are connected by just the tip of the stroke, making it appear as if the strokes are just barely touching. In contrast, a "snuggle join" is when two strokes seem to press up against each other.

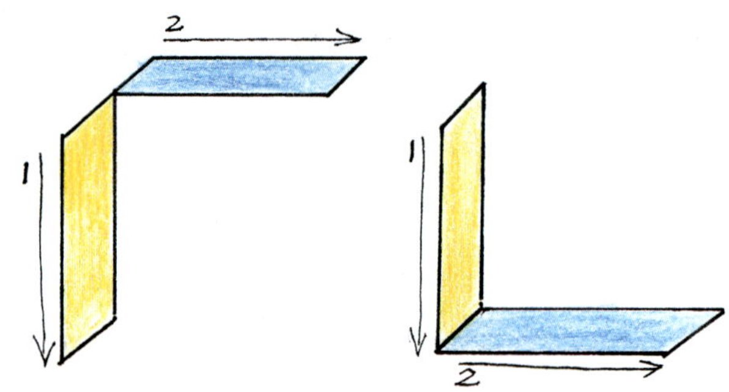


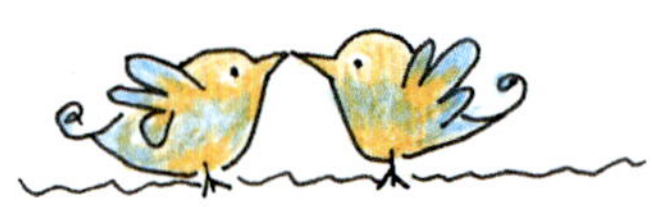

The 'Whisper Joins' are called as such
Because I made it so.
They show how pure and delicate those
joins are and you know
That once you practice carefully
The beauty starts to show
Because those crucial
"WHISPER JOINS"
Just make your letters
glow.

## WHISPER JOINS

The idea of whisper joins came to me while I was preparing to teach an Italic calligraphy class. I was trying to convey how important it was for these joins to be delicately created. I feel this join is another crucial element that contributes to the beauty of the Italic script. Joins that are heavy and overlapping create a muddy, eye-stopping spot. Instead, we want the eye to dance across the page, unhindered. These joins are illustrated in the letter *s* depicted on the right, creating the twisted ribbon appearance intrinsic to traditional Italic. Whisper joins are used in all the remaining lowercase letters. We often start with two pointy "iron bars." To achieve the look we want, the tips of these pointy bars need to barely touch. However, in order to do this, we need to begin some of our downstrokes a bit lower or end some a bit higher to provide space for the horizontal stroke to fit. We'll learn how to do this when we "activate" the whisper join in the next section.

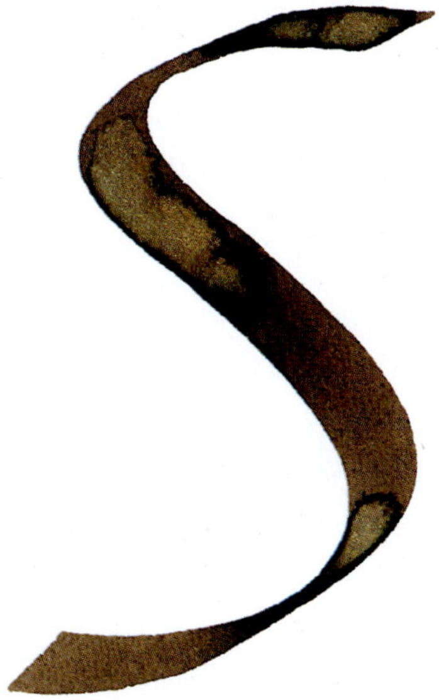

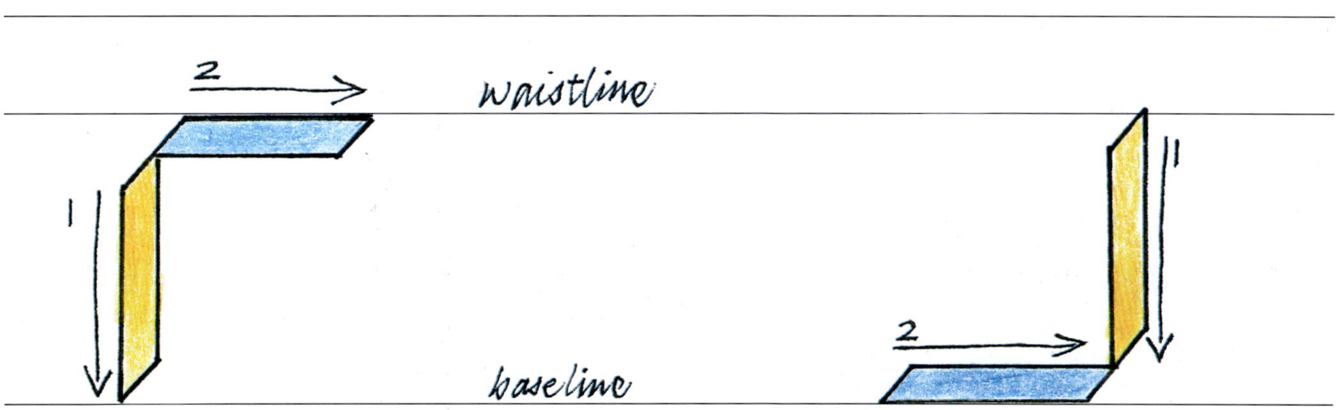

## ACTIVATING THE WHISPER JOIN

1. To create your first whisper join, start with the right tip of the nib nestled (at 45 degrees) against the underside of the waistline.

2. Slide the nib the distance of one angled nib width, with the left side of the nib leading the way, to create a fine line.

3. Having slid over to the left, proceed to make a downstroke to the baseline.

4. Now lift your pen from the bottom of your downstroke and place it where you began originally, with the right tip of the nib nestled just under the waistline. The left tip of your nib should barely touch the top point of your first downstroke.

5. Create your crossbar by making a stroke to the right. You've created your first join!

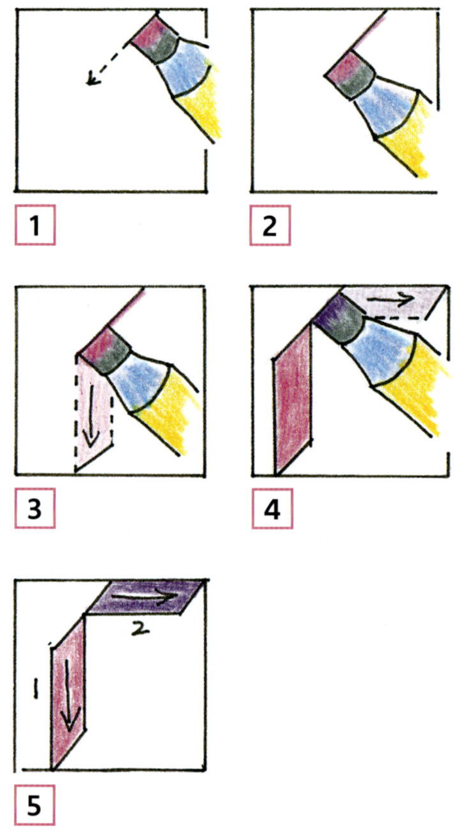


As you practice making these strokes — a page would be great — do not worry about spacing. The straight strokes, angles and delicate joins are your primary concern.

Here's a second whisper join to practice. The previous whisper join is a bit of a reversed rendition of this one.

1. Begin with the right tip of the angled nib nestled up against the waistline.

2. Draw straight down to create your downstroke but stop before the baseline one angled nib width of distance. At the angle and place where you're stopped, scoot your nib to the left and down to the baseline at the same 45-degree angle, creating a fine line that kisses the baseline.

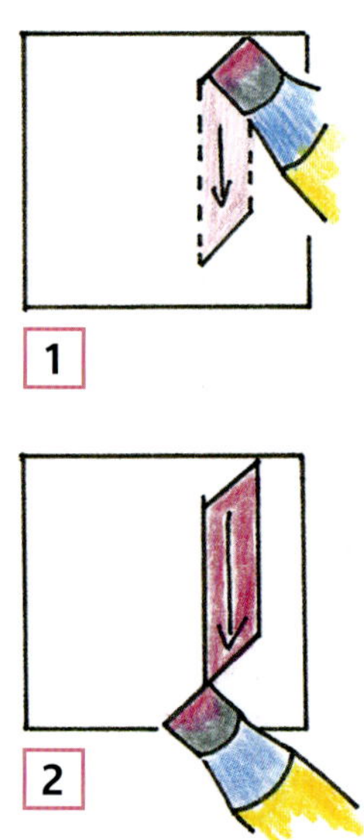

3. Lift your pen and place it to the left of your downstroke and on the baseline, making sure the angle of your pen is still 45 degrees.

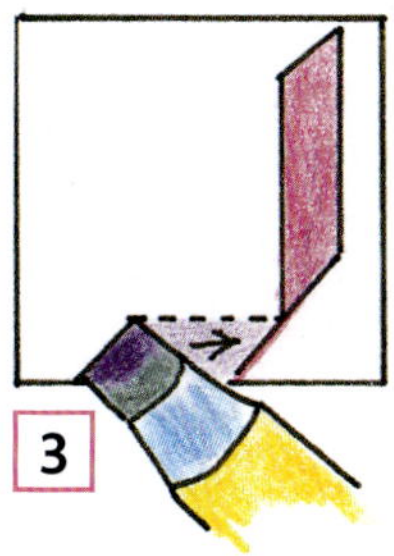


4. Draw a horizontal stroke across to the right so the points of each of the two strokes meet up in that proverbial whisper join.

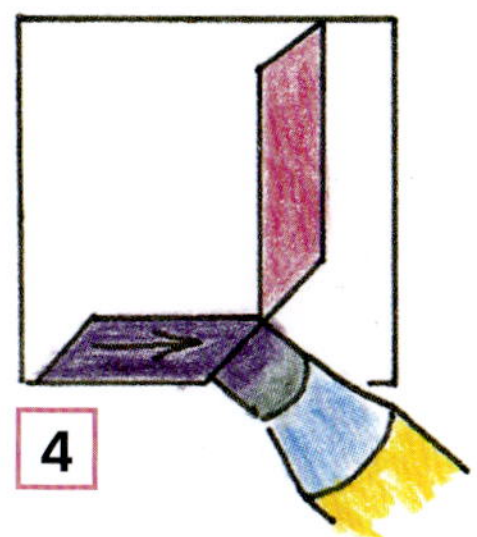


Practice a few lines slowly, aiming for the concept of barely touching joins. Try syncing the motion with your breath: breathe out for downstrokes and crossbars and in for pen lifts.

## SNUGGLE JOINS

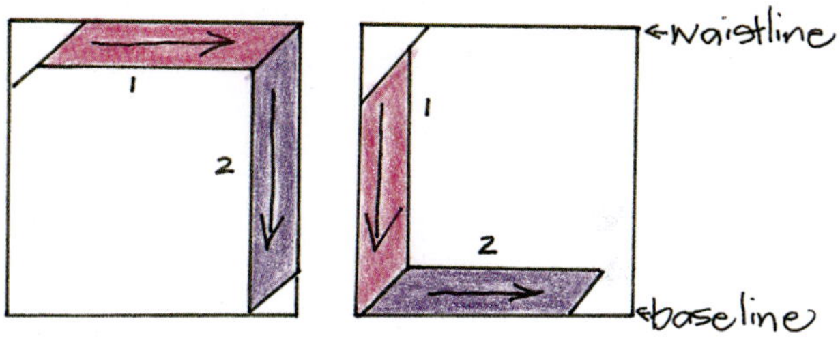


Snuggle joins, when two strokes appear to press up against each other, are a bit more straightforward than whisper joins but still require care, control and consistency of angle.

To create a snuggle join, start with a horizontal stroke just under the waistline of your practice sheet. Once you've ended your horizontal stroke, ensure your nib is still angled at 45 degrees where your horizontal stroke ended, and then draw straight down.

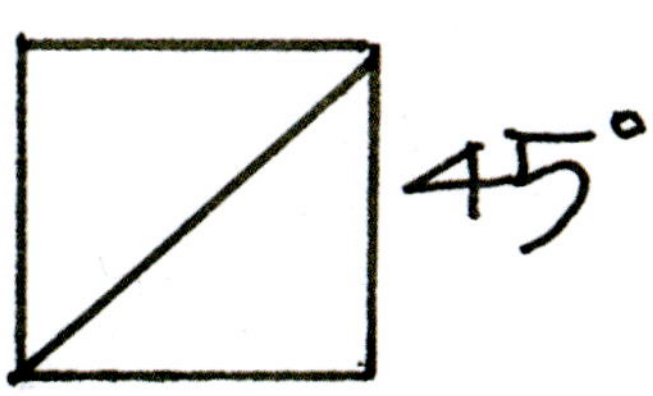


Similarly, you can start with a vertical stroke down to where the left tip of your nib is touching the baseline. Once you've ended your vertical stroke, ensure your nib is still angled at 45 degrees where your vertical stroke ended and then draw to the right.

## COMBINING WHISPER AND SNUGGLE JOINS

This exercise will help you practice combining whisper and snuggle joins.

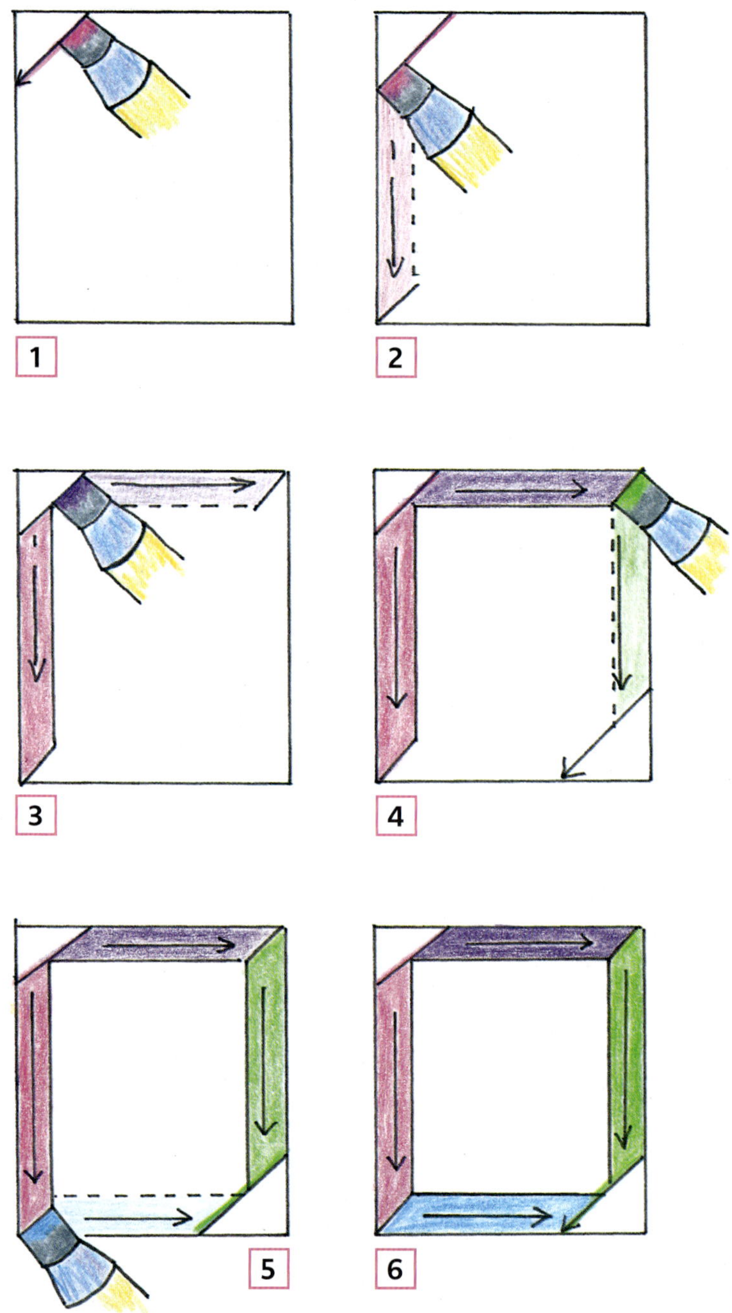


1. With your nib at 45 degrees and the right tip touching the waistline, slide your nib to the left and down about one nib width in distance.

2. Draw a stroke down until the left tip of your nib touches the baseline.

3. Once your nib touches the baseline, lift your pen up and place it where you originally started, maintaining the 45-degree angle, with the right tip of your nib touching the waistline (but not above). Draw a short horizontal stroke across.

4. Stop your pen. Adjust your hand and ensure your nib is at 45 degrees where your last stroke ended. Draw down but stop above the baseline leaving enough space for a stroke. Slide your nib left and down to create a fine line that traces to the baseline. Lift your pen.

5. Place your pen at the bottom of your first vertical stroke. With your nib at 45 degrees, create a snuggle join to begin this stroke. Holding the nib at 45 degrees, draw the pen along the baseline to meet up with the endpoint of your second vertical stroke, creating a whisper join.

6. With the box now complete, you can see two whisper joins at opposite corners and two snuggle joins at the other opposite corners. Practice this exercise on your practice sheets, remembering to sync your breathing with your strokes and lifts.

## LETTERS WITH WHISPER AND SNUGGLE JOINS

Practice a line of each of these letters that use whisper and snuggle joins: *a, q, d, f, j, y, g, b* and *p*.

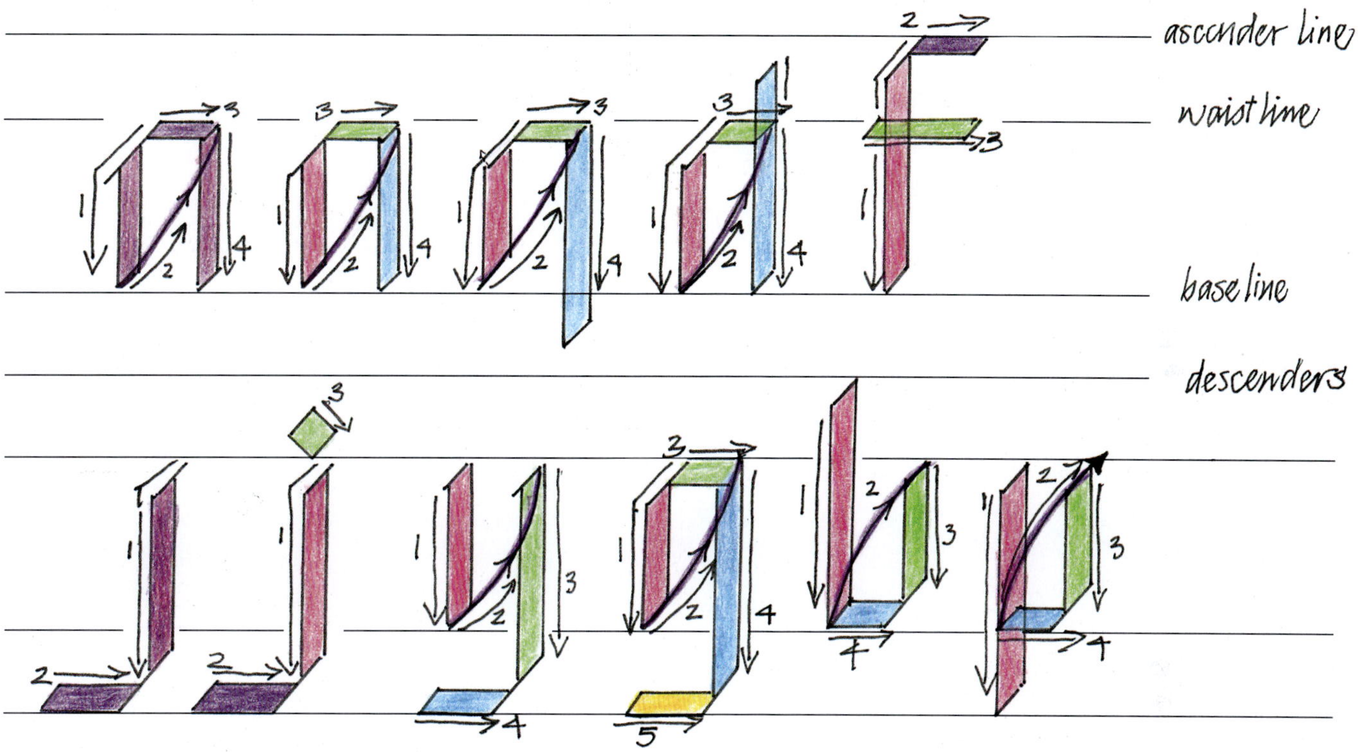

## ADDING CURVES TO WHISPER JOINS

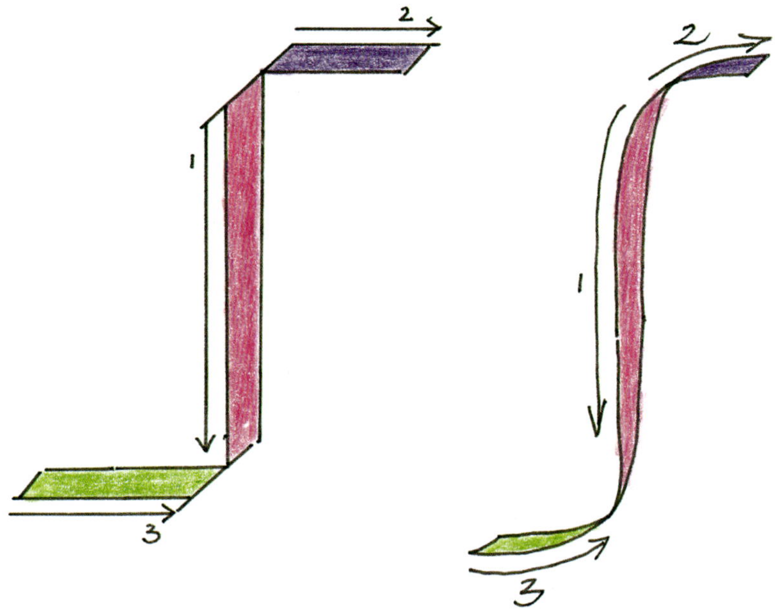


Now that you've learned how to create whisper joins with straight strokes that resemble two iron rods that are barely touching, it's time to modify them so that they look more like a twisted ribbon, which is one of the signature characteristics of the Italic script. Remember, the 45-degree angle doesn't change, just the shape of the stroke.

## THE SHAPES OF ITALIC LETTERS

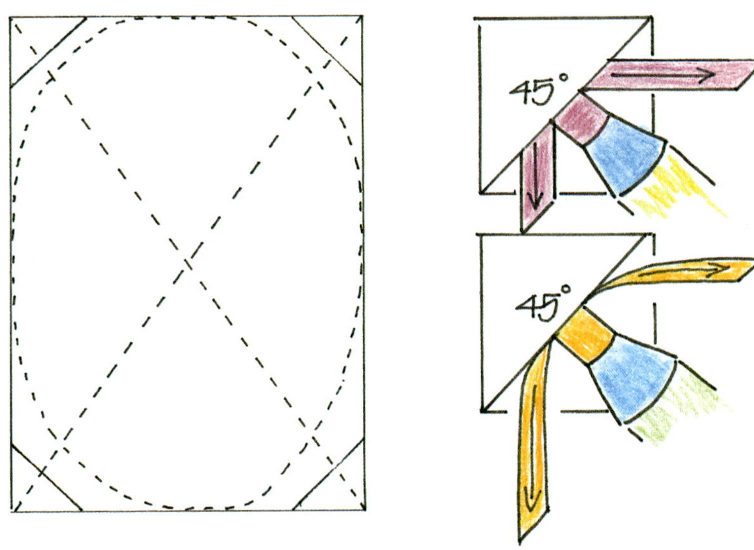


As you continue learning the Italic hand, you'll start to notice that Italic calligraphy is based on two shapes: an oval and a narrow triangular shape. Most of the lowercase letters fit into these shapes.

To develop a curving whisper join, start with your nib at a 45-degree angle one angled nib width below the waistline. To start your downward stroke, first slide over and down to the left before you draw your nib straight down. This will leave a small empty space to the left of the top of the downstroke just below the waistline. Complete the join by lifting your nib up to the top of the downward stroke, still at a 45-degree angle, and sliding the nib up and over to the right to create the horizontal stroke. This will lend a slight curving shape to the join. Practice this curved join.

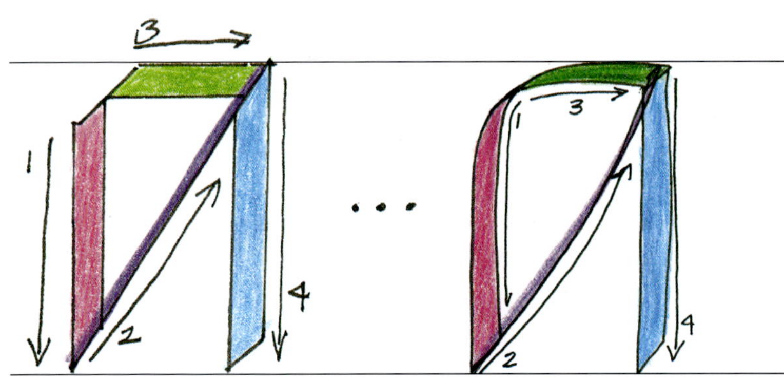


See how much more fluid the letter *a* is when you add curves to the joins?

## CREATING SHAPES WITH THESE NEW STROKES

Now that you've practiced the technique of creating a whisper join that has a curving movement, let's practice some additional shapes that will be useful in creating letters that use this join.

1. With your nib at 45 degrees and the right tip about one angled nib width below the waistline, slide your nib to the left while beginning to move it straight down, finishing the downstroke when the left corner of the nib touches the baseline.

2. Lift your nib and place it so that the left corner of the nib barely touches the beginning of the first stroke, creating a whisper join. Now slide up slightly so that the right side of your nib is touching the waistline and draw a horizontal line under the waistline until the right tip of your nib is at the right side of the letter.

3. Making sure you are at a 45-degree angle, draw a vertical line down to the baseline, stopping one curved nib width above the baseline.

4. Pick up your pen and place it at a 45-degree angle at the bottom of the first downstroke. Now draw horizontally to the right and up such that the right tip of the nib reaches up to touch the bottom tip of the third stroke, thereby creating another whisper join.

The resulting form will have a curved shape for the whisper joins, unlike the iron bars that were first shown when introducing whisper joins.

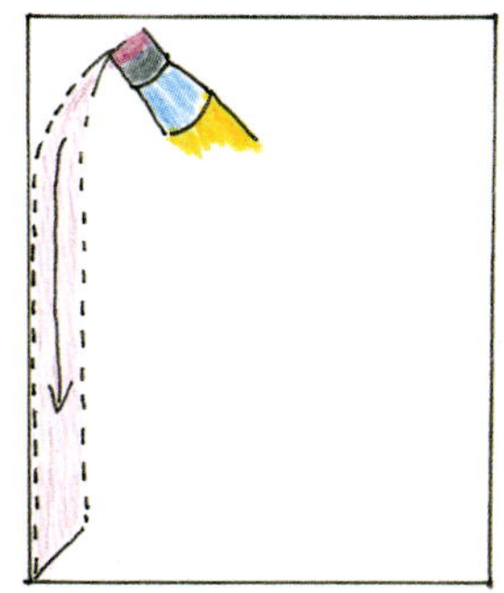

1

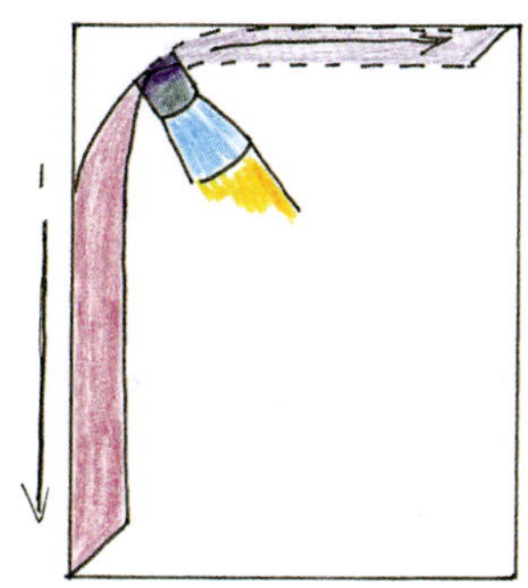


2

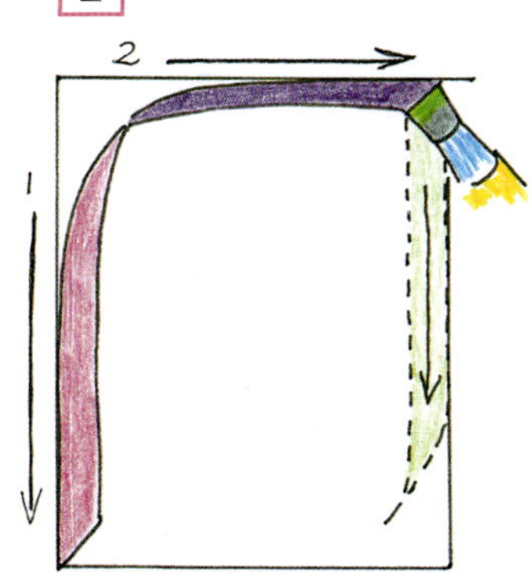


3

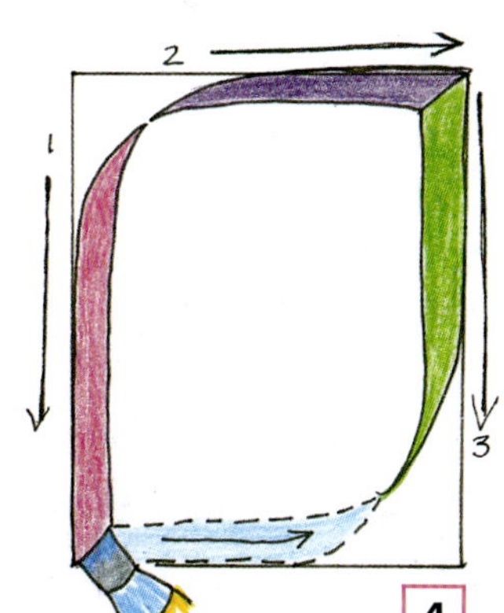


4

Next, try creating a more "triangular" shape using your curved strokes.

1. With your nib at 45 degrees and the right tip about one angled nib width below the waistline, slide your nib to the left while beginning to move it straight down, finishing the downstroke when the left corner of the nib touches the baseline.

2. Now, without lifting your pen, scoot up until the right tip of the nib touches the waistline. Make sure your pen is at a sharper angle. It will reach higher than the first stroke as a result. This stroke should bend or curve ever so slightly to allow for the letter to remain narrow.

3. Lift your pen up and place the left tip (while holding it at 45 degrees) so that it barely touches the beginning of the very first stroke. Now slide the nib up to the waistline such that the right tip of your nib nestles along the waistline and draw a horizontal stroke that meets up with the top of the upstroke in a snuggle join.

4. Finish the letter with a downstroke from the waistline to the baseline.

Once you have practiced this, work on the variation as depicted in images 5 to 8 on the right. In this case the strokes are similar but somewhat in reverse.

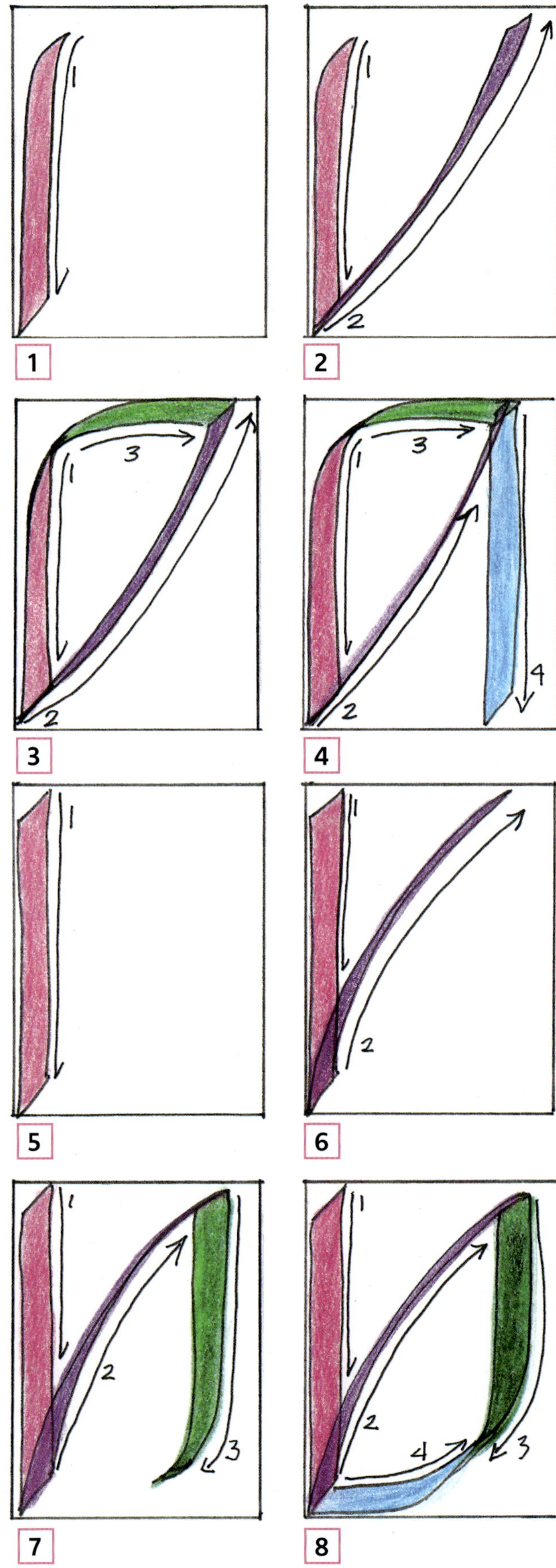

Now that you've practiced these shapes, you can try your hand at some lowercase letters that use them. These letters are grouped based on similarities in shape (i.e., family groups):

- ***u*, *j* and *y***
- ***b* and *p***
- ***a*, *d*, *q* and *g***
- ***f***

Practice at least a page of each of the family groups.

## THE U, J AND Y FAMILY

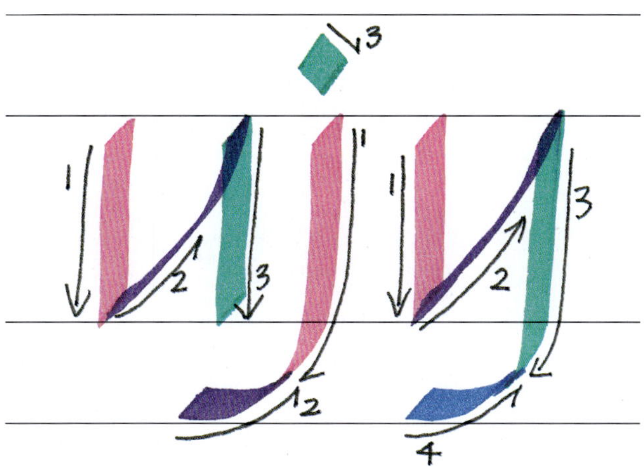


These letters are relatively simple. The *u* is created with a downstroke from the waistline that goes straight to the baseline. Then, on a steepened nib angle, the stroke scoops up to the waistline, followed by a second downstroke parallel to the first.

The *j* starts with the right tip of your nib touching the waistline and descending below the baseline and stopping one angled nib width above the descender line. The second stroke is a horizontal stroke that starts with the left tip touching the descender line. As the pen moves from left to right and approaches the tip of the first stroke, it scoops up to join the first stroke in a whisper join. The diamond for the dot is located above the waistline and should have the bottom point facing the middle of the downstroke.

The *y* is a combination of the *u* and *j*. The first two strokes are the same as the *u*; the third and fourth strokes are the same as the *j*. The fourth stroke should line up with the first downstroke.

## THE B AND P FAMILY

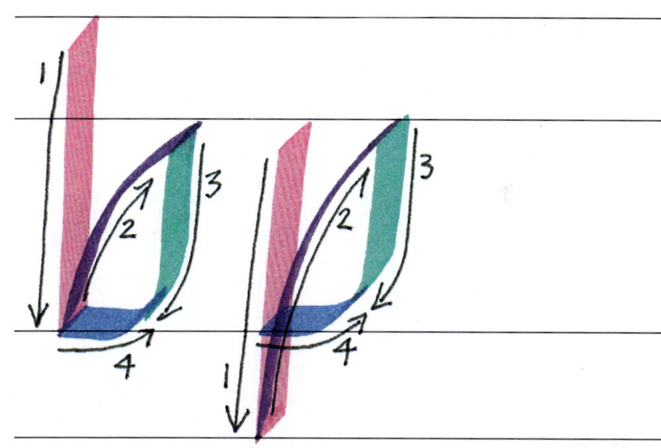


The *b* starts with a downstroke from the ascender line to the baseline. This is followed by an arching stroke up and right at a steeper nib angle to the waistline (like the *n* and *h*). The third stroke comes down but stops one angled nib width before the baseline. The fourth stroke starts as a snuggle join against the stem (first stroke) and runs along the baseline and up to join the third stroke in a whisper join.

The *p* is the same as the *b* except that the stem (stroke 1) starts at the waistline and goes to the descender line. The second stroke is a thinner arching stroke up and out to the waistline. Stroke 3 is a downstroke that stops above the baseline. The fourth starts in the stem at the baseline and moves from left to right along the baseline before meeting up with the third stroke in a whisper join.

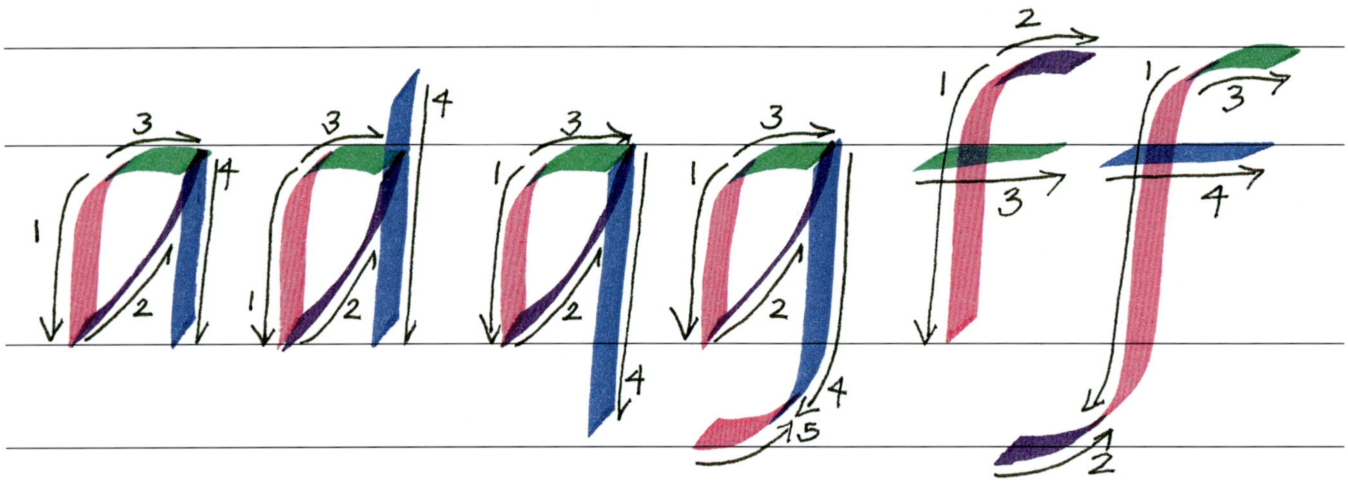


## THE A, D, Q AND G FAMILY

These letters are grouped because they all contain the shape of the letter *a*, which is where we will start.

The *a* starts one angled nib width below the waistline and goes straight down to the baseline so that the left tip of the nib just touches it. The second stroke is a scoop up to the right (like the *u*) at a steepened nib angle and stops at the waistline. For the third stroke (the cap), the left tip of your nib joins the tip of the first stroke (whisper join) and slides up at that angle to the waistline and over to join the second stroke. The fourth stroke is a snuggle join with the end of stroke three and descends to the baseline parallel to stroke 1.

The first three strokes of the letter a are the same first three strokes for *d*, *q* and *g*. Where these letters differ is the fourth stroke. For *d*, this last stroke starts about halfway up from the waistline and descends to the baseline. The fourth stroke of the letter *q* begins at the waistline (like the fourth stroke of the *a*) but goes straight down to the descender line so that the left point of the nib touches the line. The *g* is the same as the *q* except that the final downstroke stops one angled nib width before the descender line so that the fifth and final stroke can create the tail in the same way as the letter *y*. The start of this final stroke should line up with the first stroke.

## THE LETTER F

The letter *f* is discussed outside any specific group of letters. It starts one angled nib width below the ascender line and goes straight down to the baseline. The second stroke is the cap: the left tip of your nib touches the starting point of the first stroke and slides slightly up and then along the ascender line. The third stroke (crossbar) runs left to right just below the waistline, with your nib at a sharpened angle, like the crossbar of the letter *t*. The cross should go farther to the right than to the left of the stem.

A variation of *f* includes a tail at the bottom. In this case, the initial downstroke would stop one angled nib width above the descender line to enable you to make the horizontal stroke that comes up to meet the first in a whisper join.

# Oval Strokes- o,e,c,s

To begin learning the strokes that make up the letters *o*, *e*, *c* and *s*, create a line of each of the shapes on the right on your practice sheet. These shapes are replicated in this group of letters.

Once you have practiced these shapes, create a line of each of the shapes on the right with your pen and ink.

The *o* is created with two downward strokes that meet as whisper joins. The first downstroke starts one 45-degree angled nib width below the baseline, and moves downward and around from thin to thick to thin again as the stroke finishes slightly upward above the baseline.

The second stroke starts with a whisper join with the left tip of the nib touching the tip of the first stroke. The stroke moves up to the waistline before descending in what you want to be an identical curve, moving from thin (at the whisper join) to thick to thin as you curve around and down from the waistline until you meet up with the end of the first stroke, creating another whisper join. This letter is arguably the most difficult to create. As a result, I've always used an *o* when practicing spacing between words.

The *e* starts the same way as the *o*. For the second stroke you position the left tip of your nib at the tip of the first stroke (whisper join) and at a 45-degree angle you reach up in a curve to the waistline and then swoop to the left with a fine line to finish above the middle of the first stroke.

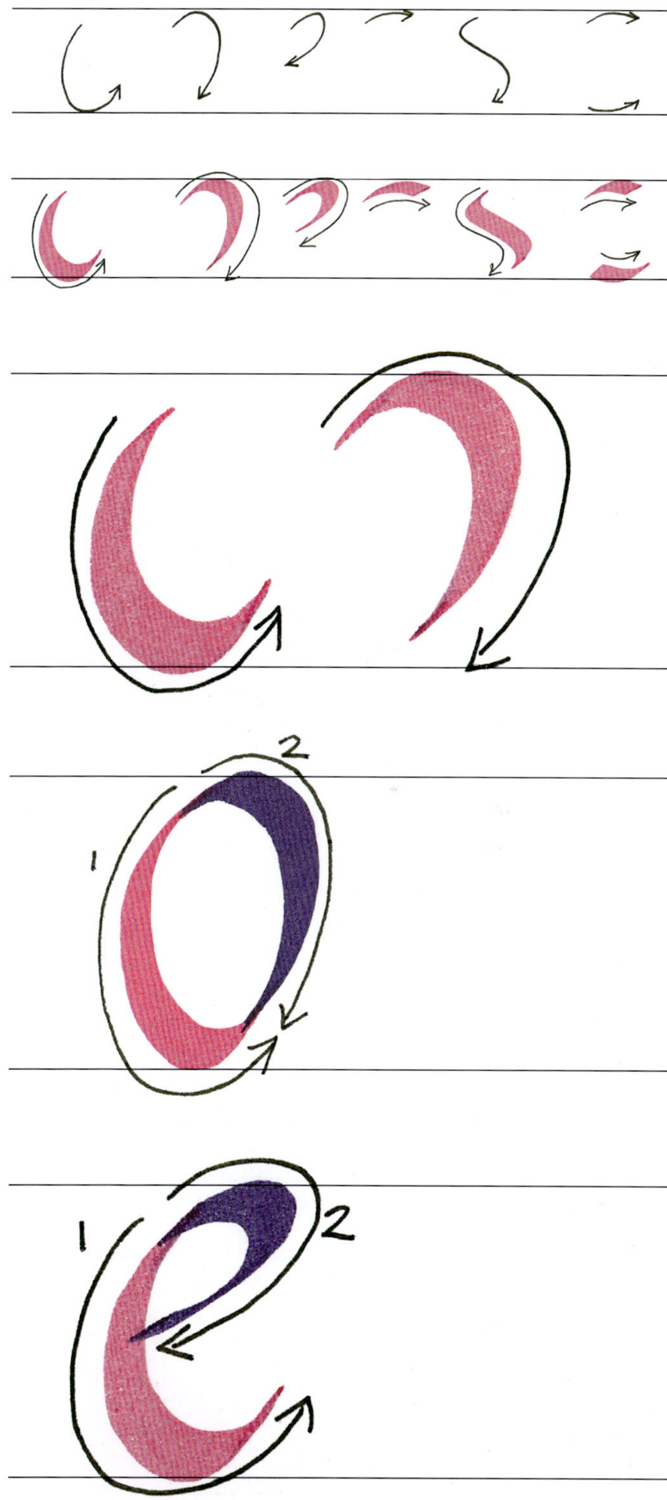

The *c* starts the same way as the *o* and *e*. As with the first two letters, the second stroke starts with an identical whisper join, then moves up to the waistline and along it, similar to the cap of the letter *a*. Make sure not to extend it too far as it will ruin the balance of the letter.

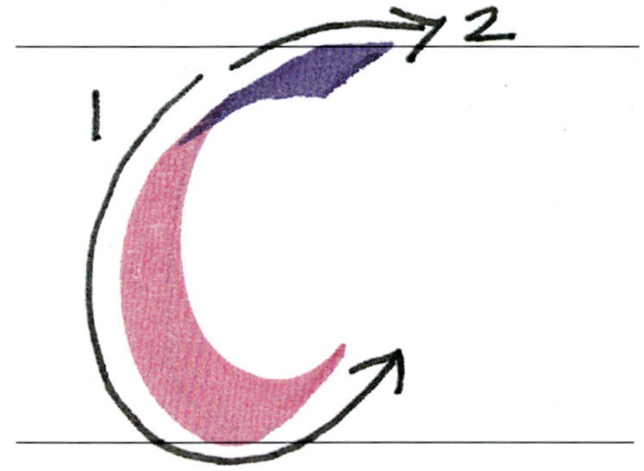


Finally, we come to *s*. Start approximately one angled nib width below the waistline (similar to the *o*). The first stroke is a curved diagonal that goes right then trails slightly to the left, finishing one angled nib width above the baseline. The stroke moves from thin to thick to thin.

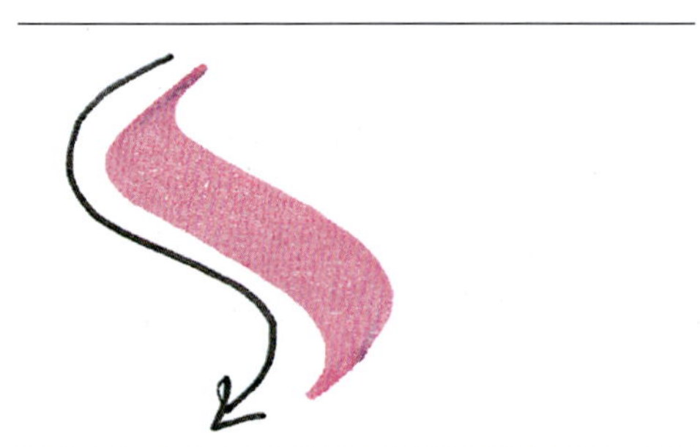

The second stroke is like the cap of the a and c. It starts with a whisper join, with the left tip of the nib touching the tip of the first stroke and then sliding up and along the waistline with the end of the stroke lining up with the lower body of the first stroke.

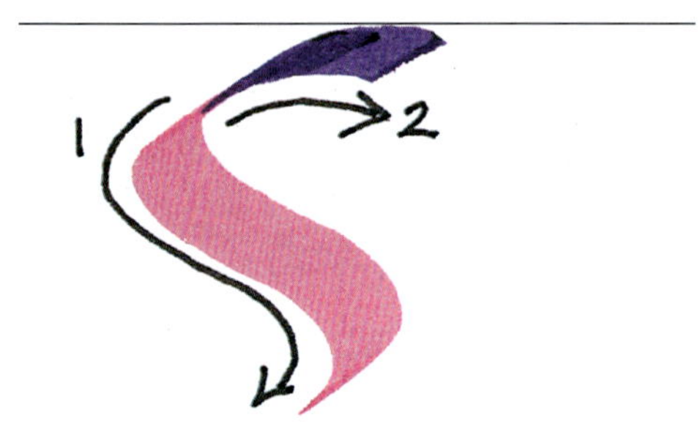


The final stroke is a horizontal stroke that rides along the baseline at 45 degrees and reaches up to the fine point end of the first stroke such that the right tip of your nib just touches it, creating another whisper join. This third stroke should start where the top left side of the body of the *s* pushes farthest out to the left. You should be able to draw a vertical line straight up to the edge of this curve. Note that when this letter is complete, the top center opening of the *s* should be slightly smaller than the bottom opening. The *s* should have more weight at the bottom to look more grounded.

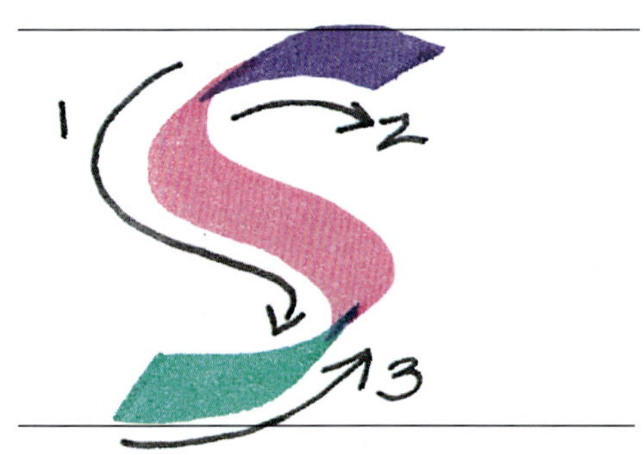

## Ductus and Fluidity

This chapter has focused on the strokes that make up each letter form, their directions and order, and the various ways to connect these strokes. Understanding this is critical to ensure proper letter form. However, it is also important that your letters dance across the page with energy and fluidity as they extend up, down and across.

As you practice, ductus will become second nature over time. Your mind, hand and eye will remember more and not need to concentrate on the mechanics of each letter. At that point the ductus will become more fluid, and what was once a hard stop at the bottom of a downstroke will start to incorporate the ensuing upstroke, thereby combining the two strokes into one. This is best described as a downstroke followed by a bounce up — either out and in, or out and away. That means ultimately the ductus becomes fewer distinct strokes, although the letter retains its form and structure.

Let's take the letter *a* as an example. As we saw earlier, this letter is comprised of four strokes. With a more fluid ductus that utilizes a bounce element, the letter *a* will have fewer pen stops as the upstroke becomes the continuation of the initial downstroke in the form of a bounce upward to the waistline. The bounce lends a bit more energy to the letter.

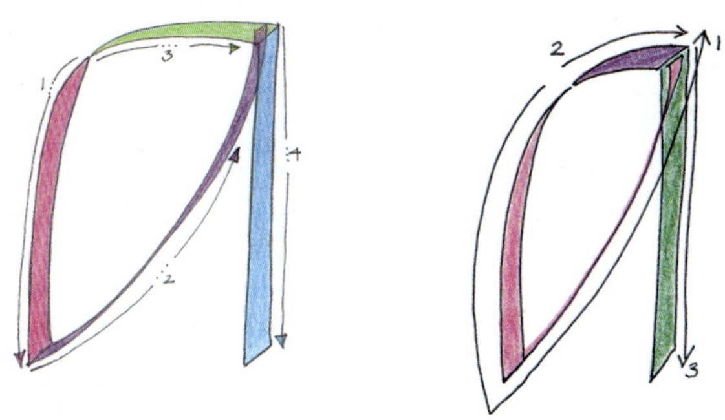

This can be seen in other letters, as illustrated on the right, first in skeletal format and then with a nib.

However, this transition takes time, practice and a confident hand coupled with a solid knowledge of letter forms. Having a careful eye to the details will result in ductus with more fluidity.

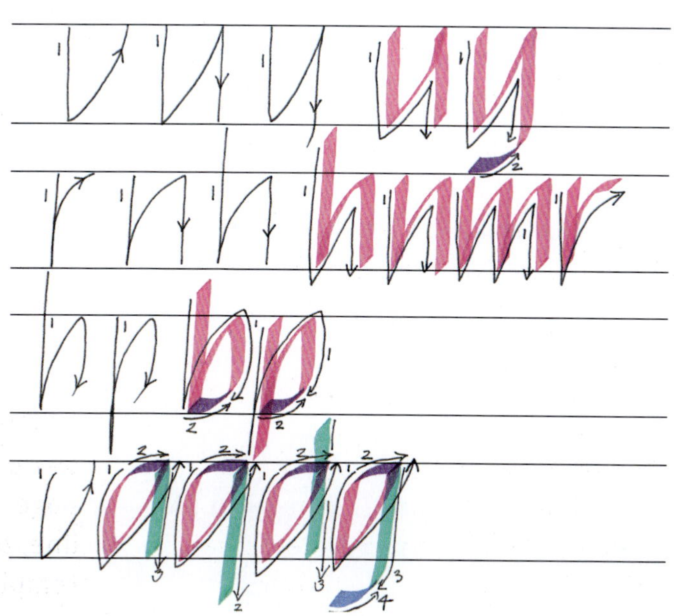

# Chapter 3

# Learning the Letters, Numbers, & Punctuation

At last, you're ready to start creating Italic calligraphy, including uppercase letters, numbers and punctuation. First, you'll update your practice sheet to include slope — a common quality of Italic — and then you'll learn how to create your letters using this slope. You'll also be reviewing spacing and noticing, and the chapter is capped with a few fun projects that utilize your practice sheets.

## Updating Your Practice Sheet

The practice sheet you lined as your template in Chapter 1 now needs to include slope. Slope is a quality of the Italic hand and historically signified an increased need for speedier writing. While experienced calligraphers may be able to execute consistent slope by eye alone, when training ourselves, it's helpful to add guidelines.

Place a ruler along the left edge of your practice sheet with a slight tilt (about 5 to 10 degrees) to the right. An easy way to figure out this slope is to measure 2 inches from the top left side and ½ inch from the bottom left side and then draw a line from the top to the bottom, connecting the two marks. After you've drawn the first line, slide the ruler to the right so the left edge lines up with the first drawn line. Draw a line along the right edge. Continue this pattern to finish this page.

If you started with a blank sheet of paper as opposed to an already-lined template page, add your lines for the ascenders, waistline, baseline and descenders to complete the template.

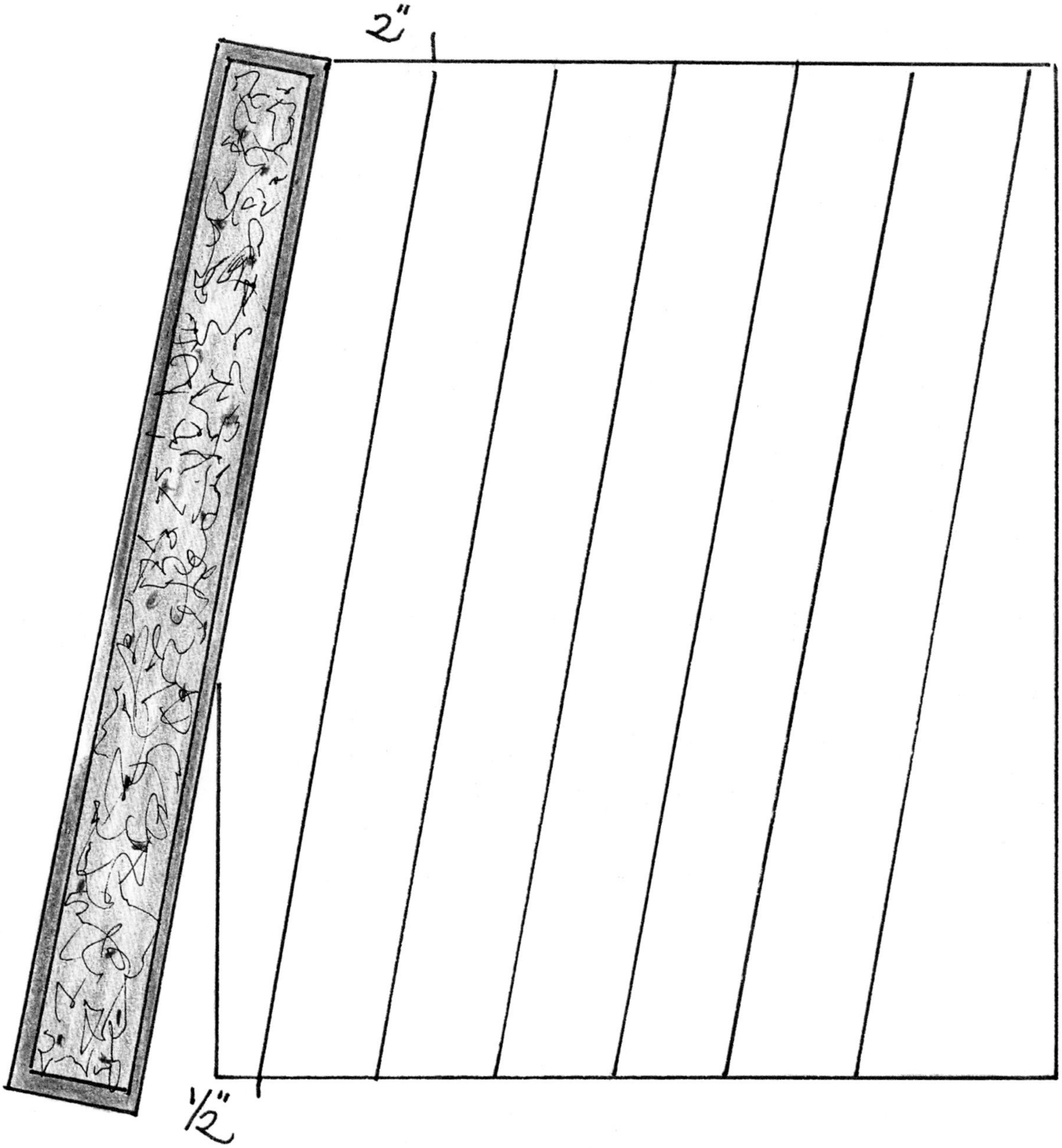


Go over everything with a black fine-liner marker. Make copies or use this new template under your blank practice sheet.

After you become very comfortable with a 5- to 10-degree slope, you can experiment with greater or lesser slopes to see what you like best. But when first learning the Italic hand, I recommend staying within this range.

# Creating Letters with Slope

Let's create the lowercase letters you learned in Chapter 2 but using the slope lines as guides.

Practice each group of letters, which are illustrated on this page and the next, for one to three lines on your practice sheets. Be sure to keep an eye on consistent spacing between letters and the blocks of letters. As well, try your best to keep your letters parallel to the slope line and each other. Remember that the way you hold your pen, as well as the angle, remains the same. You can tilt your page to the left if you find that this makes it more comfortable.

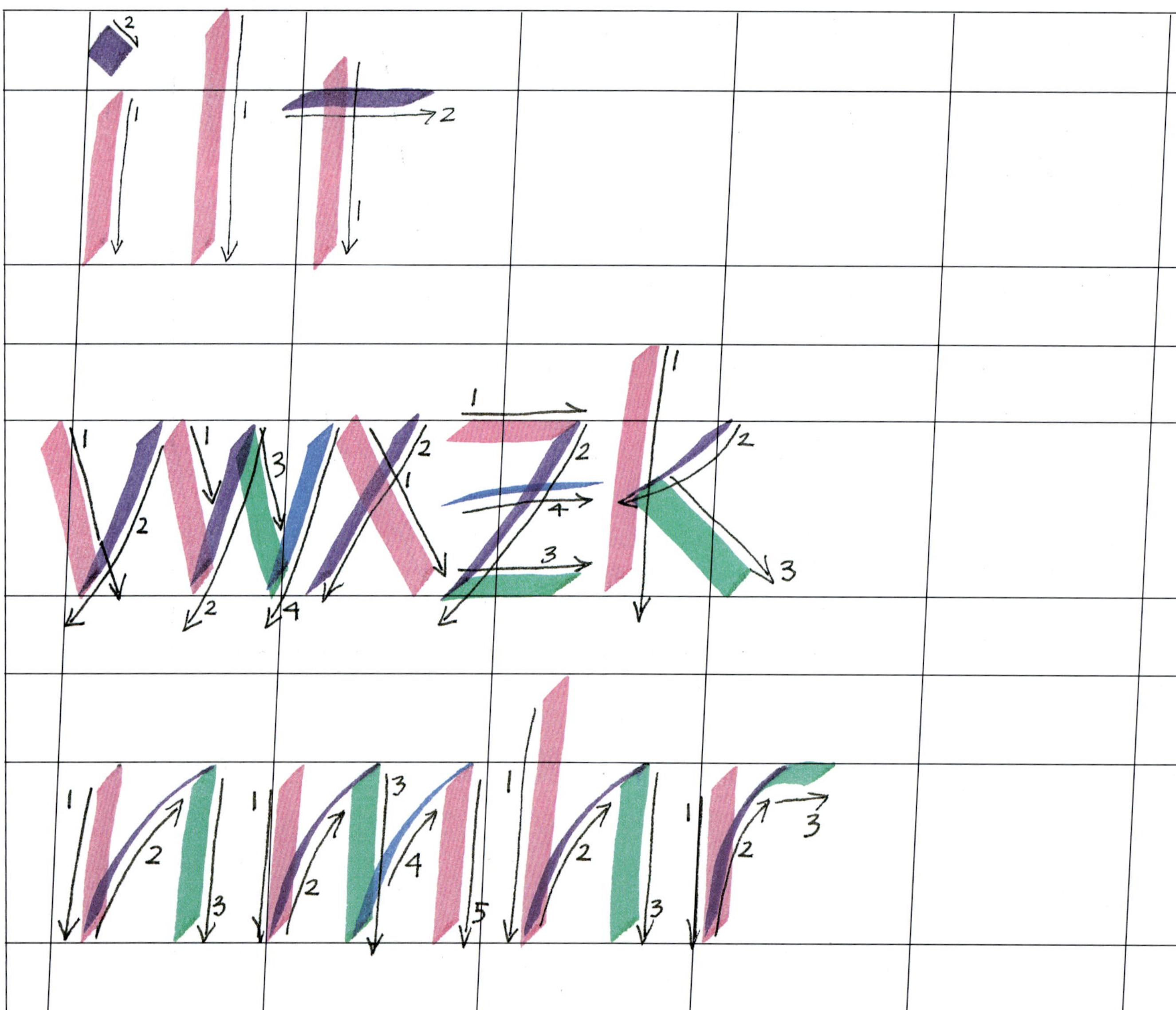

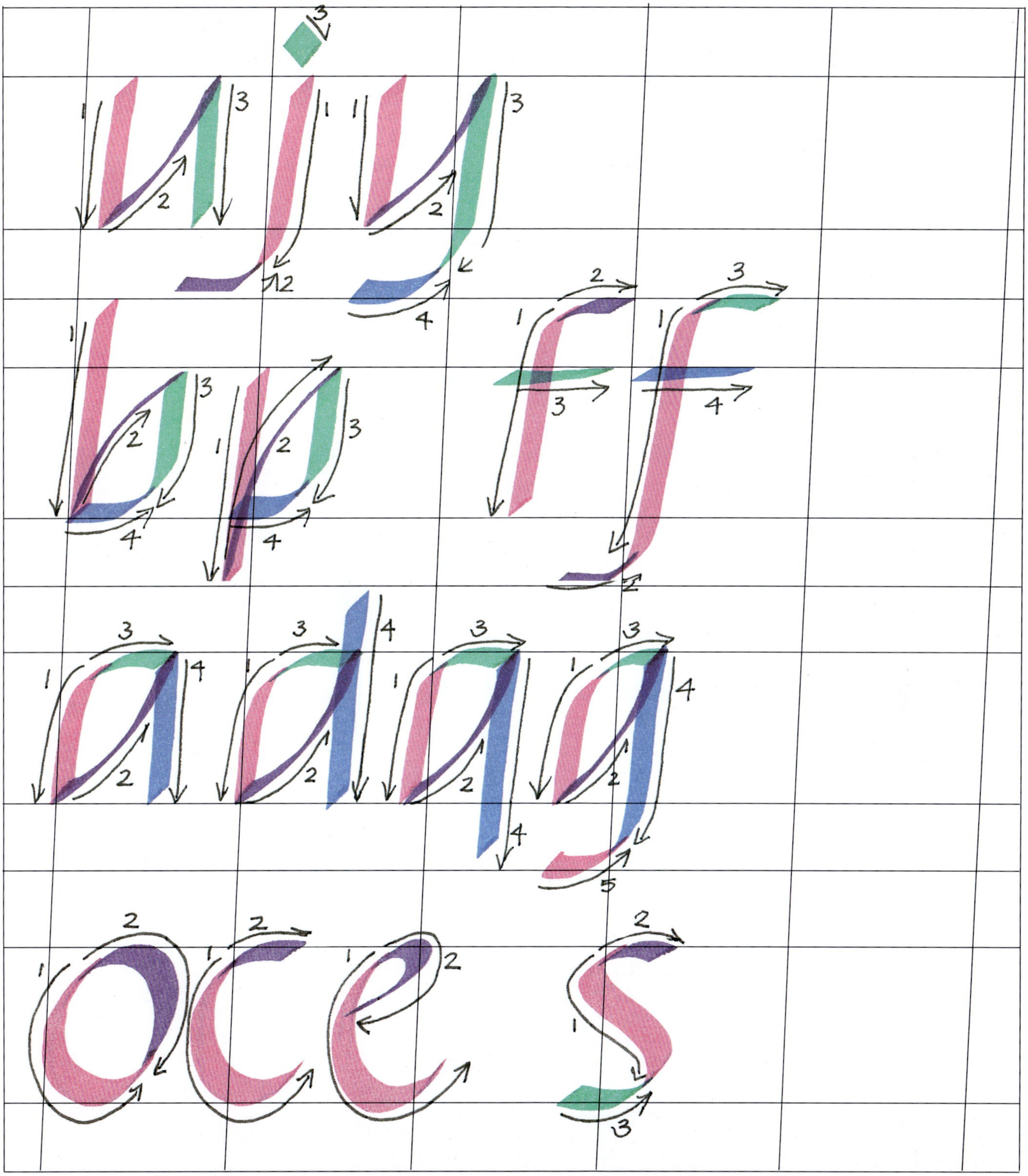

## LOWERCASE ITALIC ALPHABET

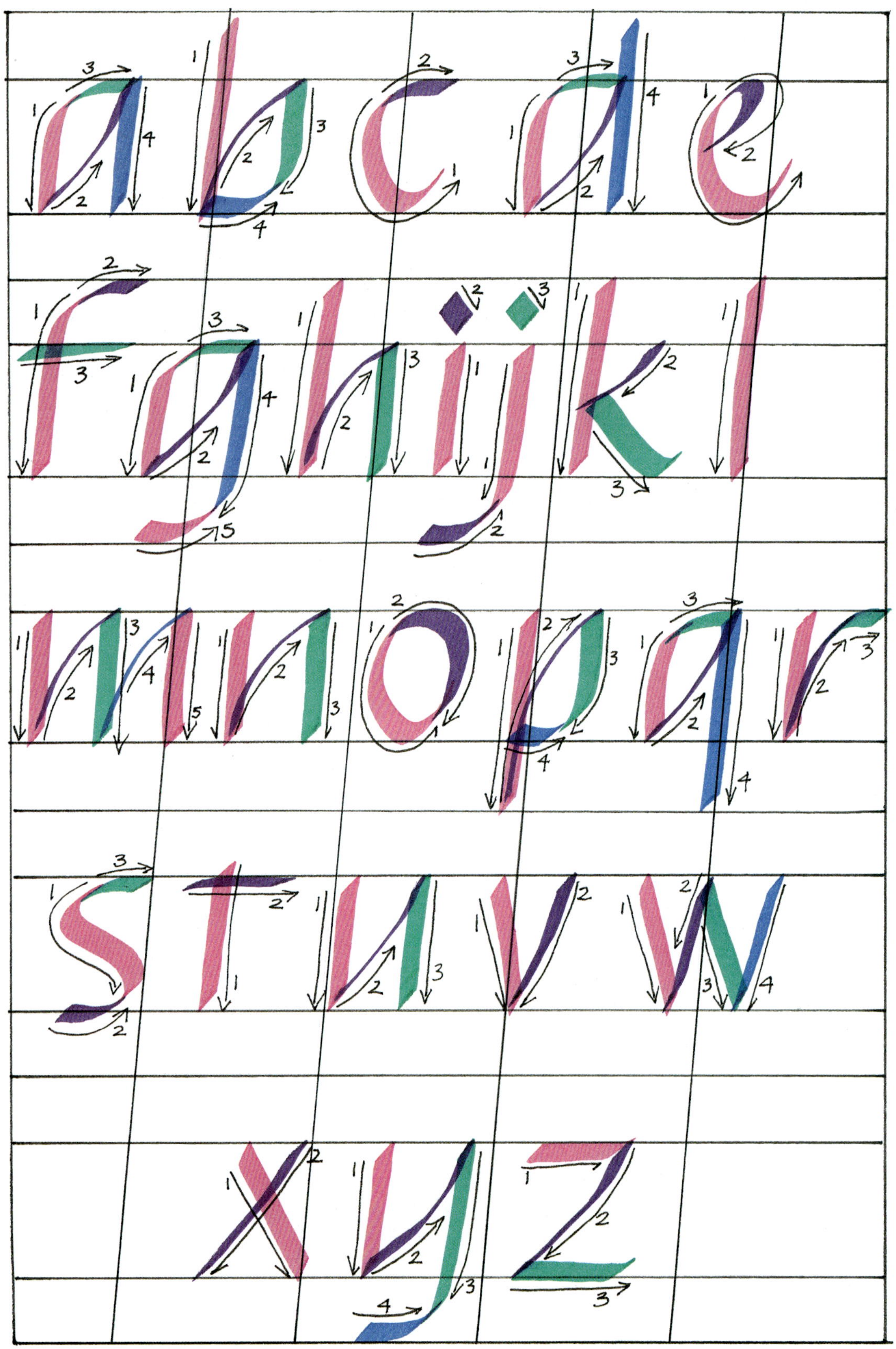

## Collecting the Goods

As you patiently practice with a strong posture, take a break after each line or every few lines.

Take a moment to look at what you've done and evaluate your work. Look through your achievements and choose one or two letters you're particularly proud of. Lightly circle them with a pencil. At the end of each practice sheet, you will have circled your favorites. Cut out the circled letters and place them in an envelope for later — there will be a fun project at the end of Section One in which you will use these special bits. (Aim for one of each lowercase letter.)

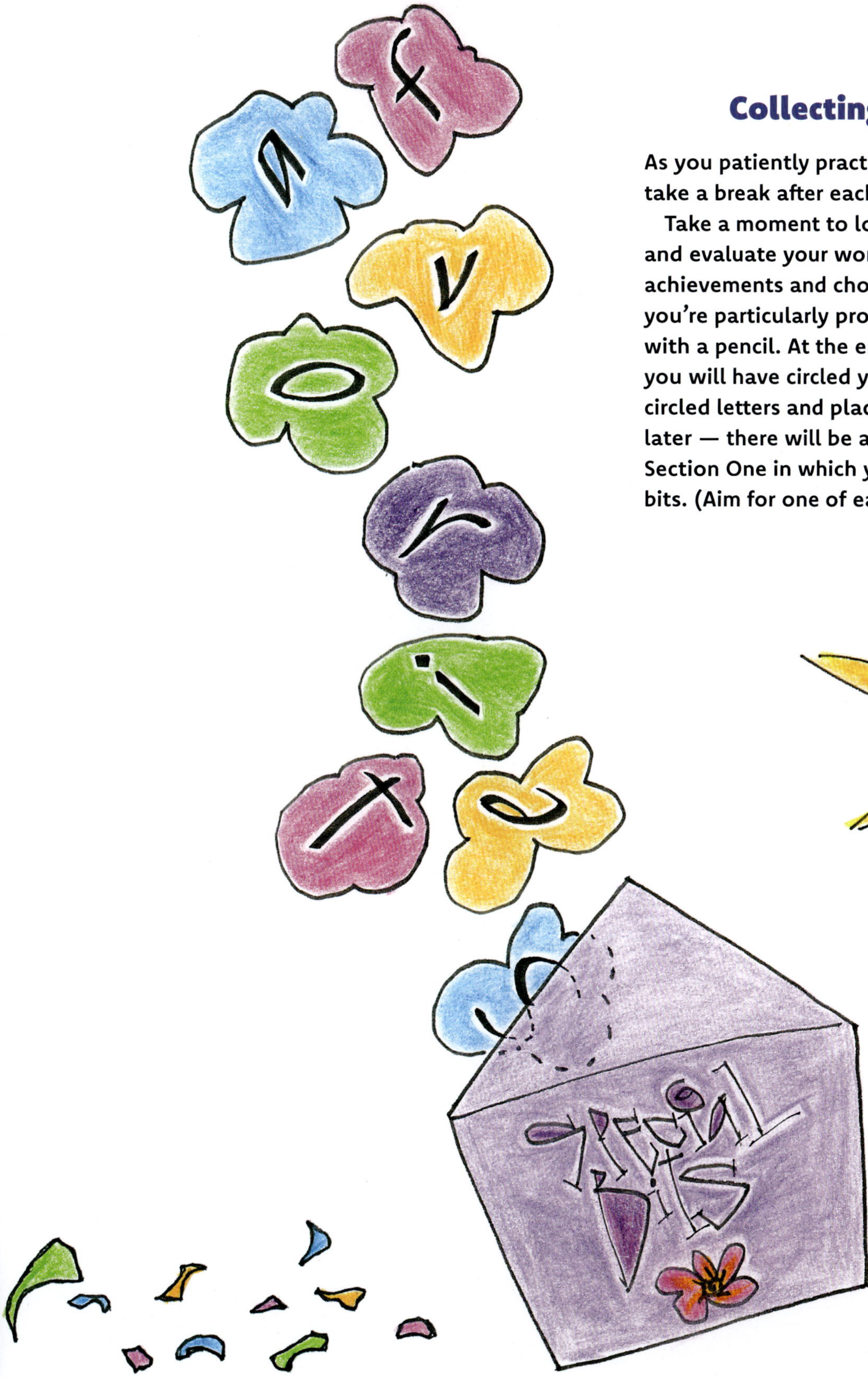

### TRYING WORDS WITH SLOPE

Let's put the letters together to create some words with slope on your practice sheets. Try completing a few lines of each word. As always, remember to notice the spacing between letters and between words, keeping both consistent.

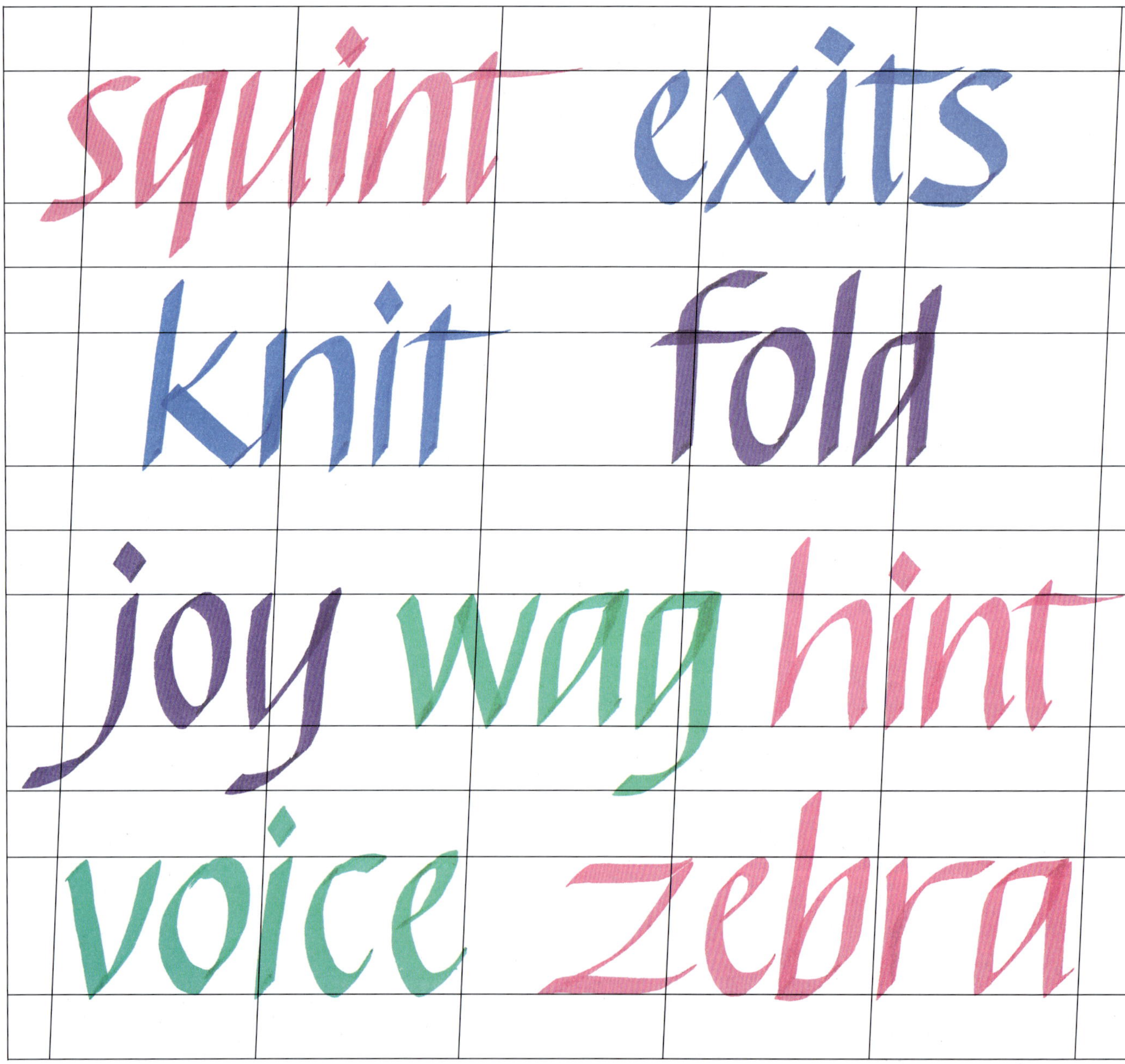

# Double Letters

Double letters, like those that appear in *puppy*, *mood* and *wobble*, can be opportunities to add a bit of flair and interest, especially if you find it difficult to make them identical. If your spacing and letters are consistent and parallel, you can, of course, create identical double letters, but some letters are particularly challenging. If you just can't get your letters perfectly identical, or you want to have a bit of fun, here are some ideas.

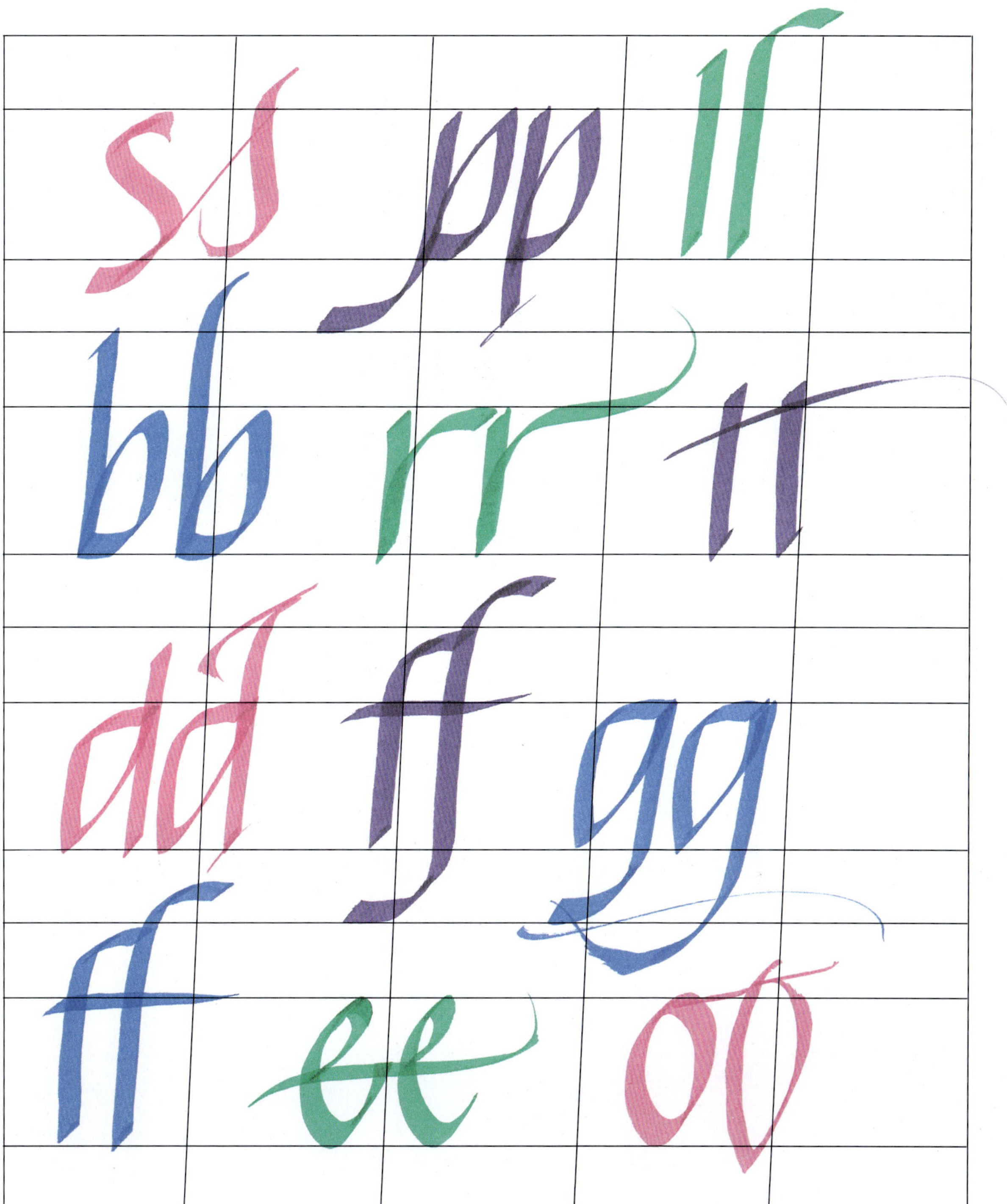

## TRYING WORDS WITH DOUBLE LETTERS

Here are some words you can try on your practice sheet that incorporate double letters.

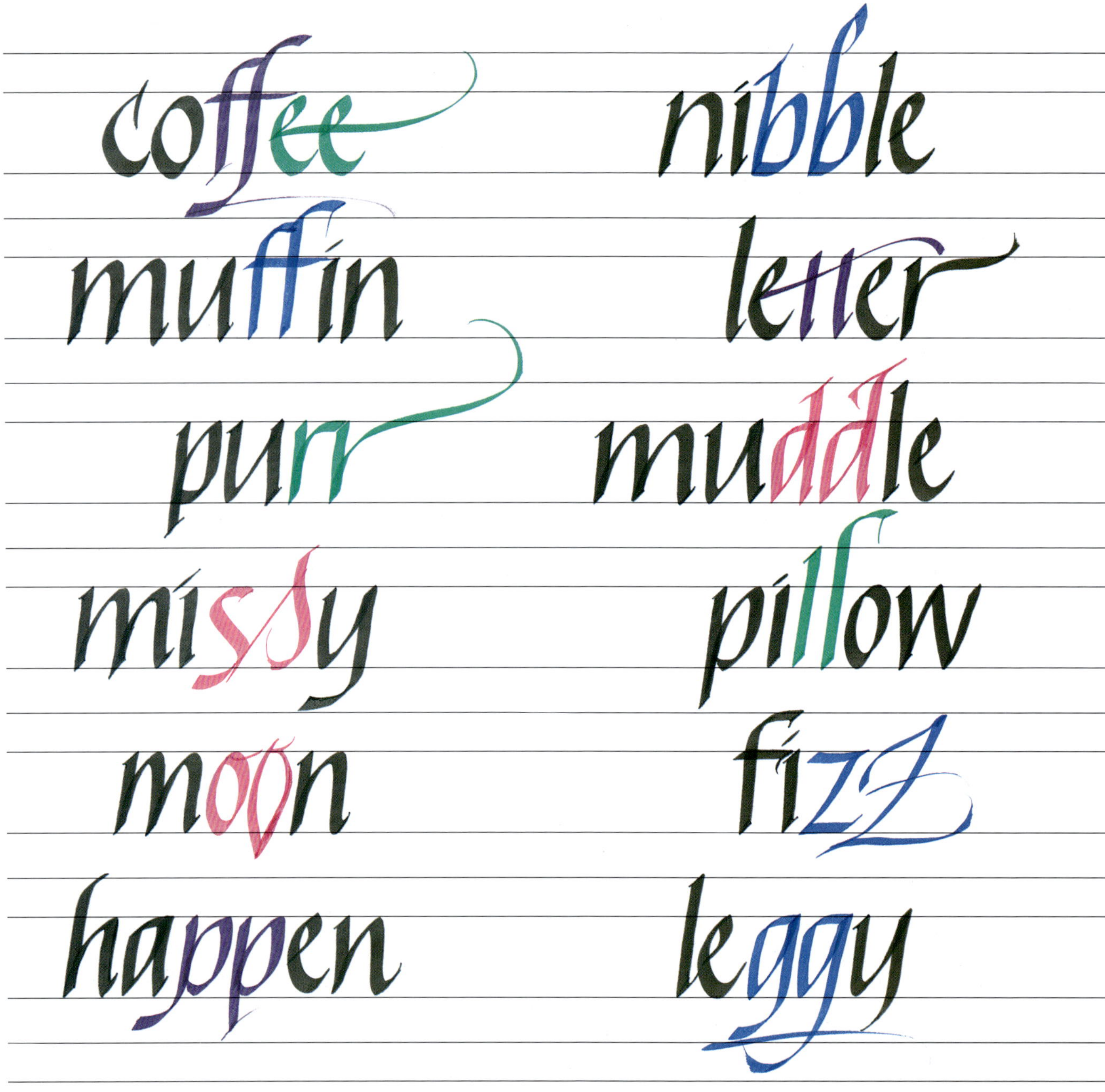

# Capital Letters

Our capital, or uppercase, letters are based on the Roman capitals. Italic capitals are narrow and on the same slight slope as the minuscules. They're also one nib width shorter than the ascenders of the lowercase letters (in other words, capitals are typically seven nib widths tall while lowercase letters with ascenders are typically eight nib widths tall). As a result, we will need to make another modification to our practice sheet template.

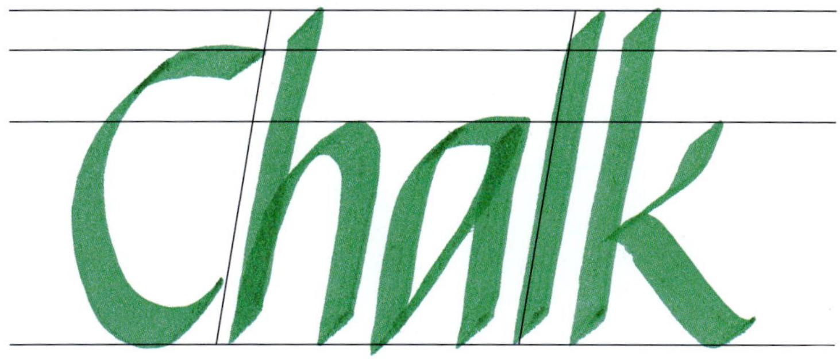


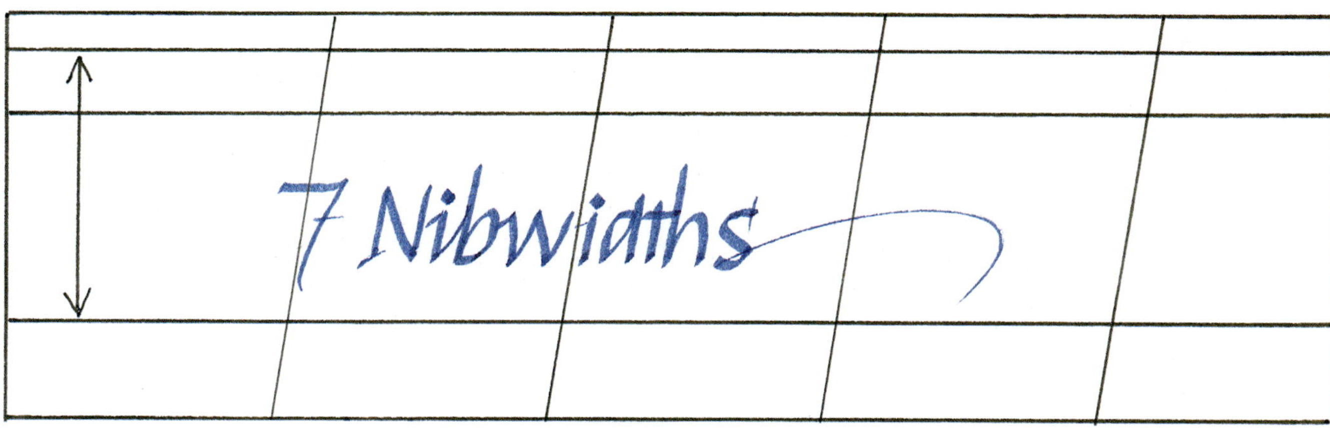


## A CAPITAL UPDATE

On your practice sheet template, measure one nib width down from the top of the ascender line. Mark the measurement on the left and right side of the page. Draw a line in pencil connecting the two marks (you could try a dashed line so it's clear which line is which). Carry on creating those lines one nib width lower than the ascender line. Once you've finished your page, go over it with a black fine-liner marker, erase your pencil marks and make copies of the new sheet or use it as a template under your blank practice sheet. See what your updated template will look like on the next page.

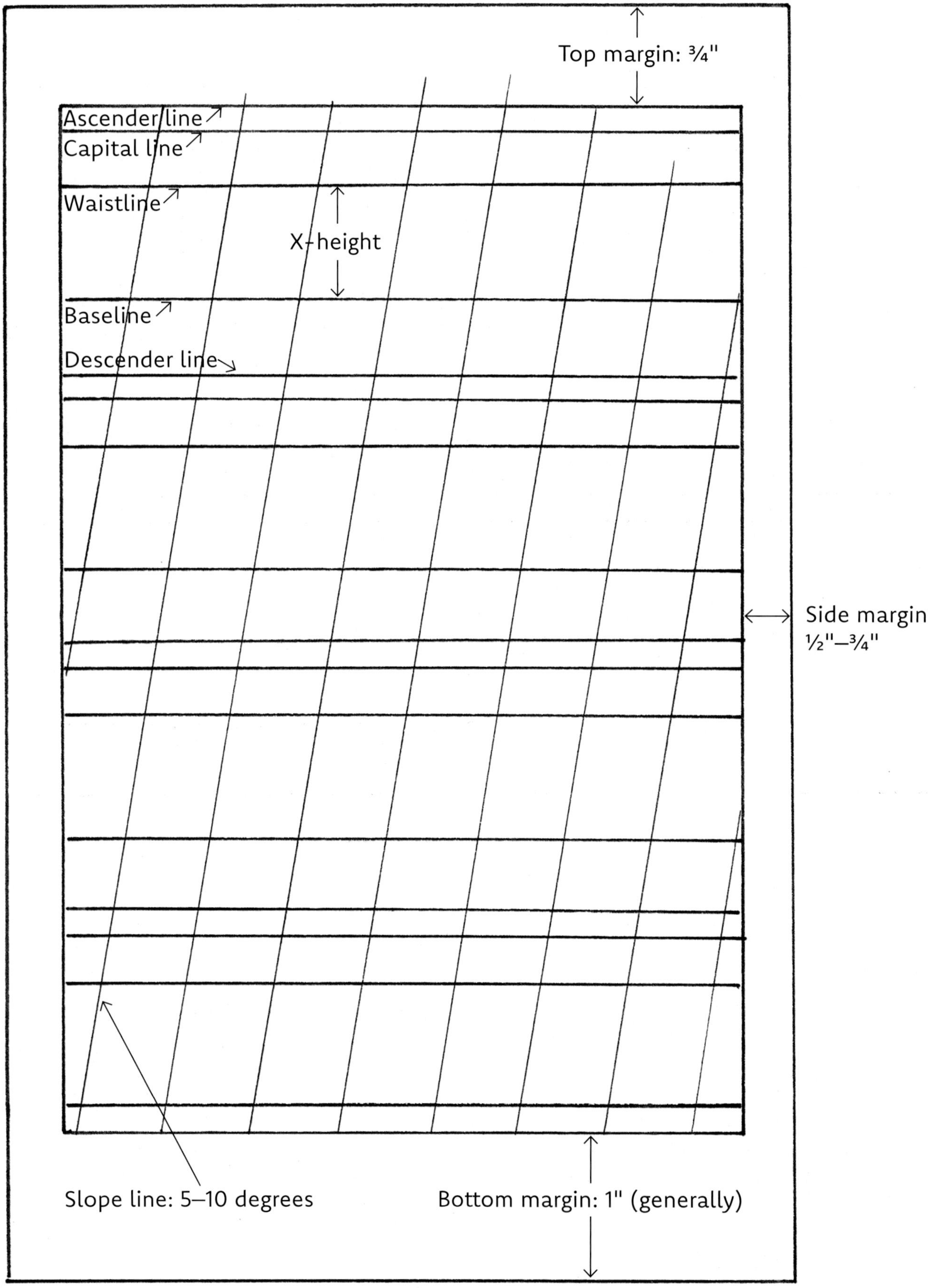
Top margin: ¾"
Ascender line
Capital line
Waistline
X-height
Baseline
Descender line
Side margin: ½"–¾"
Slope line: 5–10 degrees
Bottom margin: 1" (generally)

## CREATING CAPITALS IN LETTER GROUPS

With your practice template updated, you're now ready to tackle capitals. As you've likely noticed, I find it helpful to group letters that have similar strokes. Remember to maintain your 45-degree angle, except when the angle needs to be steeper (i.e., for diagonals and crossbars).

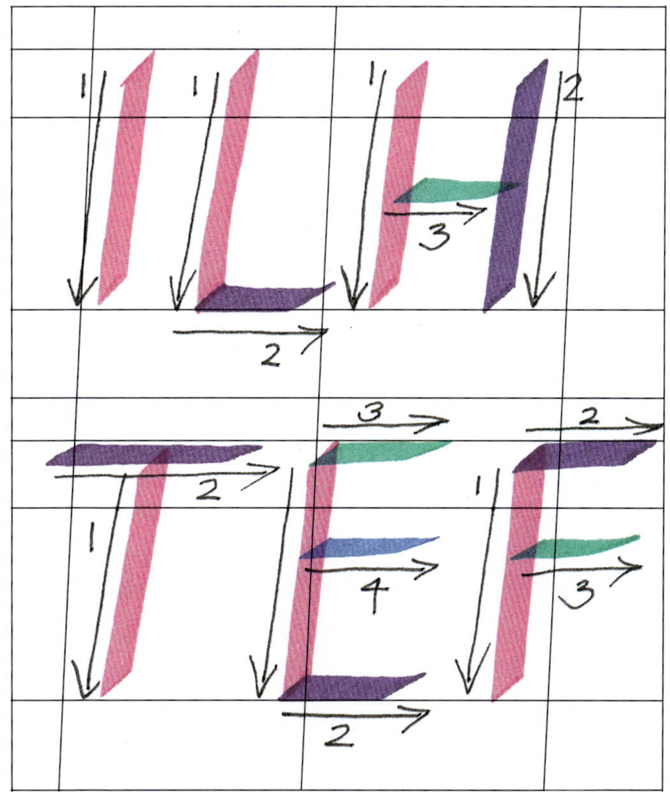

### I, L, H, T, E AND F

The first group of capital letters is made up of only straightforward vertical and horizontal strokes, and the horizontal strokes are slightly thinner than the vertical strokes.

The *L*'s horizontal stroke at the bottom carries on from the first vertical stroke after a full stop at the baseline without a pen lift. This prevents the corner from becoming rounded; you want the corner to be sharp.

For the *H*, the horizontal stroke between the two vertical strokes appears a little below the waistline. This is also true for the middle horizontal stroke for *E* and *F*.

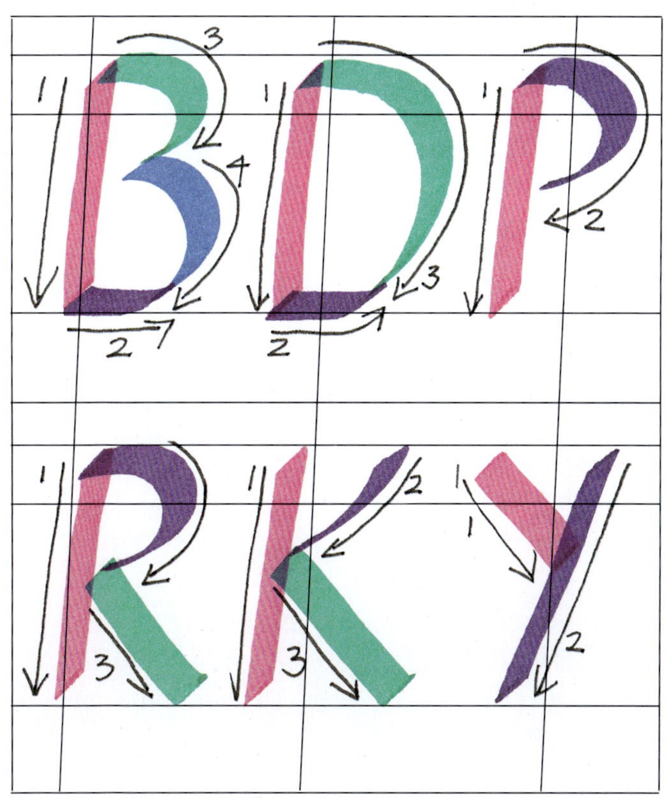

### B, D, P, R, K AND Y

This group of capital letters combines rounded strokes (*B*, *D*, *P* and *R*) as well as letters that have diagonal strokes (*R*, *K* and *Y*).

*B* and *D* use the same two-step stroke of the letter *L*, only shorter. These two letters also use whisper joins. I sometimes find creating the *D* is an exercise in blind faith. I often start drawing the third stroke and hope that it meets the whisper join at the end of the second stroke.

The round and/or diagonal strokes for *P*, *R*, *K* and *Y* should meet the first stroke slightly above its middle.

## M and W

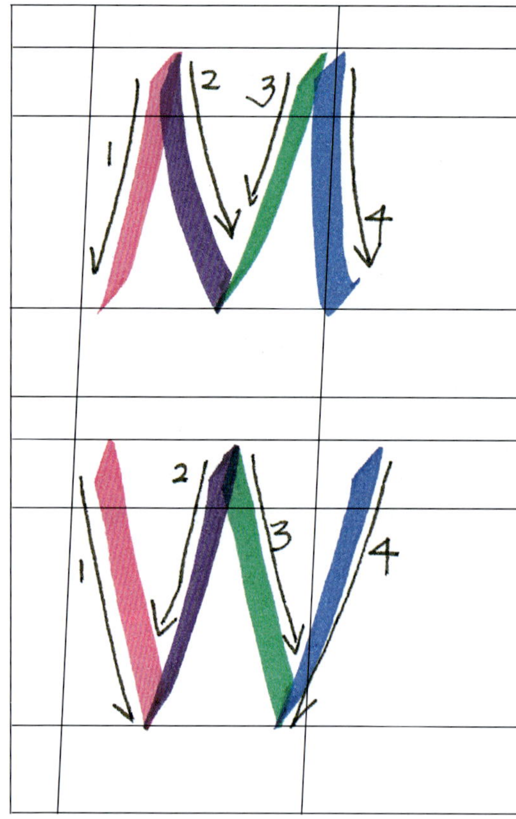

For both the capital *M* and *W*, you must angle the diagonal strokes that go down to the left at a steeper nib angle to keep the letter narrower, similar to what you did when you were learning the lowercase letters *v*, *w*, *x* and *k*. For the *M*, the first and third strokes will be slightly thinner than the second and fourth as they are downward diagonals to the left. Additionally, strokes 1 and 3 should be close to parallel, as is the case for strokes 2 and 4.

The first and third strokes for the *W* will be thick (and parallel), and the second and fourth will have narrower strokes (and be parallel as well). It is a general rule that strokes that go down to the left are the steeper strokes and as such will be thinner and will lighten the letter. Not every stroke will be thick. This will apply to the letters *A*, *K*, *V*, *W*, *X*, *Y* and *Z*.

## X, Z, A, V and N

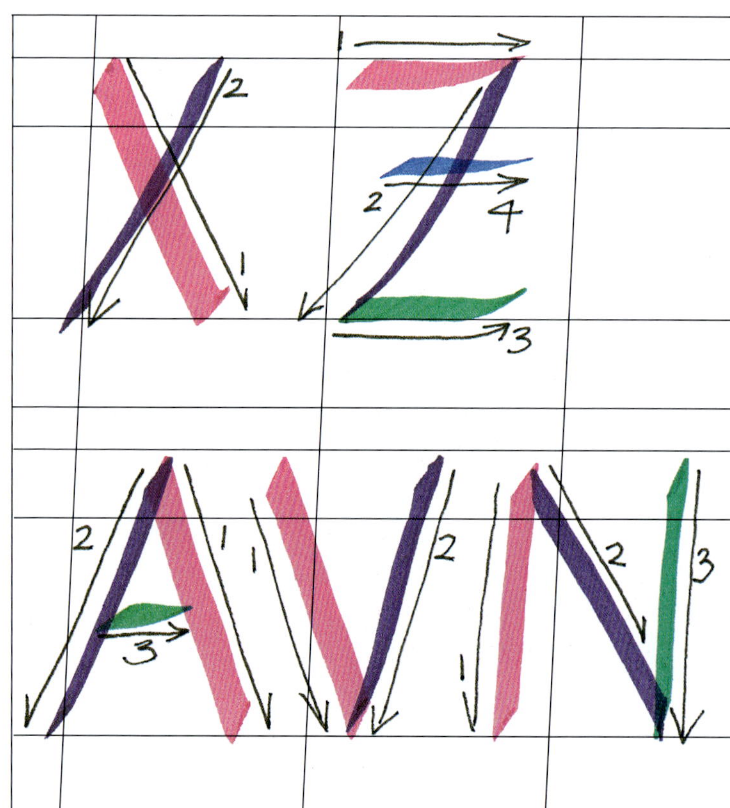

The next group of capital letters is similar to the previous group with the main difference being that these letters incorporate crossbars and verticals to go along with the diagonal strokes.

The top triangle of the *X* needs to be slightly smaller than the bottom triangle.

The crossbar for the *Z* should be slightly above mid-point. Similarly, the crossbar for the *A* should be at mid-point or only slightly above mid-point.

Remember that the second downstroke for the *A*, *X*, *V* and *Z* will be narrower (as with the *W*); however, the *N* is different in that both vertical downstrokes will be slightly narrower (i.e., at a steeper pen angle) than the middle diagonal stroke.

## J, U AND S

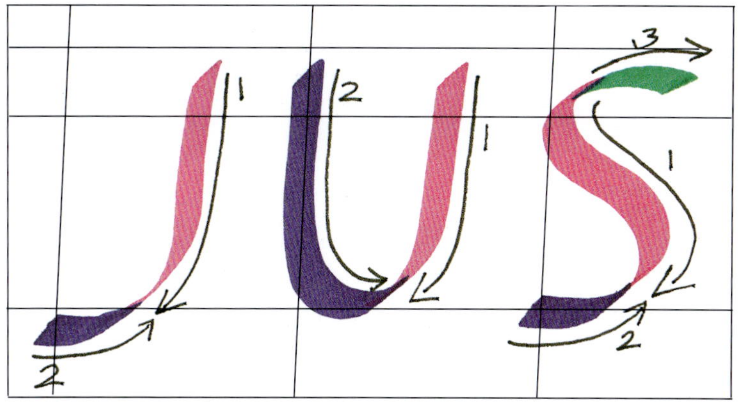

These elegantly curved letters rely on well-executed whisper joins. The second stroke of the *J* can either ride along the baseline or run just below it before reaching up to the end of the first stroke in a whisper join.

I find that the *U* is best created with the first stroke that is used when you make the *J*, with the second stroke on the left coming down and meeting up with the first stroke in a whisper join. But the stroke order can be reversed.

The *S* should be drawn the same way as the lowercase *s*, but the strokes will be stretched to cover seven nib widths instead of five. You can draw the *S* in pencil and use it as a guide as you learn the strokes.

## O, C, G AND Q

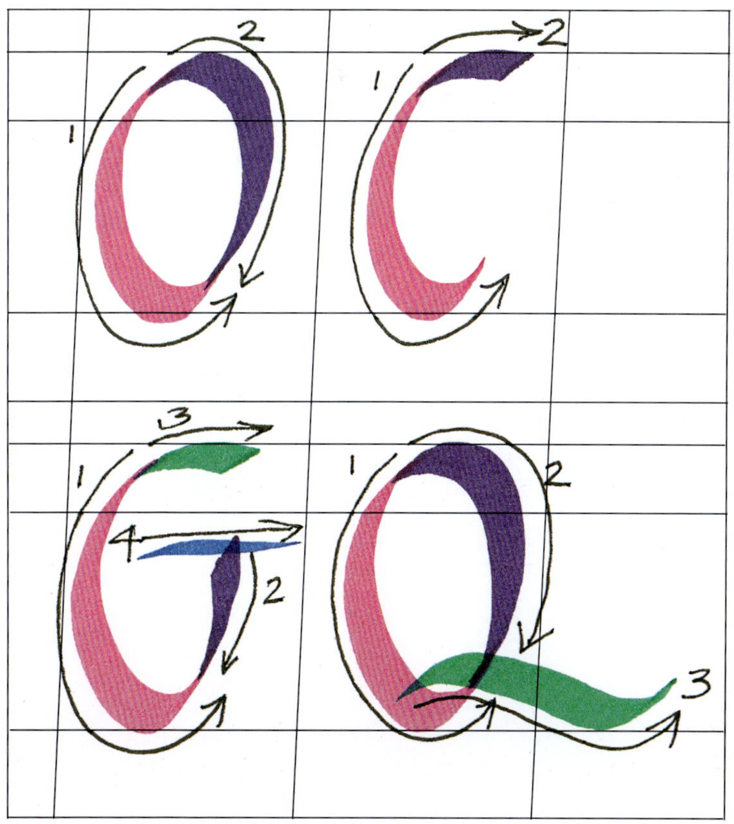

The letters *O*, *C*, *G* and *Q* are all based on the oval shape, using rounded strokes and whisper joins to connect them. The *O* and the *C* are the same as their lowercase versions, but the *G* and *Q* are very different.

For the G, the fourth (horizontal) stroke sits below the waistline and will be thinner than the other strokes, like other crossbars.

The tail of the Q starts inside the oval and ends outside, touching the baseline before flicking upward. The tail, happily, can cover a multitude of calligraphic sins — like a sloppy whisper join!

When you're first starting these rounded letters, it's helpful to use a pencil to draw an oval as a guide for you to follow, at least until you're used to creating these oval strokes.

## UPPERCASE ITALIC ALPHABET

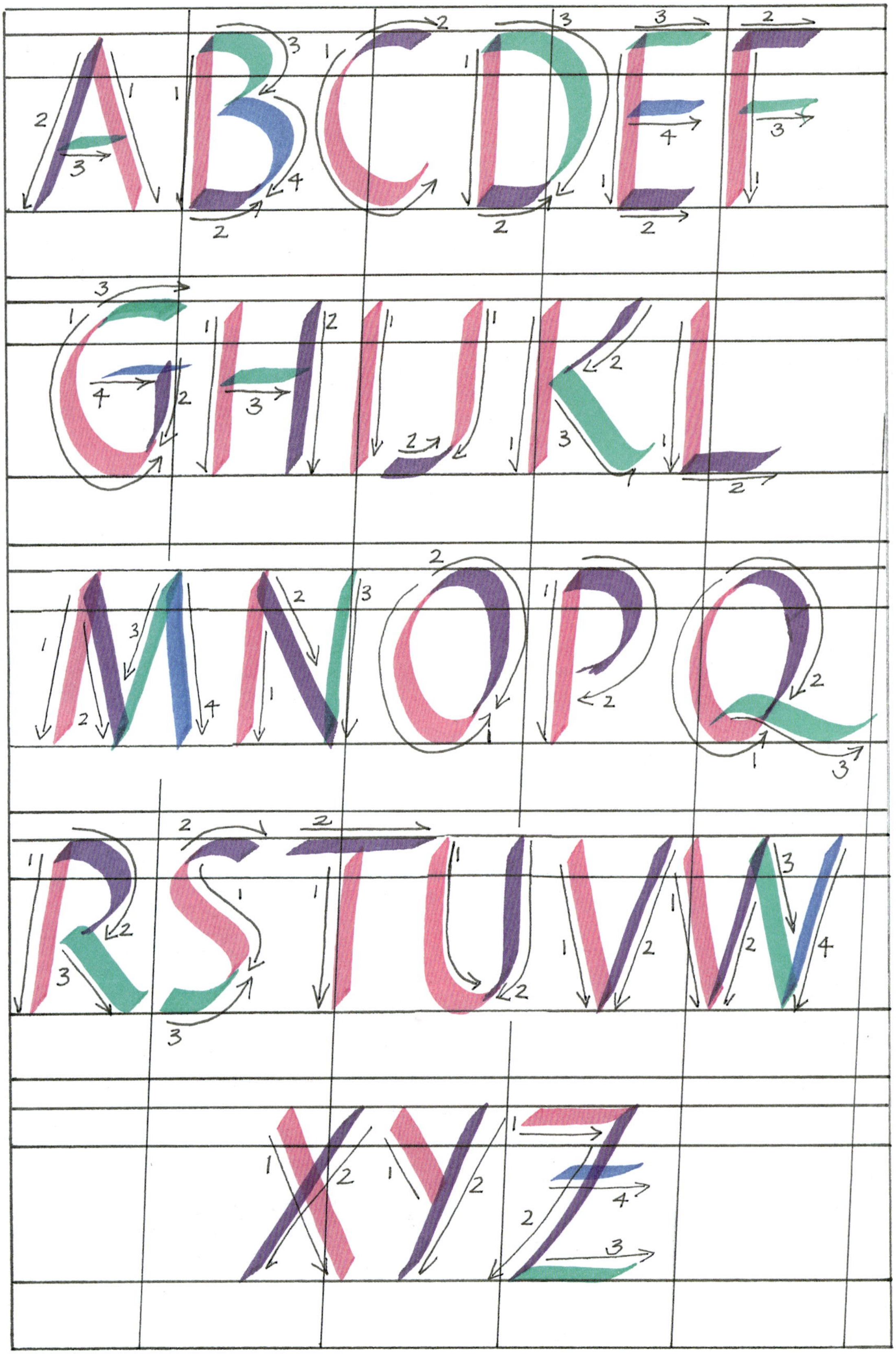

# Spacing within Letters

As you might remember from earlier, an important part of calligraphy is to understand the need for correct spacing. Spacing refers to the distance between letters, words, lines and within the individual letters themselves.

Here, we will look specifically at spacing within traditional Italic letters. Your letters need to have consistent widths if they are to look correct, though some will be naturally wider (i.e., *m* and *w*) or thinner (i.e., *i* and *l*). The examples illustrate good, bad and ugly spacing within letters. As a beginner, I always found it frustrating when a teacher would draw a "good" letter compared to a "bad" letter, as I could not really tell the difference. So I have gone to a ridiculous extreme in these examples.

The more consistent you are with the width of your letters and the distance between letters and between words and lines, the more your traditional Italic script will appeal to the eye. Of course, it is also important to recognize, as we will see in Sections Two and Three, that spacing guidelines become less of an issue as you move away from the traditional Italic hand and toward the

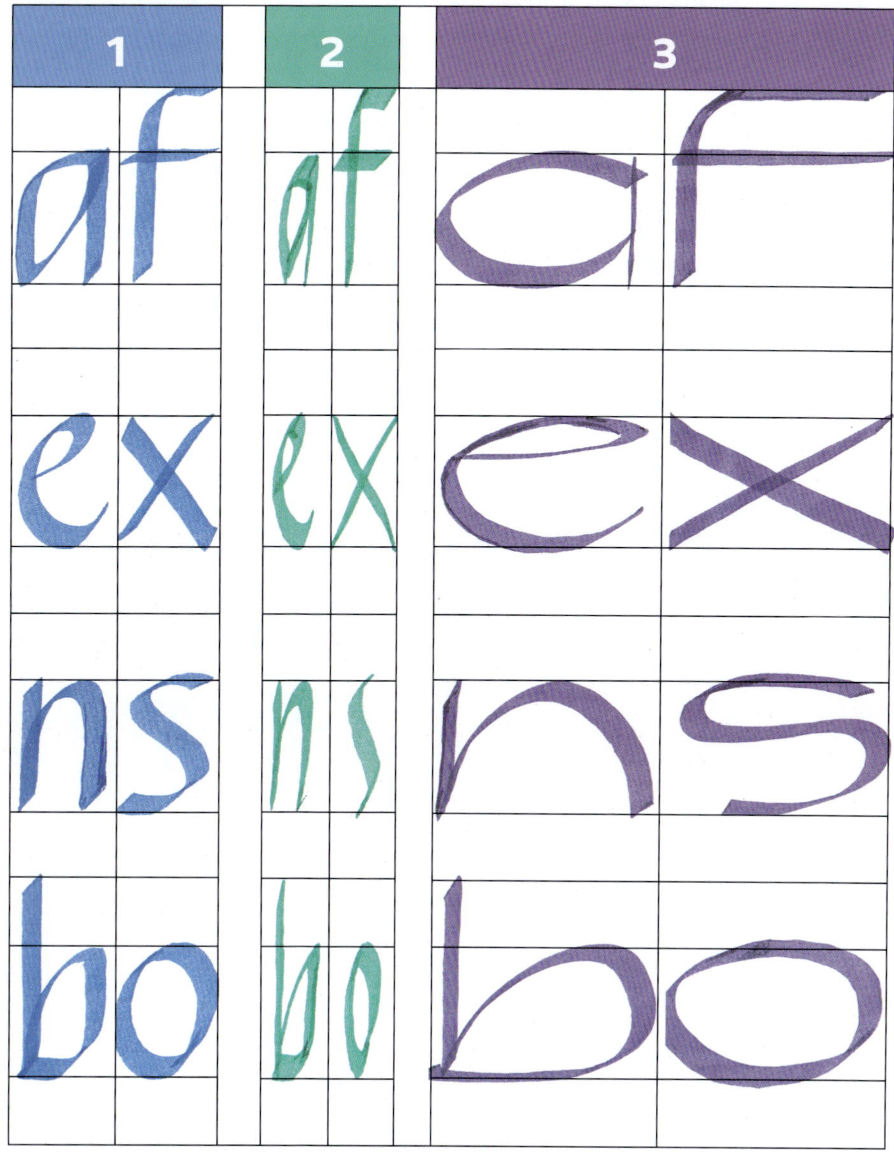


1. **good spacing**
2. **too-narrow spacing**
3. **too-wide spacing**

abstract. As such, the so-called bad letters might become quite lovely when you are experimenting with letter shapes in the later chapters of this book. However, even in those more creative expressions, spatial awareness is still crucial.

With traditional Italic, small letters are usually about two pen nib widths from the inside of the downstroke, or approximately three nib widths wide from outside to outside. This inside space is the *negative* or *counter* space, and the downstrokes and upstrokes are called the *positive* space. This is depicted in the top illustration on the right.

Capital letters have a negative space of approximately two to three nib widths. The second illustration and the chart depict the capital *A* with negative spacing of approximately three nib widths as well as examples with too few and too many nib widths.

It is important to understand that these are simply guidelines and, as my sampler illustrates, letter widths can vary slightly based on the nature of the letter. For example, the negative spacing on an *m* will be slightly less than an *n* — otherwise the *m* would appear too fat and stand out more than it should within the context of the rest of the letters in the word.

As you review the sampler for small and capital Italic letters you will see other examples where the guidelines are revised to ensure that the letter widths are not too wide. However, consistency is the key. As long as you keep the widths similar to each other, the letters will stand up to scrutiny. If, while writing, you look at your letter and think it looks ghastly, take a quick measurement of its height and negative spacing as well as the angle of your nib (it should be 45 degrees).

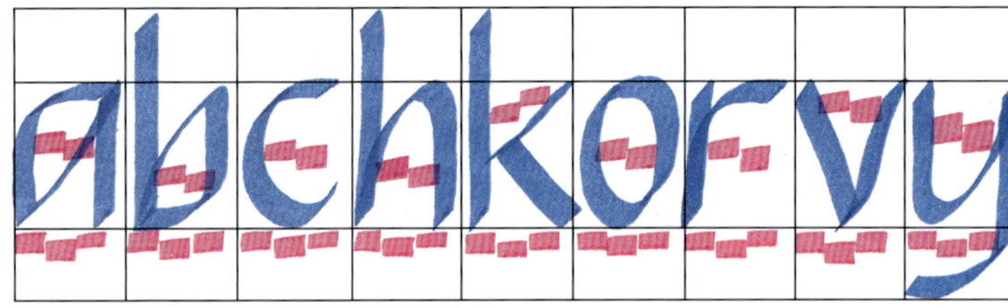

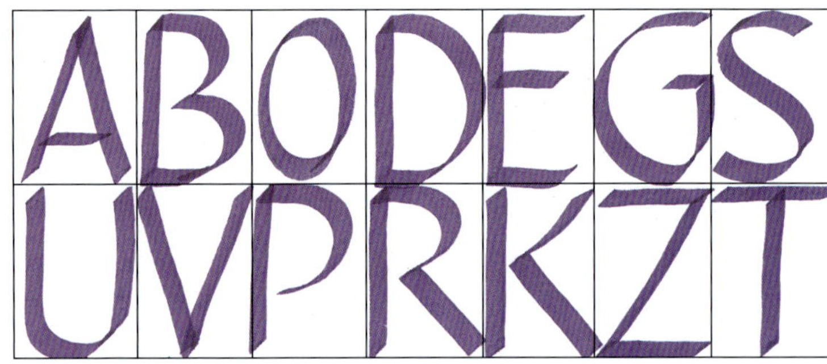

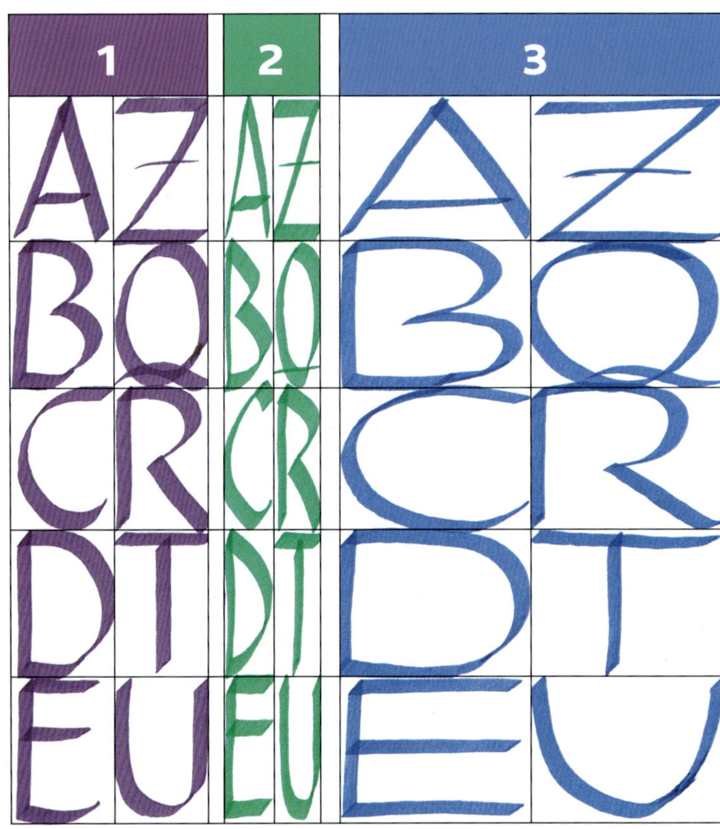


1. **good spacing**
2. **too-narrow spacing**
3. **too-wide spacing**

# Numbers

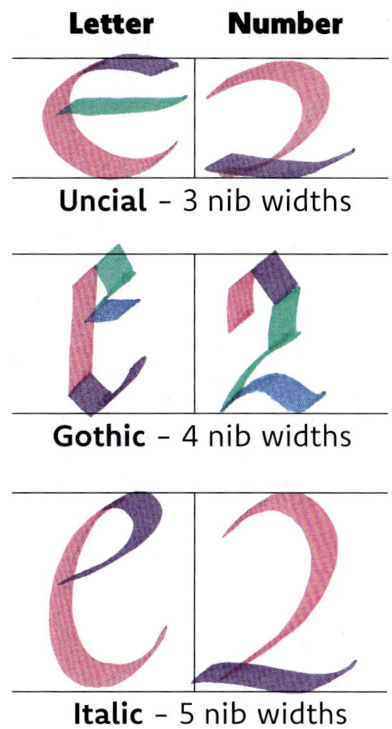


The shapes of the numbers will reflect the style of the letters they accompany. For example, Uncial numbers will appear shorter and rounder, Gothic numbers will appear narrower and more angular, and Italic numbers will look taller and more elegant.

Italic numbers use all the various types of strokes and joins that the letters use. Traditional Italic numbers all fit within the X-height — which is five nib widths high. They are all written with a 45-degree pen angle, although crossbars and diagonal strokes use a sharper angle, similar to the letters. The numbers are written at the same slope as the letters (i.e., 5 to 10 degrees).

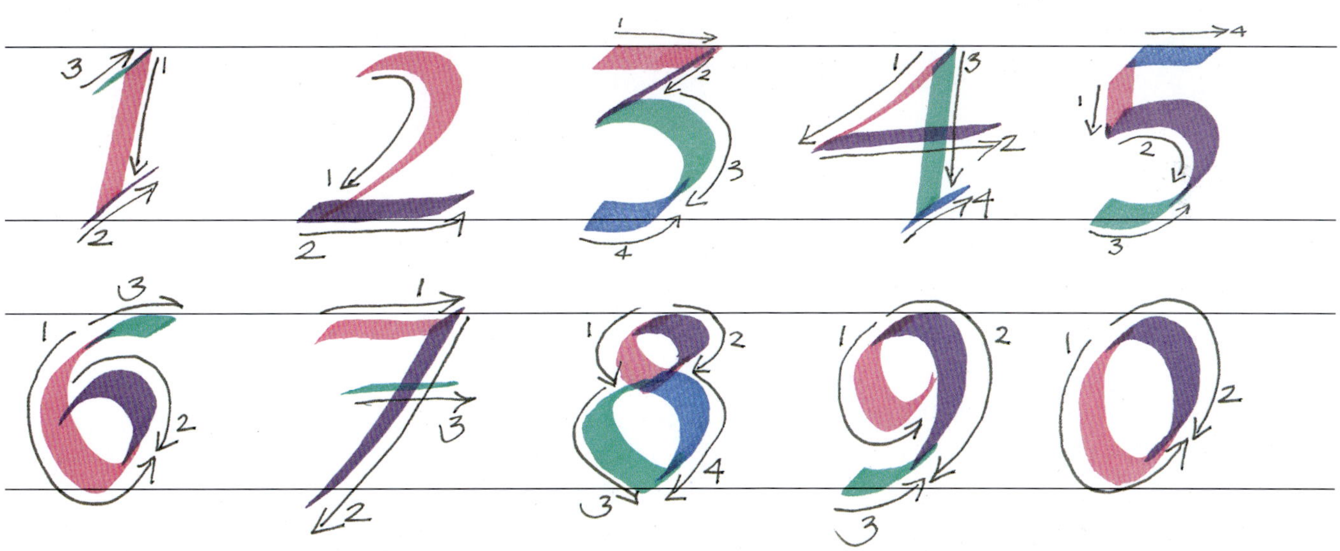

The number 0 consists of two strokes creating the same shape as the letter o. The first stroke starts just below the waistline, and the second stroke begins at the tip of the first stroke with a whisper join, goes up to the waistline and then curves down and in to meet the bottom tip of the first stroke as a whisper join.

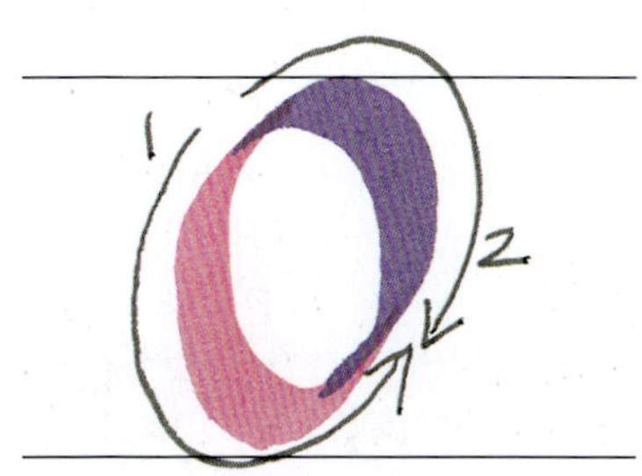

The number *6* starts out with the same stroke as the *0*, beginning just below the waistline to ensure that there is room for the final cap. Then just below the middle of this first stroke, the second stroke comes out and around, forming a whisper join at the bottom tip of the first stroke. The third stroke for this number is a small cap that starts at the tip of the first stroke with a whisper join and goes to the right. Think of the cap on the letter *c*.

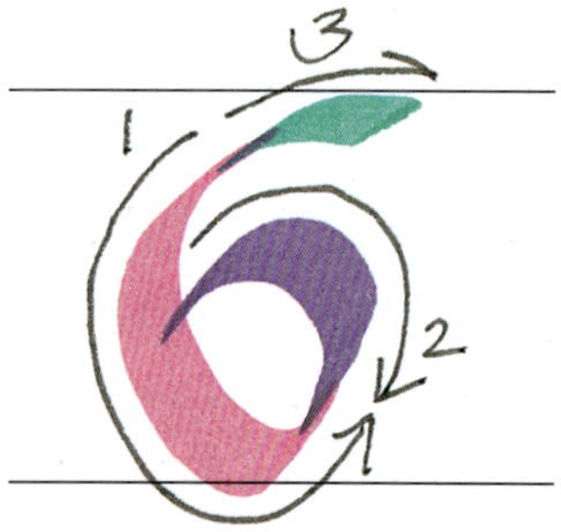


The number *9* begins just below the waist-line and starts like the oval but curves in at the halfway point. The second stroke starts at the tip of the first stroke as a whisper join and curves up to the waistline and then down-ward like the second stroke of the letter *o* to finish just above the baseline, leaving room to add the third stroke that creates the tail of the *9*. This third stroke starts to the left of the second stroke (similar to the bottom of the *j*) and comes to the right, meeting up with the bottom of the second stroke as a whisper join.

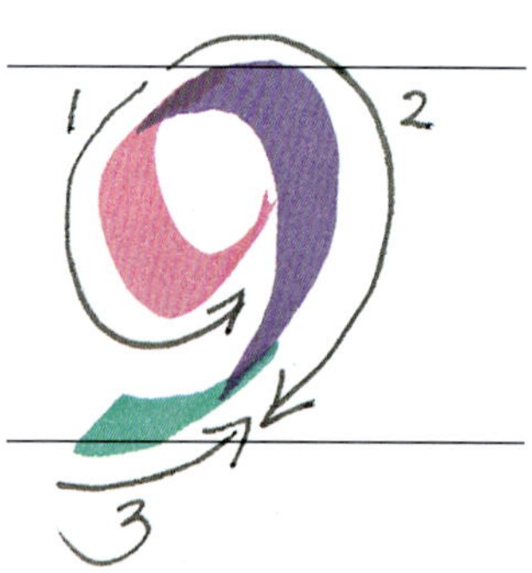


The number *8* uses rounded strokes like the *9* and the *6*. It starts just below the waistline and, like the *9*, goes down and curves in. It should curve in above the middle as the top portion of the number must be smaller than the bottom to make a balanced appearance. The second stroke starts at the tip of stroke 1 and goes up to the waistline and then curves down to meet the bottom tip of the first stroke. The third stroke starts at the bottom tip of the second stroke and curves out and down to the baseline and then curves slightly up like the first stroke of the *0*. The fourth stroke starts at the top tip of the third stroke and curves up and around to meet the bottom tip of the third stroke. Strokes 2 and 4 start and end with whisper joins. The aim is to have two centered ovals on top of each other, with the top oval being smaller.

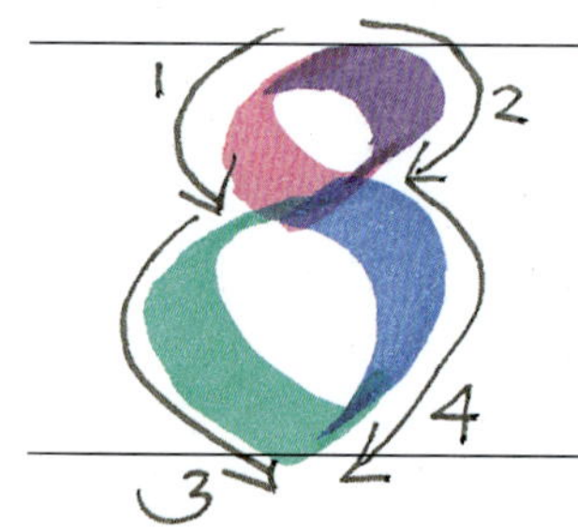


The number *5* begins with a vertical stroke straight down to above the middle of the X-height. The second stroke starts at the bottom of the first stroke and curves around just above the baseline. Similar to the bottom of the *9*, the third stroke starts to the left (lining up with the first stroke) and reaches up to the bottom tip of the second stroke to con-nect in a whisper join. The final stroke starts at the top of the first stroke and is a hor-izontal stroke to the right — like a cross-bar. This stroke should basically line up with the outside curve of stroke 2.

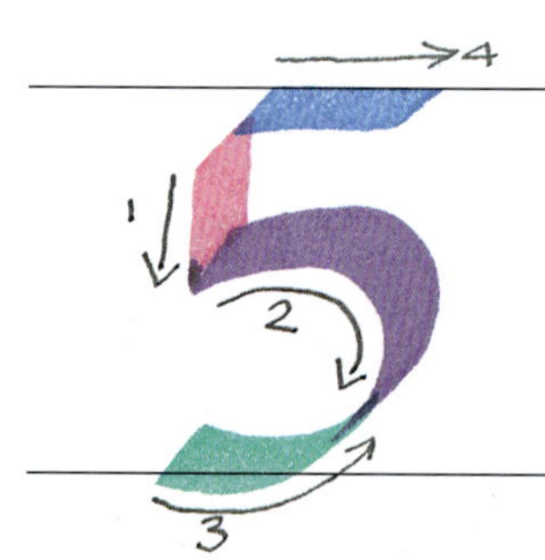


The number *3* starts with a short horizontal line along the bottom of the waistline. The second stroke is a short diagonal that starts at the end of the first stroke and goes down to the left at a sharper angle, ending above the middle and no further than the start of the first stroke. The third stroke is the same as the second stroke in the *5*: starting at the end of stroke 2, it curves slightly up and then down to end just above the baseline to allow for the last stroke, which starts to the left and finishes with a whisper join at the bottom tip of the preceding stroke.

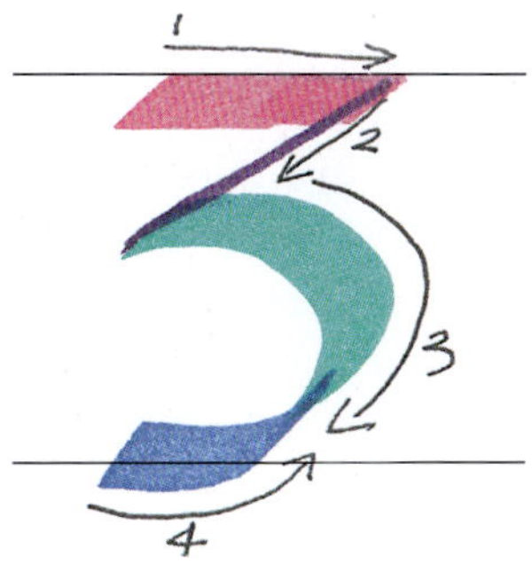


The number *2* starts just below the waistline like the second stroke of the *o*. It comes up to the waistline and then curves at a diagonal down to the baseline so that it lines up with the beginning of the stroke. The second stroke is a horizontal stroke (i.e., crossbar) along the baseline. This stroke should go just a bit beyond the outside of the curve in the first stroke.

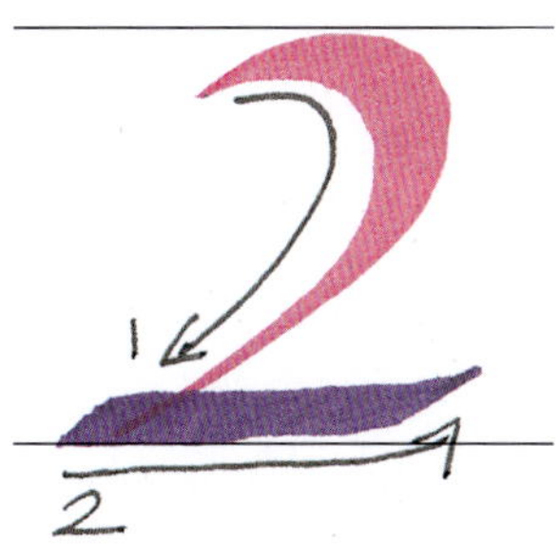


The number *1* is a simple vertical downward stroke that starts at the waistline and finishes at the baseline. Strokes 2 and 3 are simple serifs — fine-line strokes — and are optional.

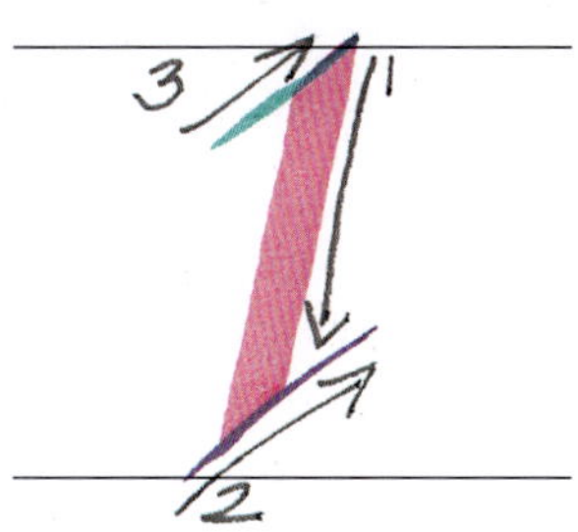


The number *7* starts as a horizontal stroke under the waistline. This stroke should be a little shorter than the horizontal stroke at the bottom of the *2*. The second stroke is a slight diagonal stroke to the left that starts at the end of the first stroke and finishes at the baseline. The third stroke starts to the left of the second stroke just above the midpoint of stroke 2 and is a short horizontal crossbar. Note: this crossbar is optional.

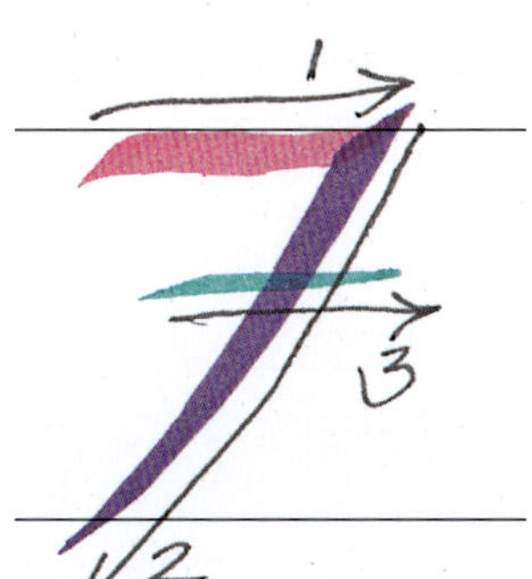


The final number is *4*. The first stroke starts just under the waistline and is a steep diagonal down to the left that finishes a bit below the midpoint. This is the thinnest stroke in this number and should angle down at approximately 45 degrees. The second stroke starts at the bottom of the first and is a horizontal stroke to the right that extends past the beginning of the first stroke. This stroke requires a sharper angle (but not as sharp as the first stroke) as it needs to be thinner than the ensuing vertical stroke. It is a general guideline that you should not cross thick with thick. The third stroke starts under the waistline, lining up with the start of the first stroke, and goes down to finish at the baseline. As with the number 1, the serif stroke (stroke 4) is optional.

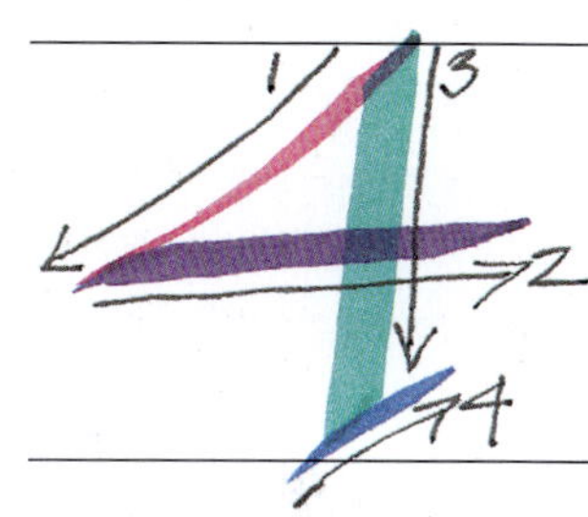


Practice a few lines of each of these numbers to become familiar with the new strokes that these numbers use.

# Punctuation & Special Characters

As soon as you're ready to start building sentences in Italic, you're going to need to add some punctuation. Here are some common punctuation marks to learn. As with the letters and numbers, all punctuation marks are created with a 45-degree pen angle and the same gentle slope.

Let's start with the period. This is a simple diamond — the same as the top of the *i*. It is placed so that it sits on the baseline and is one nib width in size.

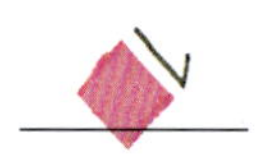

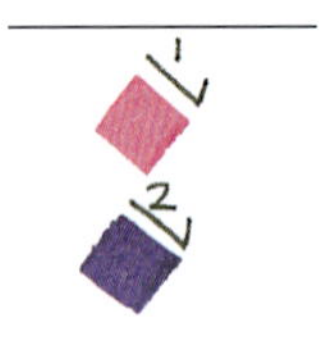


The colon is simply two lined-up diamonds that hover in the middle of the X-height, a nib width above and below the middle.

The comma starts the same way you start a period. However, as you start to pull your nib down to create the diamond, instead of ending the diamond, this stroke scoots to the left creating a very fine line for the tail. The stroke starts just above the baseline and finishes just below the baseline and is approximately one and a half nib widths in length — slightly more than the simple period.

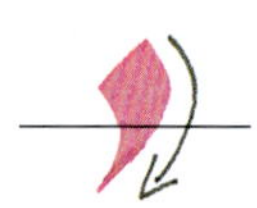

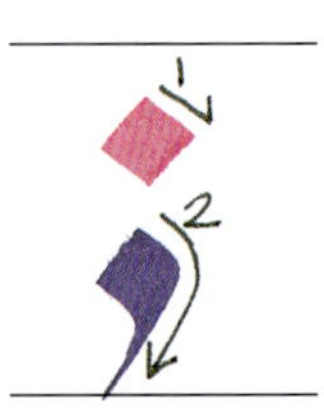


Semicolons combine the period and the comma. The comma portion sits on the baseline and the period portion is situated in the middle of the X-height or slightly higher. This is a matter of style and preference.

The question mark has a similar first stroke to the first stroke in the number *2*. The first stroke starts just below the ascender line and curves up before coming down to the left in a diagonal. Because this is a diagonal, you need a sharper pen angle and will end the stroke in a fine line slightly past the middle of the X-height. The finishing stroke is a period at the baseline, located below the bottom tip of the first stroke.

Exclamation marks consist of a simple vertical stroke that starts at the ascender line (or slightly below) and finishes just below the middle of the X-height. The second stroke is a period with the tip of the diamond pointing up to the middle of the end of the downstroke.

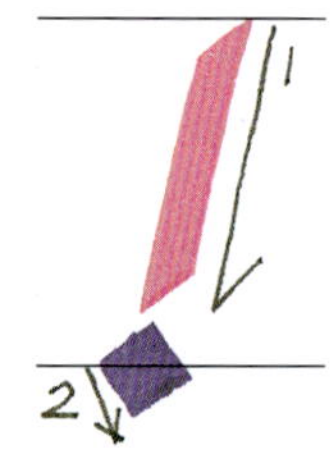


To make a dash mark you simply create a crossbar at the middle of the X-height.

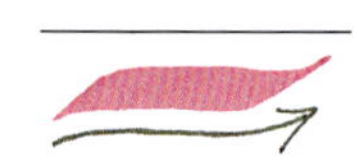

The quotation marks use the same stroke as the comma. The strokes should be parallel and are located just above the capital line although this is flexible, as long as they sit above the waistline. Your eye will tell you what looks right. The stroke is either a comma or an inverted comma. To make an inverted comma, start at a 45-degree angle, pull down and then end the stroke in the way you would finish a diamond. From thin to thick.

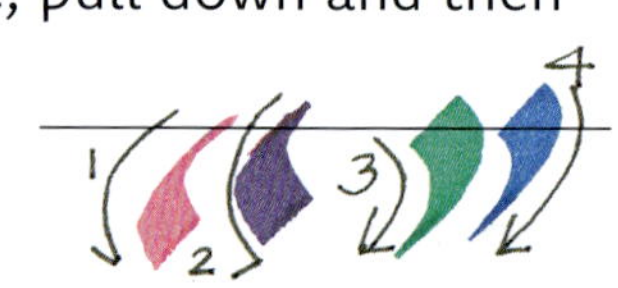


To finish off, let's look at brackets, or parentheses. The left bracket starts just below the waistline and curves out to the left in a fine line. As you curve back in toward the baseline, the line becomes thicker; so the stroke goes from thin to thick. The right bracket is the opposite. Starting your nib just below the waistline, pull to the right in a curve that matches the left bracket, but go from thick as you curve out to thin as you curve down to the baseline to finish.

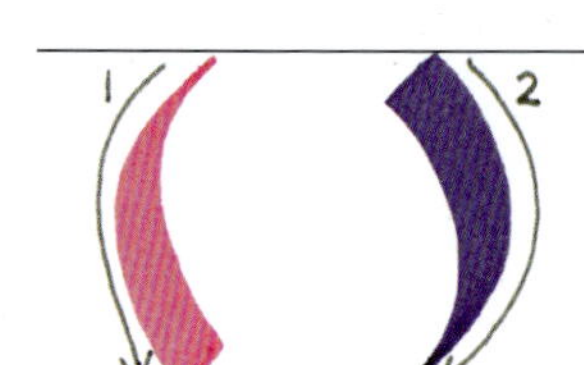

## AMPERSAND

The ampersand (&) is a combination of the letters e and t, or "et," which means "and" in Latin. (These types of characters, which combine two letters together, are called ligatures.)

The ampersand can be written in many ways. This first example on the right is a good starting point.

This example can sit within the X-height but can also go as high as the ascender line. Your eye will tell you what looks right. The first stroke resembles the left bracket. It starts just below the capital line and curves out to the left and back in to the top of the waistline. The second stroke is a horizontal stroke that can vary in length. I suggest starting with a stroke that is about three nib widths in length. This stroke pulls from left to right, meeting up with the end of the first stroke. The third stroke starts at the beginning of the second stroke. It goes down slightly and then immediately starts downward at a diagonal to the right as it continues to the baseline and then curves up as the line becomes thinner, finishing in a fine-pointed tip at the midpoint of the X-height. The next stroke (no. 4) starts at the waistline and comes downward from thick to thin to create a whisper join with the end of the third stroke. This stroke resembles the thick-to-thin right bracket. The fifth stroke is a short horizontal crossbar through the preceding stroke, just below the waistline. The final stroke is a short vertical thin line with your pen at a very sharp angle.

The ampersand is a place where you can have some fun, incorporating your own style and hand into the strokes. Here are some different styles you could try. Have some fun!

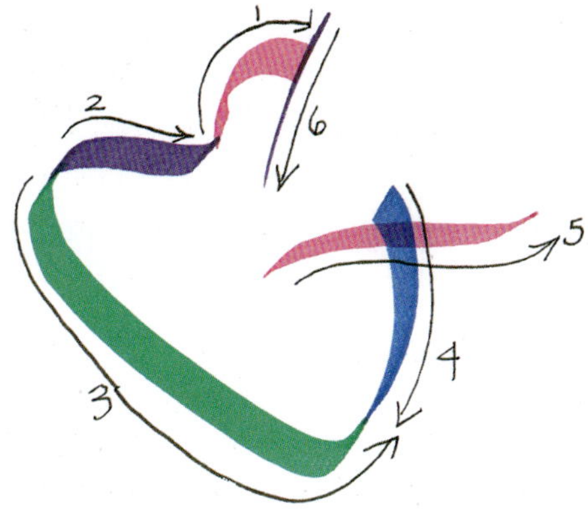
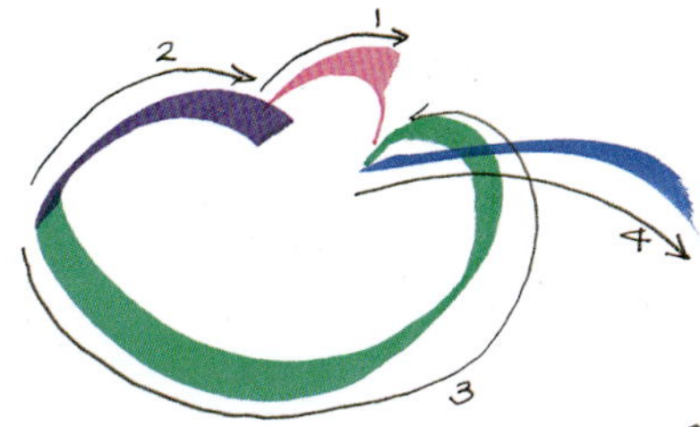
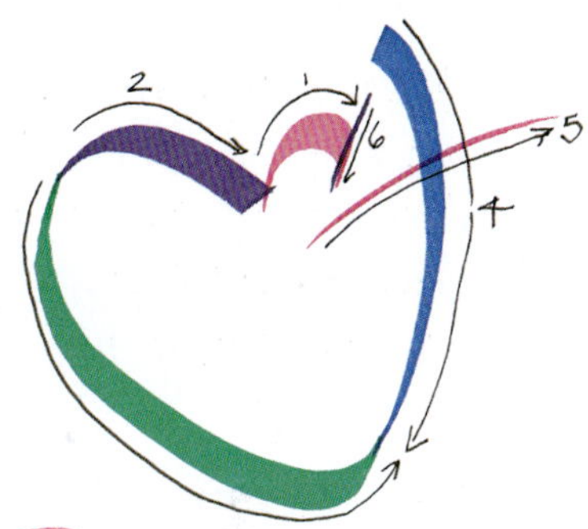
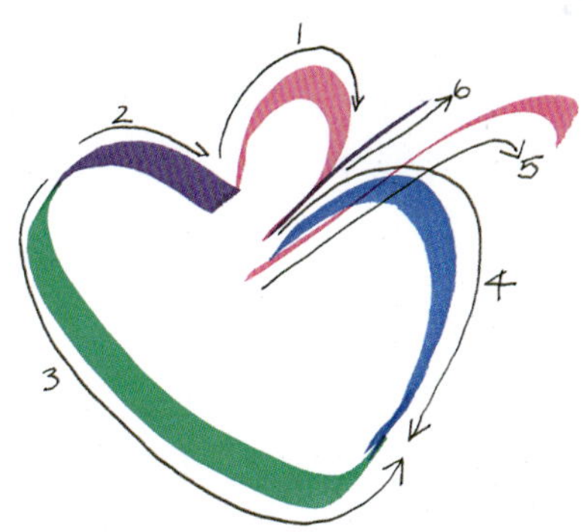
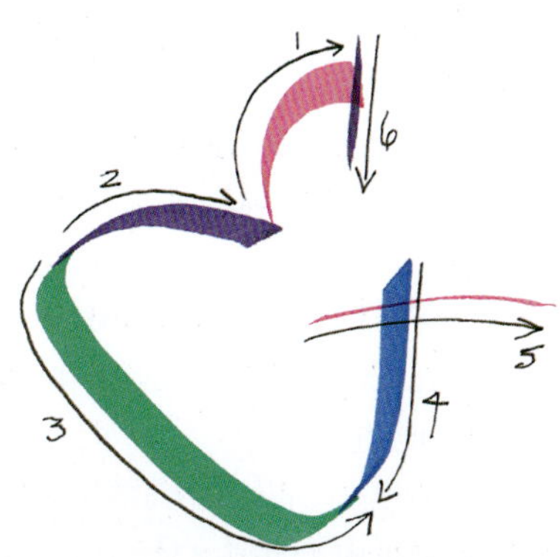

# Review: Noticing & Spacing

When teaching Italic calligraphy, I often take areas that I struggle with and dissect them into manageable portions to help others avoid the snags, which too often have tripped me up. One of those areas is spacing. This is why I introduced "noticing" right from the start.

Well-spaced letters and words will help the overall look of the calligraphy, even if the calligrapher is not experienced. But poor spacing will destroy even the grandest-looking letters.

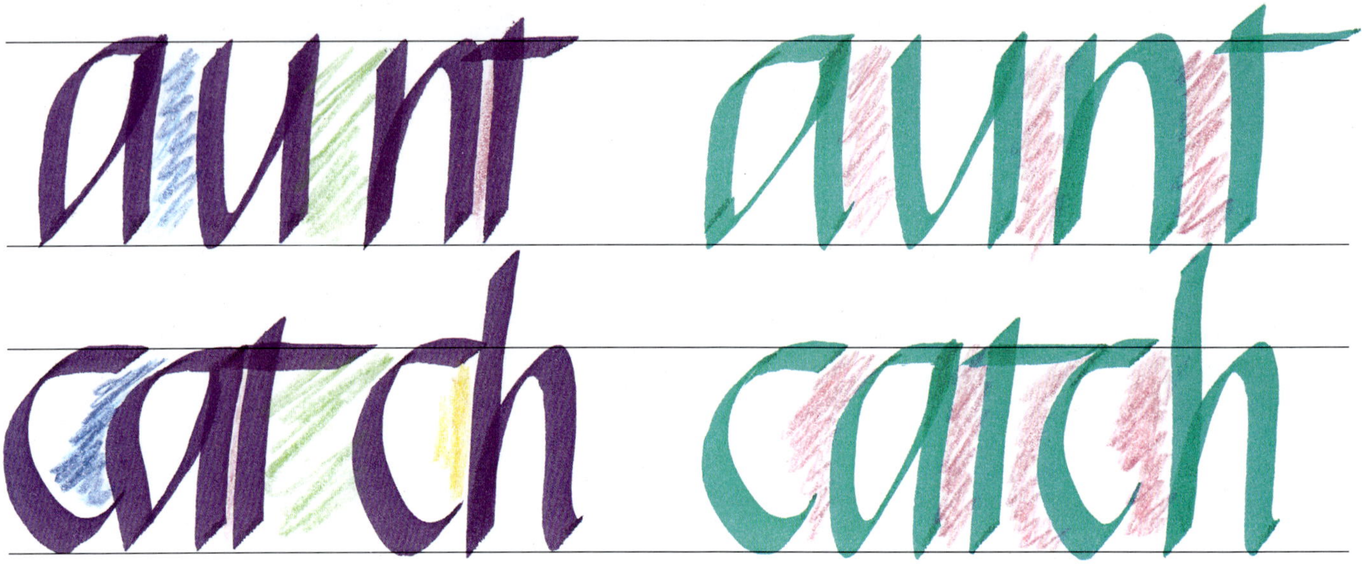


POORLY SPACED

WELL SPACED

When thinking about spacing and calligraphy, I am reminded of driving. We drive cautiously, looking ahead, keeping a good distance, glancing in the rearview mirror to see the distance behind, glancing in the side mirror and then eyes ahead once again. As with calligraphy, there is that constant glancing, discerning and deciding. A carefully drawn stroke needs to be determined in its placement in comparison to the last stroke and in anticipation of the next stroke to come.

Unfortunately, there is no mathematical equation we can rely on for this. It is something that requires attention and time for your eyes to grow critically sharp to notice errors. Let's try a few exercises to sharpen our noticing skills.

1. Draw a series of straight lines that are parallel and equally spaced on your practice sheet. As you create more lines, try to keep the space between each line even. Parallel lines are the easiest to be consistent with.

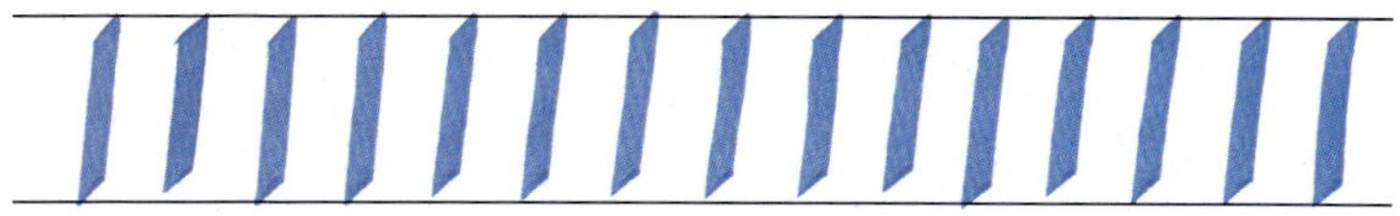

2. Next add a curved stroke between each straight line. Straight strokes followed by curved strokes will be a touch closer together than two parallel strokes to account for the spaces above and/or below the curves.

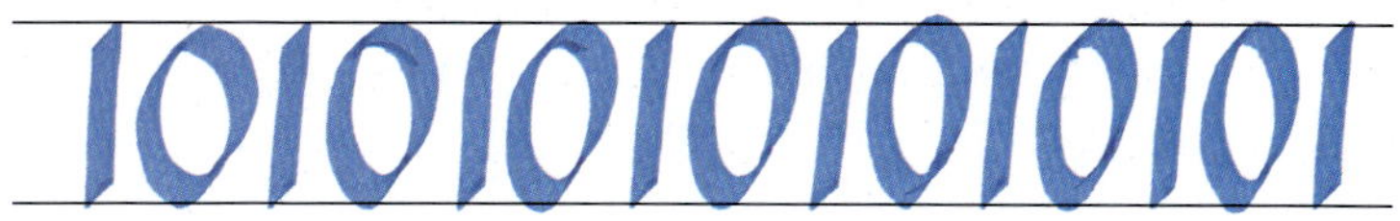

3. Now draw a lowercase *p* followed by a lowercase *a*. When two curves sit next to each other, the space between them should be even smaller. Practice another line of letters, this time a lowercase *b* and a lowercase *o*. Then try lines with a lowercase *c* and *b*, and then *q* and *r*.

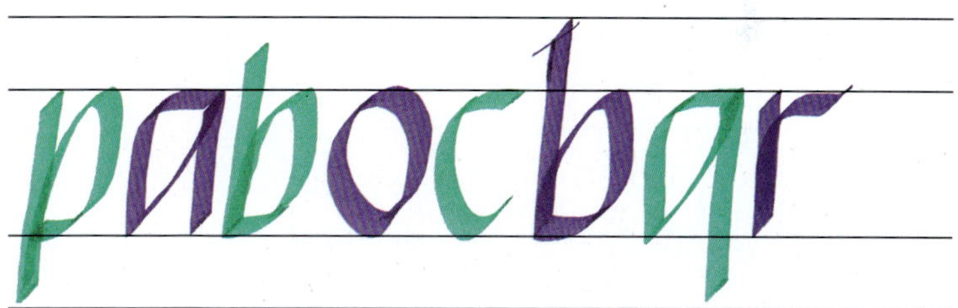


4. Certain letters, such as the lowercase *r*, *x*, *t* and *s*, sit closer because of how the letters overhang on one or both sides of each character. Practice a few lines of these letters as depicted in the illustration on the right. You can also focus on practicing a line of letters using just two letter combinations, such as *tx*, *xr*, *ot*, *ri* and *ts*.

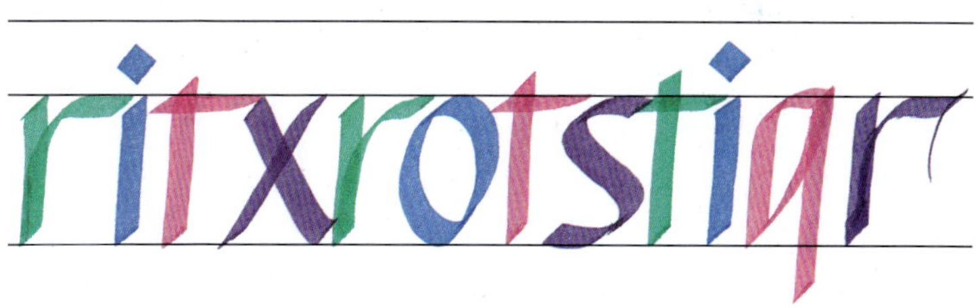


5. A final spacing exercise combines letters with curves (such as *m* and *u*) with letters with straight lines (such as *h* and *l*) and overhang letters (such as *r* and *t*). Practice a few lines with these letters, either as depicted on the right, or in small, two-to-three-letter combinations.

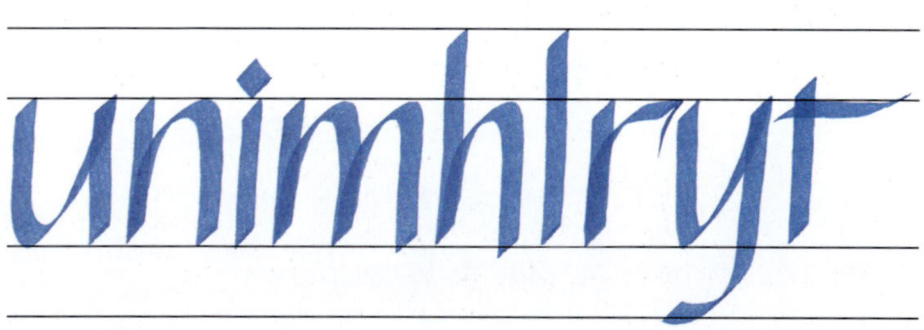

## EXPLORING SPACING WITH COLORED PENCILS

Time for a true challenge for your eyes! On one of your practice sheets, carefully write the following words in lowercase. Take your time to notice your spacing before and after each stroke. After you've written these words, go back with a pencil crayon and color the spaces between the letters to see how you did.

Another good skill to be comfortable with is writing in all capital letters. Spacing here is just as crucial. Write out the following words in all capitals. After you've done so, color the spaces between your letters.

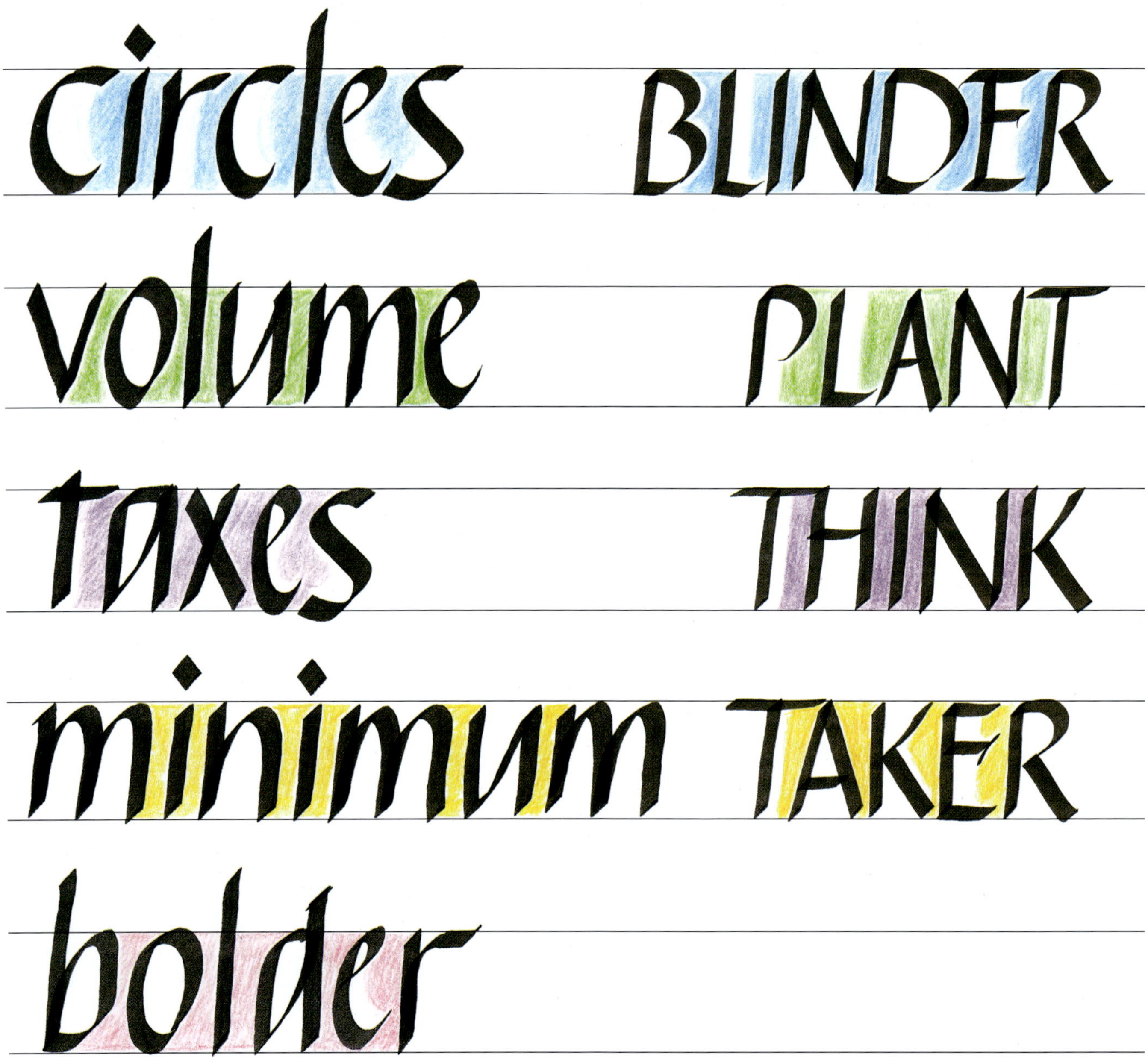

# Practicing

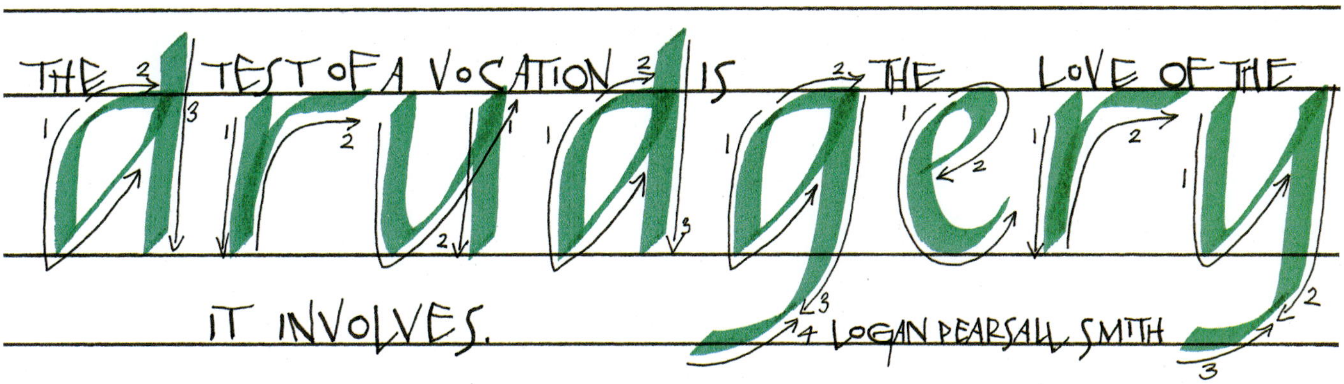


Daily or frequent and consistent practice is paramount to seeing pleasing results. Right now you are training your eyes to notice and your hand to perform. Eventually both of those skills will become natural, and then you can begin to explore and experiment. But for now, carefully carve time and space for yourself to practice.

Strong posture and deep breathing allow for this to become a pleasant experience.

This is the beginning of your perpetually learning journey. Excitement of something newly discovered will greet you at every turn. Enjoy the ride!

### Some Fun Practice: Pangrams

**Pangrams are sentences that use every letter of the alphabet. On your practice sheets, try out some of these pangrams:**

1. **The quick brown fox jumps over a lazy dog.**
2. **Calligraphy requires just a few quick things; boisterous wit, exacting resolve and much zeal.**
3. **The X-height, when very zealously created, builds the required proportion for creating just the right letters.**

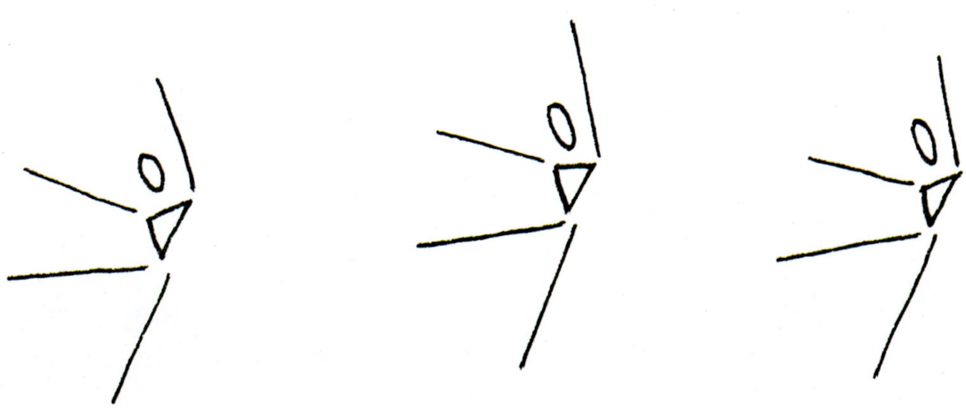

# Project: Decorative Paper

This project is all about creating interesting, colorful decorative papers you can use to adorn booklets, cards, bookmarks, gift tags and much more. This project is a great exercise for loosening your hand before starting. Because your letters will be layered and lettered over, there's no need to worry if your letters are imperfect. It's pressure-free practice in which proper spacing is basically non-existent.

WHAT YOU'LL NEED:

- **Paper**
- **Pencil crayons**
- **Ruler**
- **Calligraphy pen or markers**
- **Paint (optional if using a marker)**

1. Lightly line a sheet of practice paper just as a general guideline. Use pencil crayons instead of a pencil for more color.

2. Start writing with your pen or markers, using the alphabet or your own stream of thoughts. You're going to fill the page from top to bottom and side to side so that there's no space left anywhere. As you're writing, just think of the letter form. Don't worry about spacing. If you're using markers of various colors, start with the lightest and move to the darkest colors.

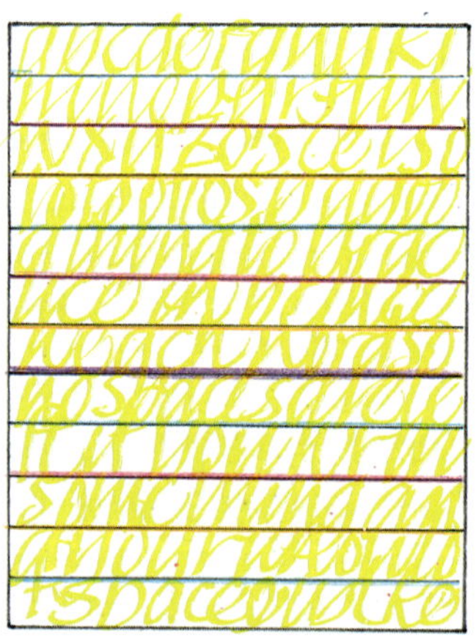

3. Once you've finished writing in one direction, rotate the paper and start writing in a new direction. Continue rotating the practice sheet over and over again until you are back in the direction where you started.

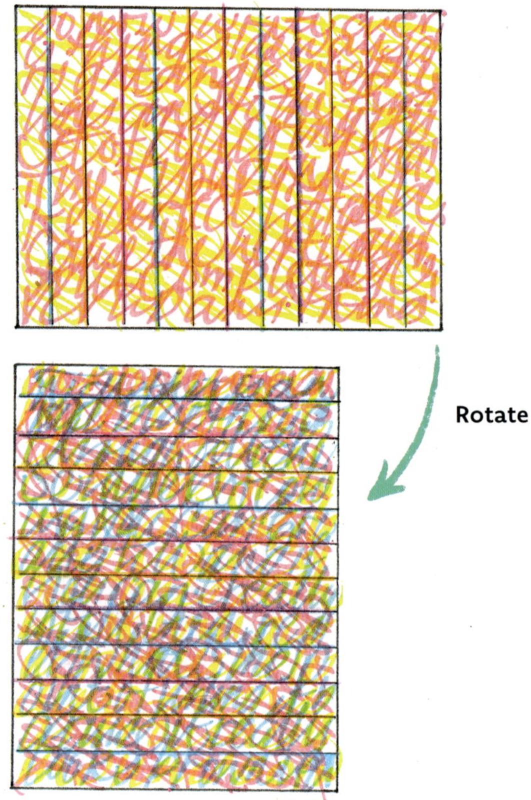


4. After you've finished your page, use your pencil crayons or markers to color in some of the white spaces between the letters. You can also try diluting some light-colored or metallic paint and splattering your page for added interest.

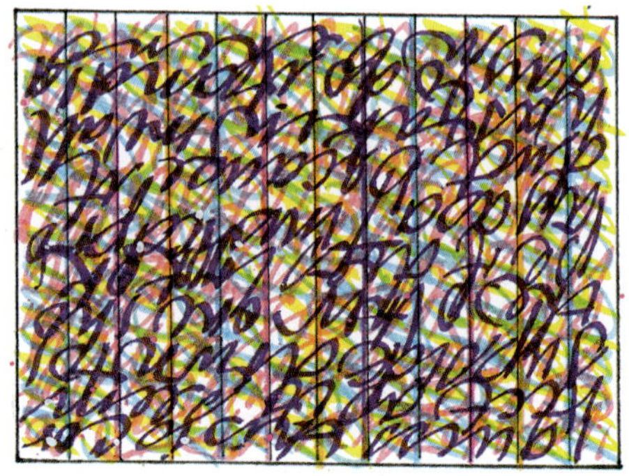

## GALLERY OF DECORATIVE PAPERS

For a bit of inspiration, here are a handful of decorative papers I've made using Italic calligraphy. This is a great way to have fun while practicing your calligraphy.

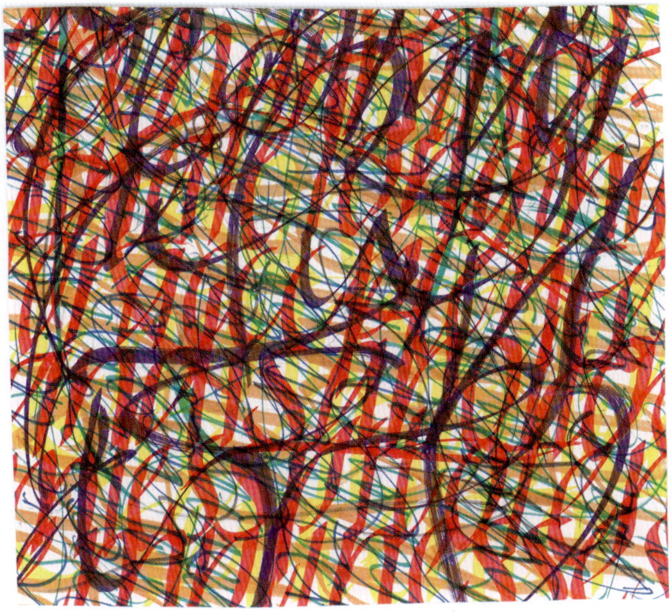

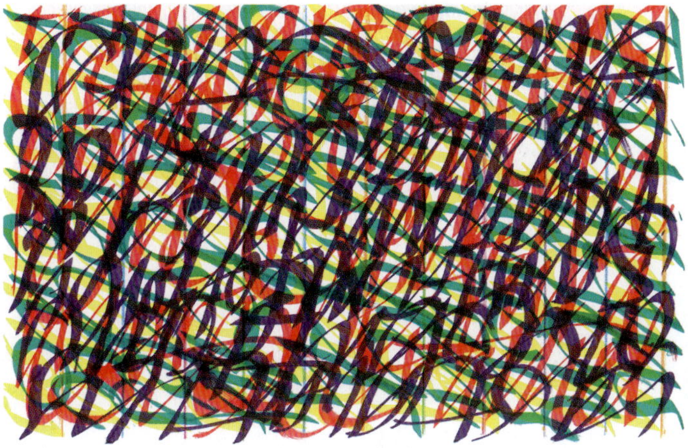

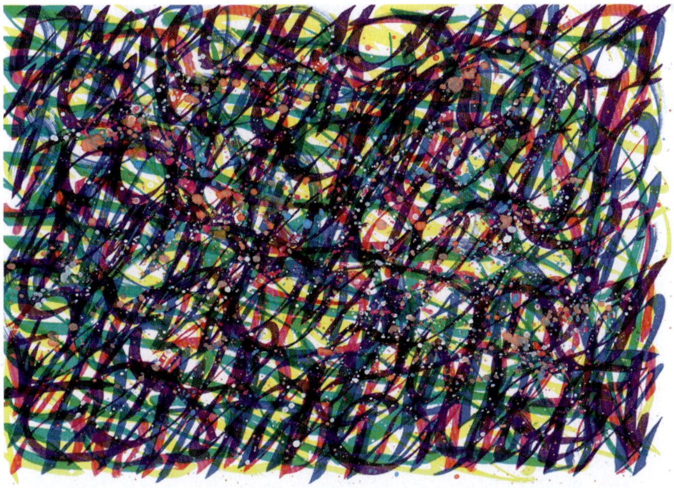

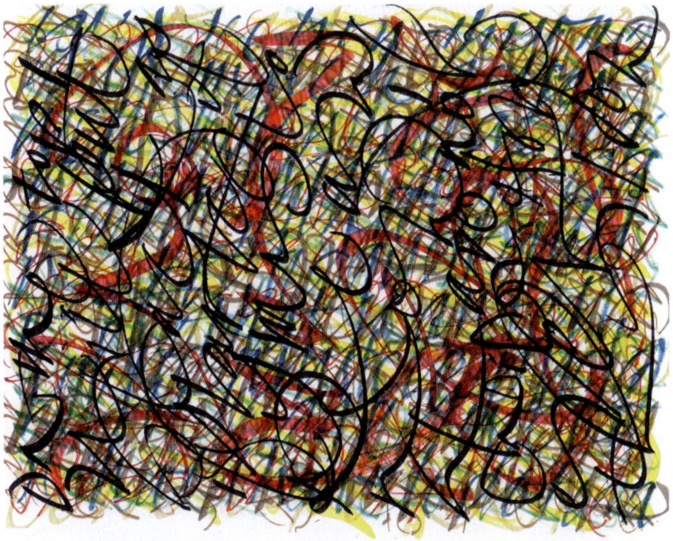

## IDEAS ON HOW TO USE YOUR DECORATIVE PAPER

An accordion book for your favorite letters (see project on pages 77–79)

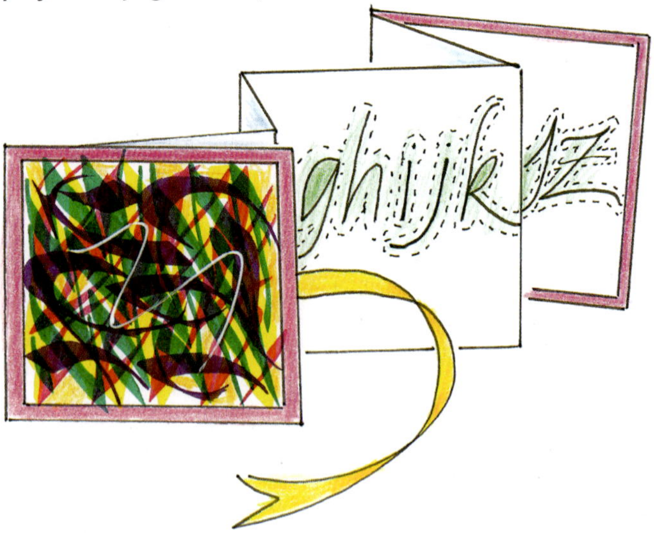

A bookmark

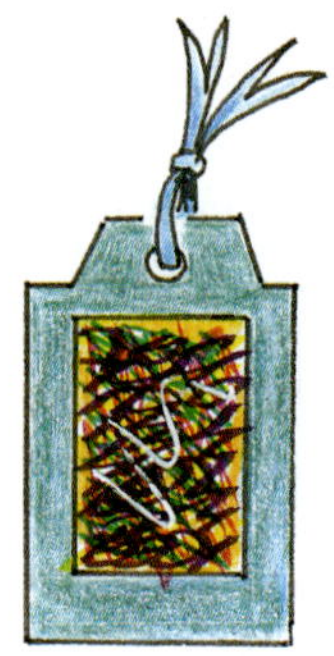

A gift tag

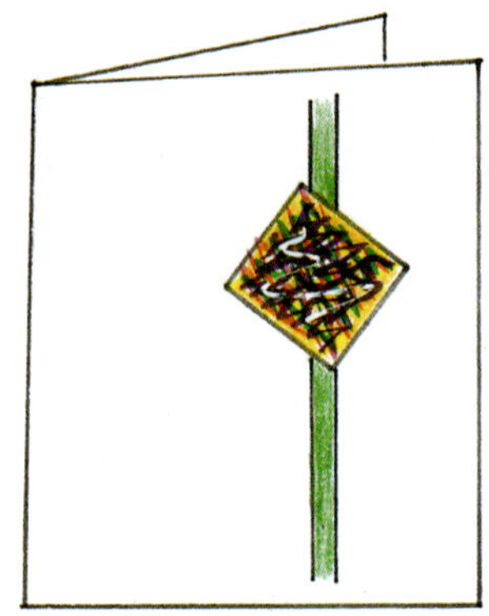

A card

An envelope, either as the lining of the envelope or embellishments on the outside of the envelope

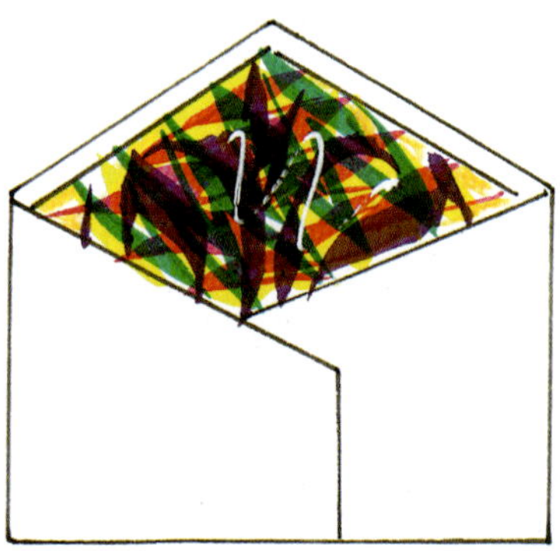

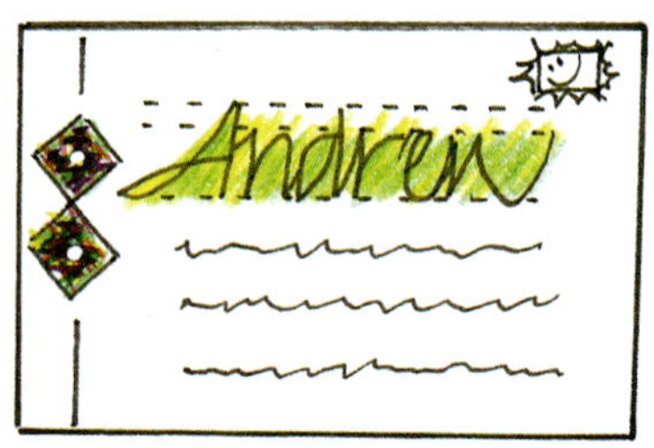


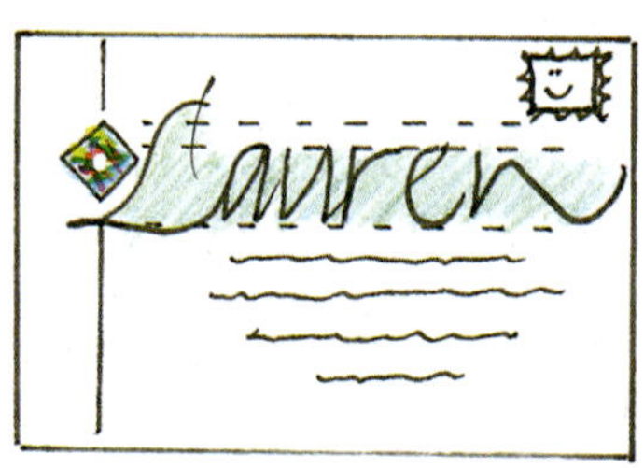


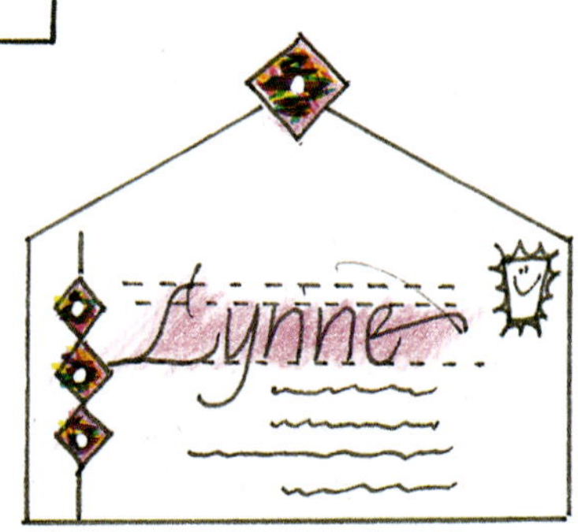

# Project: Accordion Alphabet Booklet

This accordion booklet will hold your favorite letters from your practice sheets. Having this available allows you to refer to the work you have done without the need to go through a huge pile of practice sheets. Sometimes we get discouraged, so it's nice to be able to look back to see what we have accomplished!

When closed, it stores easily, and when opened, it will inspire you to carry on.

## WHAT YOU'LL NEED:

- **Scissors**
- **Ruler**
- **Cardstock**
- **Decorative paper (see page 74)**
- **Glue stick**
- **Ribbon – 10" long**
- **Practice paper – 8 ½" x 11"**
- **Calligraphic letters from your envelope of "special bits" (see page 53)**
- **Cardboard for cutting out various template squares**
- **Pencil**
- **A few heavy books**

## FOR THE COVER:

1. Cut two 3" x 3" pieces of cardstock.

2. Cut a 2" x 2" square of your decorative paper. I recommend cutting a piece of cardboard into a 2" x 2" square and using this as a template that you can trace on the back of the decorative paper. It is much easier than measuring on your paper and allows you to choose the best section to cut into a square.

3. Glue the decorative paper square in a diamond shape to one of the cardstock squares for your front cover. Place the cover under heavy books so that it dries flat.

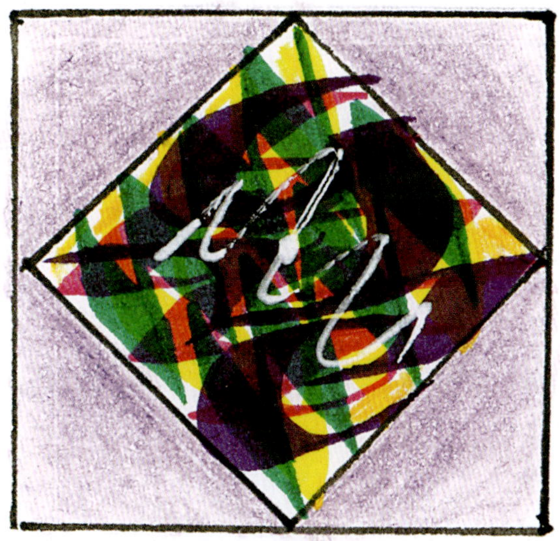

4. After 10 minutes, bring out the front cover. Position one end of the ribbon on the back of the front cover, about 1" in from the edge of the cover. Glue the ribbon in place. Press under the books again.

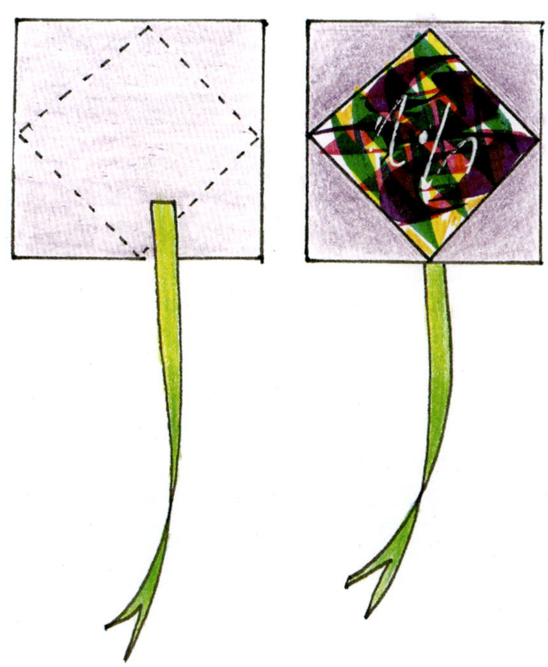

## FOR THE BOOKLET INTERIORS:

5. Using a piece of 8 ½" x 11" paper, measure and mark 2 ¾", 5 ½" and 8 ¼" from one edge at the top and bottom to create three identical strips of 2 ¾" x 11". Draw lines between the top and bottom marks with your pencil and cut along the lines.

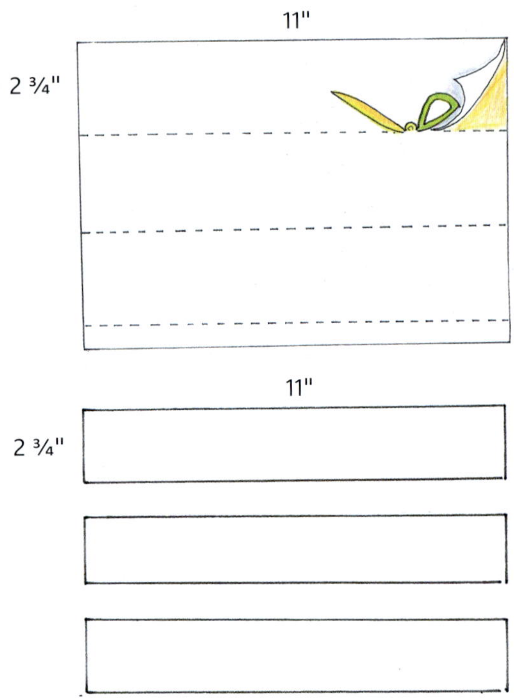


6. Fold each strip in half and then again so that each strip is made up of four squares. Unfold the strips and using your original fold lines as a guide, refold each strip so that it looks like an M or W from above.

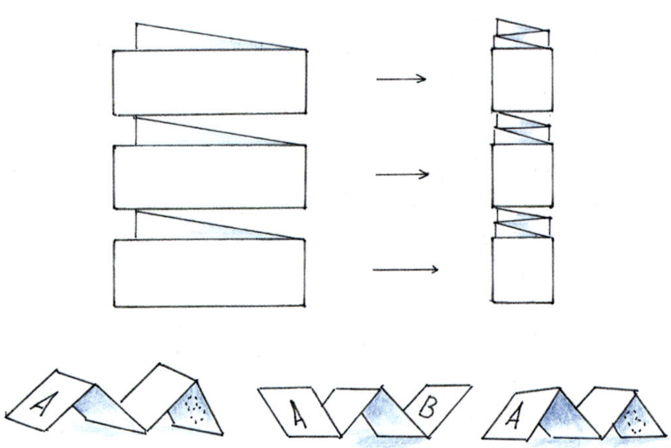

7. To make one long strip for the booklet, overlap the first and second B flaps over the second and third A flaps, as shown in the diagram. Glue the B flaps over the A flaps so they line up exactly. Fold and press the bundle under the heavy books. Go make a cup of tea while it dries.

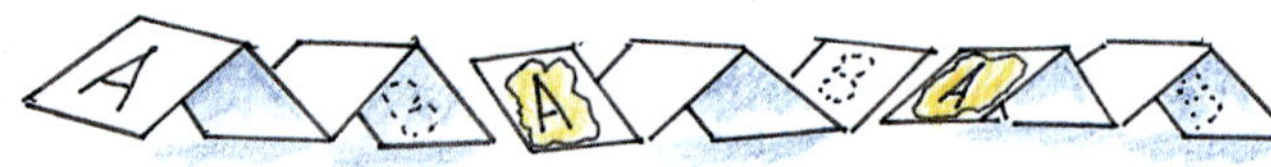

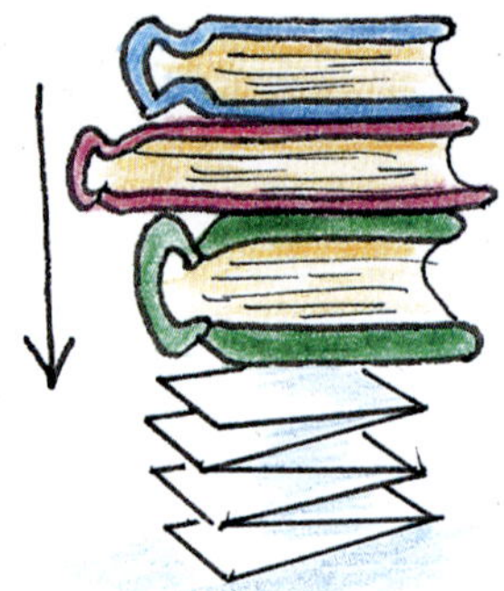

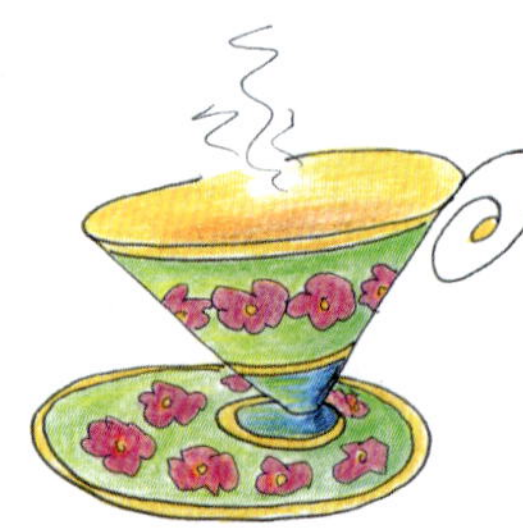

8. After you've made your cup of tea, bring out your pressed bundle. To add your covers, glue the front cover with the ribbon to the back of the first A flap, as shown in the diagram. Glue the back cover card-stock piece to the back of the last B flap, as shown in the diagram. Try your best to center the flaps in the middle of the card-stock cover pieces, and make sure the cover pieces align with each other, too. Press under the heavy books again.

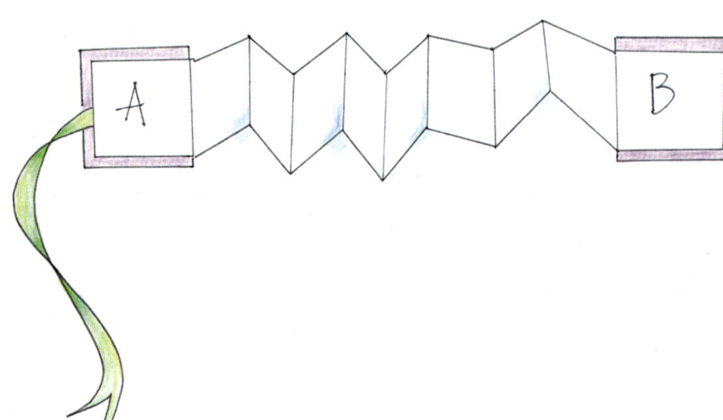

9. After you've finished your cup of tea, bring out your glued and folded treasure. Open it up and lightly draw a line with your pencil along the upper middle of the booklet as a guide.

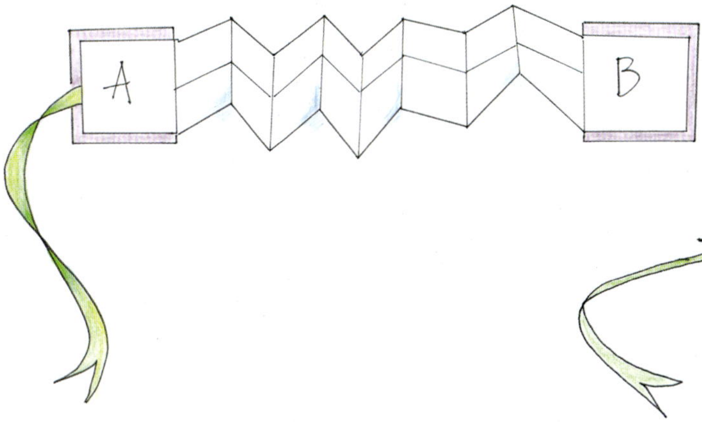


10. Now you can add your collection of "special bits" to your booklet. Find your envelope of your calligraphic favorites and spread the letters out in front of you, making sure that you have at least one of each letter. Choose your favorites of each letter. (Any letters you are missing or unhappy with can be created now, but be sure to give the ink enough time to dry.) This project focuses on your lowercase letters. If you've been collecting your favorite capitals, you can create another booklet to display them.

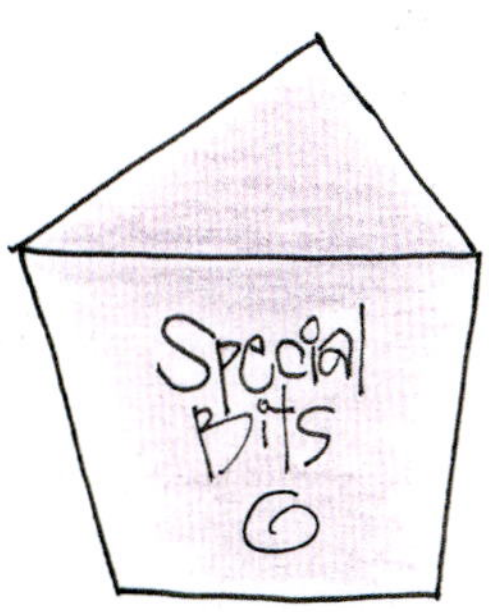


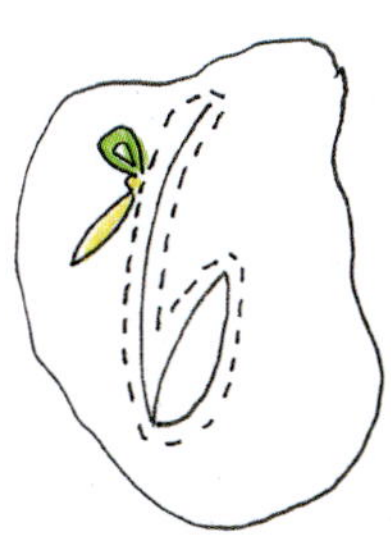

**TIP**

**Before you glue in your letters, cut closely around each letter to eliminate as much white space as possible.**

11. Once you're ready, unfold your accordion booklet fully and line up your letters in alphabetical order beneath it to make sure they fit. Glue your letters into your booklet, following the pencil line you drew to keep the letters even across the booklet. Now you have a reference for your favorite letters! You can write your name on the inside front cover and the date on the inside back cover.

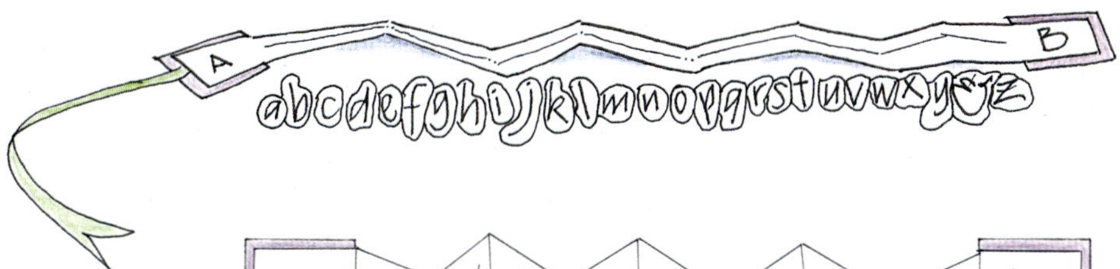


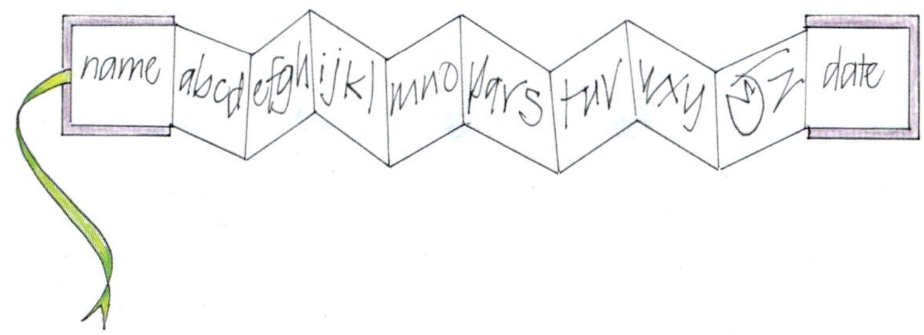


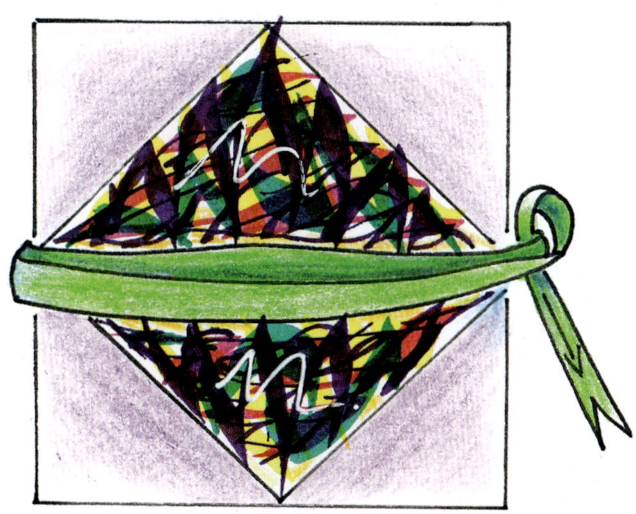

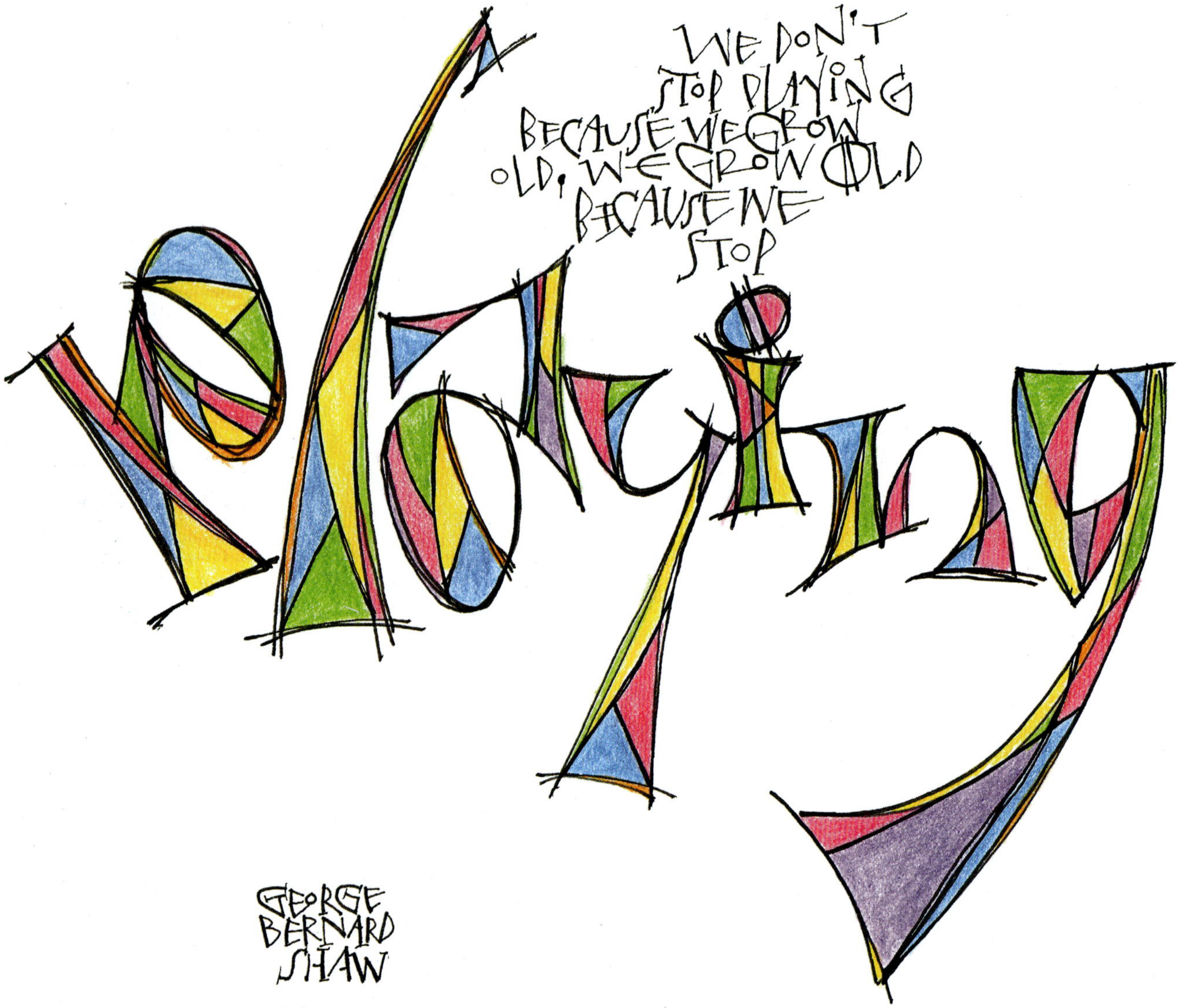
WE DON'T
STOP PLAYING
BECAUSE WE GROW
OLD, WE GROW OLD
BECAUSE WE
STOP
playing
GEORGE
BERNARD
SHAW

# Section 2

Now that you have worked diligently to feel comfortable and confident with the traditional Italic letter forms, you are ready to begin a journey of discovery and exploration.

After a review of what we learned in Section One to get us warmed up while refreshing our muscle memory, we will begin to add to those traditional letter forms. We will alter the beginning and ending of certain strokes, which will introduce the addition of flourishes.

We will also explore a new version of the Italic script with letters that bounce right out of their X-height. We will change slope, direction and angle while introducing pen manipulation.

With each new exploration, new supplies will be added that will bring life, sparkle and delight to your lettering.

The last chapter of this section introduces an informal Italic hand (called cursive Italic) that links most letters together, but not necessarily all. The cursive hand is the ancestor to handwriting, a distinct expression of each individual.

This informal Italic, because of the speed with which it can be written, can utilize flourishes freely while dancing across the page. It is most enjoyable for filling artful journals or as an additional element to abstract painting, leading us very nicely into Section Three.

But right now, let's begin to play!

# A Word on Supplies

It has been suggested by calligraphers, lettering artists, watercolorists and teachers of these arts (for whom I have much respect) that it is ideal to buy and use the best-quality supplies that your budget can comfortably afford. This suggestion especially applies to paper, paints and inks. Inexpensive paper, paints and inks can leave you feeling very frustrated and disappointed with your results. While good-quality metal nibs with plastic nib holders and decent 140-lb. watercolor pads are not outrageously expensive, it is usually the scrumptious, high-quality paints and inks that add up quickly before you've accumulated even a handful.

I suggest that you start out with a set of metal nibs with plastic holders (see page 85 to learn more about nibs), a few synthetic brushes, a pad of 140-lb. hot- or cold-pressed watercolor paper (I like Arches) and your three absolute favorite watercolor paints and/or inks. You can add to your collection over time. The best way to discover which brands you like best is to use them extensively. Good quality will delight.

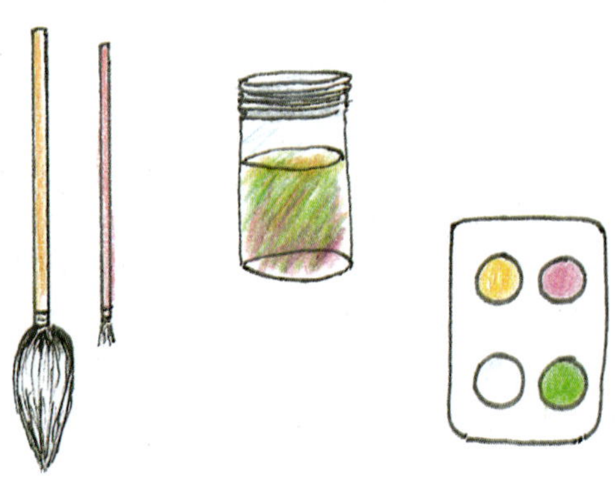

## Finding Supplies

Section Two is as much about finding and using new supplies as it is about the technical aspects of the variations of the Italic script.

When I was writing an essay for an English class at university, my professor made it her goal to teach us how and where to find excellent resources. As a result, I discovered areas of the library I had never been before — places with a wealth of resource material. This became extremely beneficial for not only my English essays but all future essays.

While outlining a supply list for the exercises and projects in this book, I have that professor's approach in mind. I encourage you to discover and explore your local art shops. Browse lovingly through the aisles of intoxicating colors. Become familiar with terms and brands. Let your eyes feast on the variety of supplies. Shop with appreciative restraint. A few quality supplies will add gloriously to your calligraphic efforts.

If shopping locally is not an option for you — it certainly isn't for me — there are online suppliers who sell quality calligraphy supplies. I have used John Neal for years as my "go-to" online seller of high-quality supplies. A simple online search will usually yield both domestic options and international options, though you might have to deal with additional costs for shipping and duties.

# All about Inks

Ink is made from pigments or dyes, sometimes with a binding agent, that are mixed with a solvent. Pigments are the solid particles that give ink its color. Binding agents (such as resin or glue) hold the ink ingredients together. Solvents, such as water, alcohol or ketone solvents, dissolve the pigments.

Ink and paint primarily differ in viscosity or thickness. Both are typically pigment suspended in a resin binder and a solvent. Ink is often made from pigment suspended in a different resin, such as PVC, gum arabic or animal glue to reduce its viscosity. Inks flow more readily than paints because they are thinner. As a result, they are absorbed more or less immediately into paper, leaving a stain. Their thinness also means they can run easily through a pen cartridge and nib.

There are numerous types of ink available. Let's briefly review the most frequently used inks in the world of calligraphy.

**Sumi ink** – This is a traditional Japanese ink made from soot and animal glue. It is rich, black and dense. This is a permanent ink that dries quickly but takes hours to dry permanently. As a result, it is a great ink to use in Sink Art (see page 176) as it can be washed with gently flowing water and manipulated to create marbled effects.

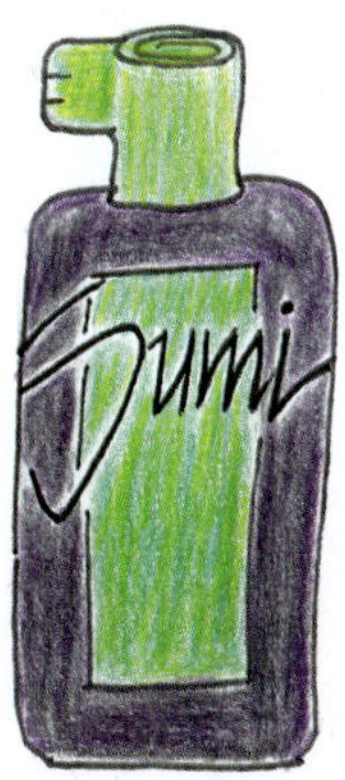


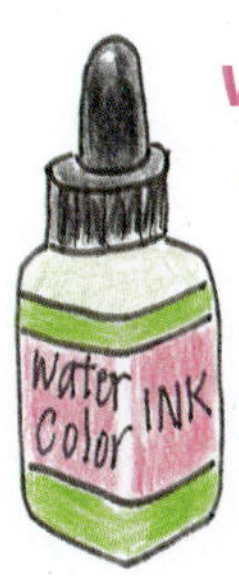


**Watercolor ink** – This is concentrated pigment often used as paint. These inks tend to be bright in color and are difficult to lift from paper as they are very quickly absorbed and dye the paper rather than sit on the surface. They are not water resistant and are usually transparent.

**Acrylic ink** – Acrylic inks are water-resistant inks (once dry) that are pigment based. They can be thicker than watercolor inks. The fluid dries very quickly and can be transparent, opaque and semi-opaque. It is essentially an extremely fluid version of acrylic paint that bonds to paper. These inks can be used for ink blending, especially when diluted, which is when you want your inks to bleed together. Acrylic inks cannot be used with a fountain pen because they will clog the pen.

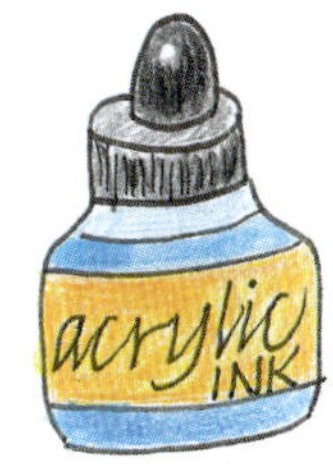


**India ink** – This is a carbon pigment (such as soot) mixed with a liquid solution of glue or gum arabic as a binder. This ink is associated with Asia — hence the name. The binder acts as a shellac, resulting in a waterproof ink. It is similar to Sumi ink, only differing because of the addition of shellac.

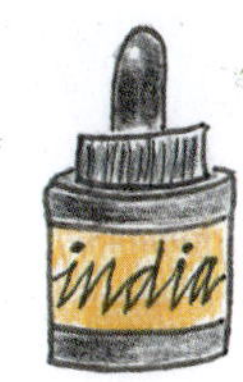


**Fountain pen ink** – Due to the fact that fountain pen nibs clog easily, they require a different type of ink that is dye based rather than pigment based. The use of a dye ensures there are no particles that could clog the nib and prevent the flow of the ink. Additionally, there is no resin or similar binding agent in these inks to further ensure the pen does not clog. These inks are thin and not water resistant, flowing very easily.

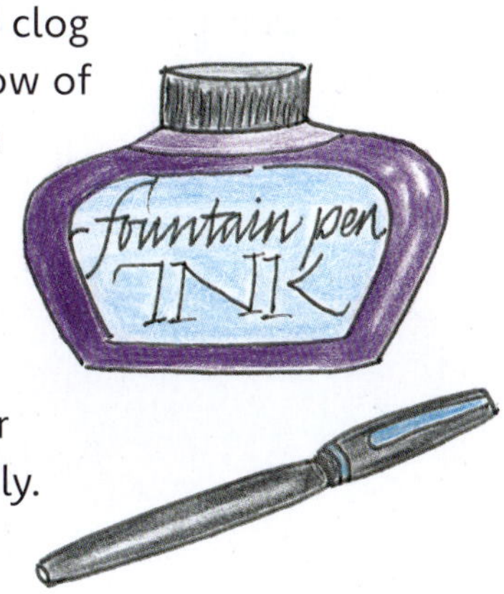

**Tech ink** – This is a pigment-based ink that is waterproof and transparent. It has an advantage over Sumi ink in that it is available in many glorious colors. This ink has great archival longevity.

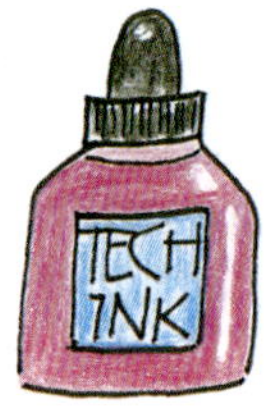


**Walnut ink** – This ink is made from either the husk surrounding the nut of a black walnut or English peat moss (in crystal form). It is a lovely warm-brown color, is not waterproof and is great for ink blending. It has decent longevity.

1 teaspoon walnut crystals to ½ cup water*

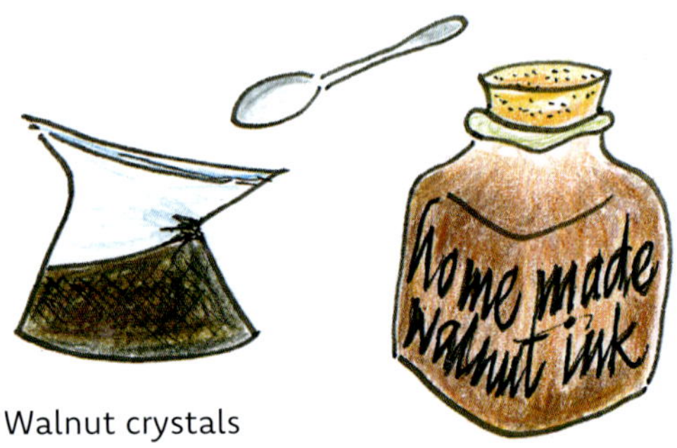


Walnut crystals

*distilled water. Keep in sealed little jar.

It should be noted that the longevity of an ink is lower when using inks that are dye-based as opposed to pigment or soot based. The terms "lightfast" and "archival" refer to inks that are not prone to discoloring when exposed to sunlight. When choosing inks for final work to be framed, keep this in mind.

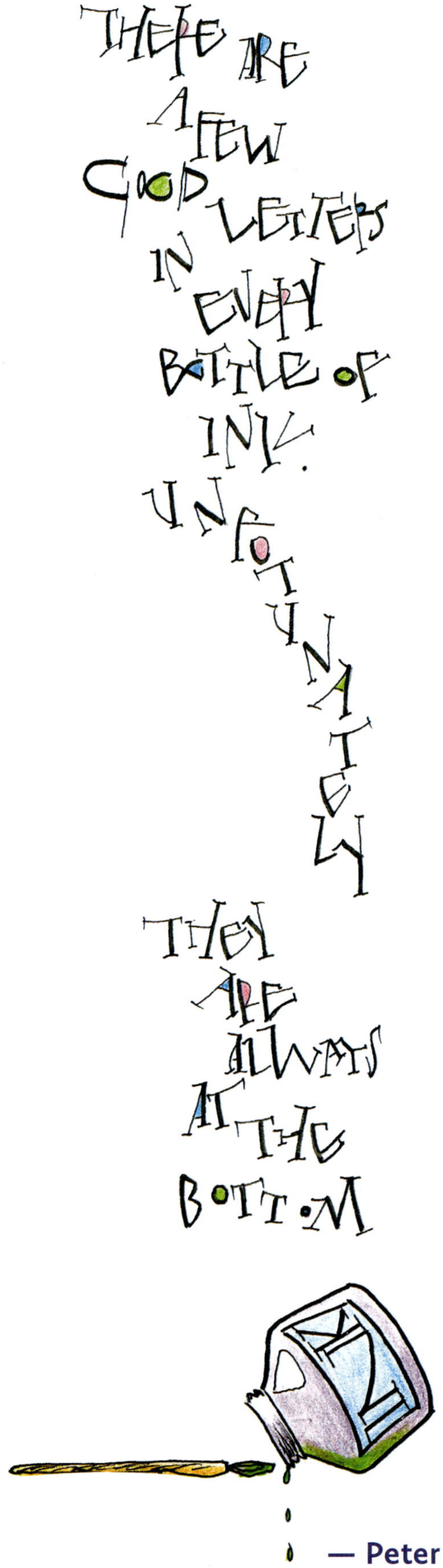


— Peter Thornton

# The Pen Nib

Your pen will include a nib that contains a reservoir. The reservoir holds the paint/ink and feeds it to the nib, thereby allowing for a longer flow before needing to refill. This loading and re-loading of the pen requires time to get used to. However, a comfortable rhythm does develop.

Some reservoirs are attached to the top of the nib, and some are on the bottom. Some are fixed permanently to the nib and some are removable. I prefer the permanently fixed ones, such as those produced by Brause, Speedball, Hiro and Tape, with the reservoir on the top. Personally, I find them easier to load. Either top-loading or bottom-loading reservoirs are good, and you will find your preference.

reservoir on top of nib

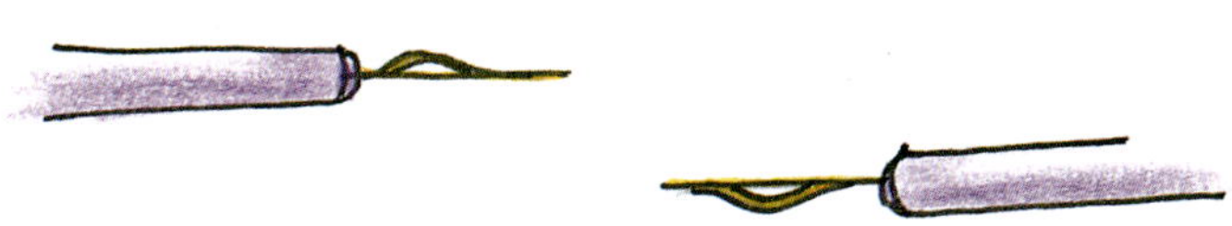

reservoir below nib

To load paint or ink onto your nib you can either dip your pen into a little container, or you can brush paint/ink onto the nib either on top or on the side. Both work.

When dipping your pen into a little container of paint or ink, try not to stick the whole nib in as you will acquire far too much paint/ink and it will begin to creep into the area where the nib is attached to the holder. Try dipping it halfway in to load the reservoir but not overload it.

Have a session with your pen, paints, inks, a brush, containers, water and watercolor paper. Load up your pen by either dipping or brushing the paint, and off you go! See what method works best for you.

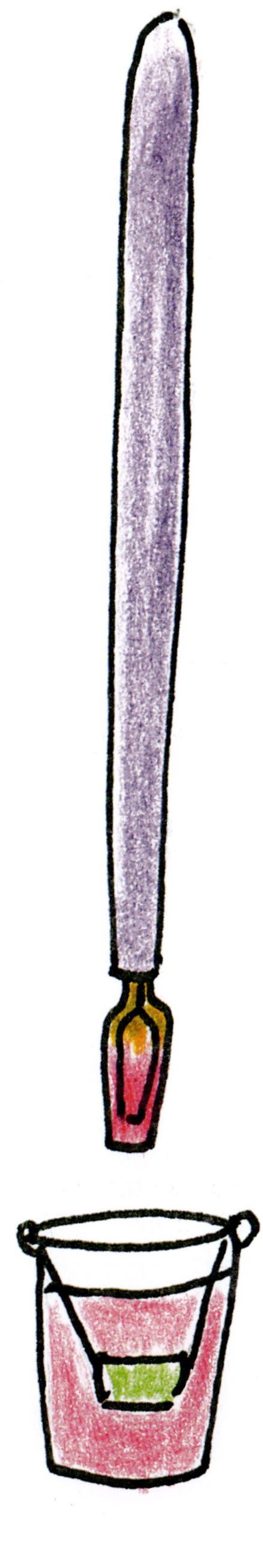

# A Wash with Gouache

Often what I recommend to you in this book is my attempt to prevent you from my mistakes, accidents or downright humiliation. This last point brings me to the topic of gouache (pronounced "gwash").

My first trip into an art store found me timidly (for I was shy and uncertain) asking for "goo-achh-ee." The woman replied, "Would you mean 'gwash,' by any chance?"

I answered with a low voice equal to the level of my sinking self-esteem, "I guess so." I left the store with nothing but a bucketload of humiliation and the determination to never do that again.

So I will save you that experience, though I am sure most other people would have seen themselves through that experience with far more aplomb.

Anyway, gouache is an opaque watercolor often used by calligraphers. It tends to sit on the surface of the paper because it has a thicker viscosity, rather than soaking into the paper the way transparent watercolor inks do.

As with watercolors, try to buy fewer but of the highest quality your budget can afford. Gouache often comes in tubes like watercolors, but there are paint sets as well, with little pucks of paint. There are many brands of tubes, and each brand has many colors you can choose from. For each color you usually have the option of choosing high-quality professional grade, or lower-quality (and less expensive) student grade. Decide how much you want to spend and choose two to three of your favorite colors within your budget. The better quality can always wait for you if you cannot afford it now. Color should be celebrated whether top quality or not.

## LOADING YOUR PEN WITH GOUACHE

When loading gouache into your pen, you will need your pen, your tubes of gouache, a little mixing tray (a cheap, plastic one will do), inexpensive paintbrushes, water and a scrap piece of paper (the same kind you will be using for your lettering). Add a small blob of gouache to the tray (keep the different colors separated) and then take your brush and carefully add individual drops of water to the gouache and stir until it takes on a milk-like consistency. An empty eyedropper (or pipette) is also a very handy tool to have for adding water to the gouache.

### Saving Some for Later

**Unlike acrylic paints, your blobs of gouache won't dry into totally useless bits of plastic (nothing against acrylic!). Therefore, you don't have to cover what you don't use while you are working. However, it is always best to put something on top of these precious paints to protect them from dust, evaporation, or, if you have many long-haired pets as I do, cat and dog hair!**

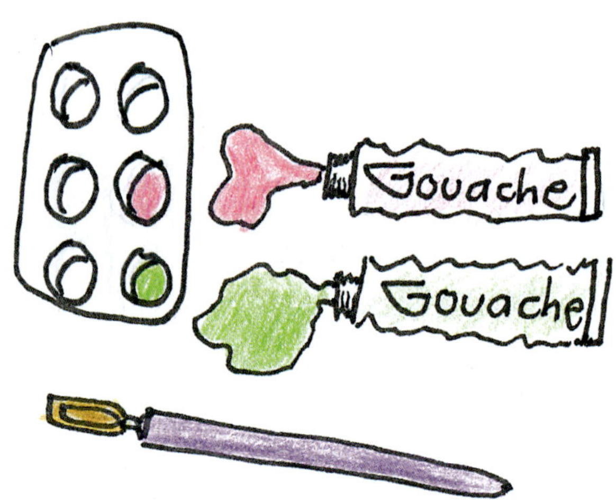

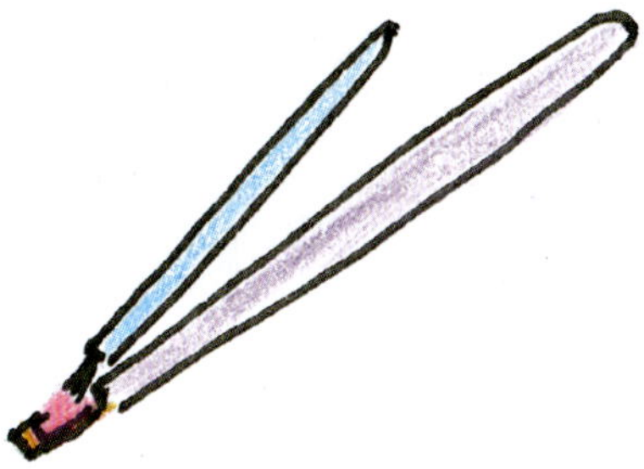

To load your pen, dip your brush so that it's saturated with gouache, and brush a bit of the gouache on top of your nib. Try the pen to see if the gouache comes through on your scrap paper. A little back-and-forth scribble will help the ink begin to flow. If nothing's coming out, dip the nib just barely into some water and try again with that same scribble motion. Sometimes the paint is shy or stubborn and requires some coaxing. Keep dipping and squiggling until it works. The gouache should be like milk, not pudding!

After your session, always clean your pen and brush.

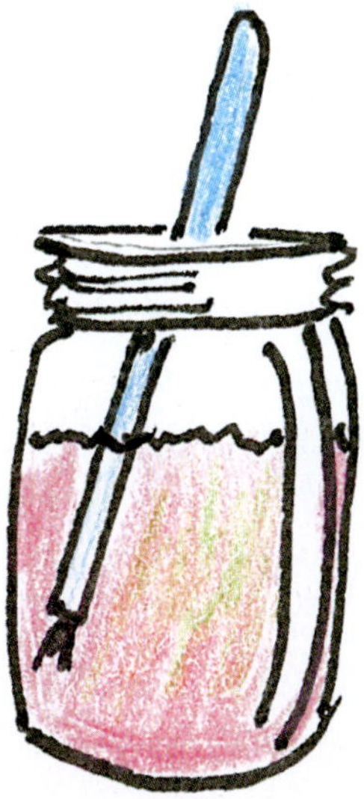

## Caring for Your Tools

As you're lettering, both pens and brushes can be rinsed and dried with a rag to keep your work clean as you proceed. However, if you are finished for the day or even for an hour, it is imperative to clean your tools carefully and thoroughly so that they will perform well, offering you the best results possible.

The pen requires rinsing under running water and wiping it dry. Then, take a sturdy piece of paper and slide it between the nib and the reservoir to rid it of any lingering paint or ink that could cause clogging, which would disrupt a smooth flow and create much frustration!

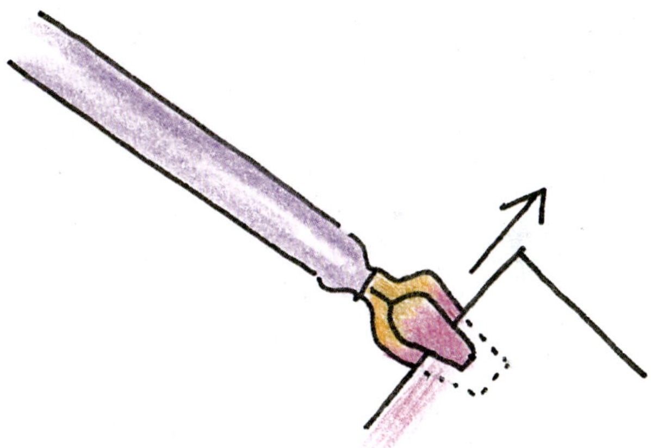

Your brushes should be run under water, then brushed in the palm of your hand with a tiny bit of soap. Rinse thoroughly and then dry with a clean rag, molding it back to its original shape so it's ready for the next time. Ideally, it is best to hang your brush vertically until it dries, then lay it flat. However, this option is not always available and you can just lay it flat to dry completely.

# Review

As you work on the review exercises provided, please refer to the alphabet samplers on pages 52 and 62, which depict the ductus for each letter in the alphabet. This will help with the review process.

## SHAPES

Fill a line of your practice sheet with each of these shapes:

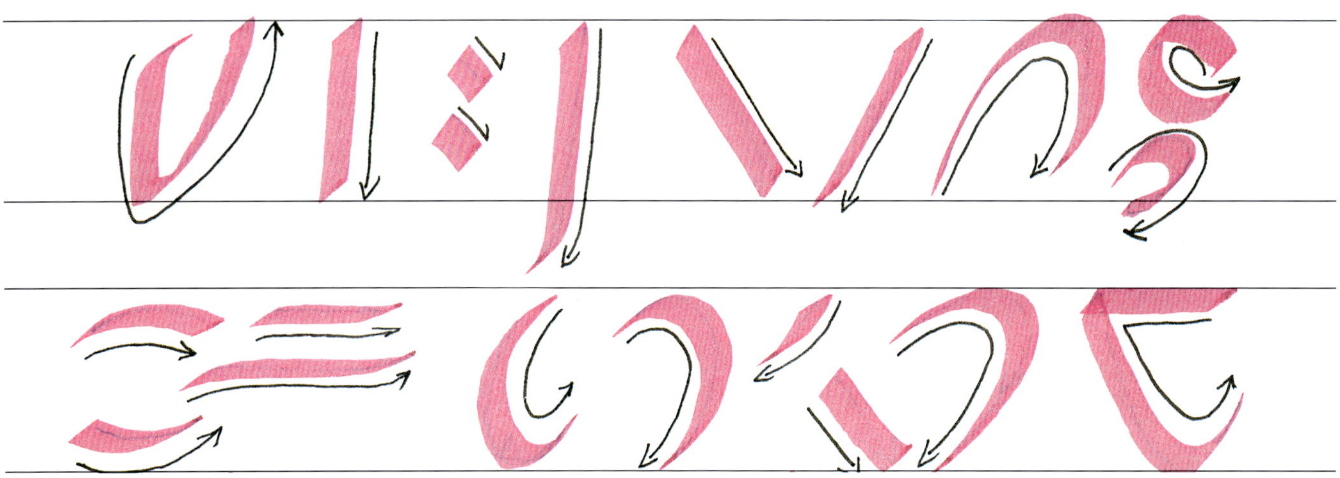

## SPACING

Since the Italic script is made up of triangles and ovals, try the following spacing exercise on your practice sheet. With a pencil, draw a variety of shapes, as depicted. As you create the shapes, keep a keen eye on the spacing between each of the shapes, having them match as closely as possible. Outline the shapes with a fine-liner marker, then erase the pencil. Color in the shapes to magnify the spaces. This will help you to see where there is inconsistency in your spacing.

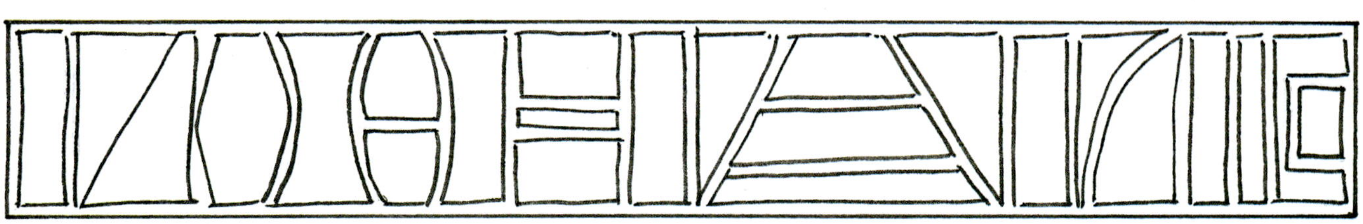

## LETTER GROUPS

Fill a few lines of your practice sheet with each of these letter groups. Remember to pay attention to the spacing between letters and between groups of letters. Remember that you will be using your template with slope.

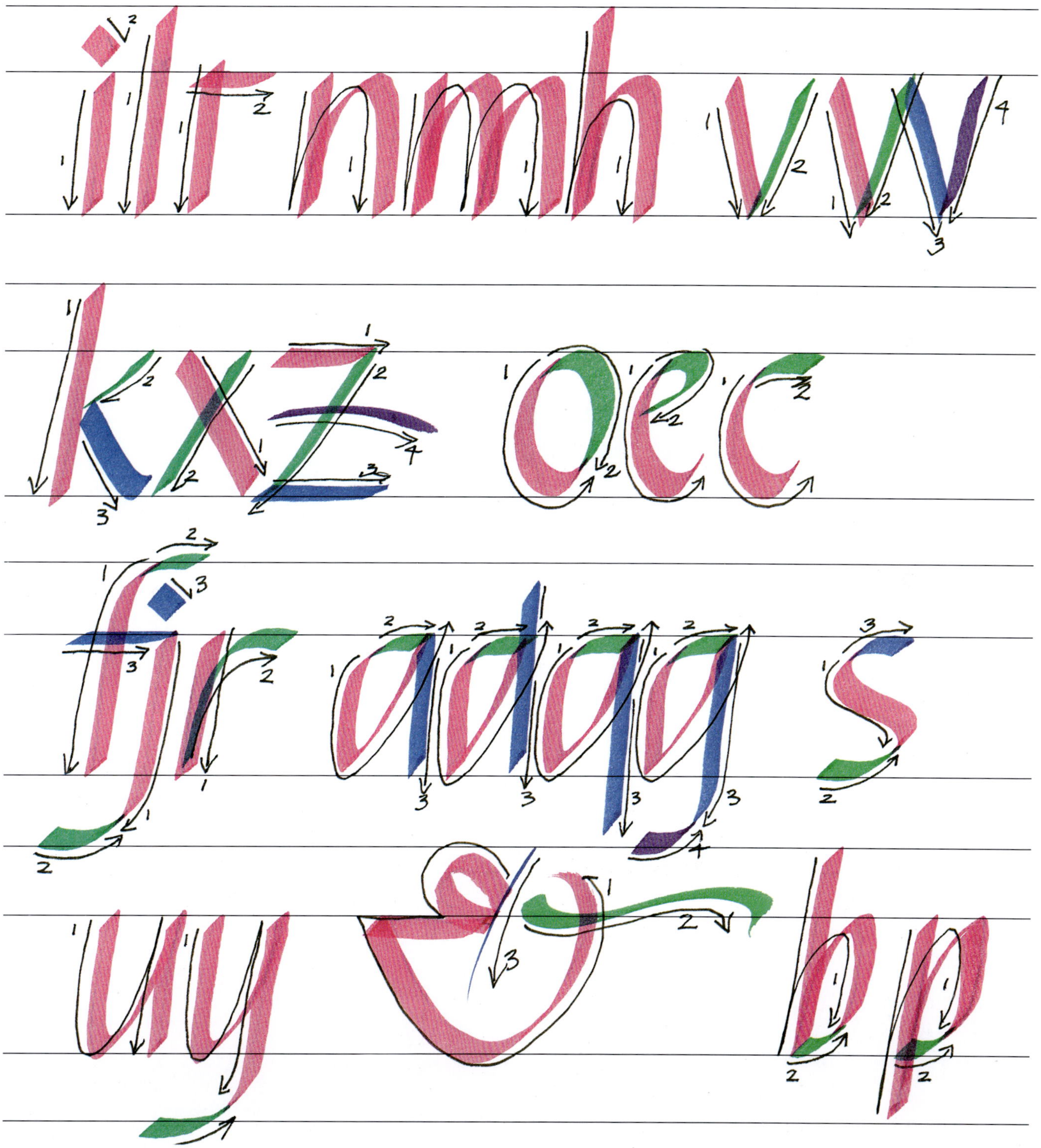

# Chapter 4

# Learning Variations & Flourishes

**B**efore we embellish or vary in any way, we must first have a firm grasp of creating the foundation. Once we're confident in our traditional letters, we can begin to alter our letter strokes and add flourishes and color.

## Altering Letter Strokes

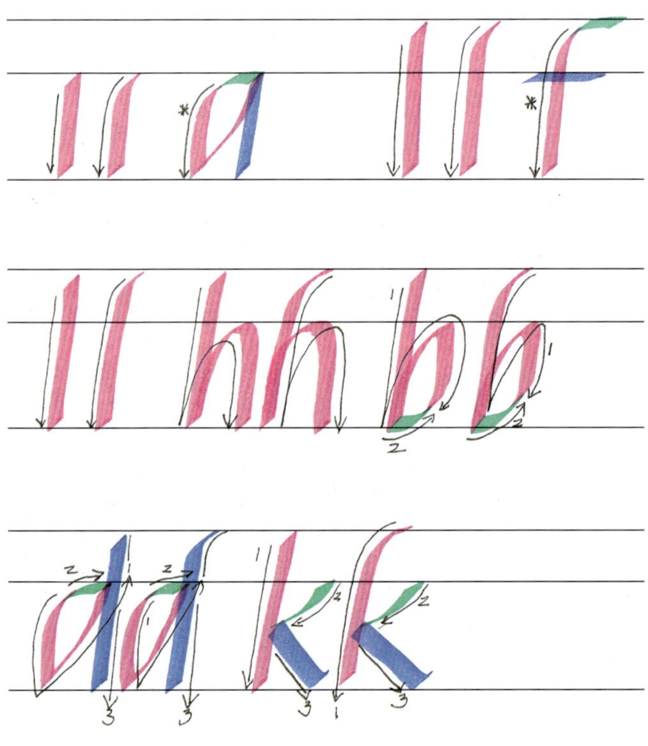

The first variation of the traditional Italic script is done in the lead-in downstroke of an ascender. This is achieved by starting the way you would start the first stroke of a lowercase *a*. The stroke is the same as the first stroke of the lowercase *f* as well. It has the same form as strokes that touch in a whisper join.

Note that these are not curves. With your nib at 45 degrees, the pen scoots to the left and then down. Practice a line of each new version of the letters with stems.

The second variation involves the final downstroke and resembles the first stroke of the lowercase *j*. It also has the same form as a stroke that joins to create a whisper join and ends below the baseline at a 45-degree angle.

Practice a line of each of the letters *h*, *m* and *n*. Make sure that the last downstroke ends with the same delicate feel as those that create whisper joins.

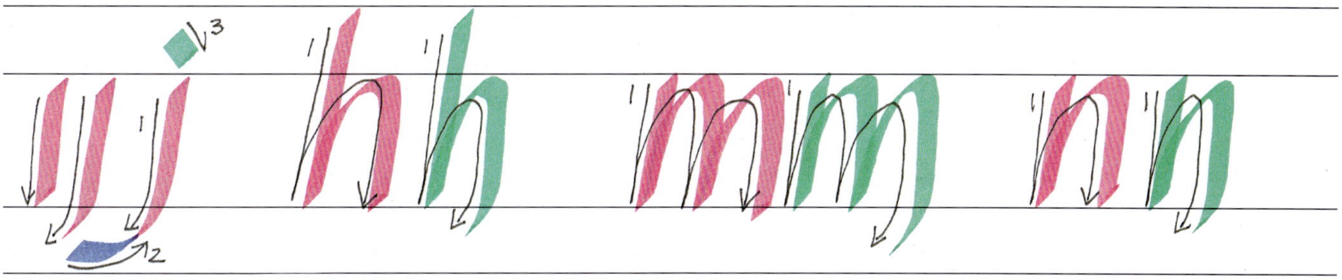

An extra stroke (called a flourish) can be added to the letter at the end of a word or sentence.

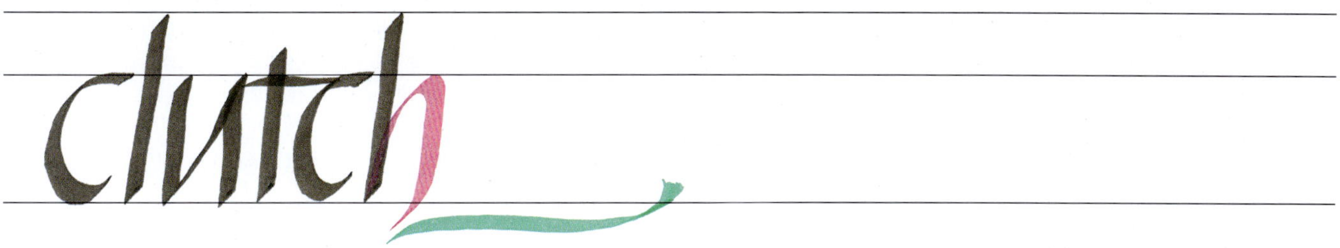


These flourishes should barely touch the last downstroke variation, although the illustrations exaggerate a gap so you can see where the join occurs. Note that the last lowercase *h* example depicts letters with variations on both the first and last downstroke and the added flourish.

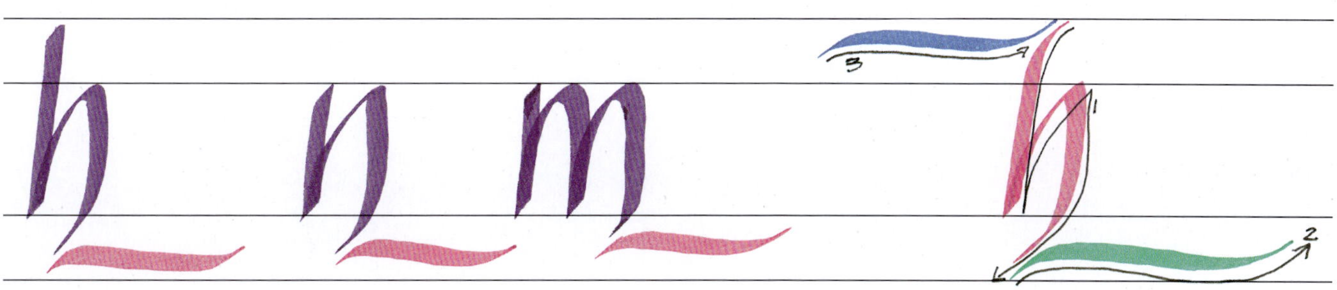

We can make another variation on the exit stroke of a letter. This stroke no longer remains parallel with the first stroke but rather resembles the first diagonal stroke of the letter *x*.

Practice the diagonal stroke of the *x* for a line, to allow for a familiarity with the feel of the angle. Once complete, practice a line of each of the below letters, slowly incorporating each diagonal ending.

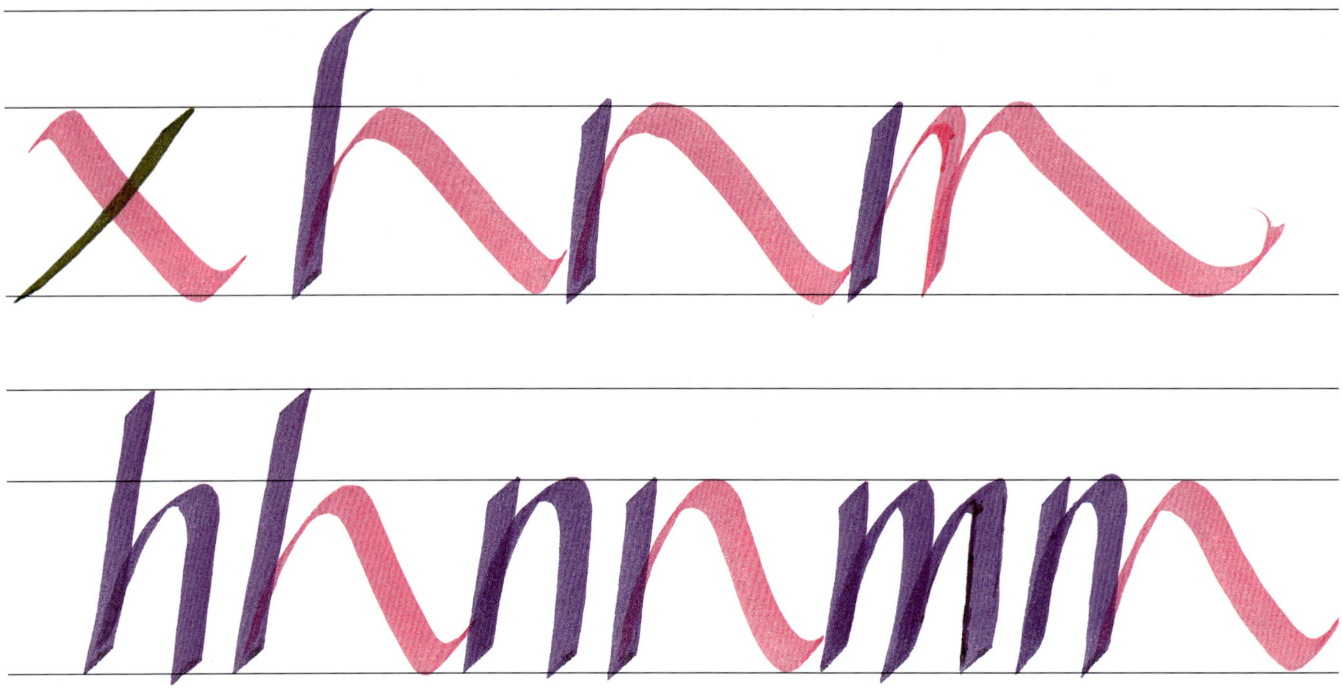

It is important to note that this variation is suited for the ending of a word. Once you feel comfortable with the angle, practice a sheet of words that end in these letters, such as *them*, *hen*, *catch*, *from*, *foam* and *than*.

As you practice, remember that the more things or versions you study, the more everything you've learned becomes apparent!

# Adding Flourishes

According to the *Oxford English Dictionary*, a flourish is "a bold or extravagant gesture or action, made especially to attract the attention of others." In calligraphy, flourishes are used to further embellish letters and words.

Try flourishing everywhere you can when you're practicing. Not only will your hand, arm and shoulder become comfortable and confident in the process, but your artistic eye will soon let you know what works well, what is lacking and what is too much and should be left alone.

With your nib at a 45-degree angle, practice a few lines of these extended strokes. They are like a crossbar and can be used to begin or extend a letter (illustration 1).

Below I have provided examples of flourishing we can add to the letters *h*, *e* and *n* (illustration 2). Practice a line or two of each of these example letters.

To further embellish a letter, you can add additional strokes to create more elaborate flourishes. This is illustrated below with the addition of a second stroke and then a third stroke (illustration 3). Practice a few lines of each example.

A well-formed letter is beautiful in itself. It does not require flourishing to be so. In fact, a poorly flourished letter will completely destroy the most wonderfully formed letter. Remember: *Artistic restraint, understated elegance.*

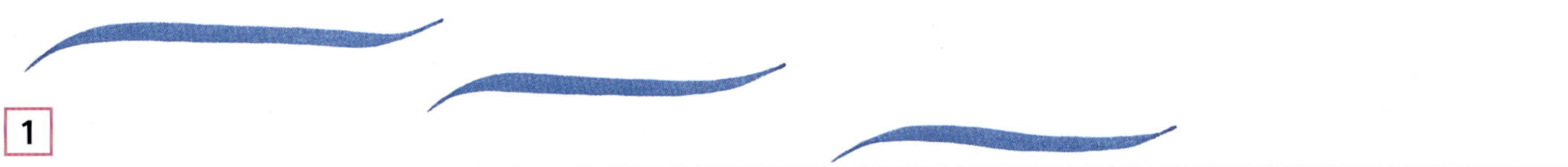

1

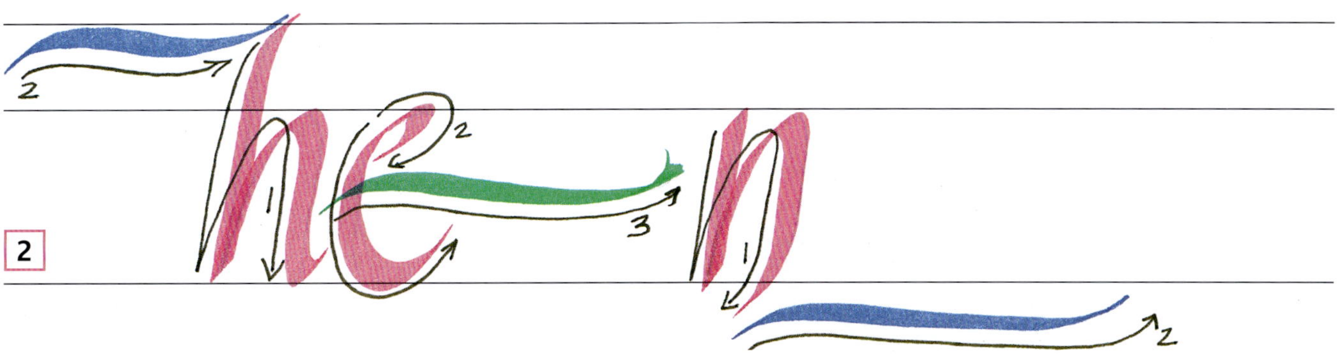

2

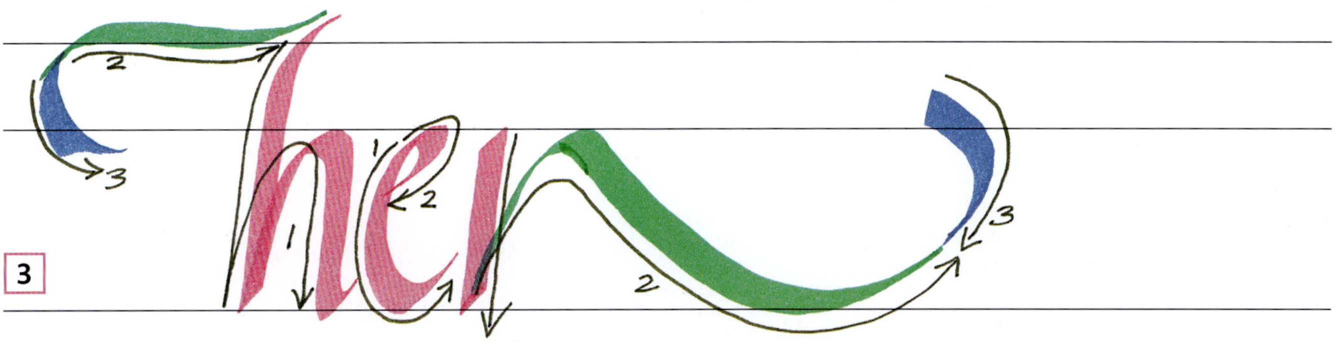

3

## CAPITALS WITH FLOURISHES

It's time to explore a new version of the capital letters. These can be — and often are — flourished abundantly.

Take some time to study the skeletal structure of the capital letters depicted below. The sampler on the following page depicts "fancy" Italic capitals, while the ones you'll be practicing below simply depict the skeletal structure.

On your practice sheet, draw the letters while following the order and direction (ductus) of the strokes, first in pencil and then, once you feel more confident, with a calligraphy pen. Try at least a line per letter. Once you have done this, try to re-create the capital letters from the sampler of "fancy caps" on the opposite page, first in pencil then with a calligraphy pen.

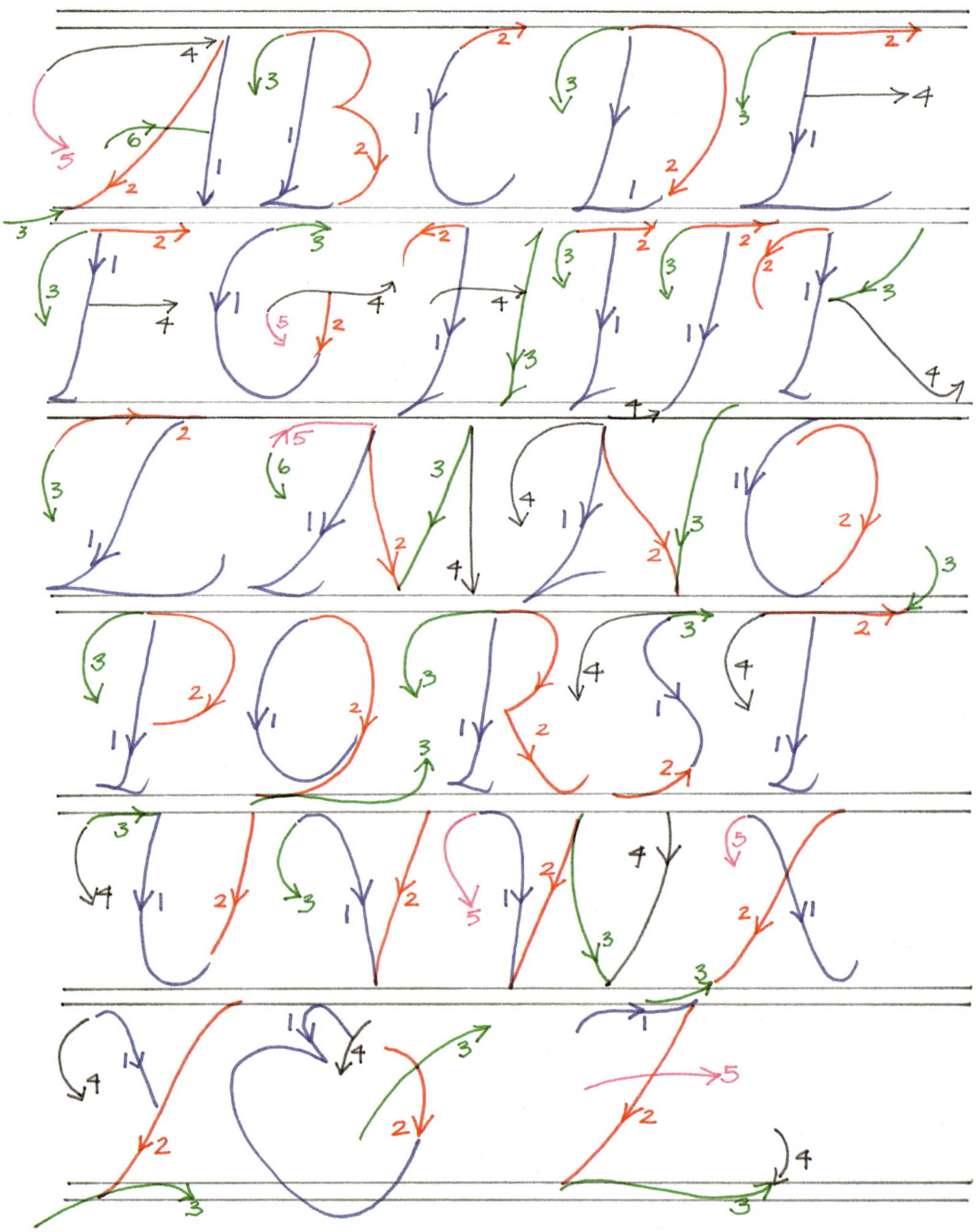

After that, create a page of words that begin with each capital letter, from A to Z. You can letter in pencil first if you wish. As you become more familiar with these capitals, you can move on straight away to your calligraphy pen or marker.

It is important to note that capital letters are like flagpoles: they must be well made and solid. Only then can the flag (or flourishes) whip and dance about with delight.

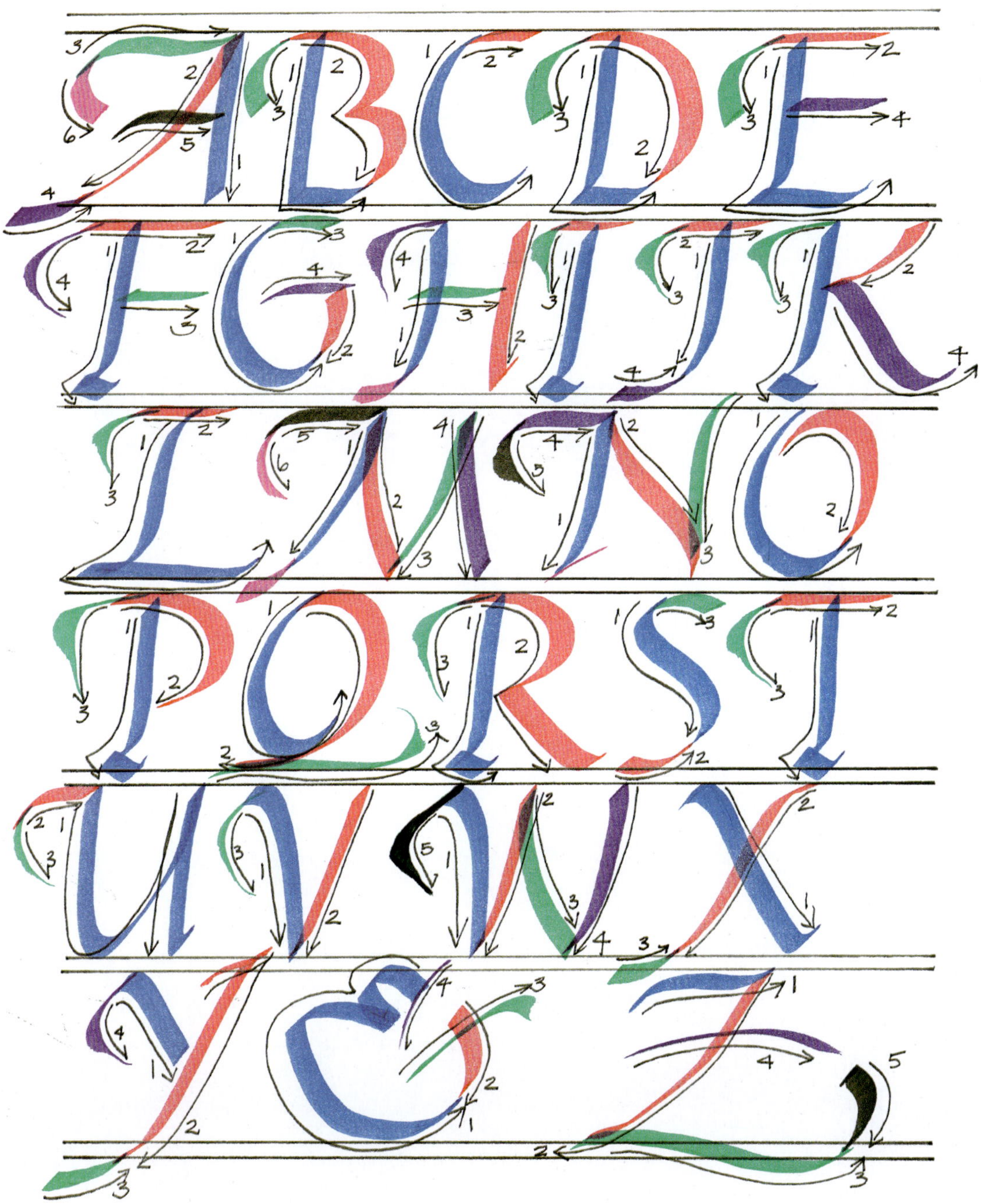

## FREE-FLOWING FLOURISHES

When we talk about free-flowing flourishing, we mean less contrived or restrained flourishes that are drawn with larger arm movements and energy. This is like incorporating dance into your calligraphy.

Free-flowing flourishing requires practice to create comfortable and natural flow. These are not preconceived strokes but rather strokes that fly like fishing lines fly off reels. To begin, practice arm movements in the air over and over, depicting the movement you want to make on paper. You may look like you are trying to conduct an invisible orchestra to anyone passing by, but that's OK!

Then, with pencil on plain paper, do a few practice lines for each of the following five flourishes.

1. Circles drawn to the left but move to the right.
2. Circles drawn to the right and move to the right.
3. Figure eights moving to the right.
4. A strong stroke sweeping up to the top to a stop, followed by a second distinct stroke down to a stop.
5. A curve up and down to the right that comes to a full stop — then continues on. As with the preceding step, this exercise requires two distinct strokes.

**Note:** For flourishes 4 and 5, you do not need to draw a dot unless it helps you to stop. It is illustrated here to signify a stop in the flow.

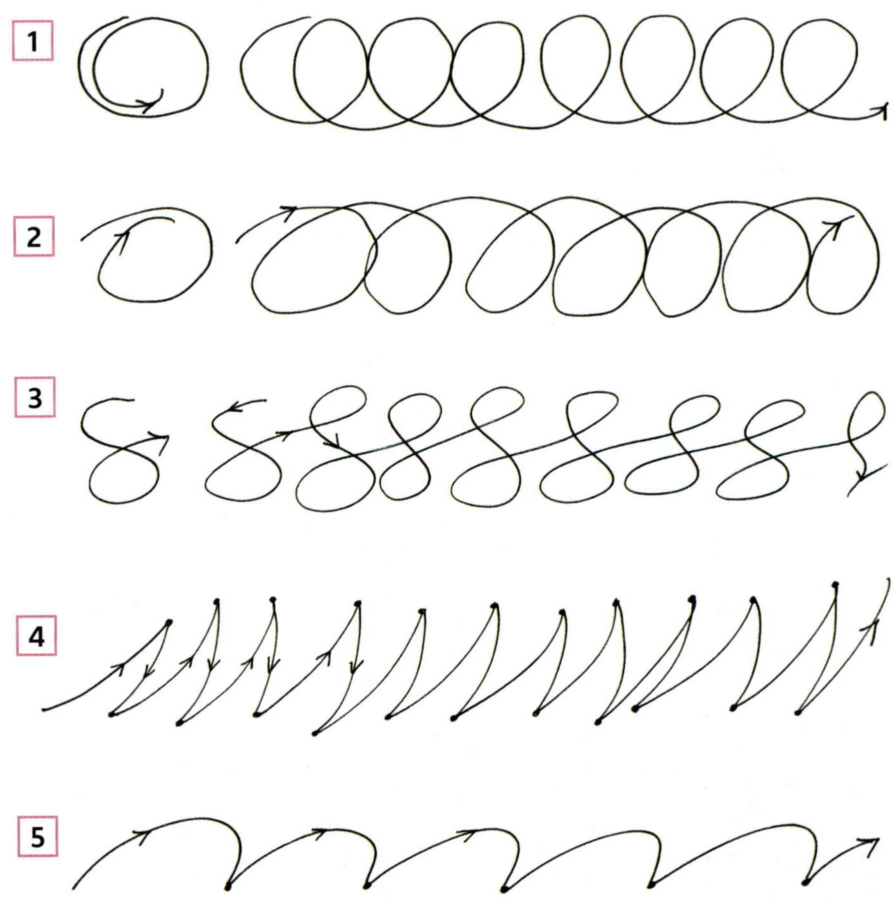

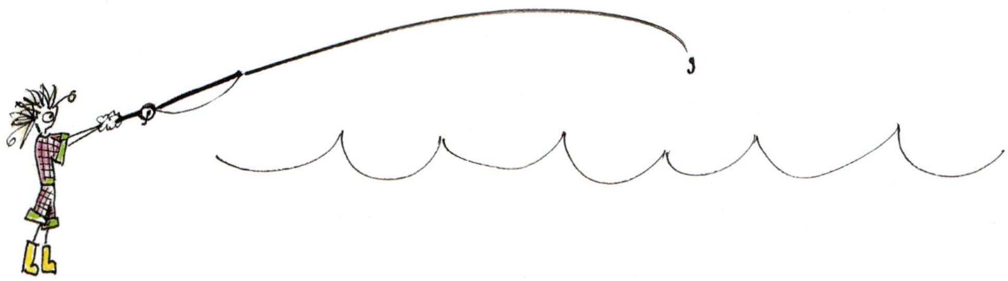

## THE MECHANICS OF FREE-FLOWING FLOURISHES

To illustrate the mechanics of free-flowing flourishes, let's use fishing as an analogy.

The fishing line arches naturally away from the end of the rod because of the energy used to throw it.

To practice, start by drawing sweeping lines with consistent pressure, using just your hand to move the pen.

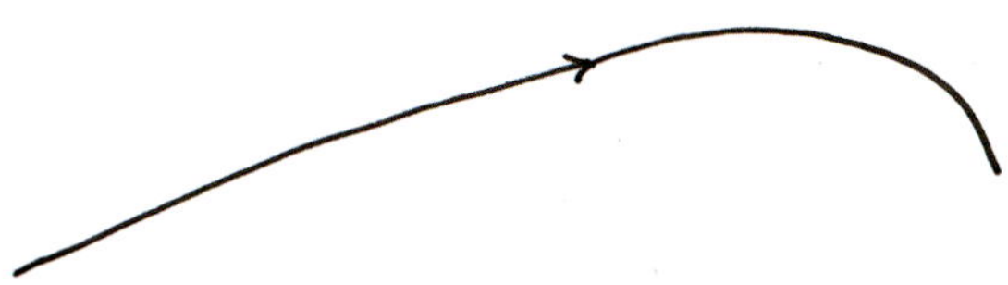

Then move on to drawing lines thrown with energy, using your hand, arm and shoulder in one sweeping motion.

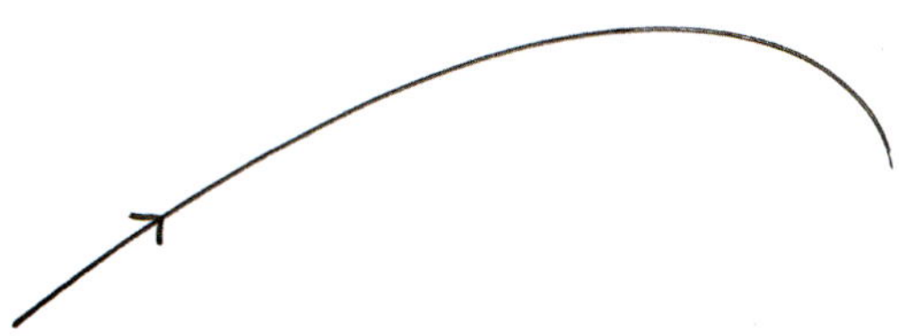

The following three exercises are created with the throwing motion. Use your whole arm to do this. These lines diminish in weight at the end, as opposed to the drawn lines, which are made with consistent pressure. The thrown lines are created with a fluid motion that will become more natural with repetition and practice. For each exercise, start with a row of lines in pencil and then do another row with your fine-liner marker.

1. On a plain piece of paper, draw a row of lines "thrown" to the right.

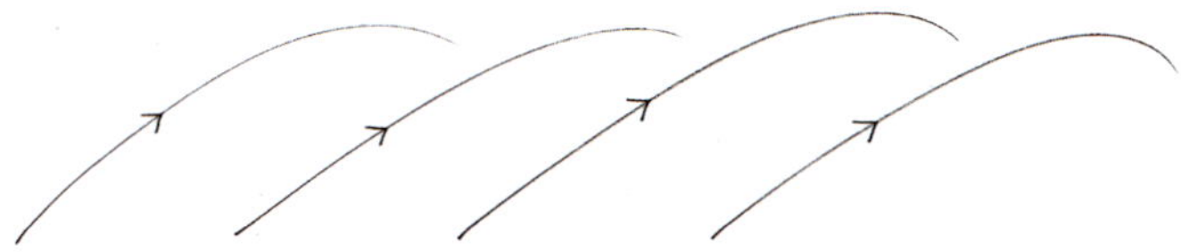

2. Next, draw lines that go up and finish either to the left, right or straight up. Think of fireworks.

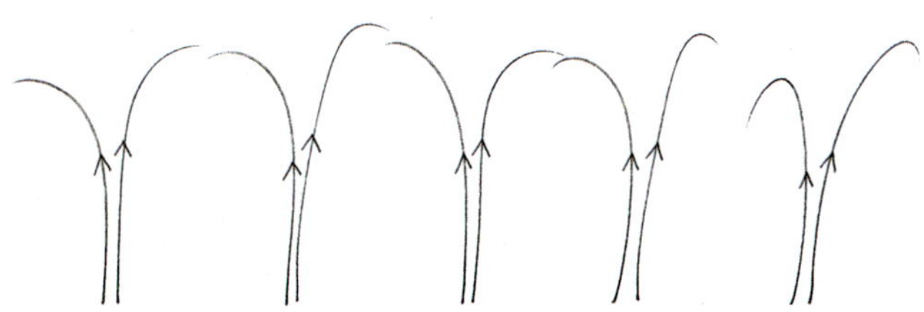

3. Lastly, try these lines, which are thrown to the left. At first you might find these awkward, unless you are left-handed.

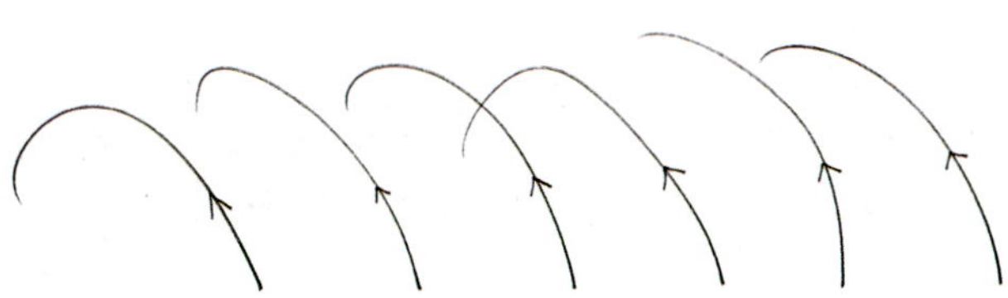

The most important result of a flourish is that it looks and feels balanced — not ready to topple. It should have energy on both sides, like the moves of a dancer. The dancer must lean enough one way to extend their limbs in the opposite direction. This is balanced energy.

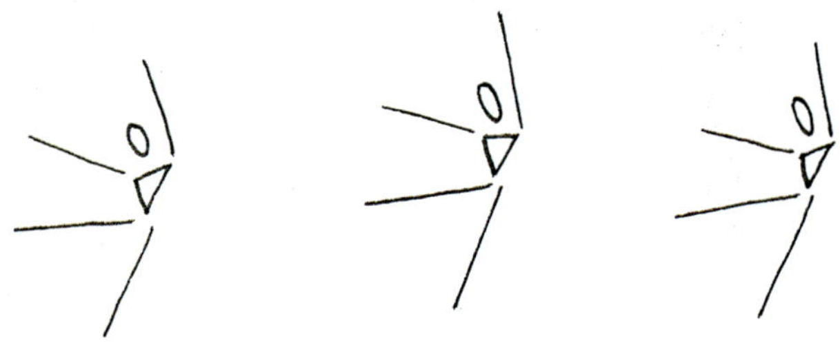

## PLAYING WITH LOOSE AND THROWN FLOURISHING

Now that you have the motion, it's time for some play. For each of the following exercises, there is a moment when you stop the energy and momentum and then throw the line in a different direction. The first line is drawn a bit more purposefully. The second line is most definitely thrown — like a fishing line.

As you proceed, start first by tracing each image with your finger. Next draw the shape on your paper *with your finger*. Then try with a pencil, and finally with a fine-liner marker. If it does not look or feel correct when using a fine-liner, begin the process again from the start. Trace with your finger until the motion is well established.

1. Draw a line that sweeps to the right, stop and then throw the line up and left.

2. Start to draw a circle to the right, stop and then throw the line down and to the right.

3. Now you're going to reverse the direction of exercise 1. Draw a line that sweeps to the left, stop and then throw the line up and to the right.

4. Lastly, you're going to reverse the direction of exercise 2. Draw a circle to the left, stop and then throw the line down and to the left.

1

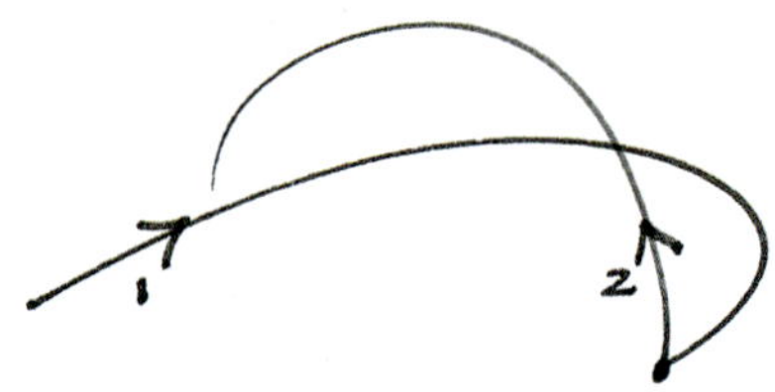


2

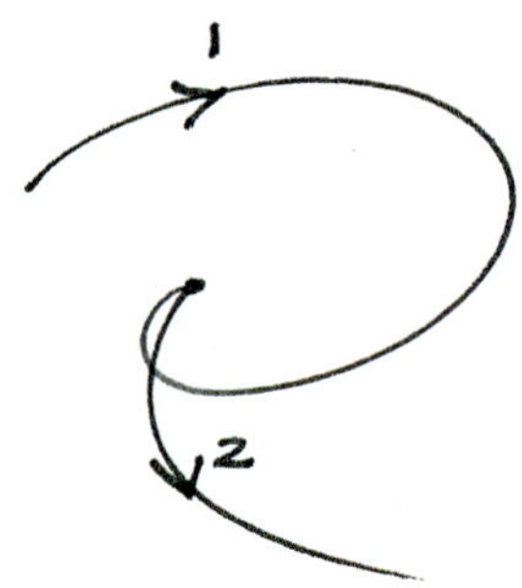


3

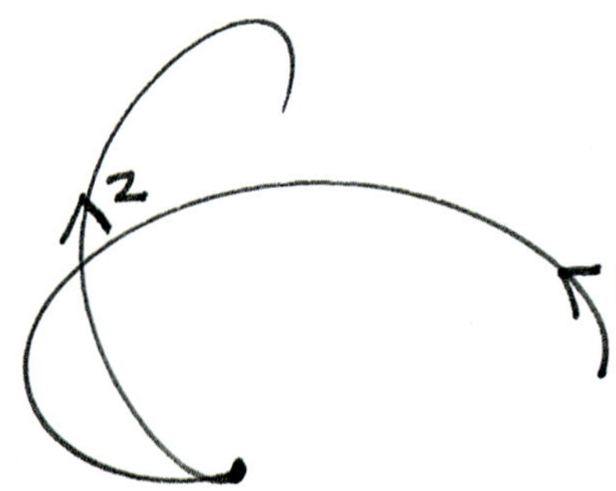


4

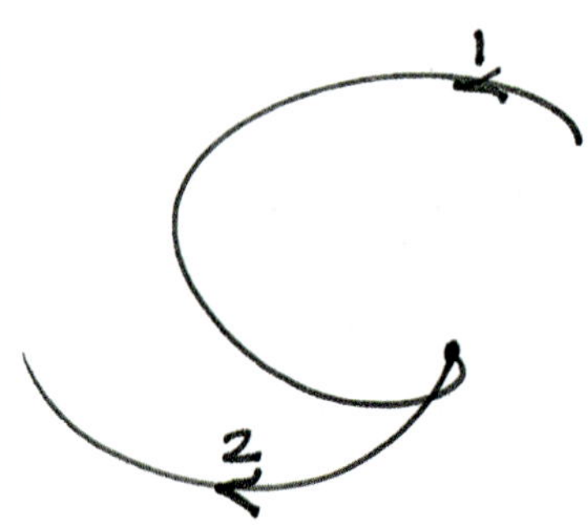

To illustrate with another analogy, when dancers listen to instruction for their next steps, they follow intensely with their eyes and minds, fingers fluttering, hands almost jerking as they strive to understand what is expected of them. Our brains must know where we are going before we begin to achieve the proper movement.

In preparation for creating the next set of free-flowing flourishes, start by loosening your hand and arm with graceful, swaying movements to feel the rhythm. As you practice, start first with a pencil, then move to a fineliner marker, and once you are comfortable and feeling more confident with the movement, I recommend experimenting with pen and nib.

Be mindful to thrust your arm and writing tool out as you create these flourishes. You are not drawing, but rather gesturing. The arrows show the direction of the flow for each flourish. Once you have practiced using the provided examples on the right, experiment with your own free-flowing flourishes.

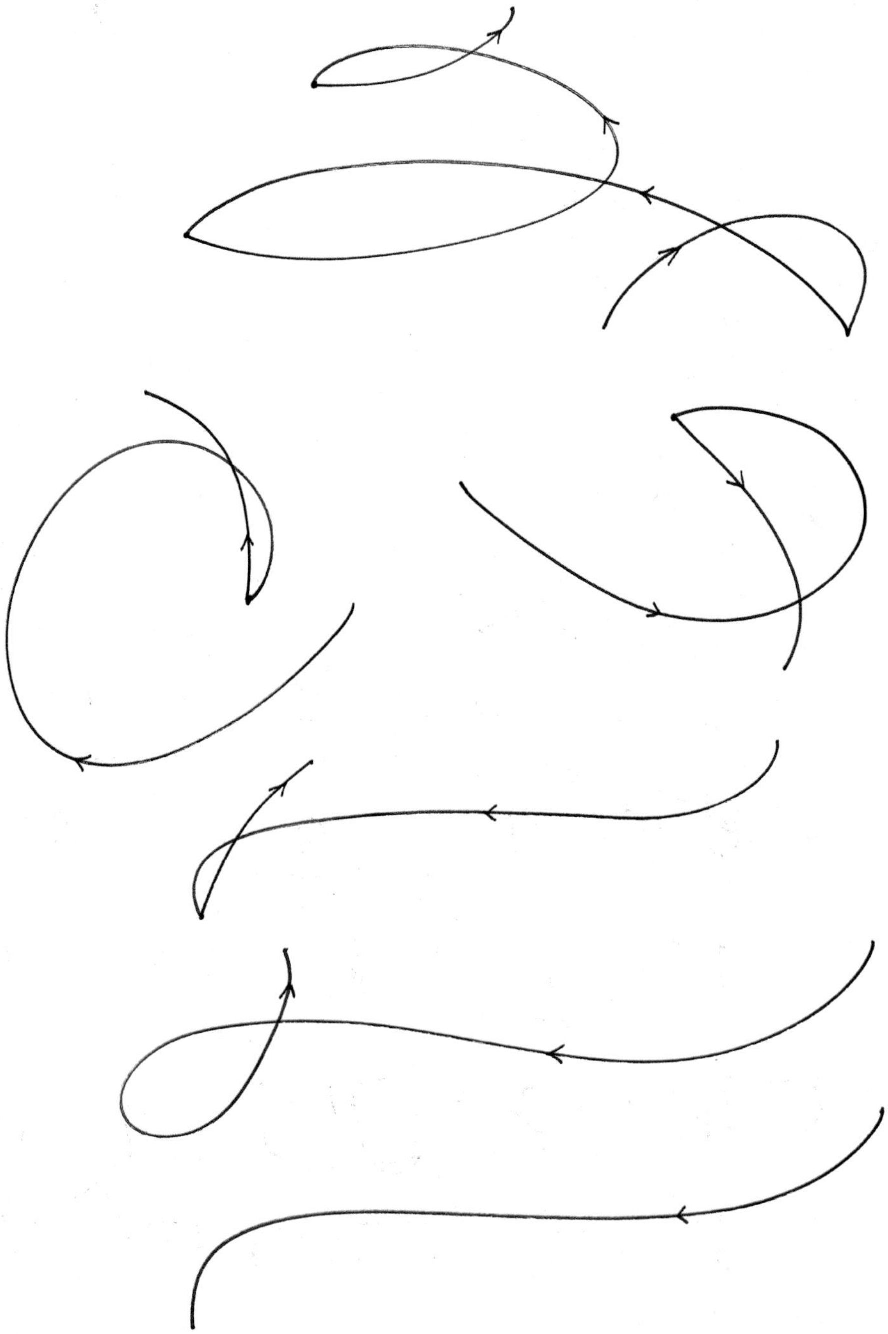

## FREE-FLOWING FLOURISHING WITH LOWERCASE LETTERS

Observe the lowercase letters below, which incorporate both one-step flourishing and two-step flourishing. One-step flourishing is when you throw your pen, hand and arm, like you're casting a fishing line. Two-step flourishing is when you throw the first line and stop, and then flick the line back, as you practiced on page 98 (also see the examples at the bottom of the opposite page).

Use one of your practice pages lined ½ inch apart to the bottom and try different flourishes on each lowercase letter. The lines will help provide guidance for your letters. Your flourishes will live predominantly outside these lines. Refer to the letters below as a starting point. You'll notice the parts of the letters in black are the familiar letter forms you've already practiced, and the parts of the letters in green and red are the various flourishes you could try. Green is the first stroke and red the second.

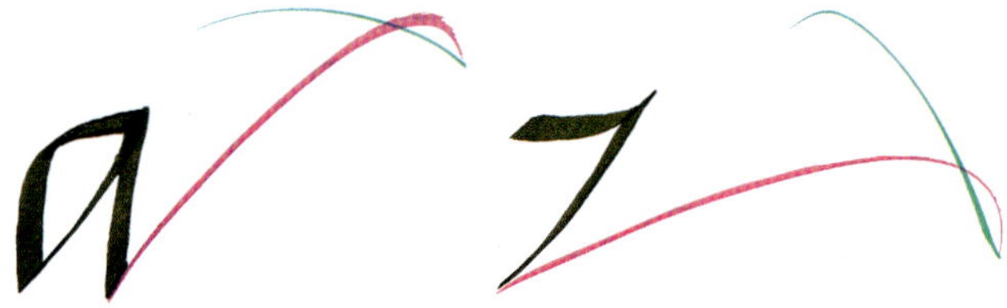

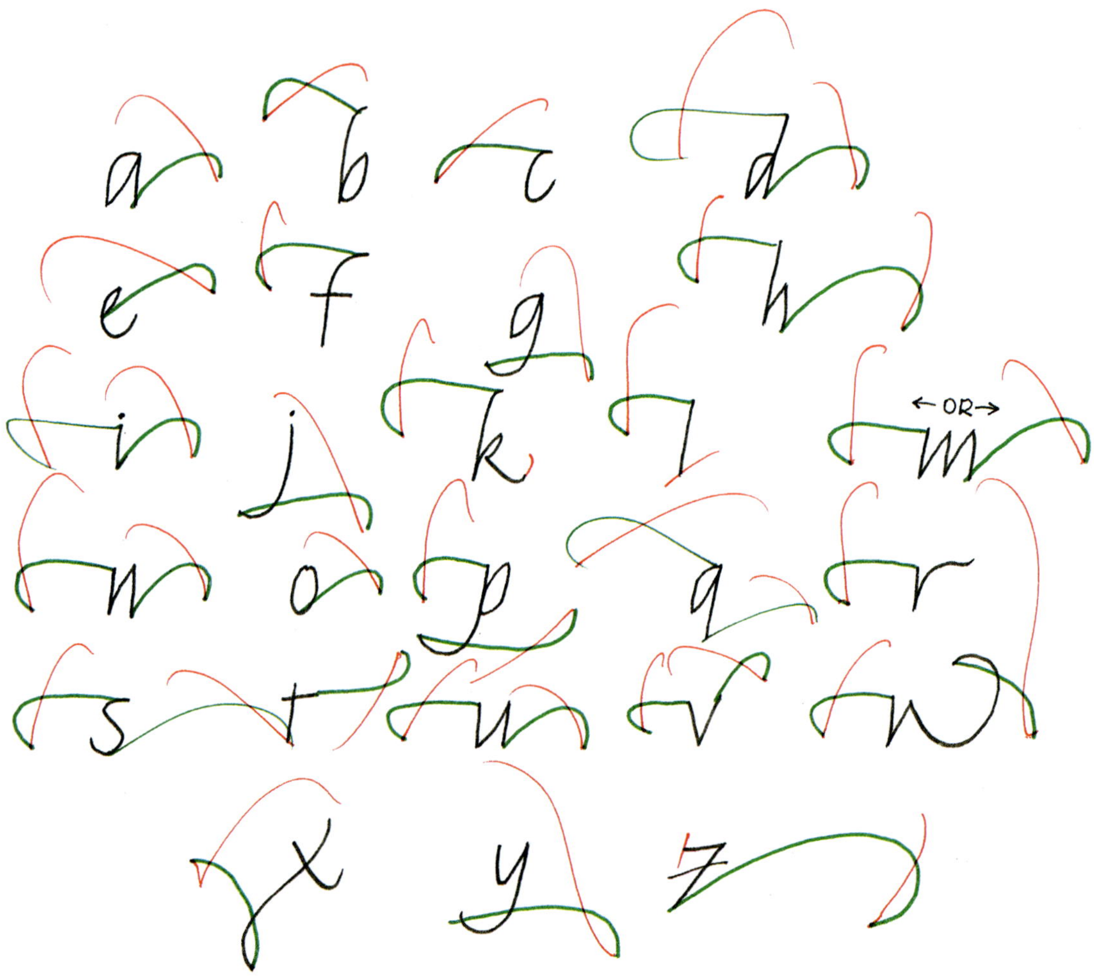


Choose one. Both would be too much.

## FREE-FLOWING FLOURISHING WITH UPPERCASE LETTERS

Sometimes you can use free-flowing flourishes with capital letters, but since these uppercase letters start a word or sentence, the flourishes would typically be a sweep to the left and up to not interfere with letters in the preceding word or the next letter in the word it starts.

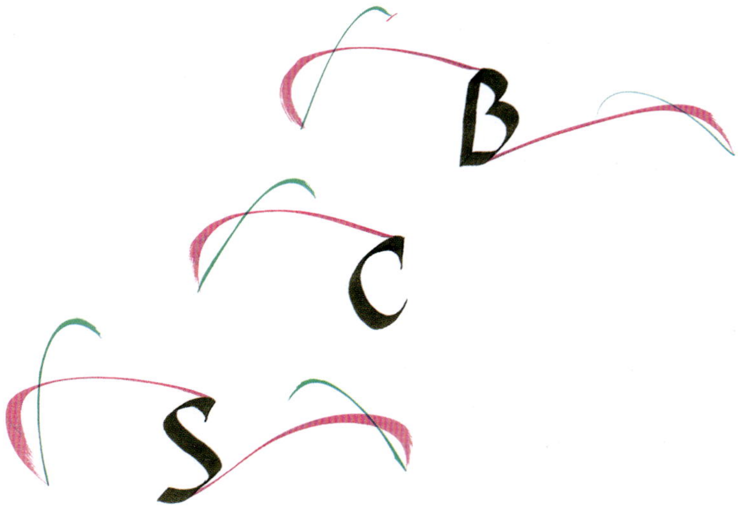

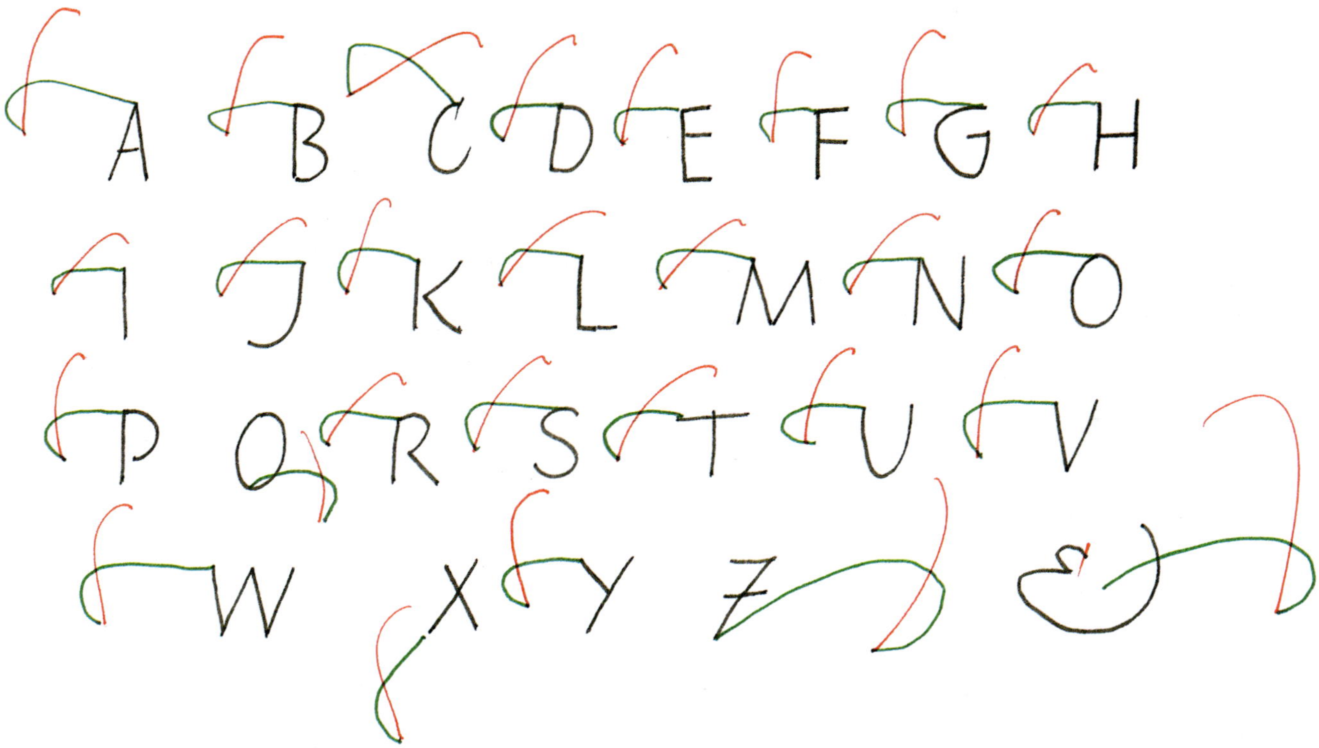

**ONE-STEP FLOURISHING**

**TWO-STEP FLOURISHING**

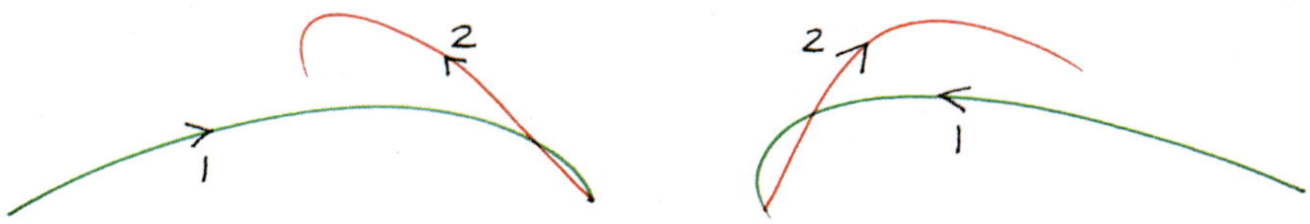

# Project: Playing with Flourishing & Color

Playing with color does introduce the need for additional tools and materials, but it is worth the investment. If this is something that is currently not practical for you, the following exercise is something that you can come back to later, and in the meantime, you can simply do the exercise with your Pilot pen and gold gouache or just a black marker and colored pencils. However, the addition of color and flourishing will most definitely morph your classic Italic script into something dynamic and vibrant, giving you great pleasure.

WHAT YOU'LL NEED:

- **Calligraphy pen with black ink**
- **Pencil**
- **1–2 pieces of 110–140-lb. hot-pressed watercolor paper (as close to 9" x 12" as possible), or a sheet of good paper from your practice pad**
- **Light table**
- **Transparent watercolor inks, either a whole set or five of your favorite colors (I recommend Dr. Ph. Martin's)**
- **Metal nibs (⅛"/3.8 mm) and holders (Brause or Tape are my favorites), or markers of the same size**
- **Fine-liner pens, ideally a couple of colors but black will do (I use Pilot Hi-Tecpoint, size 05)**
- **2" squares of any cardboard (to tape to each bottle of watercolor ink you plan to use)**
- **Masking tape**
- **Gold gouache (in a tube and a small dish to mix the gouache with water to the consistency of milk)**
- **Supplies for cleaning up: water dish, rag, apron**

## What Is a Light Table?

**A light table is a translucent surface illuminated from behind on which you can place your template. The light enables you to see your template through your sheet of watercolor paper so that you can trace over the template as needed onto the watercolor paper.**

**This device comes in many shapes and sizes, from box-like contraptions to flat illuminated surfaces that are very thin. I use mine at a tilted angle so that it resembles my work surface.**

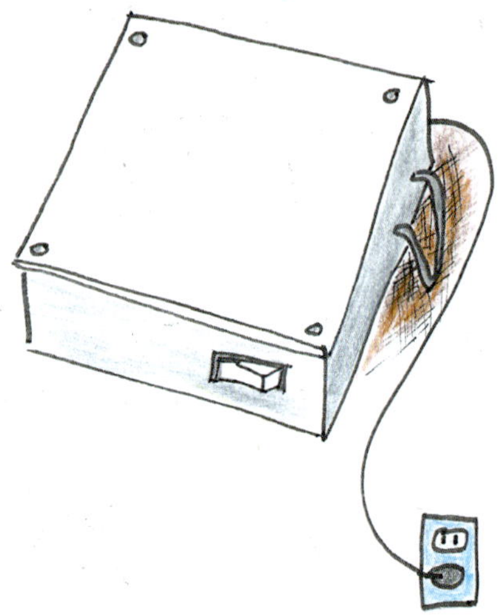

1. First you want to create a template using the word *dance* in plain black ink. Using different colors does slow down the writing process, and this can take away some momentum, flow and perceived energy. Having a template written in plain black will serve as a guide to allow you to focus on and enjoy your exploration of color, without having to worry about the rhythm and spacing of

the word itself. On a lined practice sheet (or a blank practice sheet laid over a lined template on a light table), practice the word *dance* carefully until you feel comfortable and confident in writing the word in a way that pleases you. Then take a fresh practice sheet (lined the same as the template you used to practice) and write *dance* on four different lines, as shown on the right.

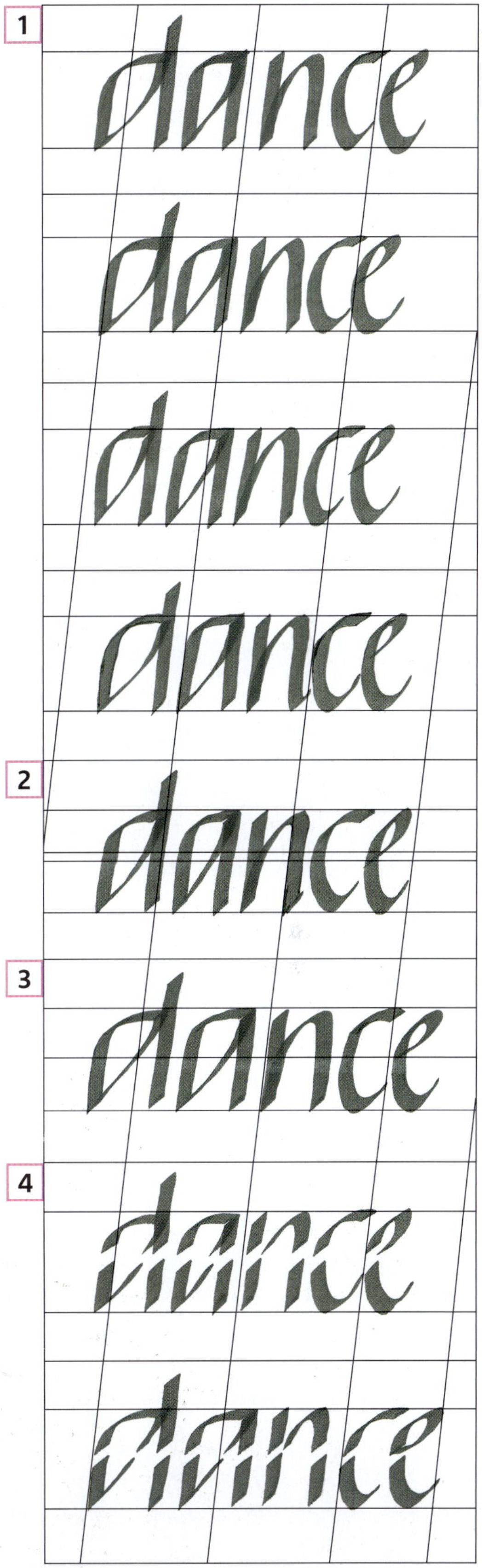


2. Once these four versions of *dance* dry, go down to the third *dance* and measure and mark halfway down the X-height on each side of the word and draw a line in pencil across the word, connecting the marks. Measure and mark ⅛" above this line on each end of the word and draw another line across.

3. Proceed to the fourth *dance* and measure and mark halfway down the X-height on each side of the word and draw a line in pencil across the word, connecting the marks. Now draw over all the lines you've made with a fine-liner pen. You now have a revised template that you will use for the next step in this exercise.

4. Tape your revised template on your light table and then place a new piece of lined practice paper over the template, making sure the lines match the template's lines perfectly. Secure the new piece with tape so it doesn't shift. Using the template for guidance, write *dance* with your pen and black ink (or marker) on each of the four lines on the new page. When you get to the third *dance,* stop when you reach the first line (the one that's ⅛ of an inch above the midpoint line of the X-height), lift your pen and then continue beneath the midpoint line. For the fourth *dance,* stop slightly above the midpoint line you've marked and then continue slightly below the line to finish your stroke. The end results will be a thin ⅛ of an inch space through the middle of the third *dance* and a thinner space through the middle of the fourth. Set the page aside to dry. You now have your final template that you will use to proceed with this exercise in color.

5. It is now time to letter the word *dance* in color. Place your final template (created in the last step) on the light table, then place your sheet of watercolor paper over it and tape the watercolor sheet securely to the light table to prevent any shifting. Have your metal dip pens (nibs and holders) ready as well as the watercolor inks you plan to use (ideally five, or one for each letter). If you are not using a pen, gather your markers. You will also need your water dish, a rag and an apron just in case you have an accident with your inks. Note: If you are only using black ink and gold gouache for this project, you will need a separate nib to add the gold color.

### Some Helpful Tips

**Many lessons, when learned the hard way, are extremely valuable. However, in the case of spilling valuable ink all over your work, work area and floor, I think I'd rather you learn from me instead. Hence why I've suggested having a rag and apron handy. This is also the reason for preparing your ink.**

**Before starting, prepare each ink bottle with masking tape and a 2" square of cardboard at the bottom. Tape each side of the ink bottle to the piece of cardboard. This little trick will help prevent spills galore while also removing the need to curse profusely.**

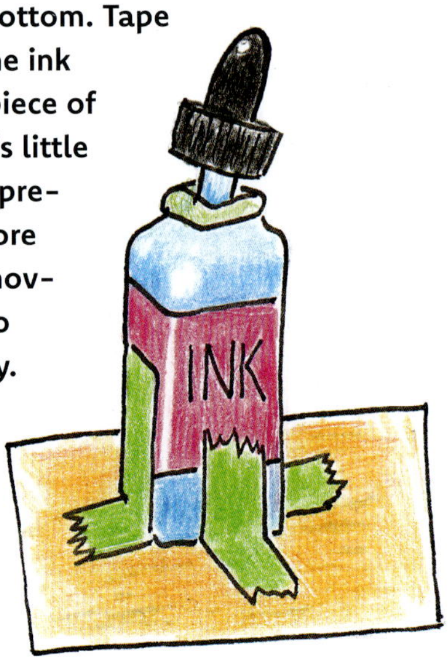


6. Now that you are set, we will take four different approaches to each word. The following examples show flourishes added to the *e*. Try out the new variations and flourishes you've learned in this chapter and have fun with the letter forms.

   **a.** Different colors – Use five different colors (one for each letter) and then flourish the *e*. If only using black and gold, alternate colors for each letter.

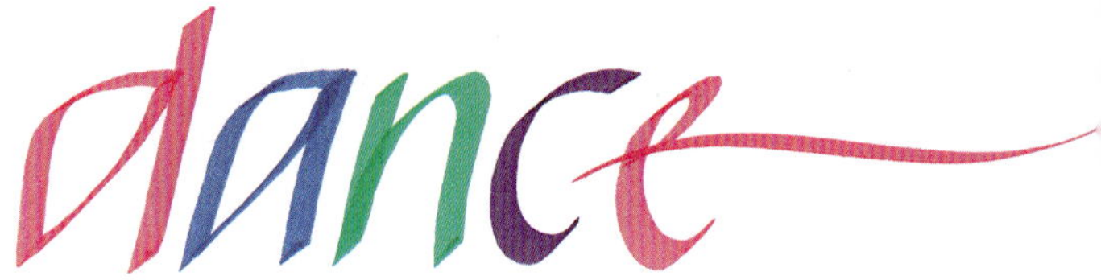


   **b.** Single color with painted spaces – Letter your word in one color and try flourishes on the *e*. Let the ink dry completely, then go back and, using your favorite color of gouache or watercolor ink/paint, fill in the various spaces in each letter.

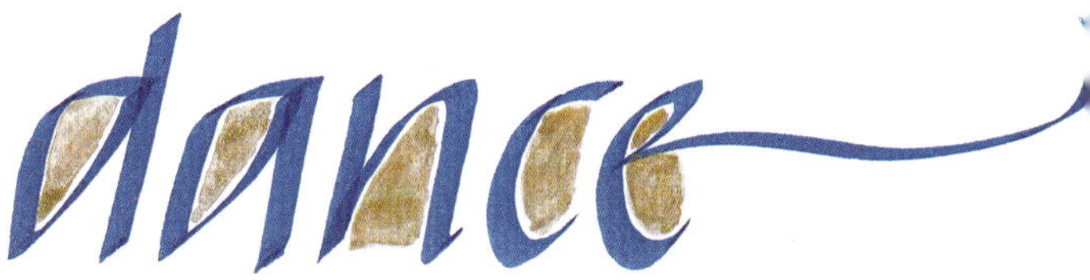


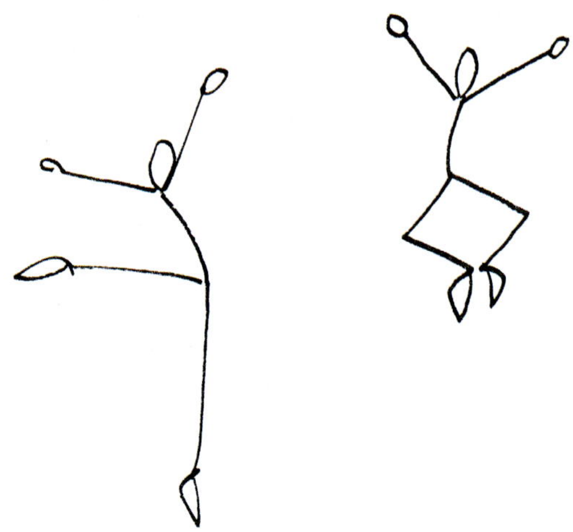

**c.** Dance with a gap – Write out *dance* in one color, but a different color than the prior exercise, trying different flourishes on the *e*. Be sure to stop your strokes when you come to the top middle line on your template and then continue the strokes under the bottom middle line. You want a nice white space across the word. Let the ink dry then take a colored fine-liner pen (or black if you don't have colored fine-liners) and fill in the gaps in the downstrokes with playful vertical zigzags to create a fun effect. Fine-liners that are size 05 or less are good for this exercise.

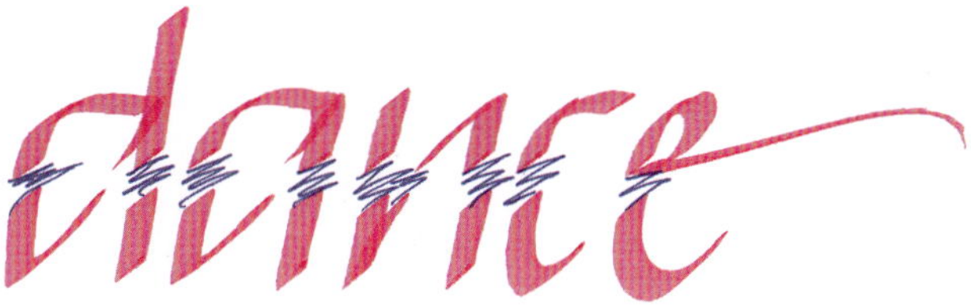

**d.** Dance in two colors with a gap – As with the prior exercises, write out the word *dance* but this time in two colors. The top half in one color and the bottom half in a different color. Make sure to stop your downstrokes slightly above the midpoint line on your template and complete your downstrokes starting just below the same line. I suggest that you do the top half of your letters first and then switch inks for the bottom half. Add a flourish or two and let dry. Then taking a colored fine-liner pen that will contrast nicely with the colors you have chosen for the letters, draw a thin line with periodic squiggles through the thin white space running through the center of the word, starting an inch or so to the left of the *d* and ending roughly the same distance to the right of the *e*. The illustration below uses what I call "barbed wire" writing and consists of a little *m* or squiggle, followed by a thin line to the next *m*/squiggle, giving it a barbed wire effect. It is a fun technique and can be used in a variety of ways to provide contrast to your calligraphy.

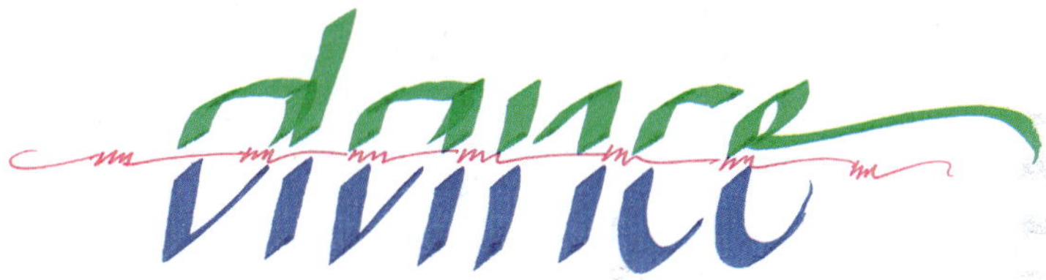

These four exercises are fun to repeat with varying color combinations and flourishes as you discover what pleases you most.

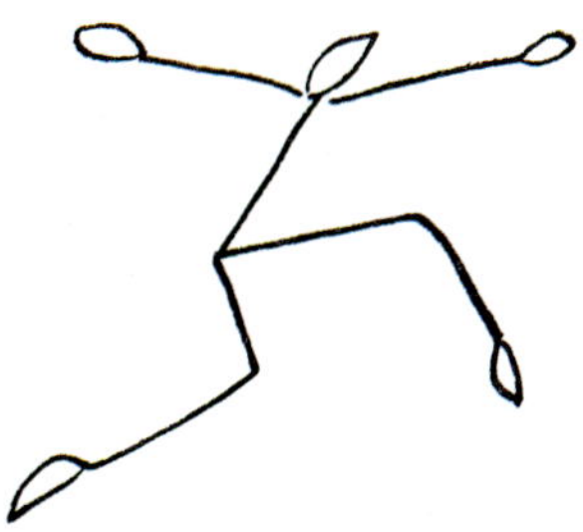

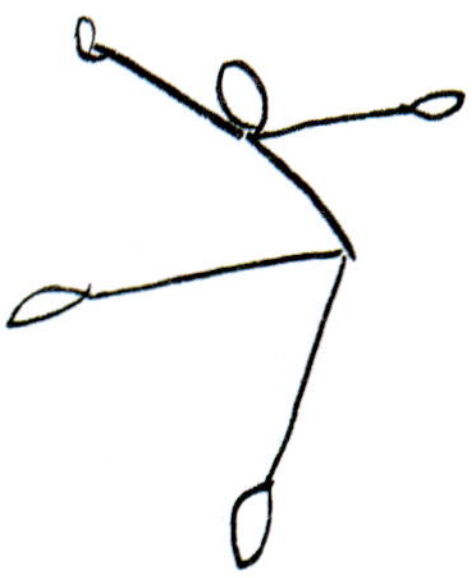

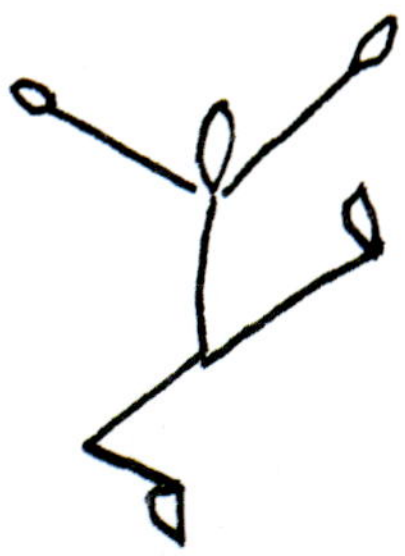

# Chapter 5

# Learning Pen Manipulation

This chapter is all about taking your calligraphy to a new level through pen manipulation techniques that will give way to a new style of Italic. We'll continue to introduce new materials, techniques and colors through various exercises, adding to your repertoire of calligraphic skills.

## Pen Manipulation

There are times when pen manipulation is a perfectly appropriate thing to do. This is one of those times!

To start, move your pen along your paper (at the usual 45-degree angle), keep the pen and your arm going, but gradually lift your nib onto one edge.

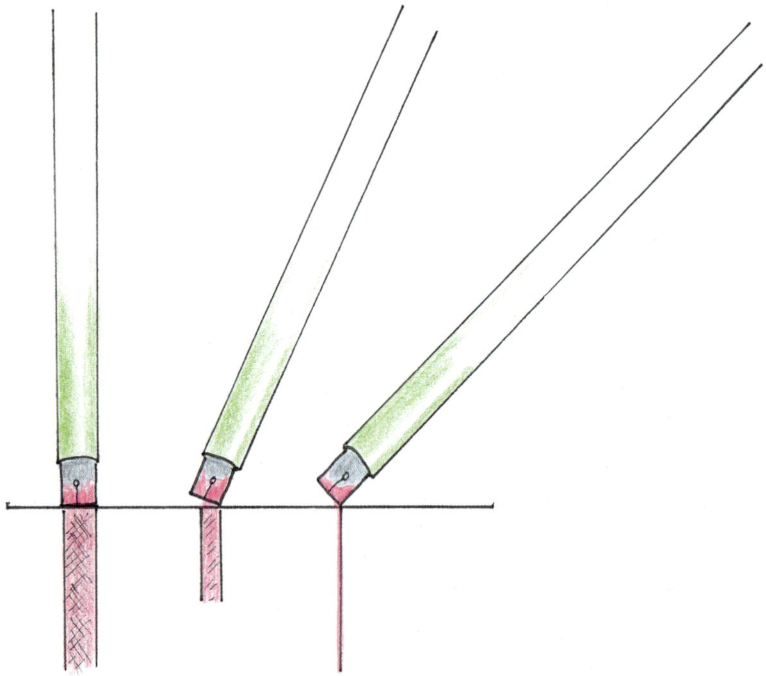

Fill a blank sheet of paper with the example strokes below, practicing them over and over to help train your arm, hand and eyes. You will get there! Start out slowly until you can create the strokes in a fluid motion. With confidence and comfort, you will be able to create a stroke that is fluid and energetic. But it is critical to take your time.

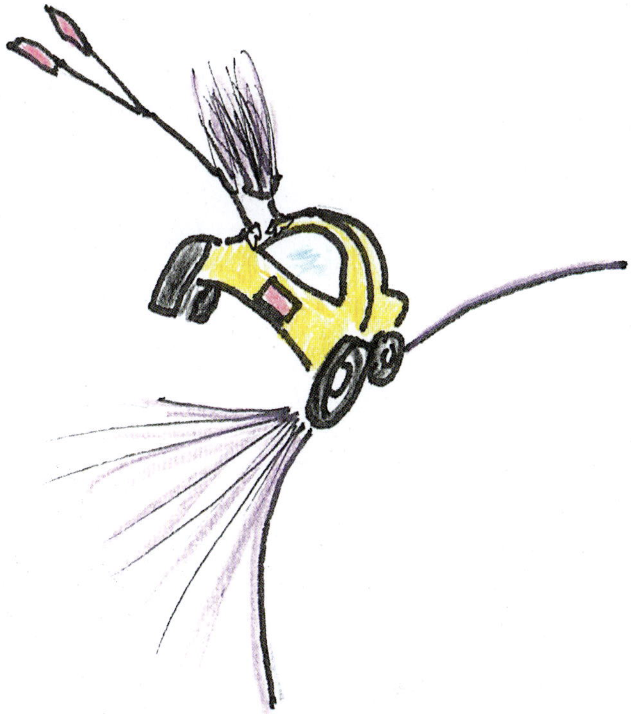

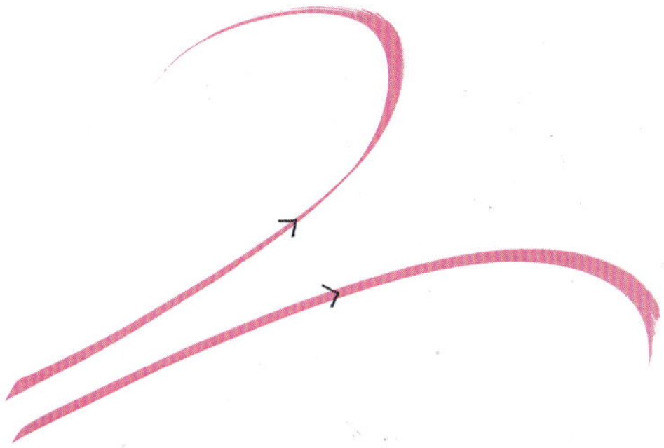

Trace over the images below to get a feel for them if you like.

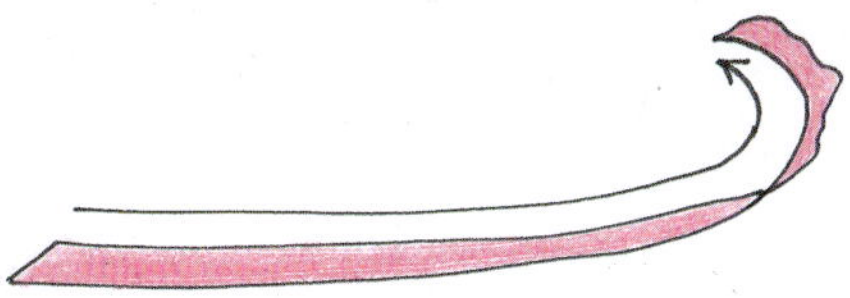

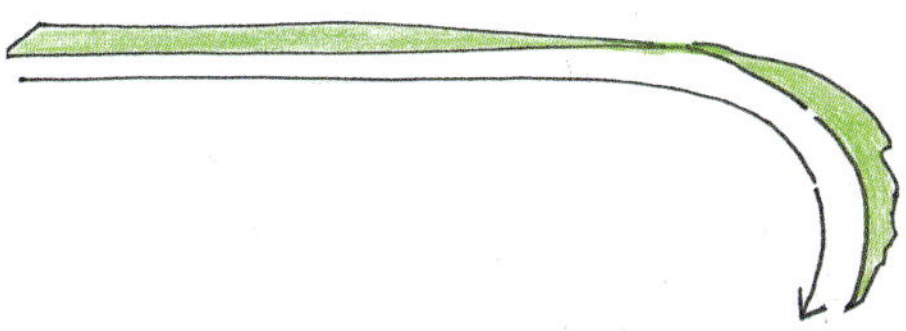

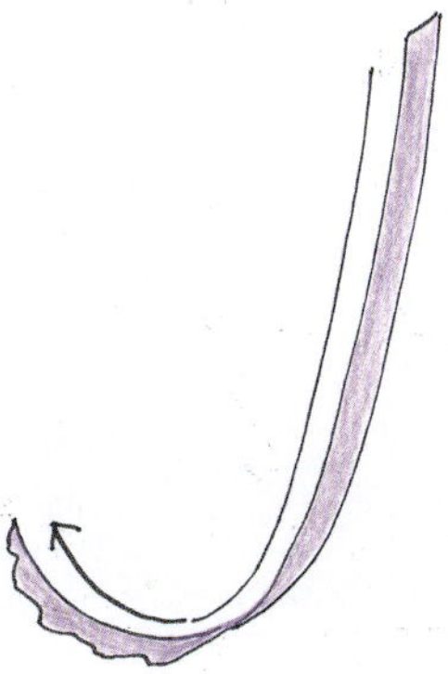

Think of a car going around a corner without slowing down and on two wheels. (My sister would say that this is how I always drive!) The inside of the nib remains in contact with the paper. In the depicted illustration, the jagged bit represents the side where the nib is lifted from the paper. Some ink gets left behind.

It is key to remember that this is done with one fluid motion. The pen is never fully lifted.

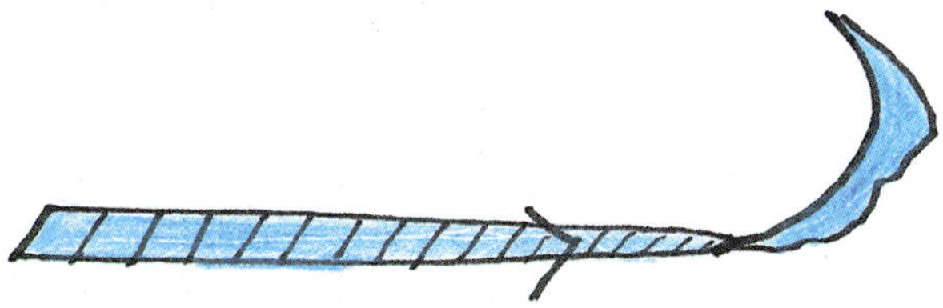

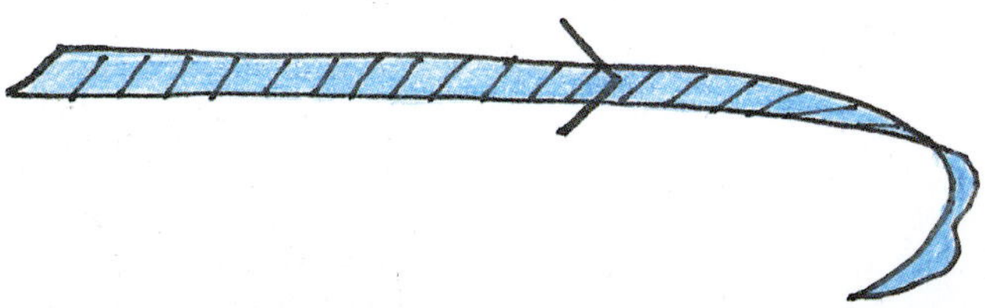

# A Variation on the Italic Script

This variation of the Italic hand, which I refer to as "snub-nosed" Italic, was taught to me by calligrapher, typographer and graphic artist Carl Rohrs. When I took Rohrs' class shortly after I began my venture into the world of calligraphy, it was a game-changer for me! I had previously struggled with Italic calligraphy, and this script made a significant difference — which I am sure you will enjoy.

**LOWERCASE SNUB-NOSED ITALIC ALPHABET**

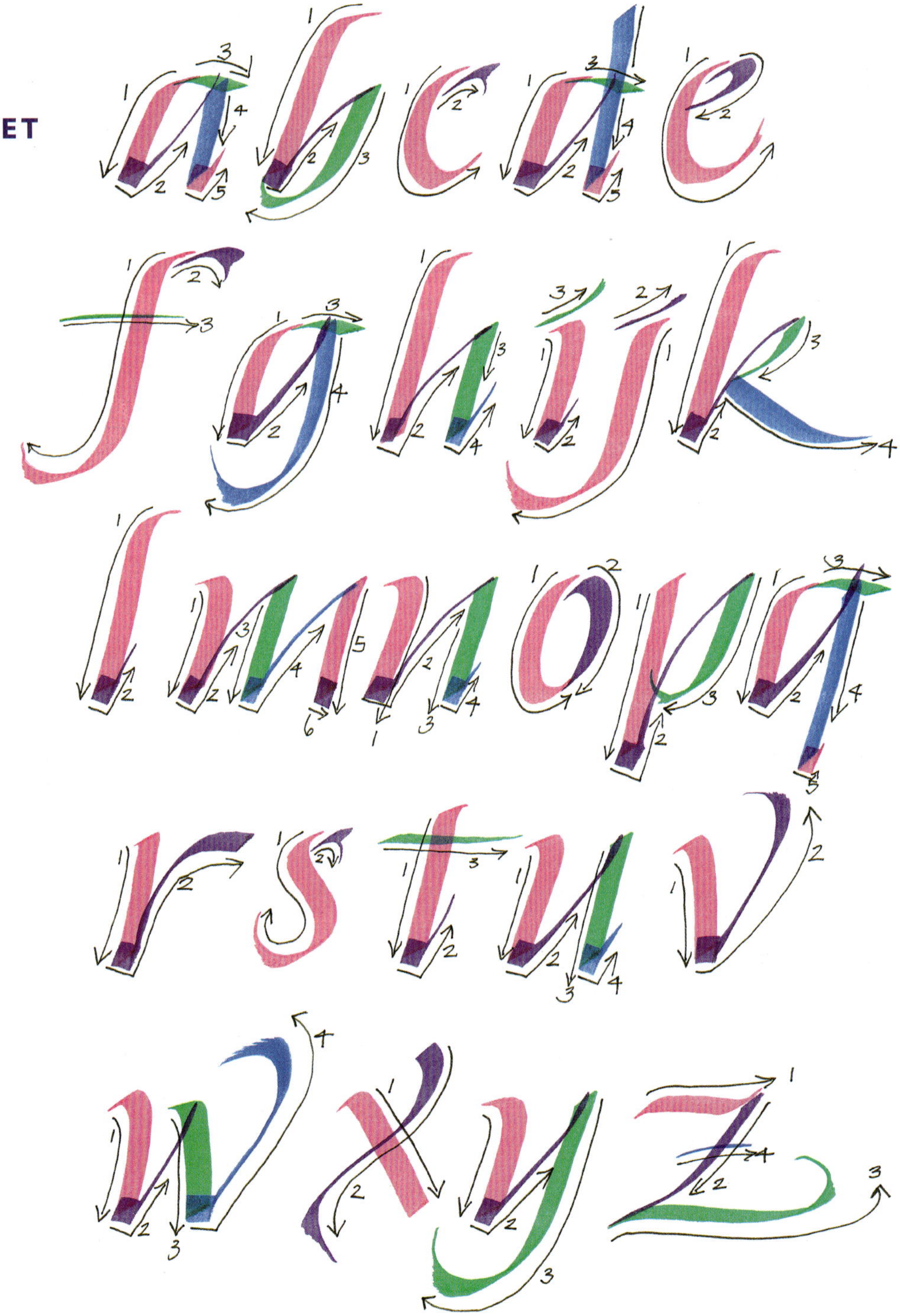

Rohrs' style of Italic features "snub-nosed" downstrokes as opposed to the pointed ends of the traditional Italic. Observe the difference between these two lowercase *a*'s. In Rohrs' version, the first and last downstrokes are snub-nosed, and the thin line of the fifth stroke is created by riding upward on the left edge of the nib.

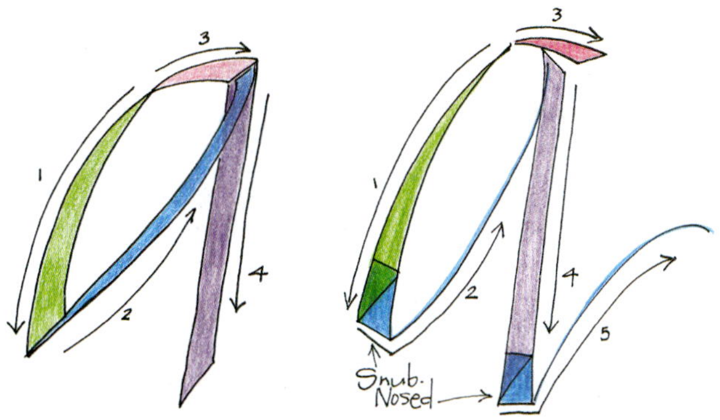


## LEARNING SNUB-NOSED STROKES

Let's begin, starting with the downstroke.

Traditional downstrokes — of which you are quite familiar at this point — differ from Rohrs' downstrokes in that his lean a bit more to the right. As you complete the downstroke, the next step comes into play — the snub-nosed blunt end and the bounce up.

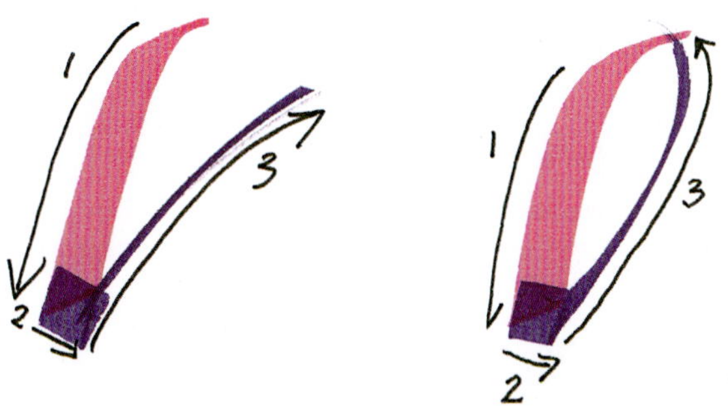


At the bottom of the downstroke, you will lift your nib and place it along the left wall of your downstroke with the left tip touching the bottom point (as shown below).

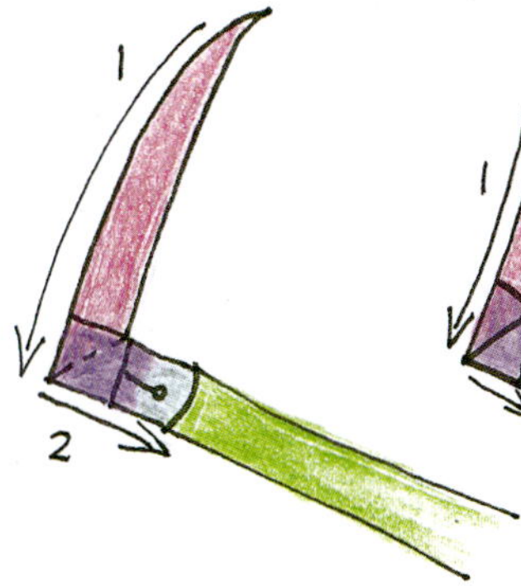


Pull down at that angle until you line up with the right side of your downstroke, resulting in a boxy end to the downstroke. The boxes that create the snub-nosed look are created similarly to the diamonds you became familiar with in Section One when dotting the lowercase *i* and *j*.

Once you have created that box at the bottom of the downstroke, it is time to proceed to the soaring part of this technique. Keeping the bottom (left) side of the nib on the page while lifting the right side off the paper, scoot up and away to create stroke 3 (as depicted below). The action is similar to creating a fine-line flourish, but it is also a connecting stroke.

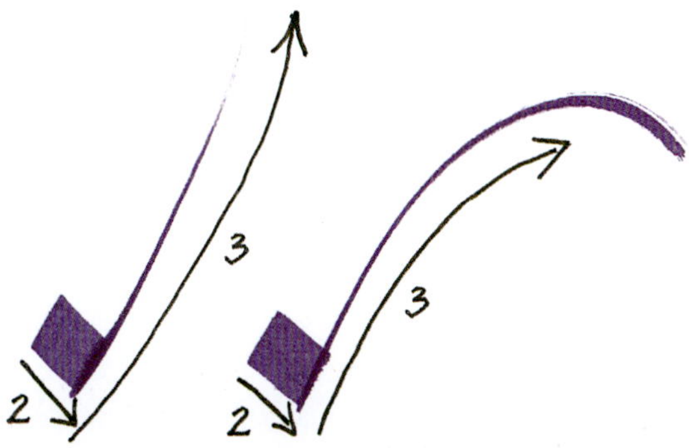

It takes a bit to feel comfortable with this technique, and it is now time to practice. Start by lining a page with ½-inch and 1-inch alternating lines all the way down the page to provide loose guidelines for your lettering. Then create a few practice lines of downstrokes and then a few practice lines of just diamonds. Once you're comfortable with the diamond motion, add the downstroke and diamond motion together.

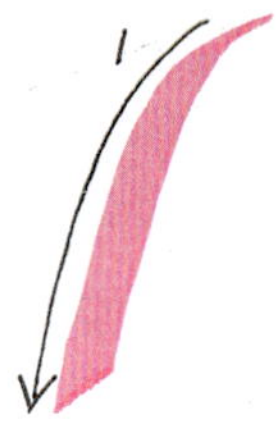

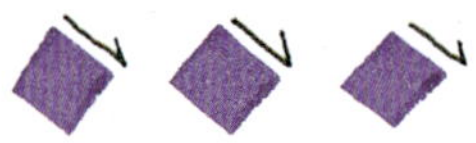

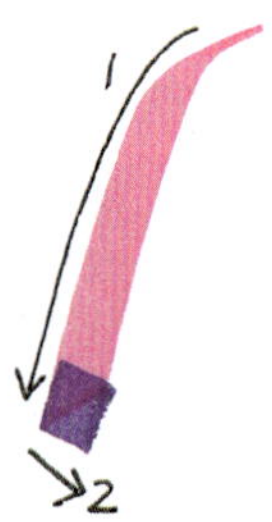

As we've already discussed with this Italic script variation, every downstroke ends with the snub-nose, typically followed by an upward fine line on the left edge of your nib. For example, if a letter has a final downstroke, it is optional as to whether you add the fine-line upstroke. To practice the fine-line upstroke, create a few lines of diamonds and then, with the left edge of the nib still in contact with your paper, lift the right edge and scoot your pen nib upward and away from your downstroke.

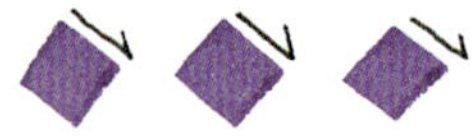

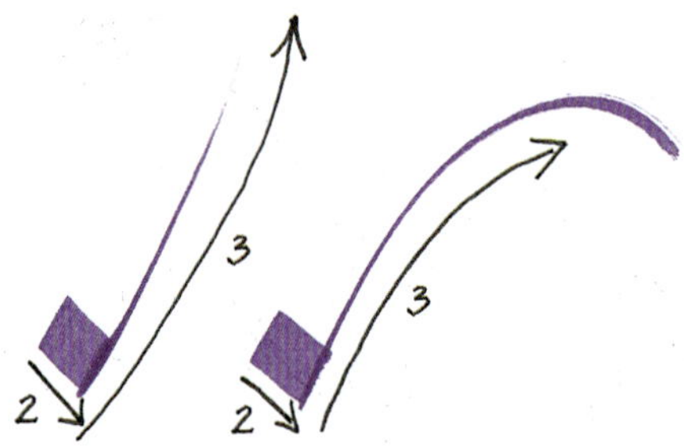

After, try all three steps in sequence: downward stroke, diamond, then a flicking upward stroke. Practice a few lines of this.

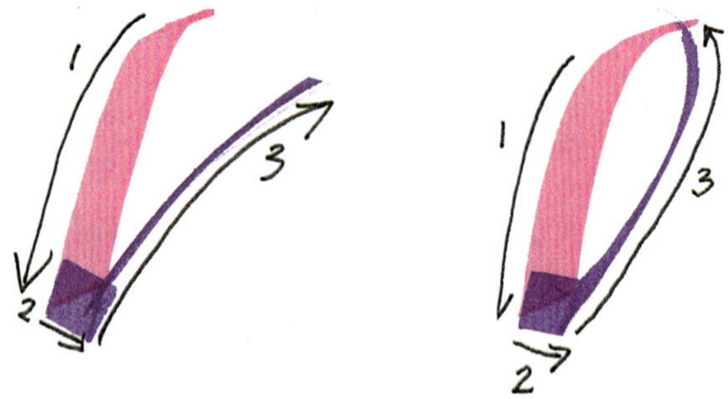

## CREATING SNUB-NOSED LETTERS

Now that you're more comfortable with the motion, let's try the *i*, *l* and *t* letter family. These letters use the following strokes:

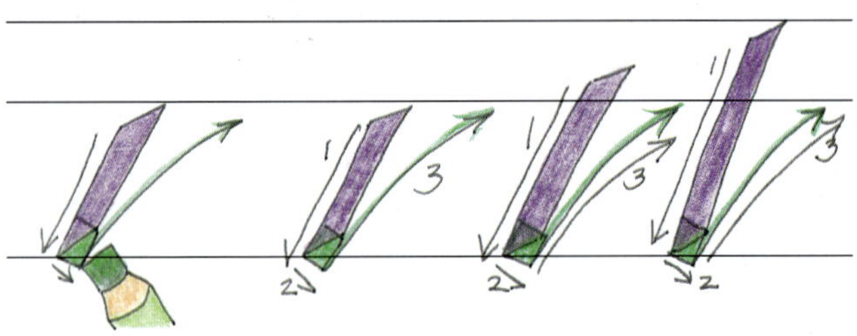

Work on keeping the letters parallel and watch for consistent spacing. When beginning each downstroke, ease into it from the left. This creates a "serif" — a slight prelude to the stroke to get the ink flowing at 45 degrees. These letters should have the snub-nosed end at the baseline and a flicking upward stroke to finish. The dot for the *i* can either be a fine line above the top of the downstroke or a diamond. The crossbar for the *t* can be a fine line using the edge of the nib.

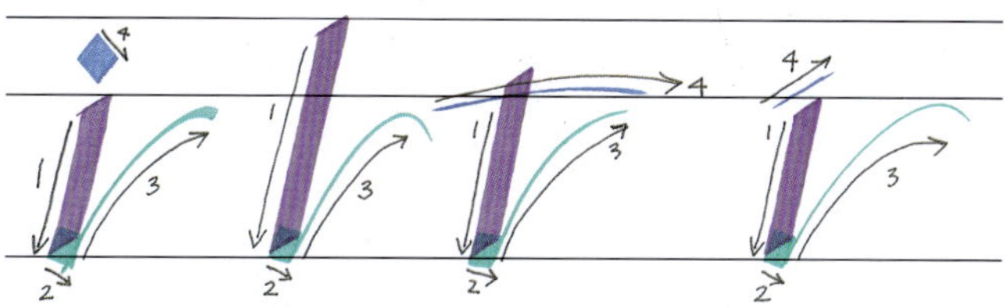

Now let's move on to some more letters, beginning with letters with two or more parallel downstrokes: *h, n, m* and *u*. These letters use the following types of strokes:

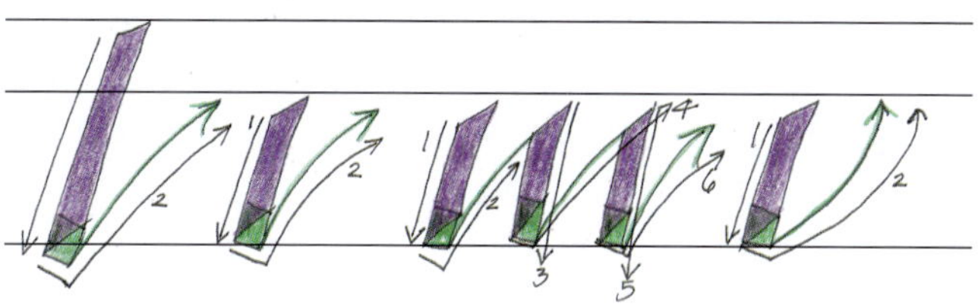

Note that with these letters, although the strokes are parallel, they are not necessarily the same length as this script is more informal than the traditional Italic hand. Practice a line of each new letter. Remember that having the downstrokes parallel establishes rhythm.

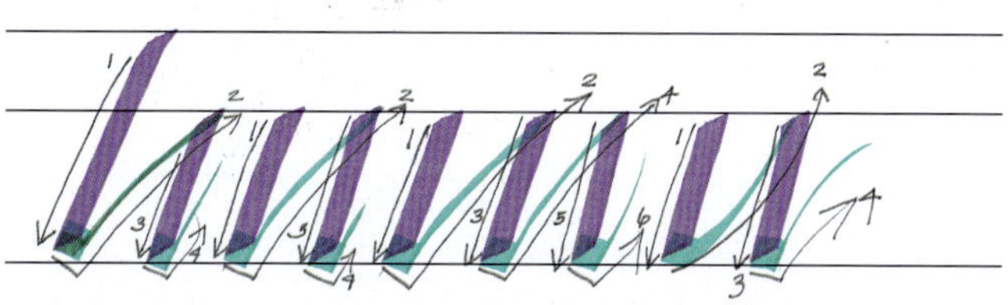

The next group of letters consists of ovals. The joins for these ovals don't quite meet, unlike the traditional Italic script in which the strokes meet. These are the letters *o, c* and *e*. Practice a line of each.

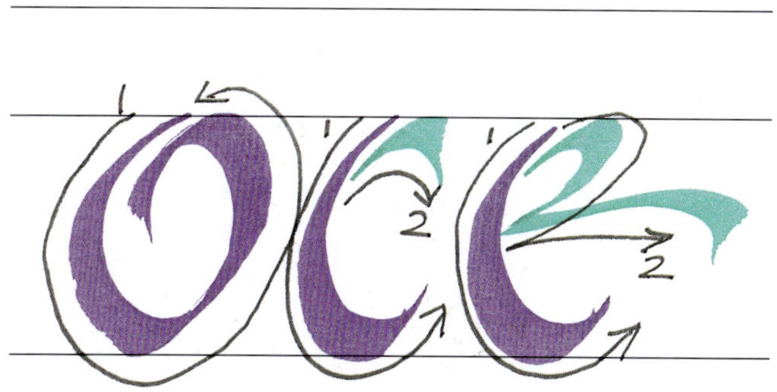

The snub-nosed Italic script introduces a variation on descenders as well. With traditional Italic, the descenders are created with two careful strokes linked by a whisper join. In Rohrs' version, you utilize pen manipulation coming down and then going to the left with the right side of the nib staying in contact with the paper. Compare a traditional lowercase *j* and Rohrs' version:

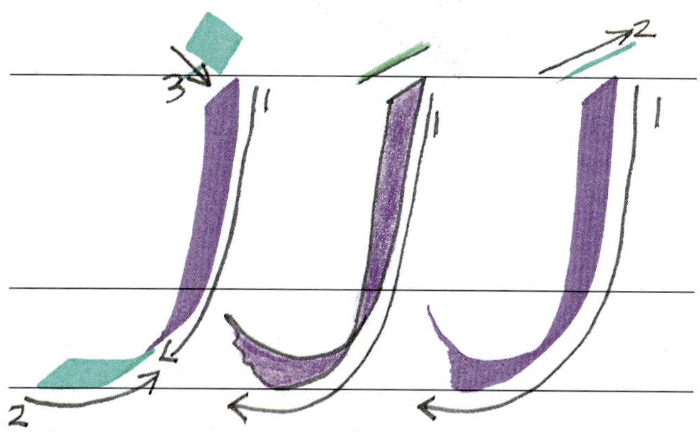

**TRADITIONAL ITALIC** **SNUB-NOSED ITALIC**

Letters with this type of descender besides *j* are *g, y* and the elongated *f*. These letters will be practiced later as they also contain additional variations in technique beyond their descenders.

Now onto the all-important letter *a*. As illustrated below, the downstroke leans more to the right. Then you create the snub-nosed box to make the blunt end. Lift the right edge of the nib off the paper leaving the left edge in contact and scoot up and *inward* on the left side of your nib creating that fine line stroke for the *a*.

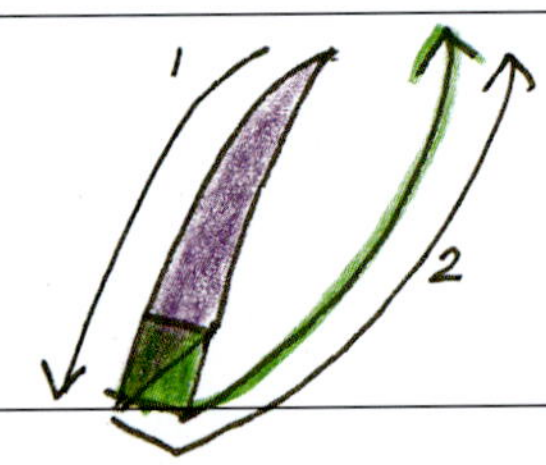


Practice this motion. Create a downstroke, then a diamond and finally scoot the line up and in on your nib's left edge.

To finish the *a*, go back to the beginning (top) of the first downstroke and create the cap with stroke 3 (as below).

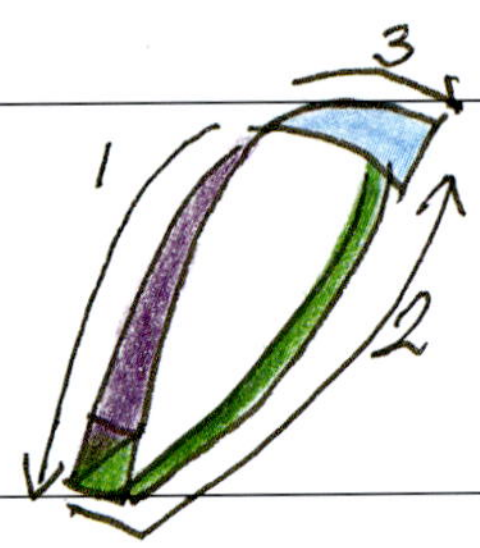


It's time to add the second downstroke. This downstroke starts where the cap ends, or just before it. This downstroke (like the first downstroke to start the *a*) leans more to the right because it is parallel to the first stroke. This slope adds acceleration, energy and movement to the letter. As with the first downstroke, the second downstroke ends with the snub-nosed box and a fine line that scoots up and out because it is an exit stroke (like a serif and/or flourish). This is illustrated here.

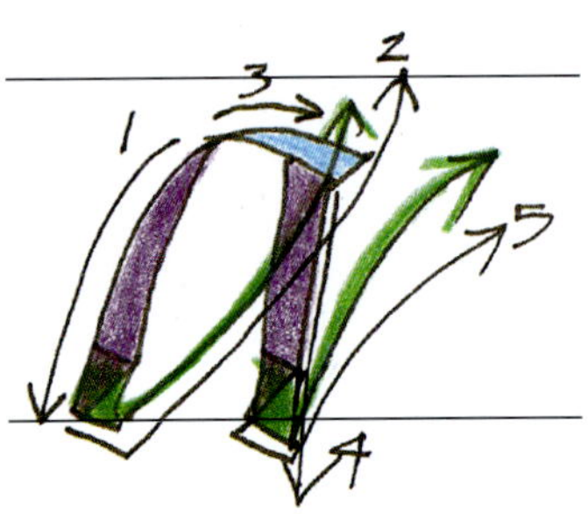


Practice a page of the letter *a*, taking careful and thoughtful time in making each one. Breathe out for downstrokes (or just breathing in general is grand). This is not an exercise to rush through. Keep the downstrokes parallel and notice the spacing between each letter.

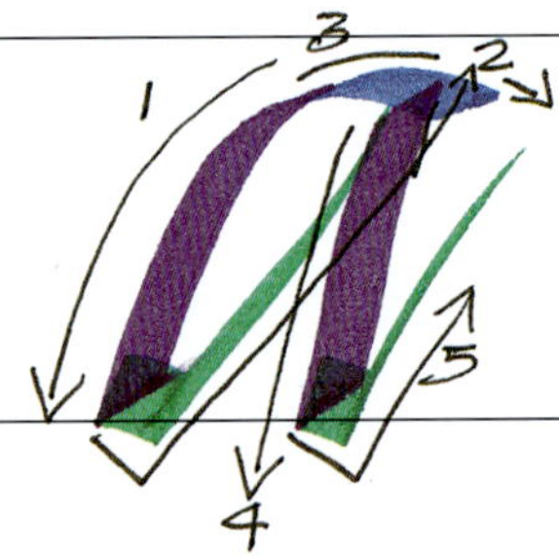


Other letters use the same structure and technique as the *a*. These are *d* and *q*. Note that the last downstrokes can end with a fine line that scoots outward or not.

Keep in mind that when you create this upward stroke it's almost like throwing it away as a fine line flourish. As you practice, take time to play and explore. Try extending upstrokes. Create downstrokes that end with only the blunt end. Have fun!

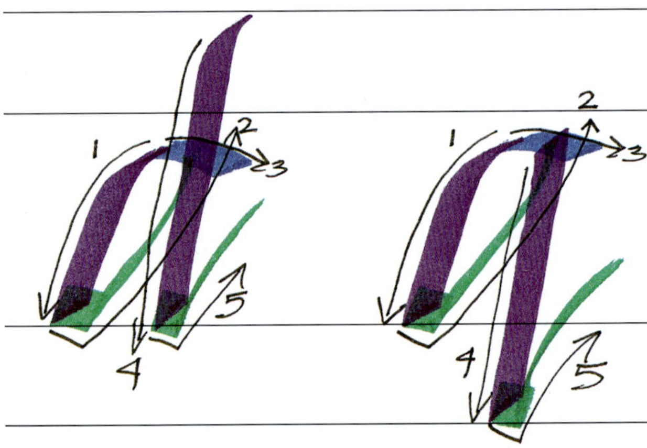

Another family of letters is the diagonal family, consisting of *k, v, w, x* and *z*. These are illustrated below with the snub-nosed blunted downstrokes and fine line upstrokes. I have drawn the stroke process in the first set of illustrations. The second set is done with my nib. Note that the diagonal downstrokes are not all blunted (i.e., *k, z* and *x*). Practice at least one line for each of these letters while noticing.

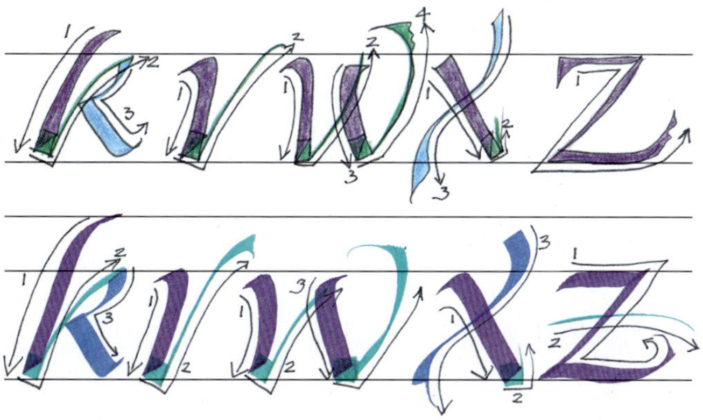

Earlier we reviewed how the pen is manipulated for the creation of the descenders and how the snub-nosed Italic script differs from the traditional Italic by making the creation of the tail a one-stroke process, not two. This same pen manipulation is also used as part of the bodies of the lowercase letters.

The letters that require pen manipulation are *b, p, j, y, g, r, s* and *f*.

The letters *b, p, j, y* and *g* all utilize a final downstroke ending in a pen manipulation. As you move to the left for the descender, the right side of your nib carries through while the left side of the nib gradually lifts until it is fully lifted by the end of the stroke. By doing this you are combining what would be two strokes in the traditional Italic hand.

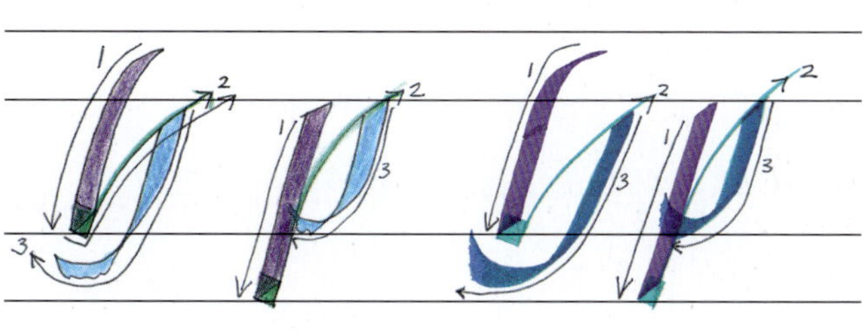

Practice one or more lines for each of these letters, focusing on the movement and motion of coming down at an angle and then lifting the left side of your nib. As with the other letter families, the stroke process is depicted first as hand-drawn illustrated letters, and then with my nib.

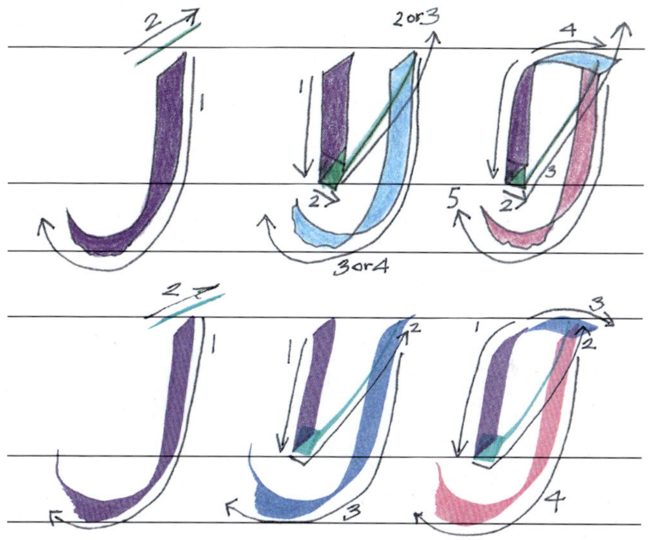


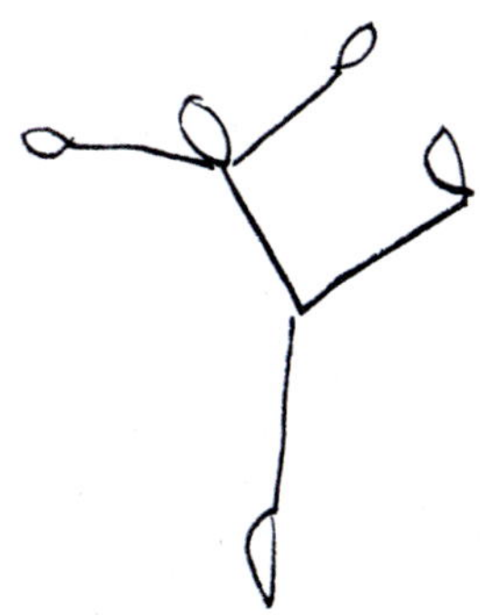

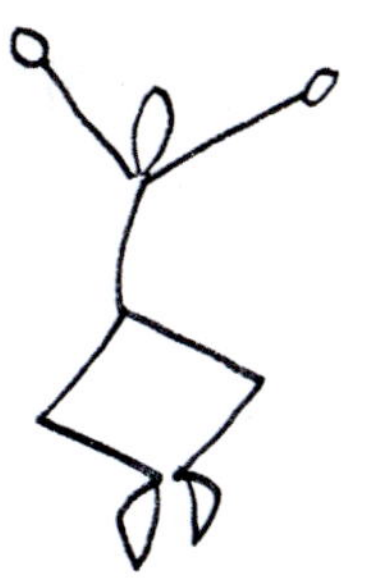

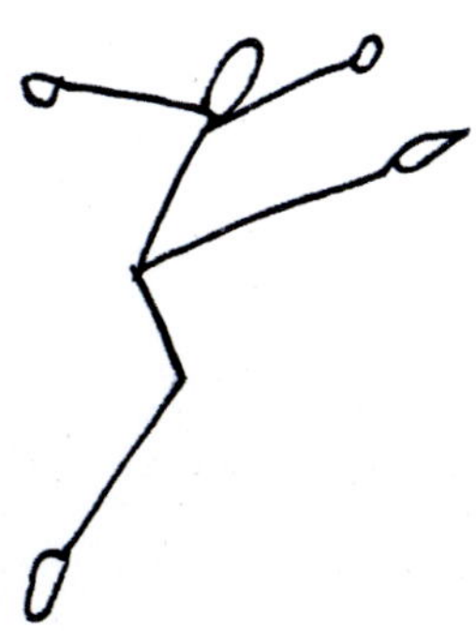

The letters s and *f* incorporate this same ending to the downstroke, but have a second manipulated stroke that, like the letter *c*, starts underneath the top of the first stroke but without touching it as it rides up and then curves down a little, riding on the left side of the nib and imitating the cap of the letter c. This stroke goes from thin to thick.

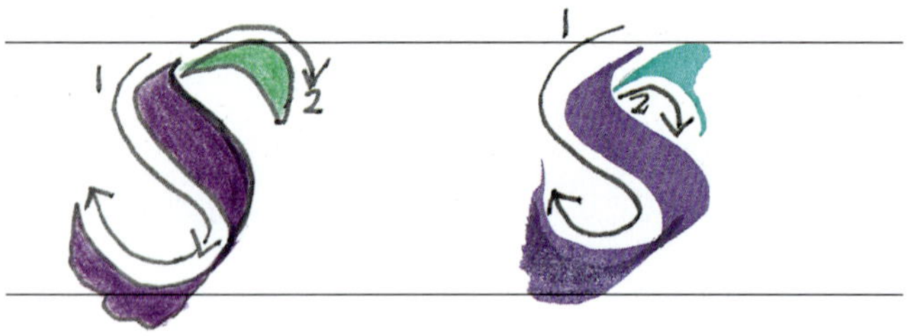

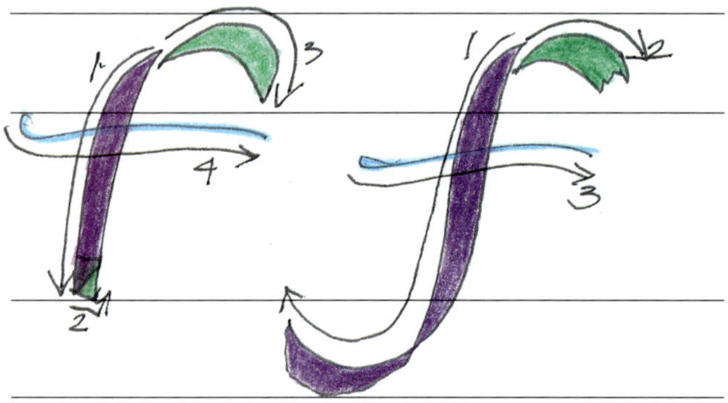

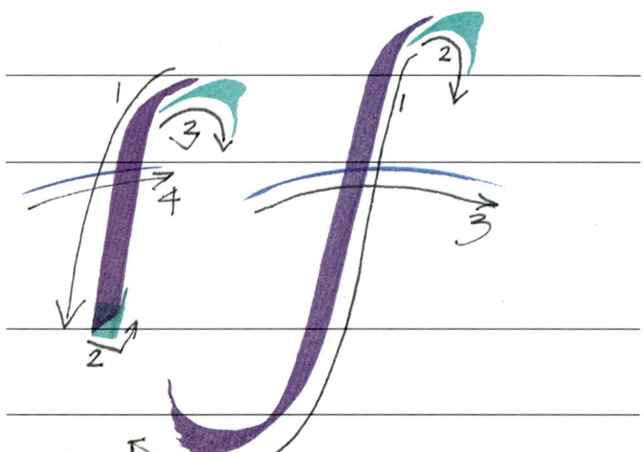

The last stroke of the *r* rises from the snub nose and before the waistline arcs out, riding on the left side of the nib and going from thin to thick as it moves away from the stem.

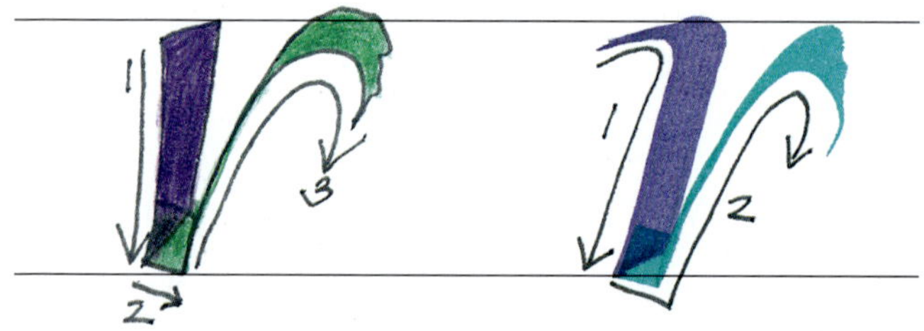

Practice one or more lines for each of these letters, focusing on the movement and motion of going up at an angle and then lifting the right side of your nib. Aim for a natural fluidity and graceful lines.

You will doubtless have noticed that I emphasize practice a lot. I do so because it is key to improvement. But please be mindful to take your time and be patient and practice correctly. Practicing something incorrectly is of no value. Make a point to focus on letters that give you more difficulty, while still ensuring that those that are easier are not neglected. Be careful to examine letter forms to ensure they are accurate and that your pen utilization is fluid, confident and correct in its rendering of each letter form.

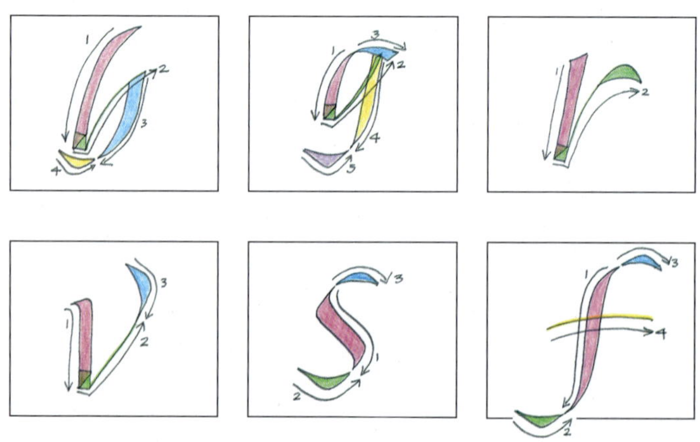

# About those Ampersands

On this page, you'll see a variety of ampersands created with pen manipulation. The first set of ampersands are hand-drawn. The second set are illustrated using a nib. The hand-drawn ones will help you see where you can try pen manipulation techniques (observe the jagged edges), and the ones using a nib let you see these techniques in practice. Create a page of ampersands, experiment with the different stroke styles and decide which you like best.

**HAND DRAWN**

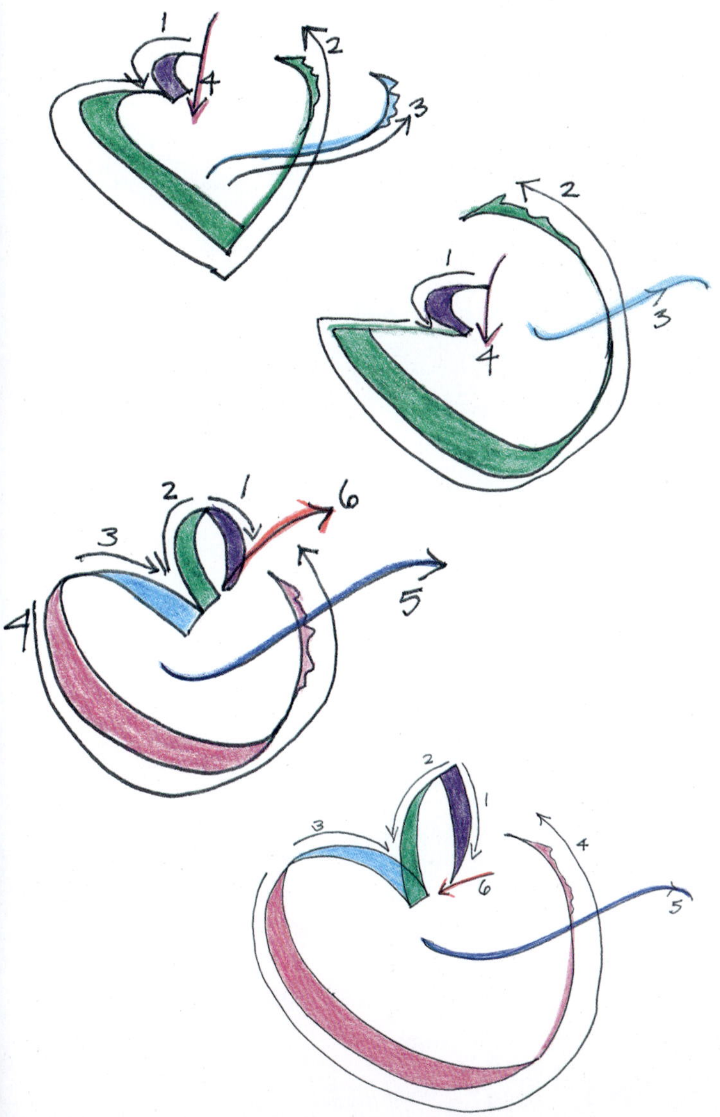

**ILLUSTRATED USING A NIB**

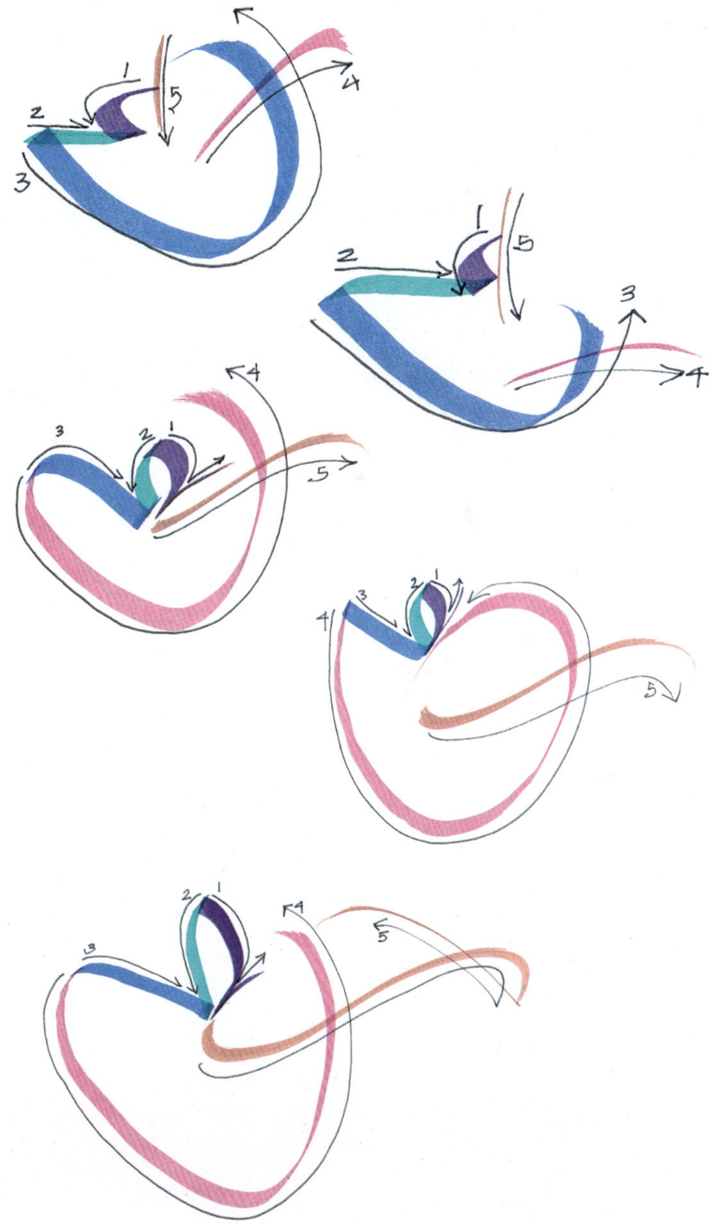

# Project: 'Snub-nosed' Italic Booklets

This project focuses on using new supplies with the snub-nosed version of Italic you just learned, and will help familiarize yourself with mixing and using gouache — which is a skill in itself.

## WHAT YOU'LL NEED:

- **A few sheets of black 11" x 14" mixed-media paper (I recommend the brand Canson)**
- **White or lightly colored chalk pencils (I find Rexel Derwent the easiest to erase)**
- **Ruler**
- **Scissors**
- **Eraser**
- **Water dish and rag**
- **Tray for mixing gouache**
- **Dr. Ph. Martin's Bleedproof White ink, or white gouache**
- **Calligraphy pen with ⅛" (3.8 mm) nib**
- **Small brush for putting the gouache on the pen, optional**
- **A few colors of gouache (pink, gold, white, green) that look good against black**
- **Large brush (i.e., Chinese calligraphy brush)**

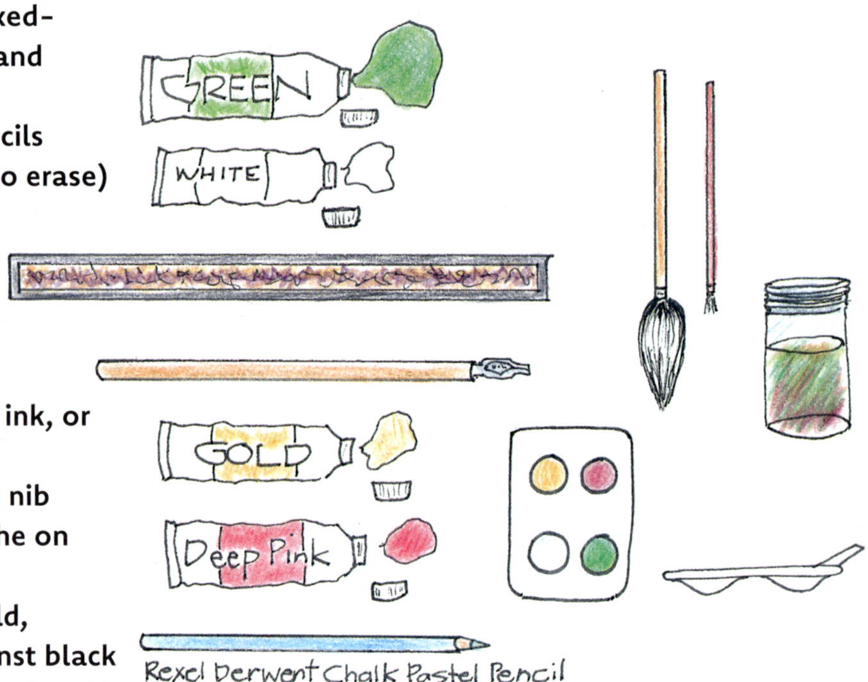


## FOR THE FOLDED STRIPS:

1. Turn your first sheet of black paper horizontally and mark it at 3 ½" intervals at the top and the bottom across the page. Then draw (using your chalk pencil) a line from top to bottom for each of these intervals to divide the page into three equal strips (with a small portion left over at the right). Next cut the paper into three strips along your lines. You will now have three strips of paper measuring 3 ½" x 14".

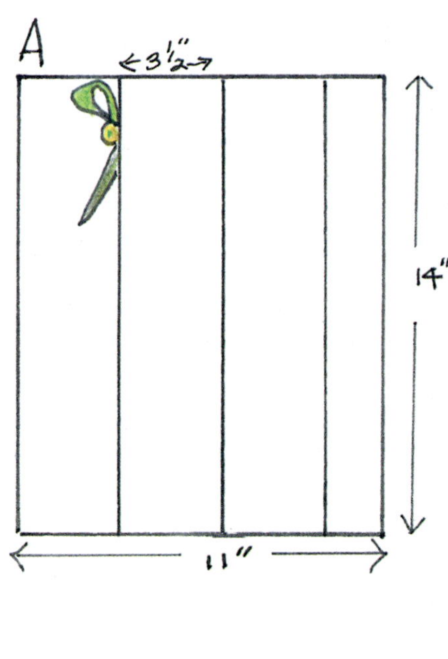

2. These strips of paper will be used to write out, respectively, the alphabet, a word, and a quote.

**'A' cut into strips**

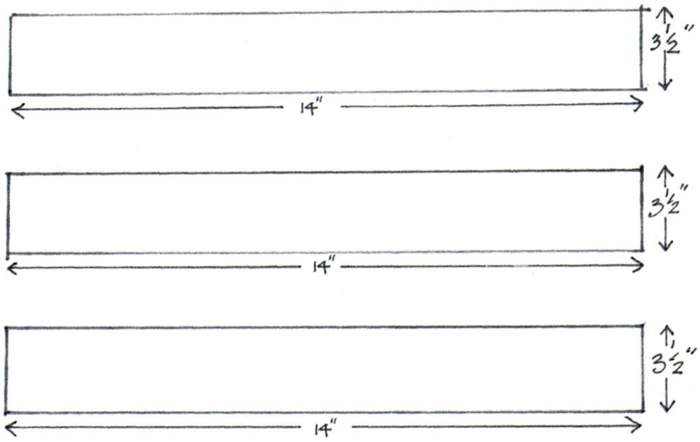


3. Lay out a strip horizontally, and from the top measure down 2" on the left and right, mark and lightly draw a line across the page with your chalk pencil connecting the marks. Next mark ½" below this line (on the left and right) and draw another line connecting the marks. Then measure and mark a ½" above the initial line drawn and draw another line connecting the marks. Finally measure and mark another ½" above this new top line and draw another line. You will now have a strip with four lines (the initial line at 2" acts as your baseline on which you will write). Repeat this process for the other two strips.

4. Before proceeding to write on these black strips of paper, it is best to practice. Cut three strips of your regular practice paper to the same dimensions (i.e., 3 ½" x 14") and line them the same way as in step 3. In pencil (you can use a regular pencil for this practice) write out the alphabet on the first strip, a short quote on the second, and a repeated favorite word on the third. This practice is important as you work on spacing and word/letter placement. Keep in mind that you will be writing using the snub-nosed Italic you have learned in this chapter. You may have to make several attempts before you are happy with how the letters and words fall across the strips and you may need more than three practice strips before you are satisfied. But pencil marks are easily erased and three strips may be sufficient.

5. When you are ready to write on the black strips, proceed using the ⅛" (3.8 mm) nib and either bleedproof white ink or a light-colored/white gouache.

6. Test your pen and ink and/or paint by trying a few scribbles on a scrap of black paper (this scrap should be the same as the paper you previously lined). Make sure you have a protective sheet of paper in place before you start lettering.

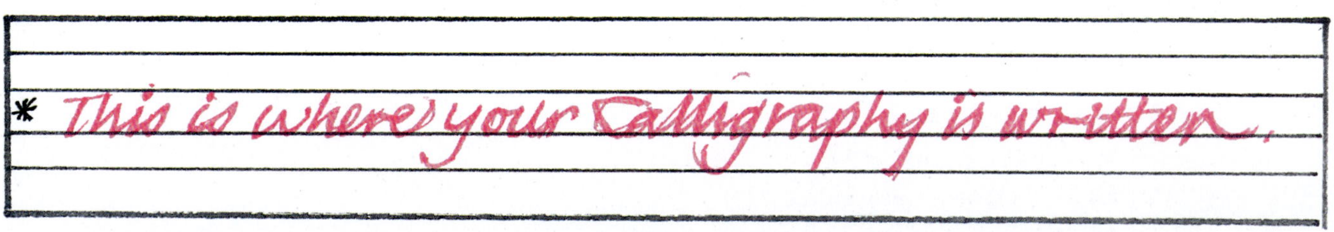

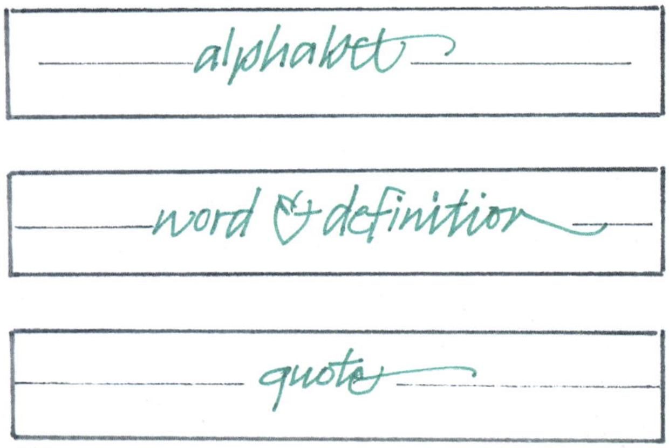


7. As mentioned previously, the line that you drew in chalk pencil at the 2" point will be your baseline. The line ½" above that is your waistline. Your letters with ascenders and descenders will go above and below these two lines. Write the alphabet for the snub-nosed Italic hand on the first strip, reloading your pen as needed. Then on the second strip write a favorite word. Try for one that has a fair number of different letters and includes at least one ascender and descender. I personally like *aequanimitas*. Finally, write out a favorite quote on the third strip. A nice final touch is to splatter a bit of gouache (in a different but complementary color) on your calligraphy. Then set aside to dry.

8. Once the ink or gouache has fully dried (I suggest 24 hours or more) gently erase the chalk lines. If you erase too soon you risk smudging your work. You may not be able to fully erase the lines as some chalk pencils erase better than others.

9. It is now time to fold the strip. This is the same technique you used for your accordion book in Section One. Fold the strip in half and then in half again. Then open it up and work the folds back and forth until the strip opens and closes like an accordion.

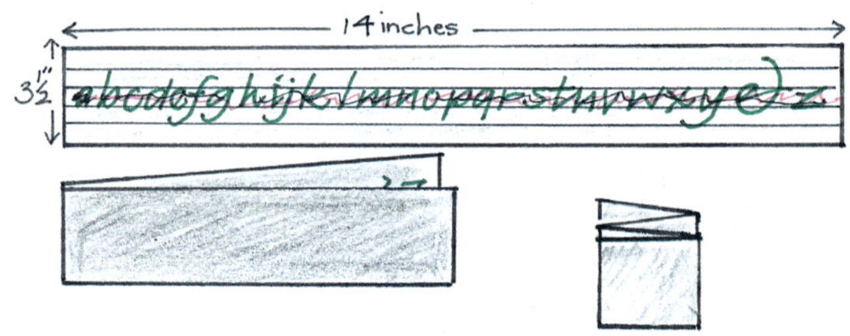


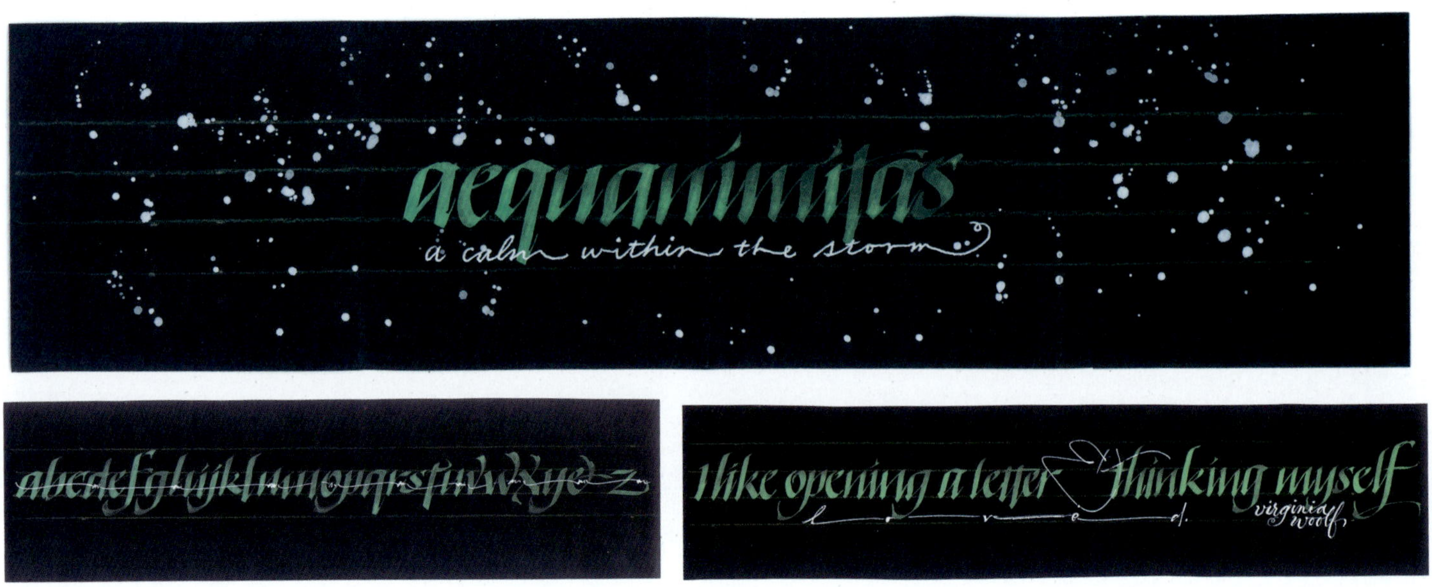

**FOR THE COVER:**

10. To make a cover for your folded strips, take a piece of black paper measuring about 11" x 14". Turn the paper horizontally and mark the page at 4" intervals along the top and bottom. Connect the marks vertically with your chalk pencil so that you have three 4"-wide strips marked. Mark the remaining portion on the right with ½" intervals and lightly connect the marks so that you have another three ½"-wide strips.

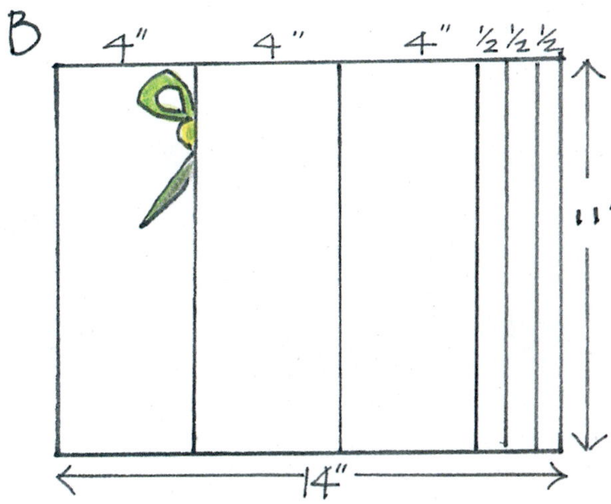


11. Flip your lined page over and using your large brush, proceed to decorate the whole sheet with gouache. I recommend starting with white, creating random lines and patterns that stand in stark contrast to the black paper. Then clean your brush and add a second color to complement the white, but don't use nearly as much as the white you started with. Add splatters, dots, additional streaks, etc. Clean your brush and add yet more color, but make sure that the black is not overwhelmed by the color you add. When finished, set the sheet aside to dry until it is not sticky to the touch.

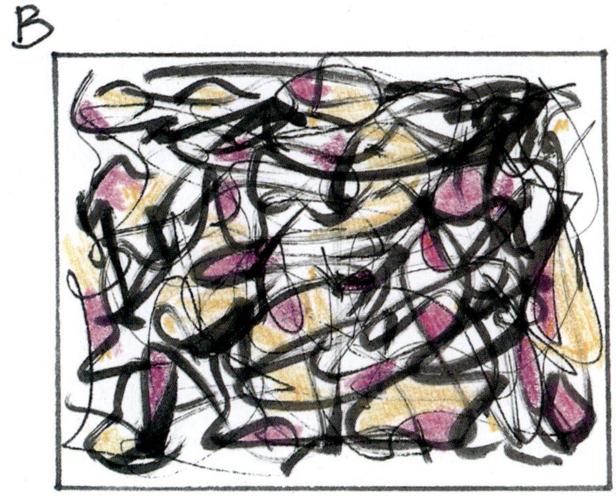


12. Once your cover is dry, flip it over and cut along the chalk lines you drew previously. You will now have three 4"-wide cover strips and three ½"-wide strips that will be used to create bands for your covers.

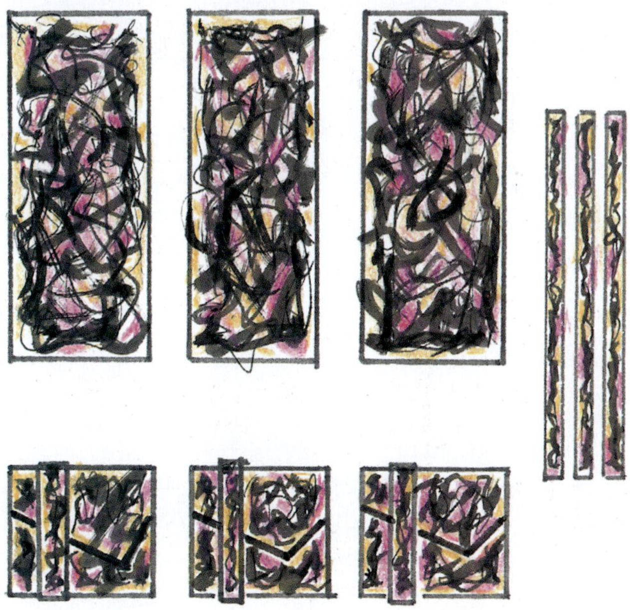

13. To complete the book, position the cover vertically such that the 4" side is at the top and bottom. Place the folded accordion booklet in the center on the inside of the cover and fold the bottom edge of the cover so it almost covers the accordion booklet. Then fold the top down to cover the bottom flap. Now fold the band around the cover (top to bottom), and once it fits glue the two ends of the band together to finish it. The accordion booklet should sit loosely inside the cover you just made.

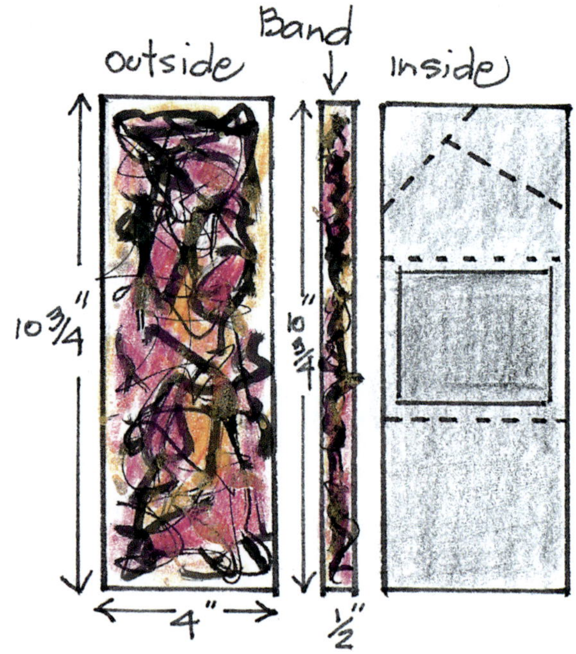


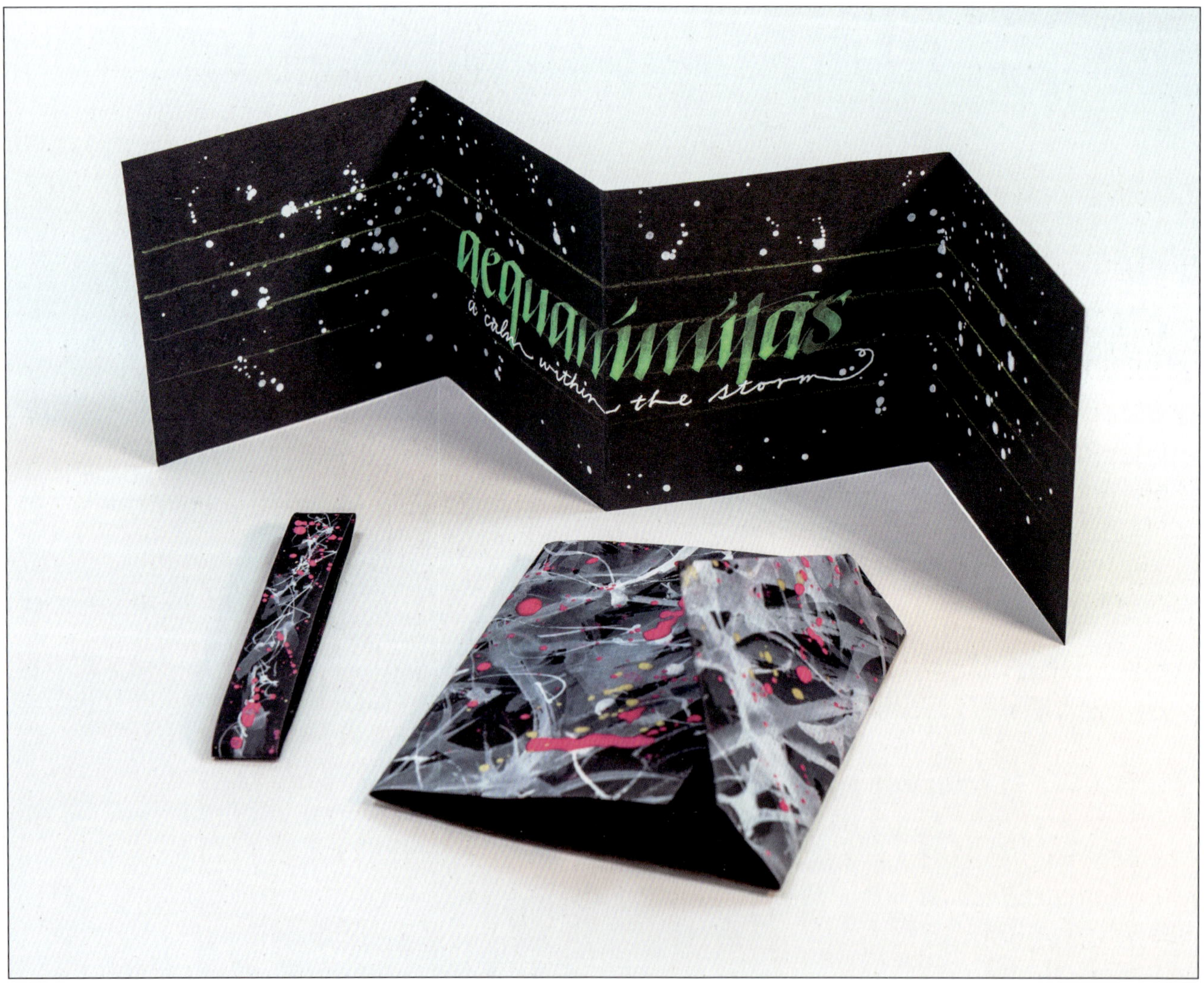

# Chapter 6

# Exploring Cursive Italic

The word "cursive" is derived from the Latin word *carrere*, which means to run. It is a hand based entirely on the Italic script and created for less-formal uses when speed is the higher priority.

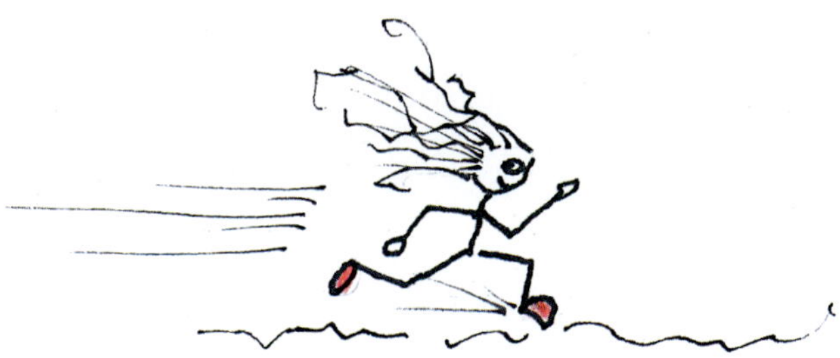

This is a less-formal script, more akin to our handwriting. There are very few pen lifts as most letters join. This allows for more momentum.

For this chapter, you'll need a few new supplies:

- **Fountain pen or small Pilot Parallel Pen (2.4 mm with the orange cap, or 1.5 mm with the red cap)**
- **Small calligraphy marker, similar size as the pens**
- **Ink (for the pens)**
- **Pencil, eraser and ruler**
- **Practice paper to go over your lined template**

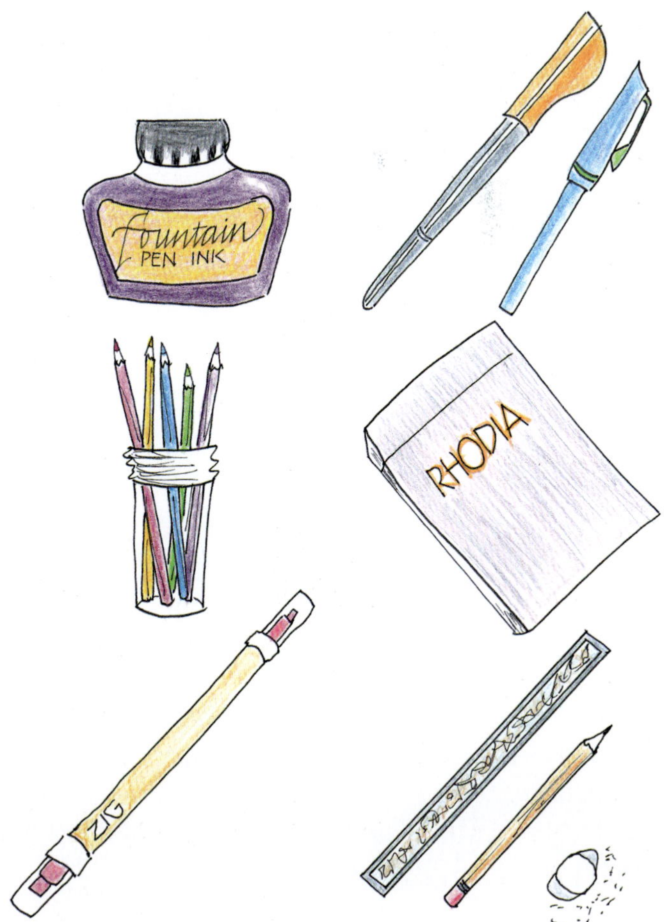

In addition to some new materials, we must line a new template page for this script. Because I use a smaller nib (around 1⁄16-inch/2 mm), I only require ¼ of an inch for my smaller letters with ⅛ of an inch above and below. That means I mark ⅛ inch, then ¼ inch, then ⅛ inch all the way down the page. Mark off ¾ of an inch for the top margin and sides, and 1 inch for the bottom margin. Use a pencil to make your lines, then outline the necessary lines with a fine-liner marker and erase the pencil lines. The lined template is critical so that you don't have to guess about the placement of the letters.

A 1⁄16-inch/2 mm nib (or a bit smaller) is a good size, but it must be a metal nib — either a fountain pen or a small Parallel Pen — or a new, sharp calligraphy marker. The sharpness allows for good, clean, light upstrokes, which will improve the overall look.

With pen, ink and lined template in hand, and with an intent to focus on rhythm, consistent spacing, angle and slant, we are set to learn the delightful ways to link our letters together.

One of the biggest differences between traditional/formal Italic and the cursive/informal Italic is the number of pen lifts. An entire word written in cursive will most likely require fewer pen lifts than one letter of the more formal version.

As you know, the formal Italic letter *g* takes four to five strokes to complete, whereas in cursive writing the entire word "linking" can be executed without any pen lifts (other than the dots on the two *i*'s). This is why cursive is faster.

However, time must be taken at first to ensure proper letter forms as well as proper links between letters. Let's take a closer look at the generally used guidelines behind this script.

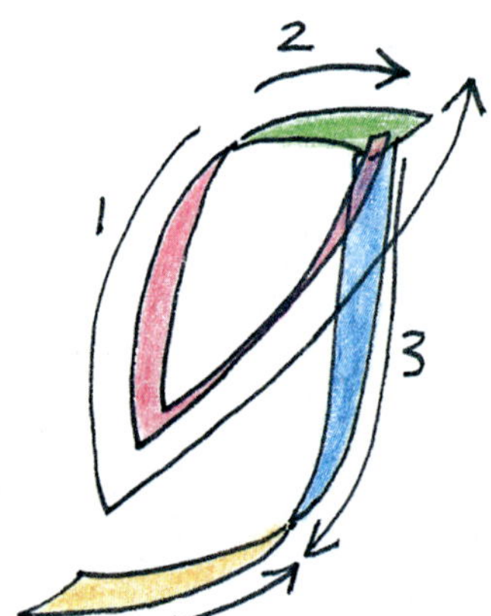


**Formal Italic:** Letter *g* takes four to five strokes and several pen lifts.

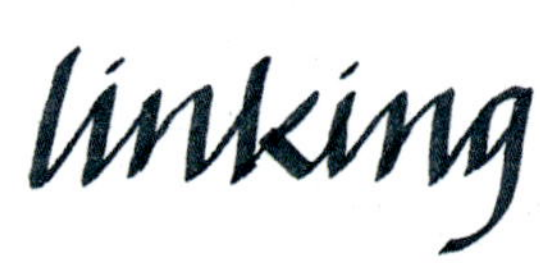


**Cursive Italic:** The word "linking" requires no pen lifts (except for the dots on the *i*'s).

# General Guidelines

There are a few different ways to link letters, and there are letters that should just not be linked at all. As with the formal Italic script, there are no loops or scoops. Consequently, descenders never join the following letter. The letter *t* uses a crossbar that is as understated as possible to avoid any dark, muddy eye-catchers.

Remember to set yourself up on a slanted work surface. This is still very important, if not more so, because you can write longer without a break. Shake your hand out once in a while to avoid cramping.

## A VARIETY OF JOINS

Because the letters are shaped differently, resulting in different strokes to begin the letter and exit from the letter, there are naturally various ways to link them together. The following depicts three specific joins you will need to learn:

1. **Rollover:** With this join, the stroke goes up and over the following letter, as depicted in the example word *an*. You can also see this in the letter combinations of *in, im* and *ir*.

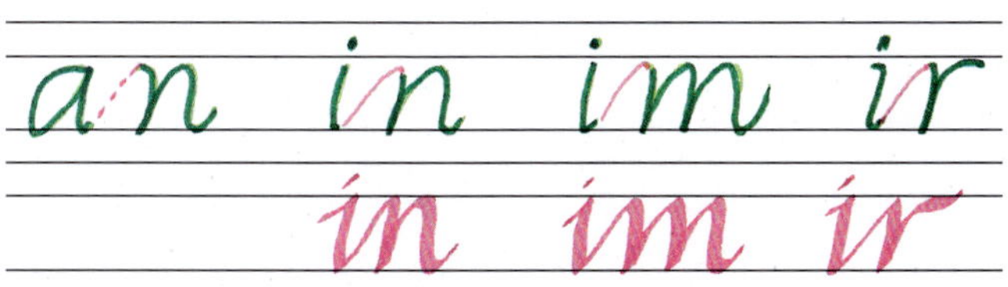


2. **Diagonal:** With this join, the stroke swings up to attach at the top of the following letter as illustrated in the example *ai*. You can see this same diagonal join with the letter combinations *aj, ao, si, ci* and *ei*.

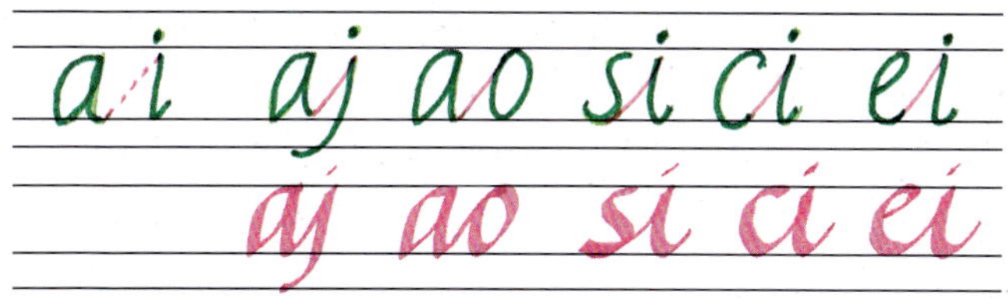


3. **Horizontal:** Here the join is a horizontal line connecting the first letter to the next as depicted in the illustrated example of *owvi*. Good words to practice with are *moon, grove, broom, from* and *bring*.

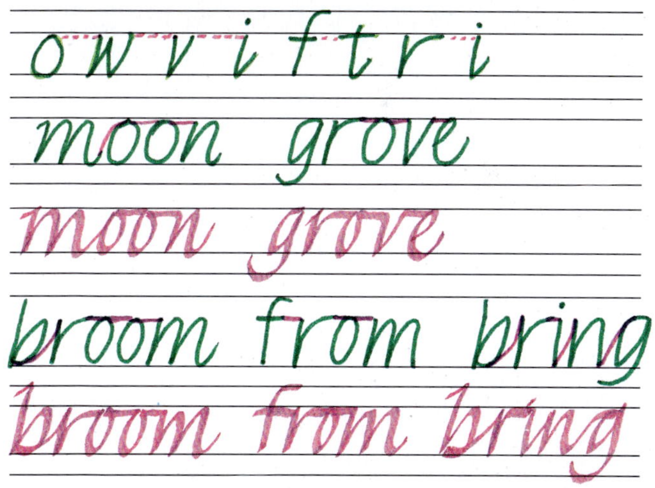

The capital letters are based on the simple (as opposed to fancy) Italic capitals and can join the next letter if it is smoothly done. Here are some examples:

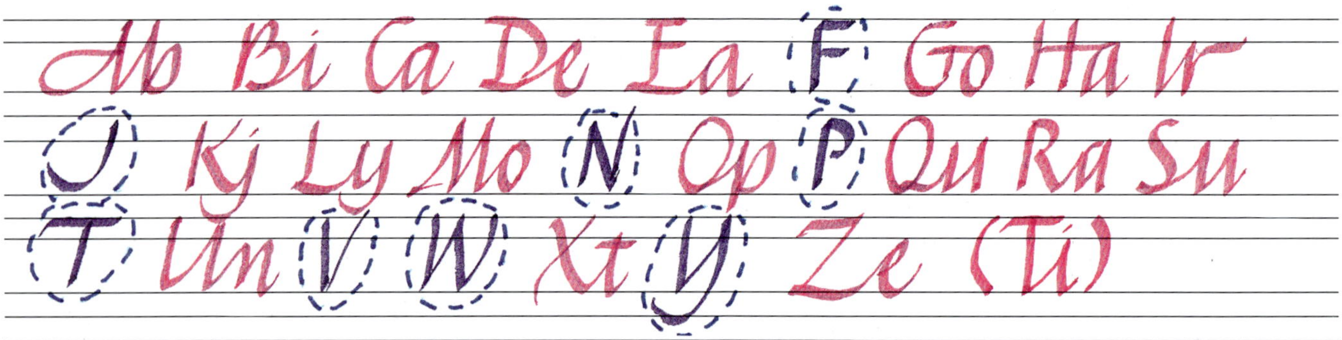


The capitals in purple are letters that cannot be joined.

### LETTER JOINING EXERCISES

Now let's practice! Try these exercises.

1. Create a row across your page of each letter of the alphabet, focusing on making the joins look as similar as possible for each row and taking careful time to form the letters well. For example, *aaa* would use a rollover join, *bbb* would use a diagonal join, while *ooo* would use a horizontal join. These letters should closely resemble the traditional Italic letter forms from Section One, but the join technique enables greater speed with the removal of pen lifts from the strokes.

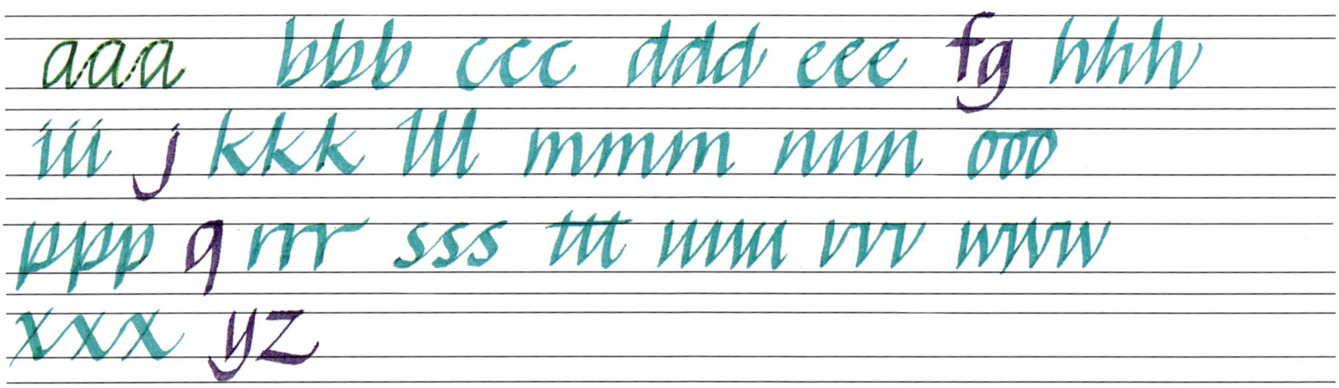


The lowercase letters in purple are letters that cannot be joined.

2. Link an *n* between every letter of the alphabet as follows: *ana*, *bnb*, *cnc*, *dnd*, etc.

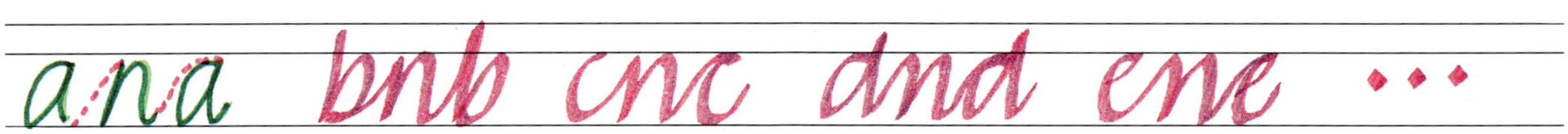

3. Join the entire alphabet together in a single line. You may not achieve this on your first attempt, but you will soon find the correct letter widths and spacing to accomplish this. As illustrated below, there will be points where you need a break between the letters, such as between *g* and *h*. This is because, in cursive, you do not join a letter with a descender to the following letter.

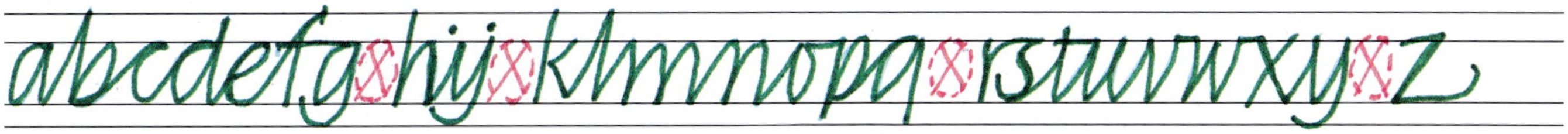


4. Link a capital and lowercase letter, as depicted in the illustration below.

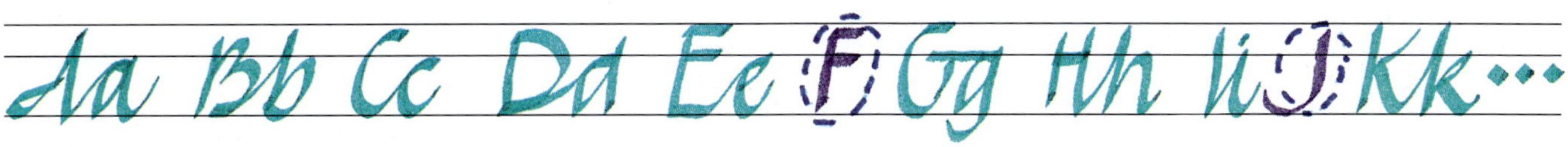


5. Letter a word with a capital for each letter of the alphabet, such as *Apple, Banana,* etc.

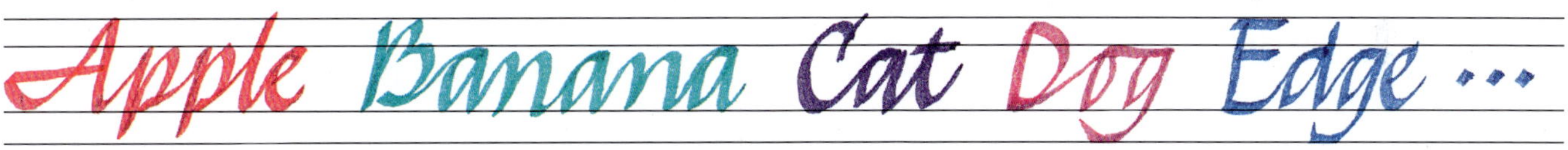


6. Practice combining words to create sentences. Practice initially with a pencil to lessen the pressure so you can first attain a rhythmic flow. Then pick up your pen and work at attaining the rhythm once again. The following are good sentences to practice with:

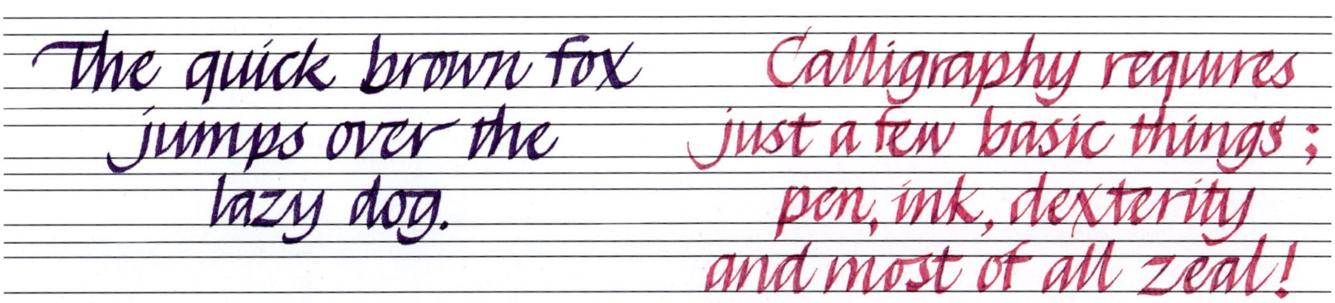

## PLAYFUL PRACTICE

When you have the rhythm of joined Italic letters with an increased naturalness, there is much play that can result. Try these experiments:

1. Link the whole alphabet again.

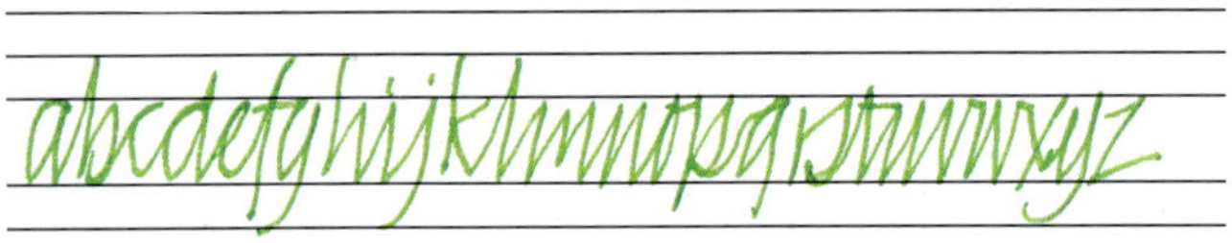

2. Repeat this but work on squishing the letters, forcing a more upright form with tighter angles as you write faster across the page.

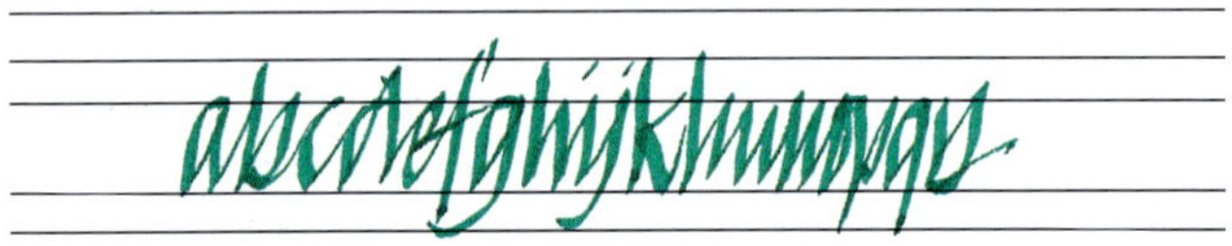

3. Now do the opposite. Extend the letters, making them shorter and the links longer.

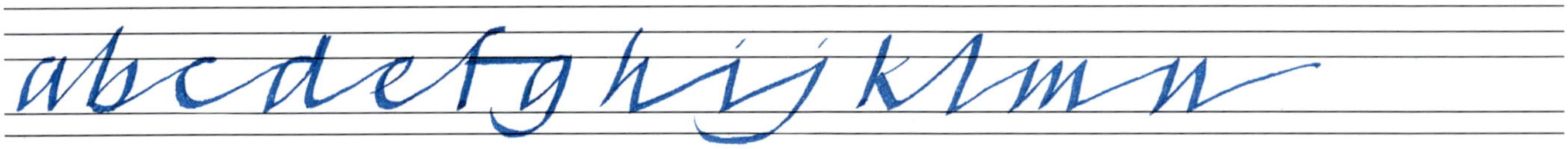

4. Now combine exercises 2 and 3, with three squished letters followed by three extended letters, and so on.

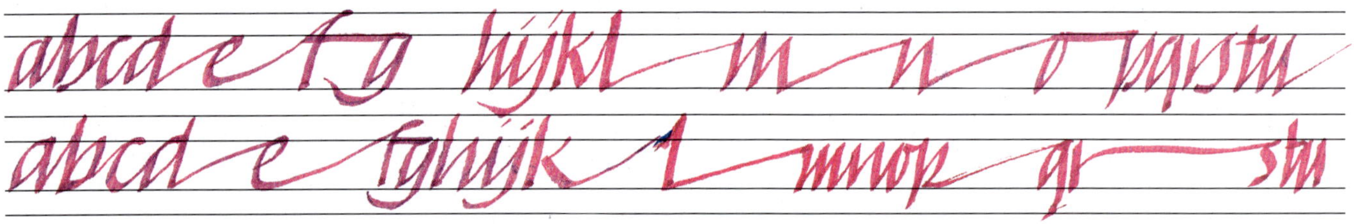

5. Try your hand with ampersands. These are fun to letter with the cursive hand and allow for much playfulness.

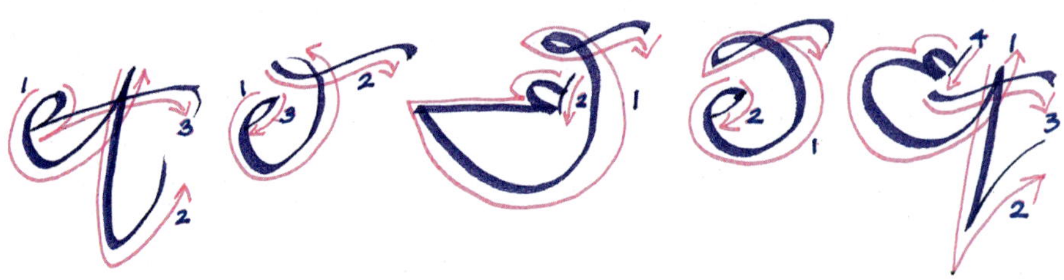

### The Misfits

**Remember that most letters with descenders (i.e., *g*, *j*, *q* and *y*) do not join the next letter, but there are times when a join does work, such as the letter *p* (because the end of the letter is at the baseline and can therefore connect to another letter). However, if it doesn't look right, don't do it. You will develop an eye for what works. The surrounding context of the word will help dictate that.**

# Project: Cursive Decorative Paper

This project is similar to the decorative paper you made in Section One. Utilize every space with cursive Italic practice, but leave a circle in the center of the bottom right quadrant of your practice sheet blank. Be sure to place your cursive template under your practice sheet as a guideline. This is a good time to practice the cursive hand in its compressed state as well as the elongated version. This project would work well with markers or ink, if the paper holds ink well.

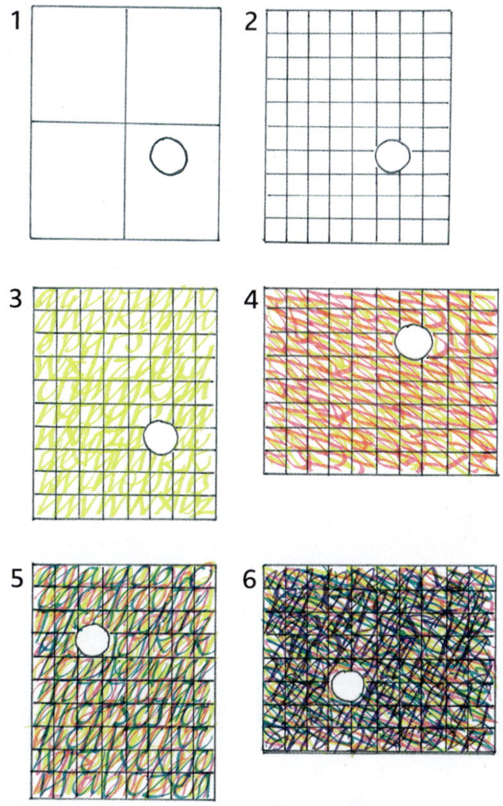


WHAT YOU'LL NEED:

- **Paper**
- **Pencil and eraser**
- **Ruler**
- **Calligraphy pen or markers**
- **Ink, if using a dip pen**
- **Black fine-liner marker**
- **Paint or colored pencils**

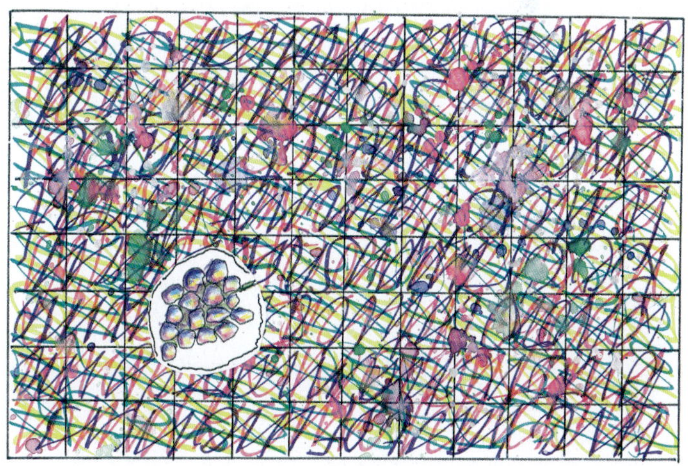

1. Draw a circle in pencil somewhere in the middle of the lower right quadrant of your practice sheet, using a round-based object as a guide. You might also draw a grid on the paper with a pencil. The grid can be used as a guide for your lettering. Fill your sheet with practice lettering in one direction, but avoid lettering in the circle. Then turn it 90 degrees and fill the page again. As you work, start with lighter colors and move to darker colors with each rotation. Practice shapes you are struggling with. Try some ampersands, too.

2. Rotate the sheet another 90 degrees and fill it again. The final 90-degree turn could be a page of flourishes.

3. Once your page is packed with practice, sketch a drawing in the circle. Perhaps a sleeping kitten curled up, a daisy, an apple or a bunch of grapes. Whatever you prefer. After you have sketched in your drawing with pencil, outline it with a black fine-liner marker and erase the pencil lines. Color in as you please.

# Project: Journal

## Write the way through

This little journal is meant to be used for your own private thoughts and recollections. The above phrase "write the way through" suggests how we can cope with a difficult time — sickness, depression, loneliness and trauma of any sort. It proposes that writing could possibly help you *right* the way through by *writing*. Of course, writing about something wonderful you're learning or experiencing is appropriate as well!

### WHAT YOU'LL NEED:

- **One 7" x 20" piece of Bristol board (or 140-lb. cold-pressed watercolor paper)**
- **Ruler**
- **Scissors**
- **Painter's tape or low-tack tape**
- **Calligraphy pen or markers (various sizes)**
- **Ink, if using a dip pen**
- **Six 11" x 5 ½" sheets of text wove paper (or paper from your sketchbook)**
- **Bulldog clips**
- **Awl (optional)**
- **Needle and embroidery thread**
- **Glue stick**

### FOR THE COVER:

1. Cut a 1" strip from the bottom of your 7" x 20" piece of Bristol board/watercolor paper so that the larger piece measures 6" x 20". The 1" strip will be used as a band for your journal.

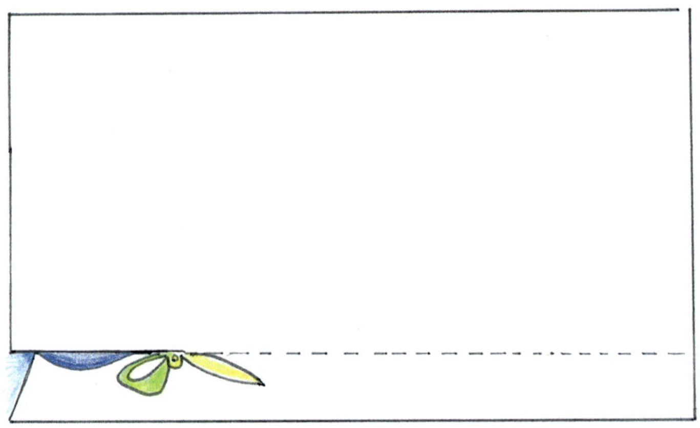

2. Fold the larger piece into three equal parts, then flatten it out again. This sheet will be used as the cover for your journal.

3. Place the 1" band across the flattened-out sheet and tape it with low-tack tape at each end to hold it in place.

4. Cover the entire sheet (including the band) with large and small letters using the cursive hand and various pen/marker sizes. Play with lots of color. Go wild!

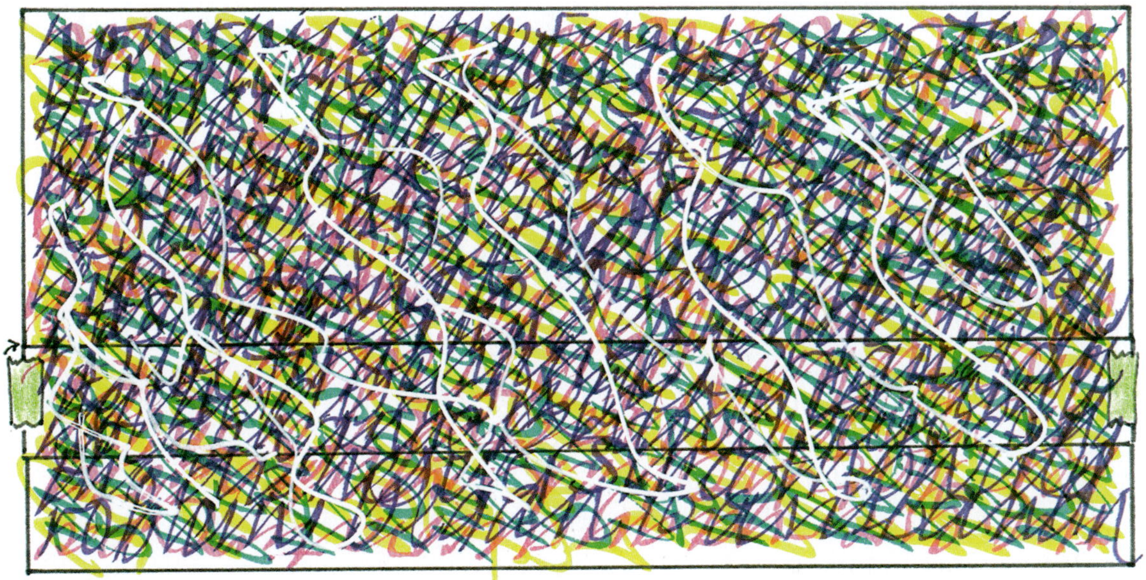

5. Once the sheet is completed, let it dry and then remove the 1" band, revealing a white unlettered strip.

6. You can write your name and date in the white space, a title for your journal or maybe a quote (see below). You will need a small nib for this step, such as the fountain pen or Pilot pen you have used in this chapter.

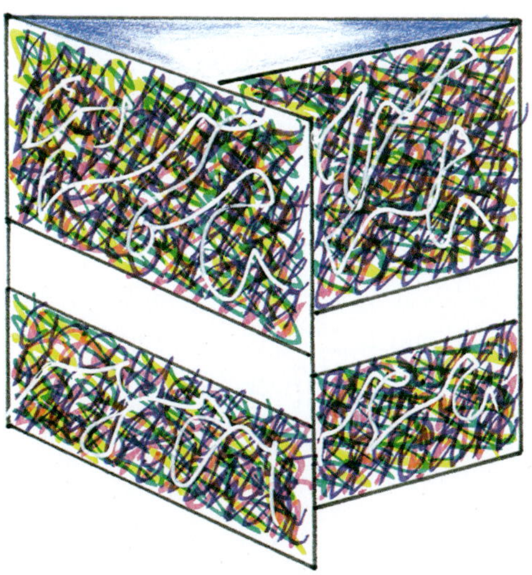

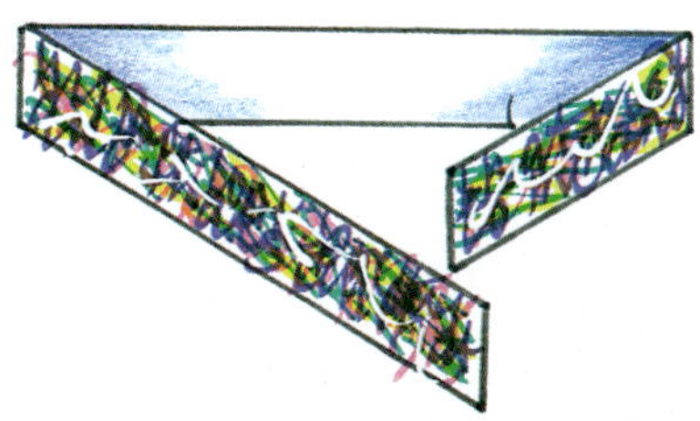

Here are a couple of my favorite quotes from Oscar Wilde:

*I keep a diary in order to enter the wonderful secrets of my life.*

*A writer is someone who has taught their mind to misbehave.*

## FOR THE JOURNAL INTERIORS:

7. Stack three 11" x 5 ½" sheets together and fold them in half to create a signature.

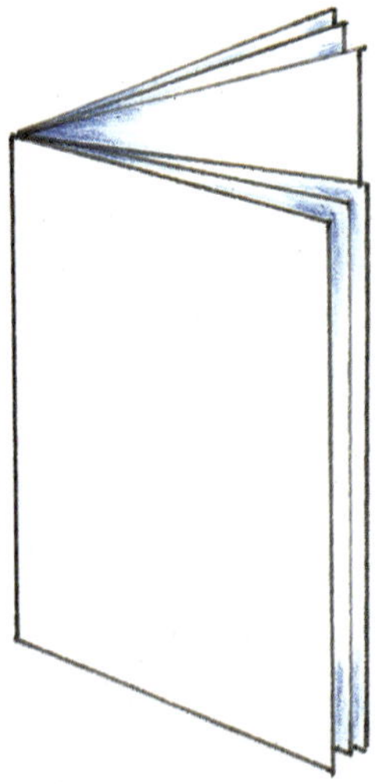

8. Repeat this with the remaining three sheets of paper to create your second signature. These signatures should be 5½" x 5½" in size and will be contained within your folded cover.

9. Line up the folded edge of one signature with the first fold of your cover. Keeping it in position as best you can, open the signature to reveal its center crease/fold. The fold of the signature should be nestled into the first fold of your cover. Clamp the top and bottom of the left side of your opened signature to the cover using bulldog clips.

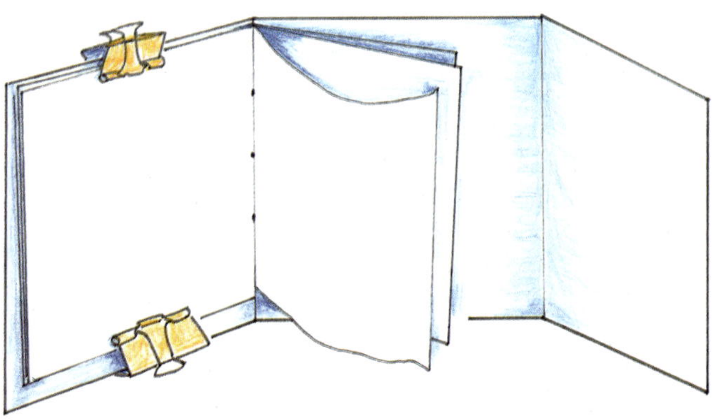

10. Pierce three equally spaced holes through the signature fold and cover fold with your needle. This job is even easier if you happen to have an awl. Exercise caution either way as the ends will be sharp!

11. Now it's time to sew! Thread your needle with embroidery thread (or whatever you have available).

12. Send the needle through the middle hole (hole B) from the inside. Pull the needle and thread most of the way through, leaving a dangling tail on the inside of the signature approximately 3" long. This tail will be used to tie the knot at the end.

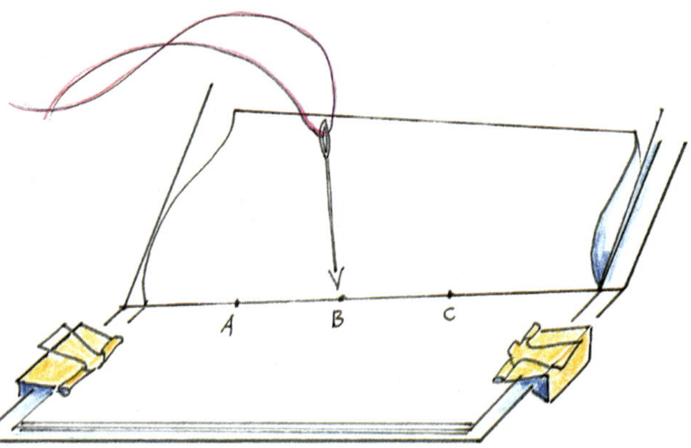


13. From the outside, send your needle and thread through hole C so that it's back inside the signature. Pull your needle and thread right the way through to the inside, but make sure you do not pull the 3" tail with you. (If you accidentally pull the tail through, you can simply start again.)

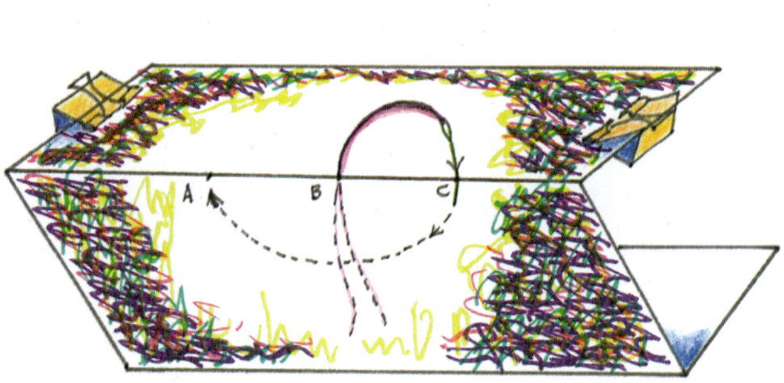

14. Now take your needle and thread and send it through hole A from the inside to the outside. Pull the thread taut while holding onto the tail to ensure that it stays in place.

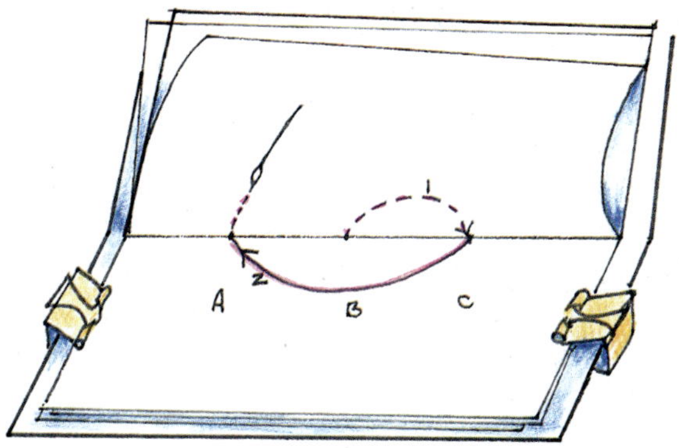


15. Now from the outside, go back inside through hole B so that the 3" tail meets your needle and thread.

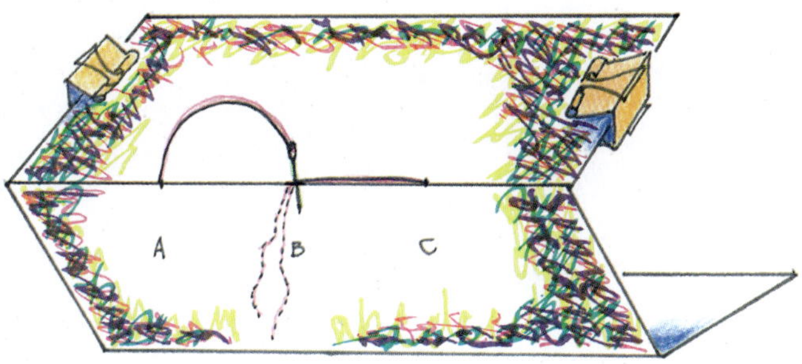


16. Pull the thread snugly and cut it, leaving a second 3" tail. Tie the two tails in the middle with a simple knot.

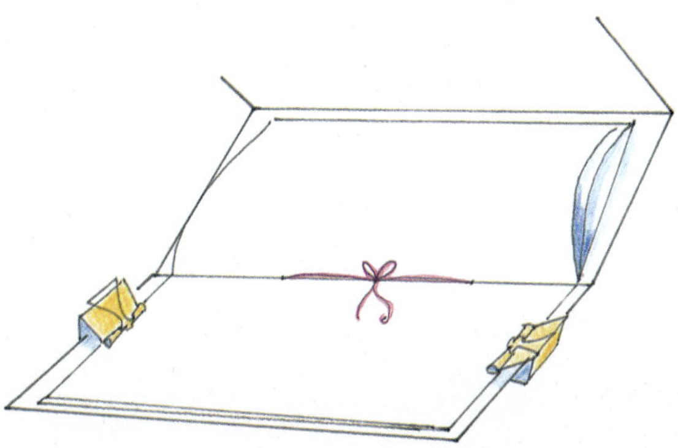

17. Once you have completed the first signature, take the second signature and sew it into the second fold of your cover, using the same steps. The final journal will look like the illustration depicted here.

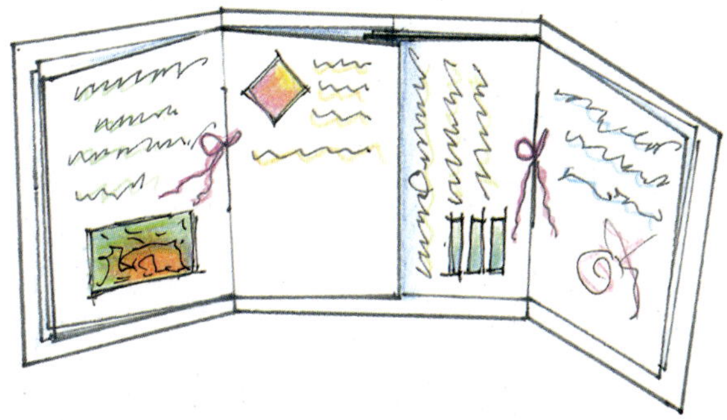

Bookbinding is one of the many delights that can be incorporated into the world of calligraphy. Once you start, you'll find many variations on how to create books, from simple to complex. One simple variation is to start your stitch from the outside going into the signature (leaving the tail on the outside) and tying up your threads on the outside of the cover. This will allow you to add a simple decoration to the knot, such as a small bead or bauble.

Now that your journal is complete, you can take the 1" band you cut, fold it into three sections, as you did for your cover, and glue together the overlapping portions of the band to create a sleeve to slip your journal into.

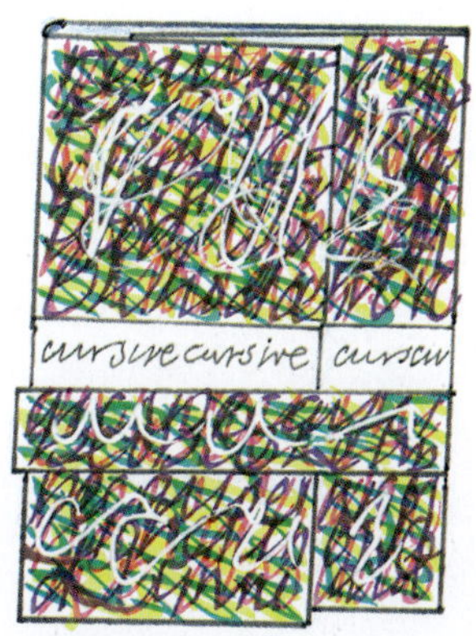

# One Last Word on Italic

Now you can play endlessly with Italic and its variations. Be sure to keep practicing correctly, and you'll become more and more comfortable and confident with ductus, spacing, angle, linking, pen manipulation and the other key components that create beautiful and correct letter forms, words and sentences. As you reach this point, you will be set for Section Three, where we will take the rules we learned in the last two sections and break them artistically.

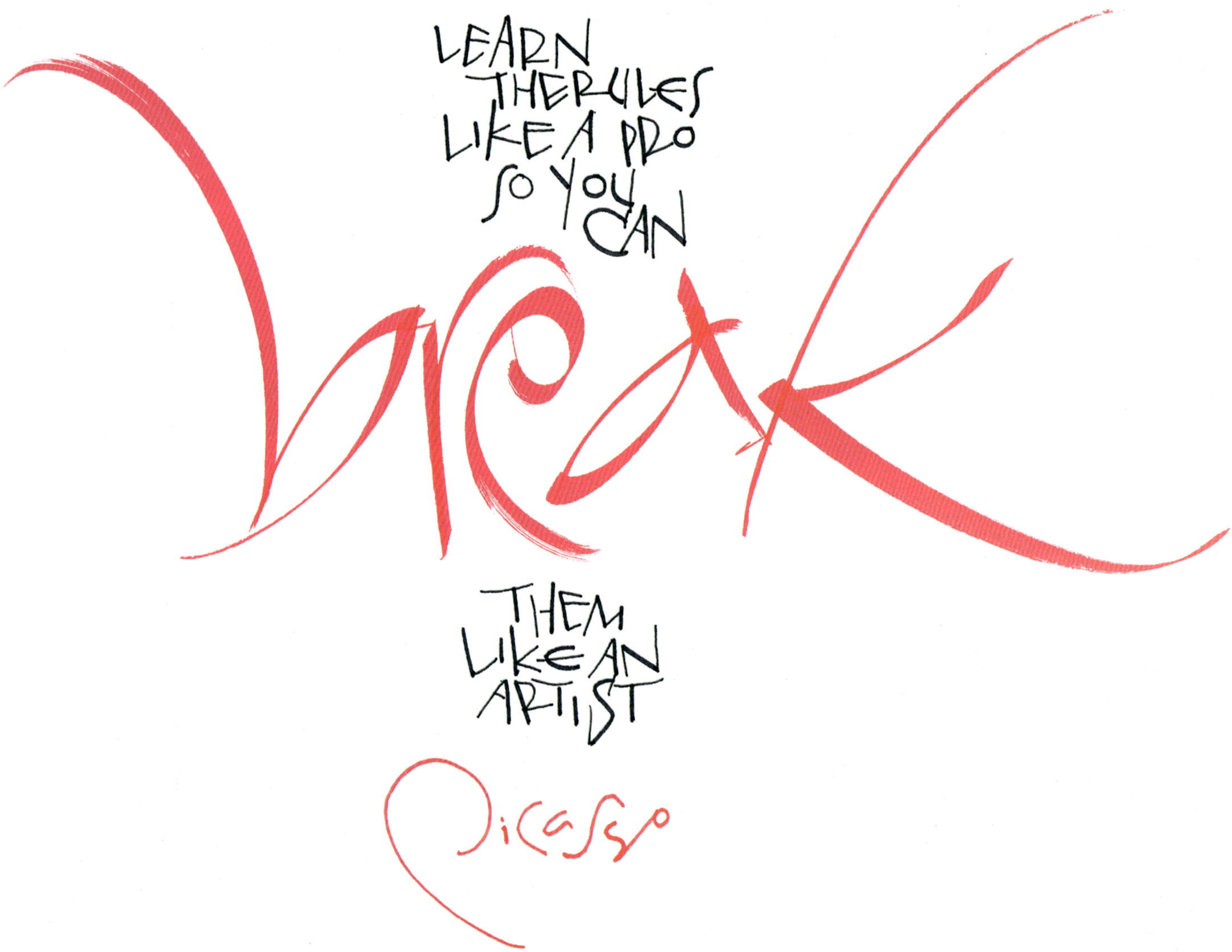

# Section 3

Moving from traditional Italic calligraphy to a gestural and abstract version is not a leap of faith with the hopes of grabbing something solid on the way down. As with the traditional, there are steps that help you move from one place to another. In the end, when you desire to create and splash and gesture and fling, all your training comes into play, although it is your gut that leads, conducts and dictates your movements.

Speaking of movements, one of the main differences between the Italic calligraphy in Section One and the Italic you are about to explore is the use of full-body gestures. When practicing, you will need large sheets of paper on which you will apply your ink and paint with both large and small tools. The traditional Italic lowercase *a* below was created with my hand and forearm, whereas the letter *a* depicted beside it utilized my whole arm and shoulder.

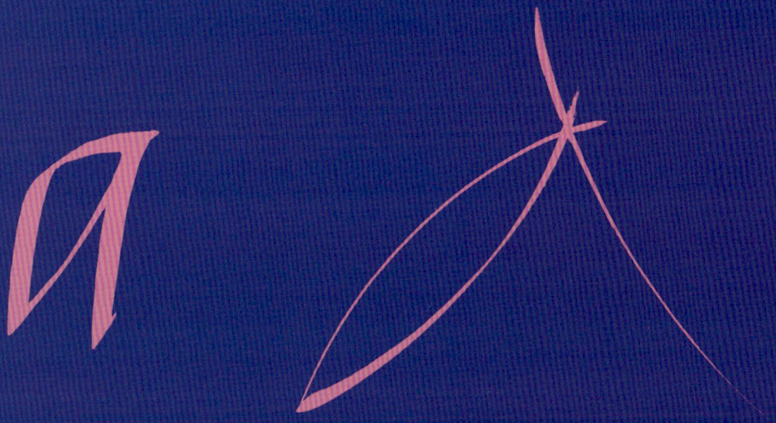

In the first chapter of this section, after a review of the traditional Italic, we will proceed to break down boundaries and walls, taking each letter through several variations, while having the letter remain recognizable.

The next chapter explores the use of another tool that creates letters in a wonderful way — the pointed brush. This tool emulates the basic letters, but by nature of its form, it begs to exaggerate.

The final chapter is the culmination of this book, pulling the various techniques and skills that you have learned over the course of the preceding chapters and combining them with an eye for what works from a design perspective. The focus is going wild with Italic, moving more and more into the abstract.

Throughout, you'll be given projects, new and familiar, as well as be introduced to new tools and media to play around with. As always, detailed supplies are listed with the exercises and projects.

One thing I want to emphasize is the importance of play and experimentation as you develop your own unique style. The examples I illustrate for the more stylized letters are merely that — examples. While you might try to imitate what I do in an effort to learn, don't be afraid to try new things, altering the letters and words as you see fit.

## A Bit of Background to This Section

It was perhaps the hottest and most humid summer in Ontario I've ever experienced. My sister and I headed to York University in Toronto for my dance audition to get into its dance program. Back then, I was on the heavier side, I had only small-town dance instruction, and I had less-than-average flexibility.

We all waited in the changeroom, eyeing each other surreptitiously. I sensed I was the least fit and skillful of the group. We had two auditions. One was as a group, where we knew nothing of what to expect. The other was a solo audition that we had prepared for in advance.

The group audition is where I thought my lack of skill would stand out, so I tried to hide in the back. I may have been tall, but there were so many of us, so I assured myself I wouldn't be noticed. The instructor looked at the bumbling group with consternation and commanded that we form ourselves properly, in alphabetical order. I almost laughed out loud when she pointed me to the center, indicating that was where the *M*'s should be. As my last name starts with an *M*, I was inevitably stationed front and center.

I didn't feel I would excel at this audition as I had very little training. What I did have, however, was rhythm and an aptitude to catch onto things quickly. I was eager. I loved to dance and I knew I had good balance. However, that describes nearly every dancer auditioning for entry into a university dance program.

The group audition came and went and has not remained in my memory at all. Back we all went to the changeroom to await the next call — the solo audition, our chance to present our hearts and souls and our position on the spectrum of skill.

I had worked very hard on my solo and I loved it. It was somewhat akin to rock ballet, though I had training in neither. I knew ballet movements but longed to express them through rock music. I performed to the best of my ability despite seeing who I perceived as far more capable dancers returning from their performances crestfallen, or downright angry. Based on their expressions, I believed I wouldn't achieve my goal, so, with nothing to lose, I went out — unusually calm because of my diminished expectations — and simply danced.

In the end I was accepted to the program. Everything — other than the unbelievably excellent news — was a blur. My sister recalls them saying that I needed work, but that I had potential.

Now, you have every right and reason to wonder why I am telling you this story in a calligraphy book. It is because not long after this audition, I discovered calligraphy and realized that I could also dance with my pen. However, as it is with all who are skilled at something, you have to start at the beginning.

Now, as I dance using my pen and brush, I find it similar to enjoying the structure of ballet but let loose to rock music. I take the traditional Italic script and let it soar. And this leads us into Section Three.

Section One celebrates the simple beauty of Italic, which can stand proudly on its own. All success hangs on learning this foundation. Section Two adds a bit of icing, but only if the cake is well made will it taste splendidly. While the icing dazzles and adds playfulness and color, the most important thing about a cake is still the cake!

Section Three, however, is different. It is not better than or superior to the traditional Italic, snub-nosed Italic or cursive Italic hands. It is just a different approach, a different way of looking at what you can do with these wonderful letters.

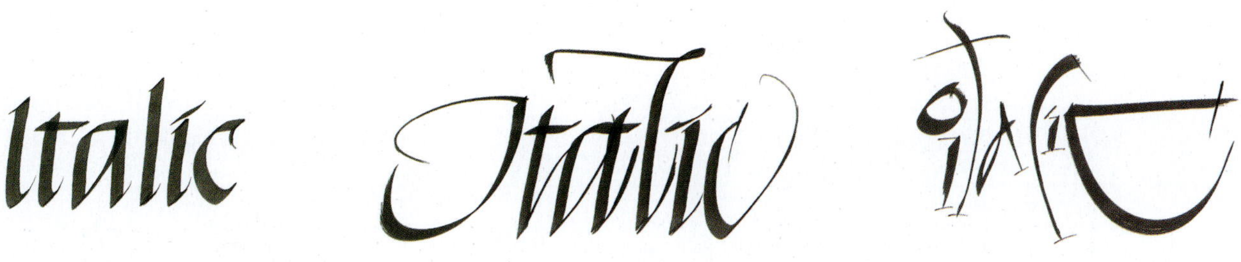

# Chapter 7

# Linking Letters & Backward Strokes

In this chapter, we will take each letter through a number of variations, while having the letter remain recognizable. This includes four exercises that are of the utmost importance in this process, as they provide the opportunity to manipulate letters as well as words. At the end of this chapter, you will make another accordion booklet to record the alphabet in which each letter has been pushed beyond its traditional boundaries.

In terms of supplies, you'll need lots of practice sheets (with paper that will take ink), a 2.5-mm to 3-mm metal calligraphy nib (that would be just bigger than 1⁄16 of an inch) and holder, a practice sheet template created for your nib size, ink for dipping (if you're using a dip pen), water and a rag.

Before altering the traditional Italic hand by incorporating linking and backward strokes, first take some time to practice this hand without alteration. Based on the size of your nib, create a template that you can place under your practice sheet as a guideline and practice each letter of the alphabet in the traditional Italic hand.

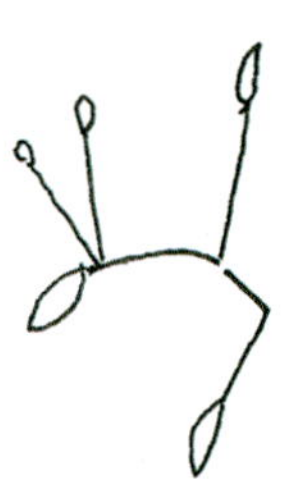

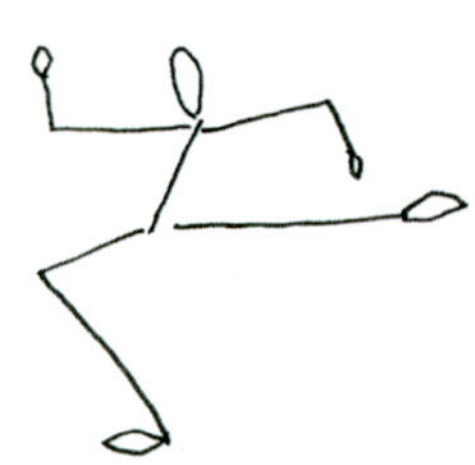

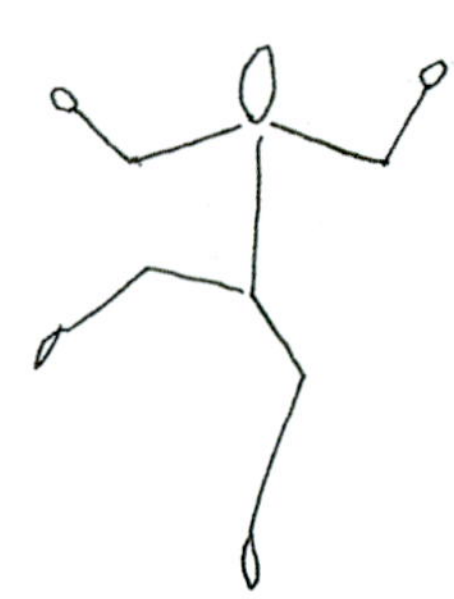

# Practicing Linking Letters

Once you feel comfortable, the next step is to link letters together, such as *ab, cd, ef* and so on, right the way through to the end of the alphabet. Unlike cursive Italic, where there are very few pen lifts *and* the letters are linked, this approach still incorporates all the pen lifts for each letter stroke in the traditional hand but also adds a link to the next letter. This is a new element and is non-traditional.

Now practice several lines of various letter combinations, altering the links as you deem appropriate. Recall the cursive Italic exercises with compressed and elongated joins to create variety (see pages 126). Experiment, working to develop an eye for what works.

Now move on to words, again being sure to keep your practice sheet over your template for your guidelines. Here are some suggested words for practice and experimentation: *before, after, cats, devoid, enough* and *family*. Try words in all lowercase or starting with uppercase letters. Include some form of alteration while linking these letters, again keeping an eye on what looks good and what creates fluidity and artful motion. For example, in the word *family* illustrated on the right, I used a combination of compressed and elongated links to play with the word, giving it an altered non-traditional appearance. One thing you will notice is that I have thrown out the rule about never using loops, which we observed when learning cursive Italic.

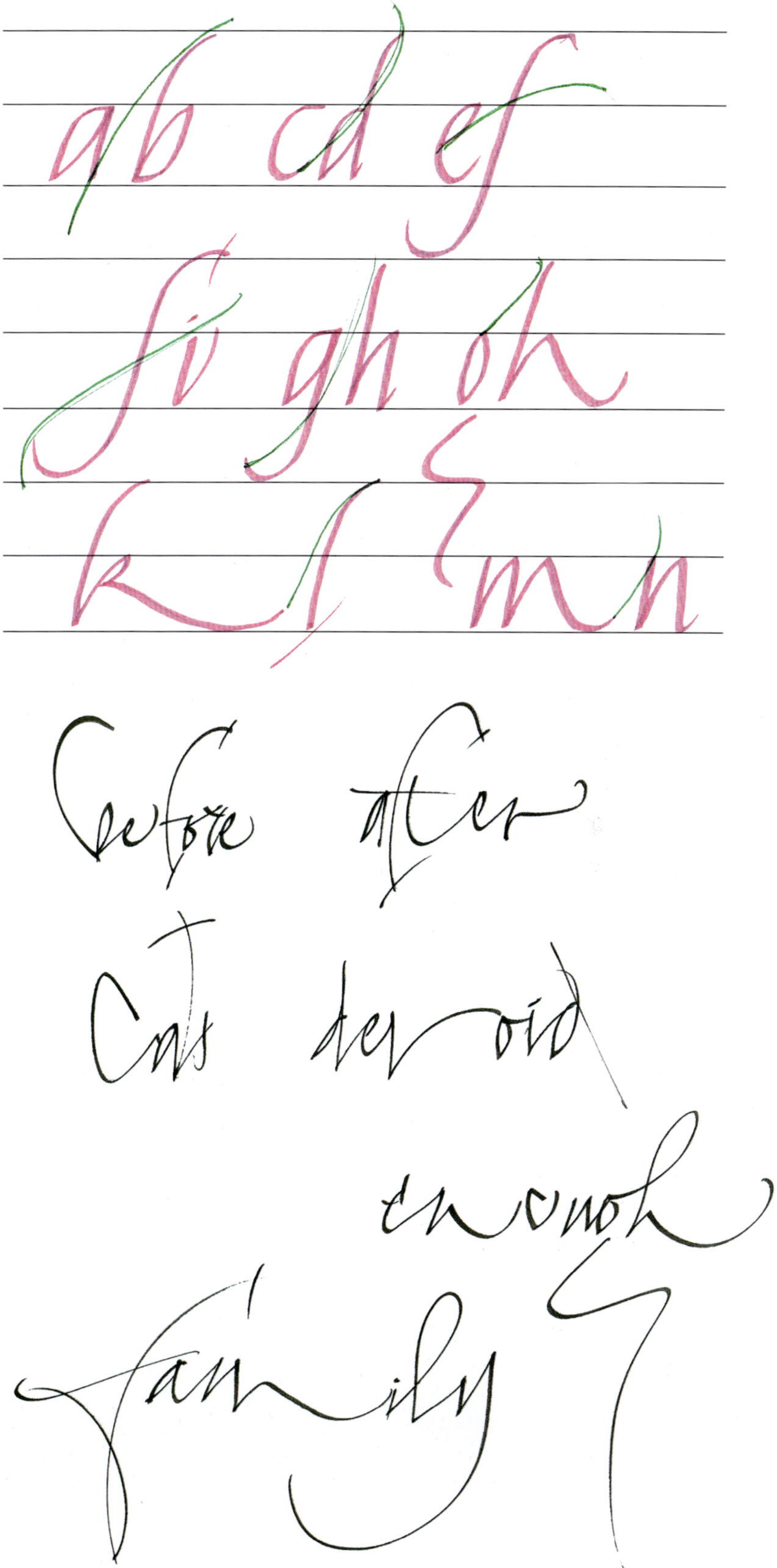

## EXERCISE ONE

The following exercise will help you to think more creatively about pushing the limits of each letter. The purpose of the chart is to incorporate variations for each of the letters. This chart is crucial, so take time to create it. I suggest you keep it for future reference. This is a fun exercise, and I wish I could see what you come up with!

**Note:** The four exercises in this section all require the same supplies, so refer to the list below if you decide to break up the exercises.

### WHAT YOU'LL NEED:

- **Practice sheets**
- **Pencil**
- **Ruler**
- **Calligraphy pen and ink, or a calligraphy marker**
- **Eraser**

1. Create a practice sheet with space for ascenders and descenders. You will need 26 rows in total (one row for each letter of the alphabet). Divide your practice sheet into five columns. Note: You will likely require two to three practice sheets so that your letters will not be crowded (consider photocopying your template).

2. Create five versions of each letter using the following guidelines. Pencil your letters in first, then follow up with your pen. Let the ink dry completely and erase any pencil lines you don't want. You may want to keep some of the pencil lines if you find you prefer the penciled shape but your hand could not quite execute it with a pen.

**Column 1** – Fill in this column with the traditional Italic hand.

**Column 2** – In this column, make one change such as a longer-than-typical downstroke.

**Column 3** – In this column, make two changes and try fewer pen lifts.

**Column 4** – In this column, write your letter with a different slant and forget about the 45-degree pen angle.

**Column 5** – Try to write your letters with your strokes opposite to the traditional ductus (both in order and direction of strokes). This is the "go crazy" column where you can do things like changing the direction, angle and shape.

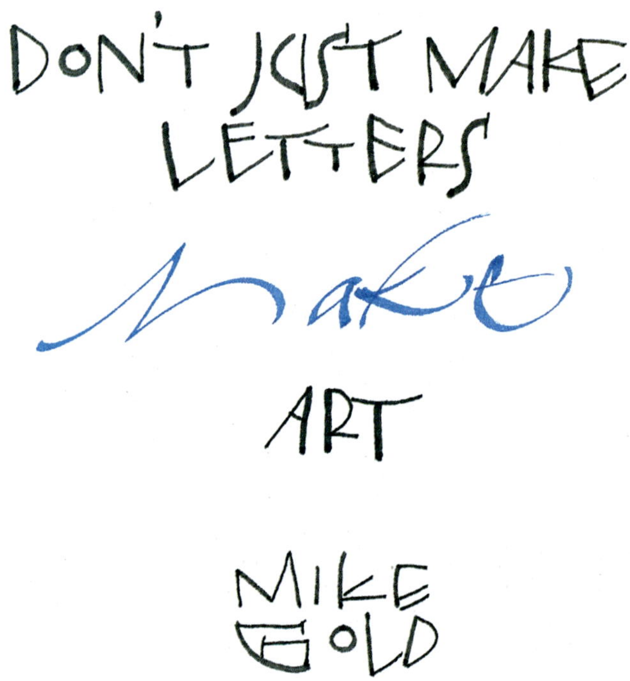

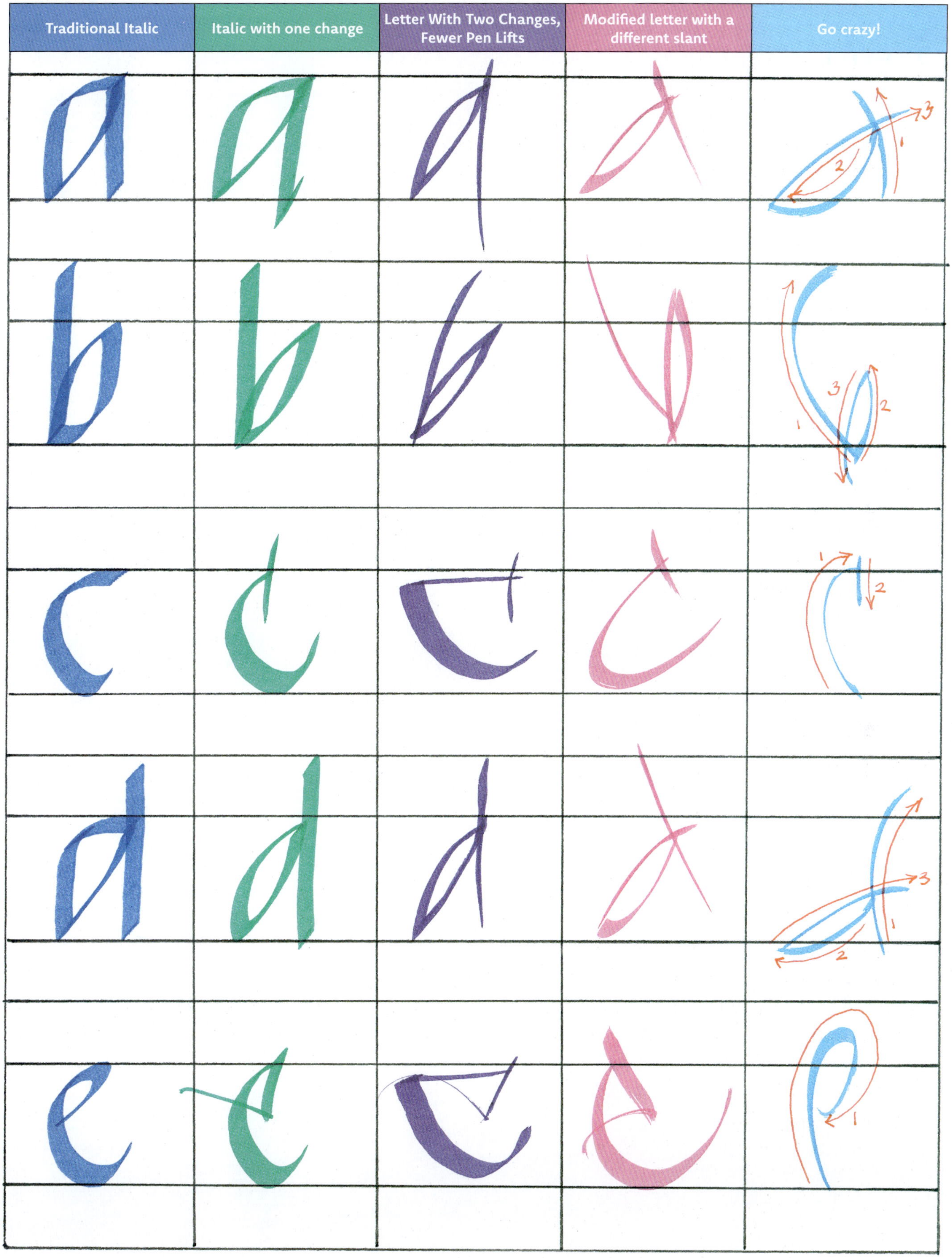
Traditional Italic
Italic with one change
Letter With Two Changes, Fewer Pen Lifts
Modified letter with a different slant
Go crazy!

## EXERCISE TWO

This second exercise will help you alter the traditional Italic by playing more with the links within words.

1. With your template under your practice sheet, divide your practice sheet into three columns.

2. Letter the words *wisdom, color, dance, pencil, magic, secret, rhythm* and *party*. Create three versions of each word following the guidelines below. Start with pencil, then follow up with your calligraphy marker or pen.

   **Column 1** – Join letters with a simple link.

   **Column 2** – Add one change.

   **Column 3** – Add two changes.

3. Once you have completed this chart, choose your favorite word from the lot. This will lead us to exercise three on page 142, where you will change that specific word numerous times.

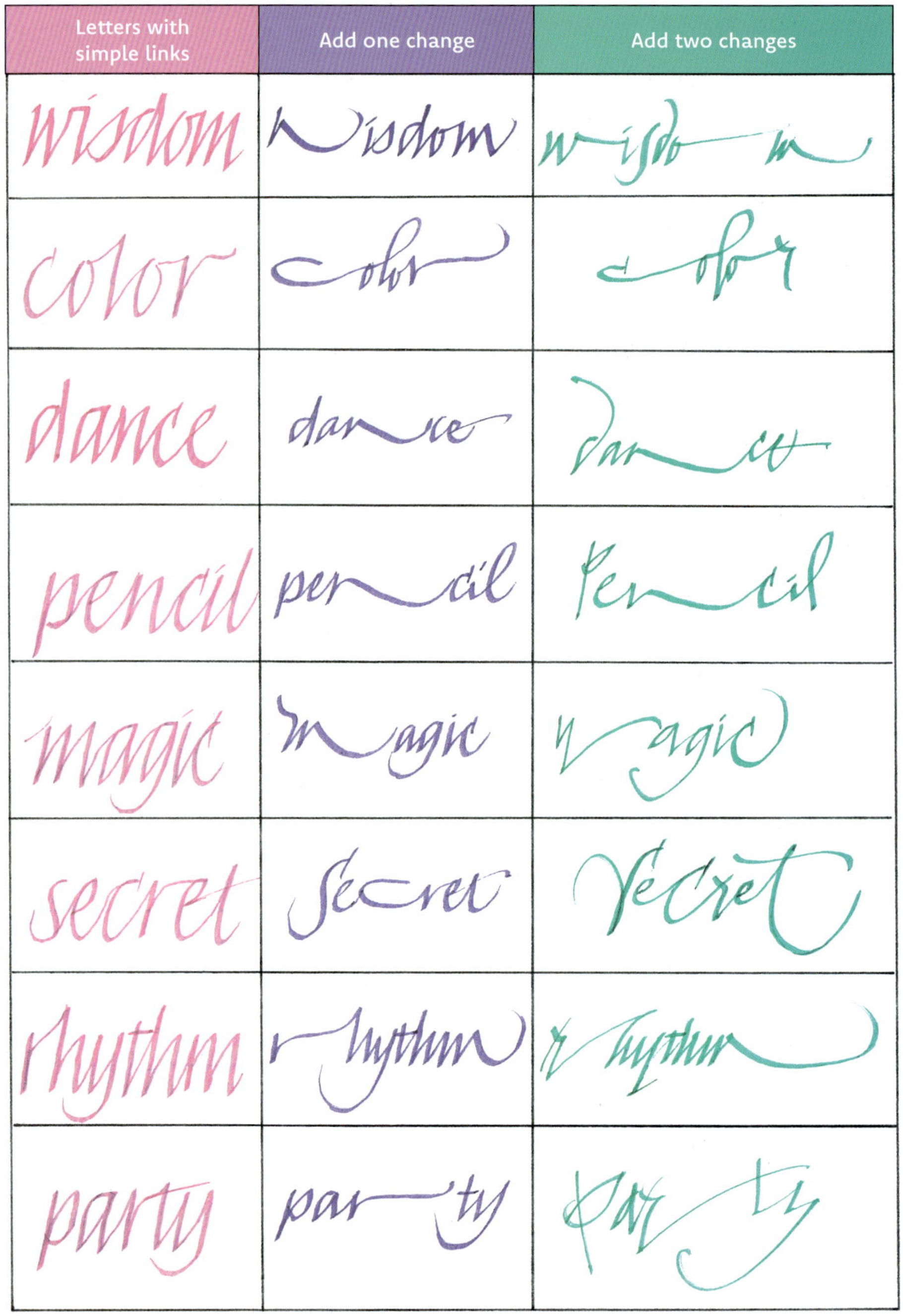

# Backward Strokes

The next exercise incorporates a different approach to your calligraphy — going at it backward. Typically, when doing calligraphy, you start at the top and go down with a downstroke of sorts. However, I have found it instructive to start from the bottom of the letter and go up with your strokes.

To start, try to letter the entire alphabet in this way, creating strokes in the opposite direction of what you're used to. I suggest practicing this technique with pencil before moving to pen and ink. Work on your freedom of movement as you experiment with different strokes, enjoying the different letter forms you create. On the right are some examples of letters made with backward strokes.

Some letters may look ridiculous, but others may look kind of cool.

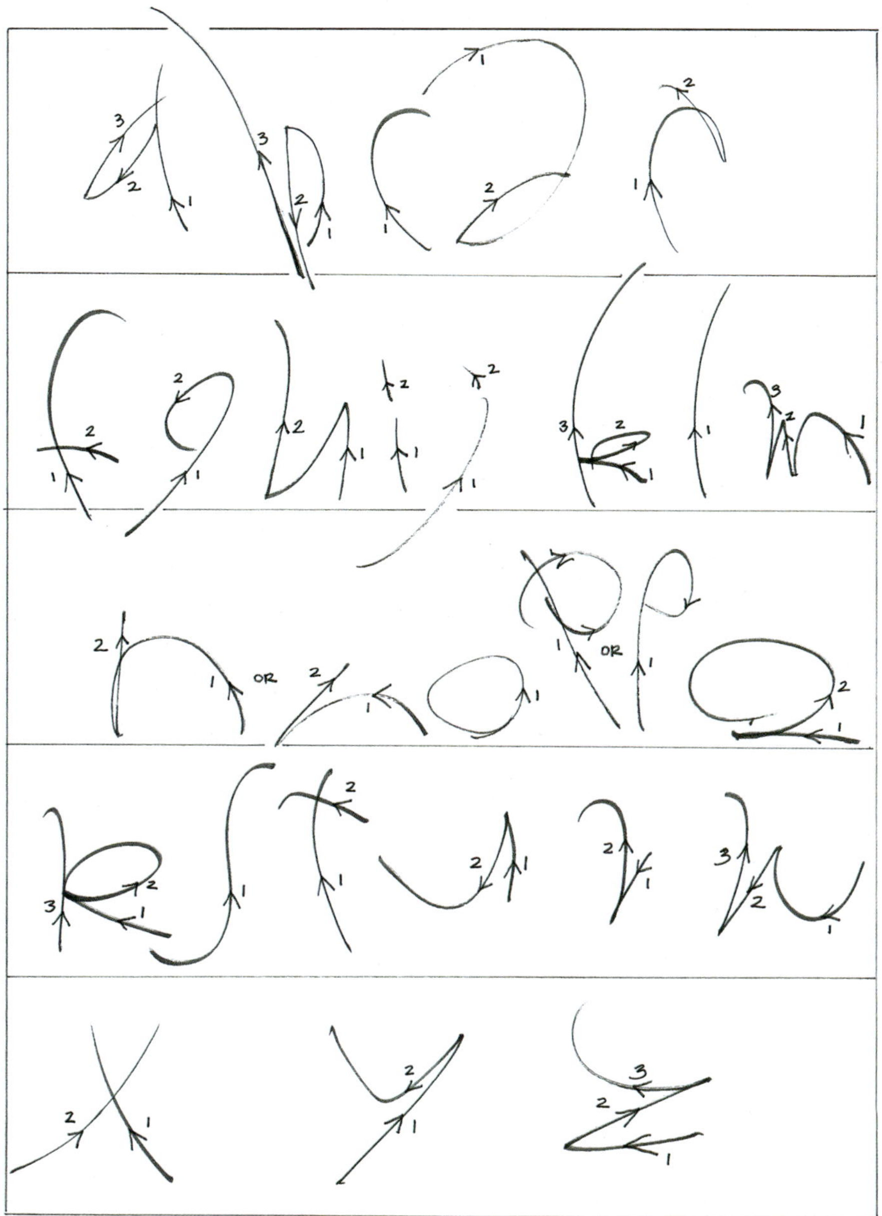

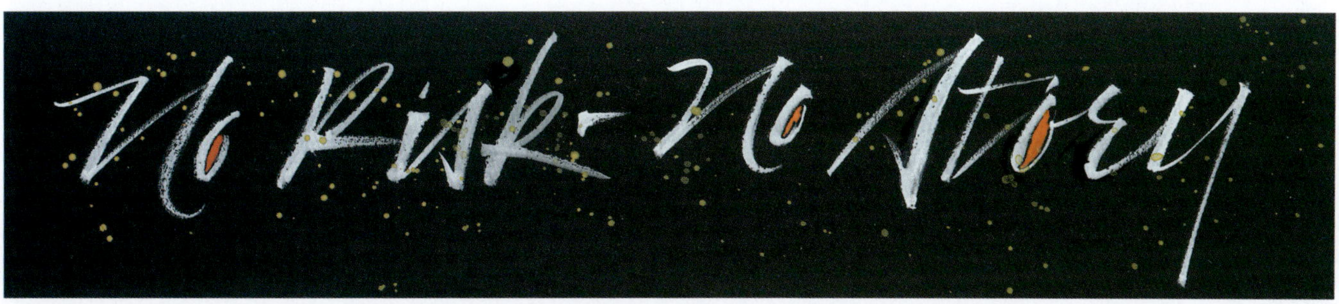

## EXERCISE THREE

In this exercise, you will take your favorite word from Exercise Two and create at least 10 variations of it, applying some quite outlandish letter forms to the word, including the backward stroke variation.

1. Take your practice sheet and divide it into two equal columns and five equal rows aligned to your template. Now add your favorite word to the top left box. In my example, I have used the word *wisdom*.

2. Now apply some quite outlandish letter forms to the word, including the backward stroke variation. This provides the opportunity to learn when to let outlandish rule and when to apply restraint. Sometimes it feels like quite a stretch, but some results will be quite pleasing and worth imitating again. You are training your artistic mind, eye and body to understand what works and what does not work. As with the previous exercises, start with your pencil, then move to your pen.

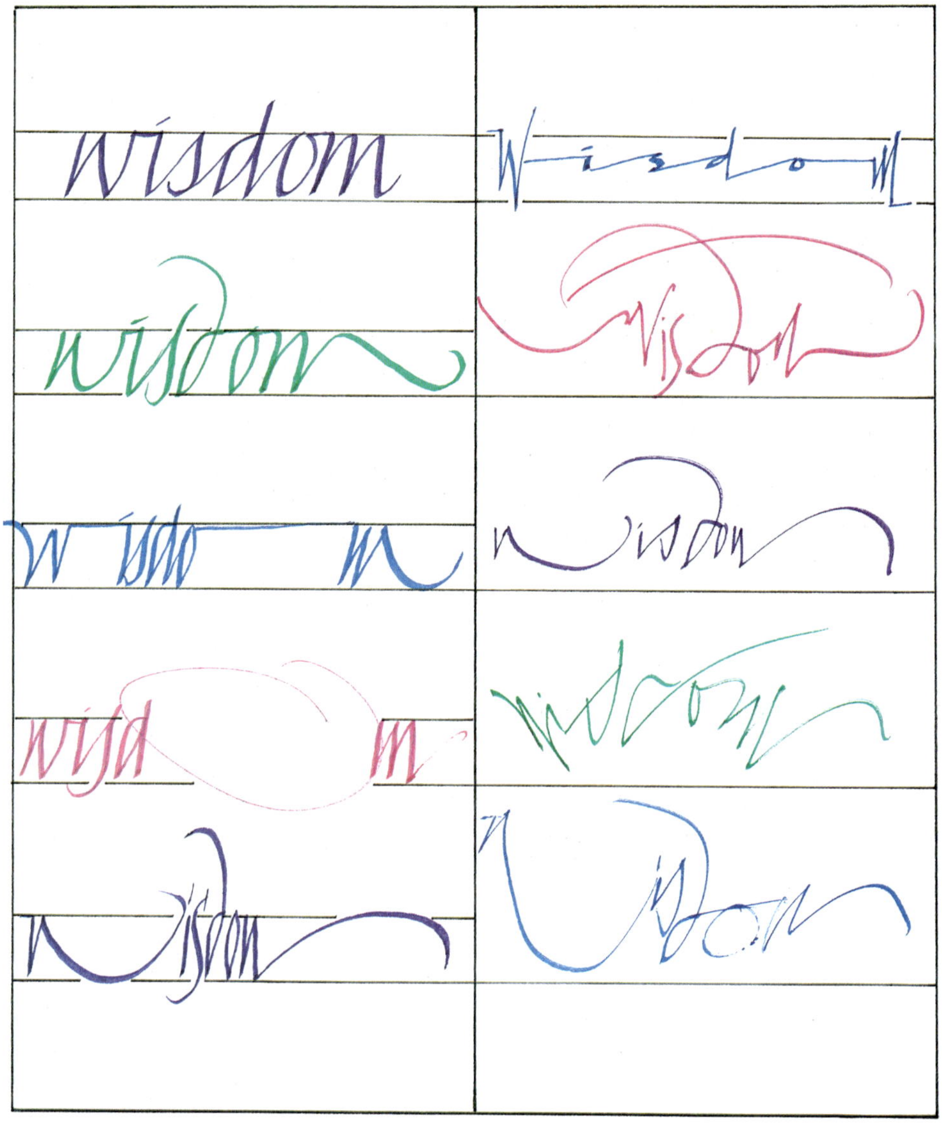


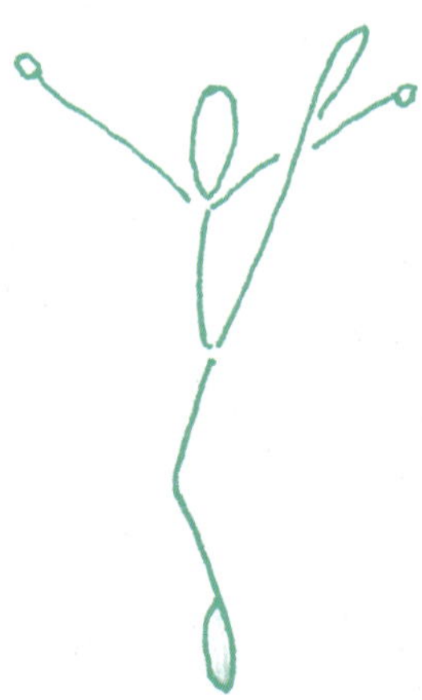

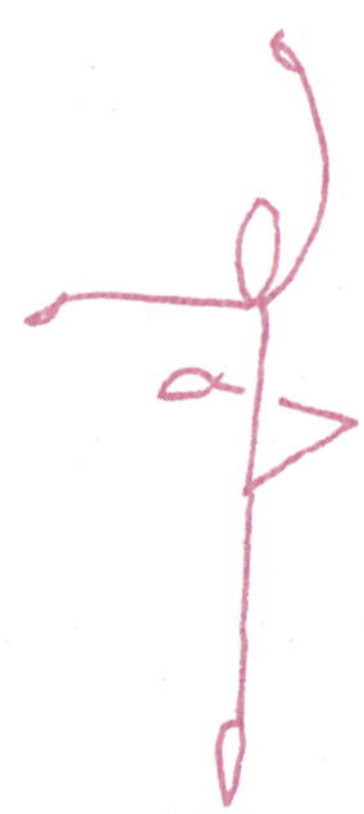

## EXERCISE FOUR

It is fun and rewarding to create letters that step over legibility or words that are challenging to read. However, it is artistically difficult to make the words meld together into a cohesive design. It does not happen as easily as transforming a letter or word, so let's spend a bit of time putting a few words together and then working up to a full sentence.

1. Write a practice page of each of the phrases on the right, trying to place each word well so it creates a pleasing whole. Try different approaches to each word as well as to fitting the words together. Then proceed to incorporate more words. I suggest you do this in pencil first to experiment with placement before proceeding to pen and ink.

The more you practice the four exercises in this chapter, the more you will see improvement and your work becoming more dynamic. I recommend saving your best practice sheets so you can look at your improvement over time. That is always an encouragement!

**The quick brown fox**

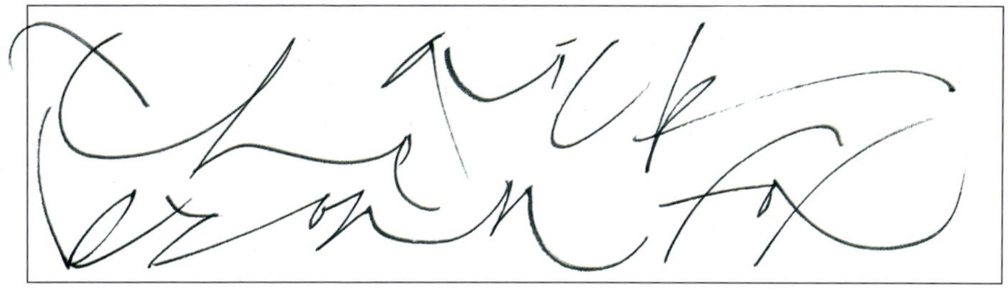

**The quick brown fox jumps**

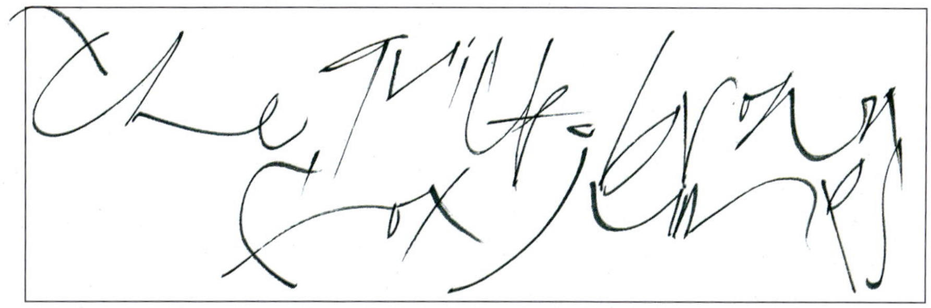

**The quick brown fox jumps over**

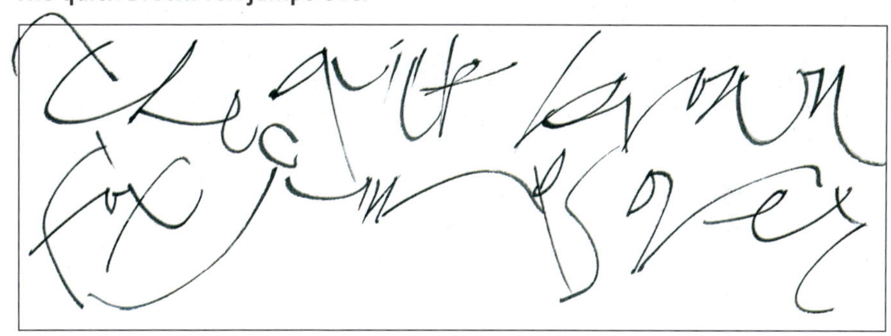

**The quick brown fox jumps over the lazy dog.**

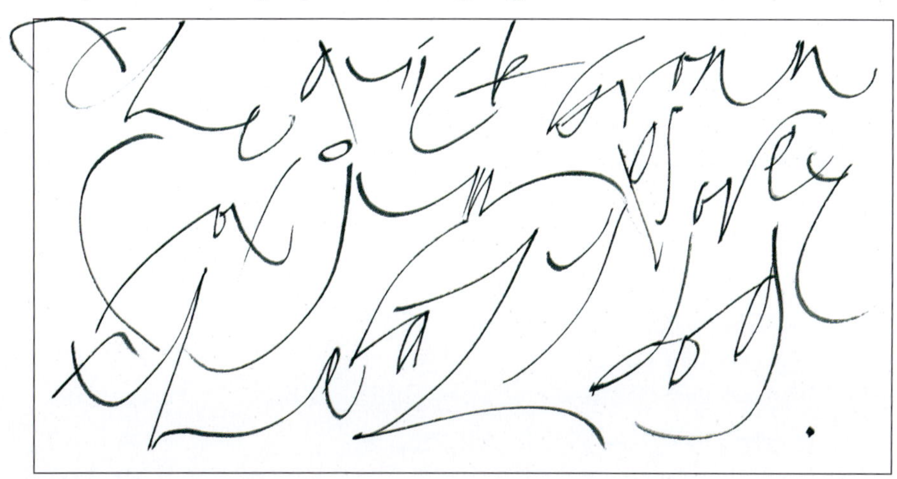

# Project: Updated Accordion Book

In this project you will make an accordion booklet to record your favorite letters from the first exercise you did in this chapter. (This is similar to the one you did in Section One, with a few changes to the materials and process.)

When completed, this booklet will provide you with a gratifying reminder of what you can do, as well as a reference if you need an alternative letter when working on a calligraphy project. I recommend making these kinds of booklets over simply storing your worksheets. It is a very compact and accessible reference, and I find that I use my little booklets quite frequently. Plus, they are much more aesthetically pleasing than a pile of worksheets!

### WHAT YOU'LL NEED:

- **Scissors**
- **Ruler**
- **25" x 40" sheet of Arches Text Wove paper**
- **Pencil or chalk pencil and eraser**
- **Chart of letters from Exercise One (see pages 138–139)**
- **Calligraphy pen with nibs of various sizes**
- **Ink (multiple colors, if you like)**
- **Bone folder**
- **Hot- or cold-pressed watercolor paper**
- **Various inks, such as Sumi ink, walnut ink, tech ink, gold gouache, Dr. Ph. Martin's Bleedproof White, etc.**
- **Access to a sink**
- **White craft glue or glue stick**
- **Ribbon – 9" long**
- **A few heavy books**
- **Bulldog clips (optional, but required if you plan to sew the booklet together)**
- **Thread and needle (optional if you prefer to glue your booklet together)**
- **Plastic sheet, rags, water**

### FOR THE BOOKLET INTERIORS:

1. Cut one 3" x 39" strip of the text wove paper. If you don't have a sheet of paper that long, make sure that your strip of paper's length is divisible by three as you want each page in your accordion booklet to be a 3" square.

2. Lightly draw a horizontal line at the 1 ½" mark of your strip, going from left to right with a pencil. Then mark your paper vertically at 3" intervals across the strip. These vertical marks will be your fold lines as you create the accordion booklet.

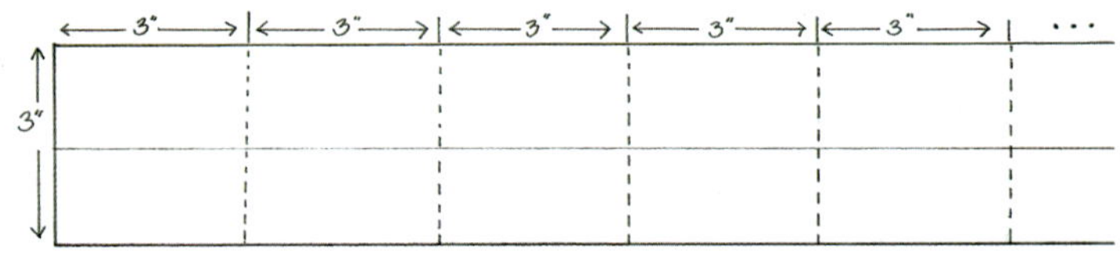


3. With the charts that you created for Exercise One in front of you, study the last two columns for each of the letters and draw in pencil your own version of each letter in the alphabet on your strip of paper using the horizontal middle line as your guideline. Be mindful of spacing as you do not want to leave too much empty space at the end, nor do you want to run out of space. You want to see the entire alphabet running across the strip of paper.

4. Once you have penciled in your letters, take your pen with your preferred nib and your ink and go over each of your letters. You can use multiple colors or a single color — whatever you prefer. Let it dry completely and then erase your horizontal pencil lines, but *not* the fold lines.

5. Now, with a bone folder, fold the strip of paper at the 3" marks, folding the strip back and forth as you move from left to right to the end of the strip. Once folded, lay the strip out flat and carefully erase the fold lines/marks. Now that you have created your booklet interiors, it is time to give them a cover.

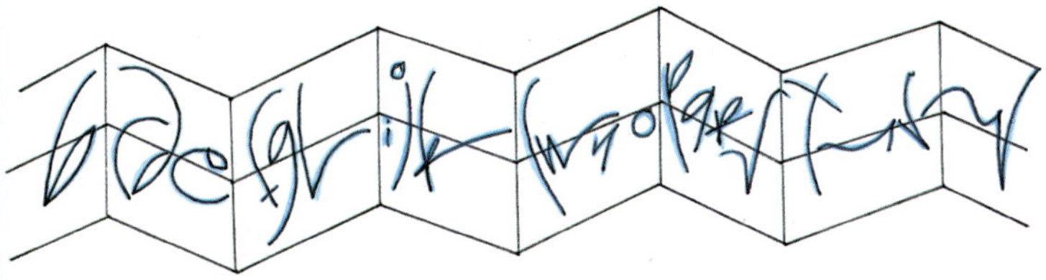

## What's a Bone Folder?

**Bone folders are an essential bookbinding tool for making strong, sharp creases. They are also used for burnishing. Though they used to be made of bone or from antlers, they are now often made from plastic. These tools are typically 4 inches to 6 inches long and approximately 1 inch wide. The surface is polished and the blunt edges of the folder are used to create creases.**

### FOR THE COVER:

6. Cut out a 3 ¼" x 6 ½" piece of watercolor paper. This will be your cover.

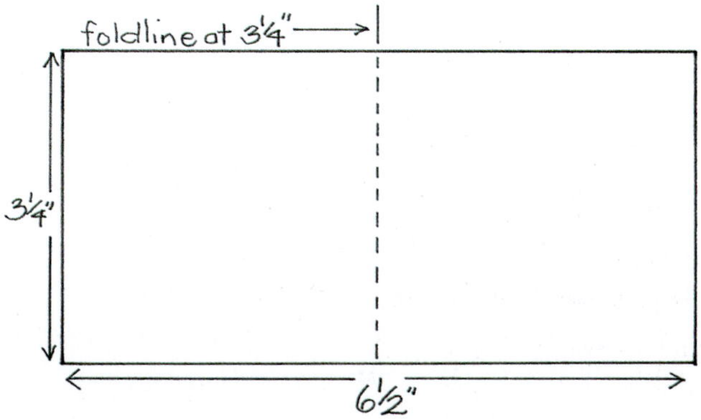


7. To decorate your cover, first lay down a piece of plastic to protect your work area. Take out your various inks and have a jar of water and your rags at the ready. With your largest nib, dip into your Sumi ink and make marks, random letters or a word. Try to have some of the letters or marks run off the page. This adds an element of energy to the piece.

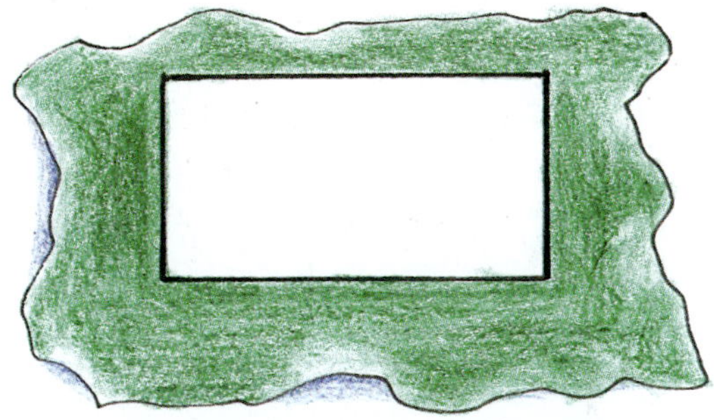

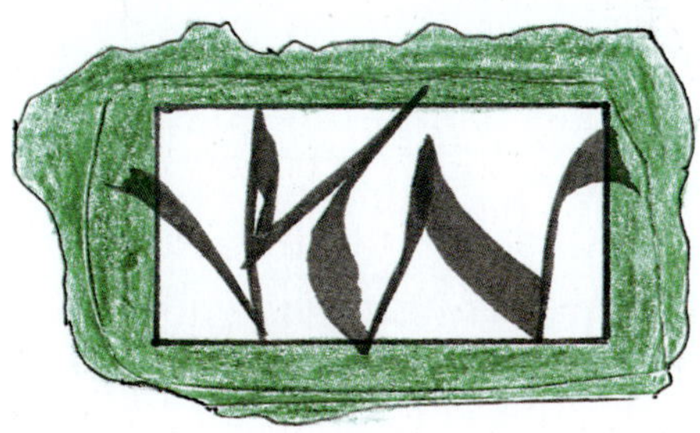

8. Let the ink dry for 30 to 60 seconds. Take your paper to the sink and rinse your page for 2 to 3 seconds under lightly running water (like a trickle), swishing the paper around to let the water play with the ink, but not so much that it causes the ink to run off the page. Work to create a marbling effect, watching for ebbs and flows in the ink as it interacts with the water. Don't leave too much water standing on the page once you have what you are looking for. Set your page aside to let it dry completely.

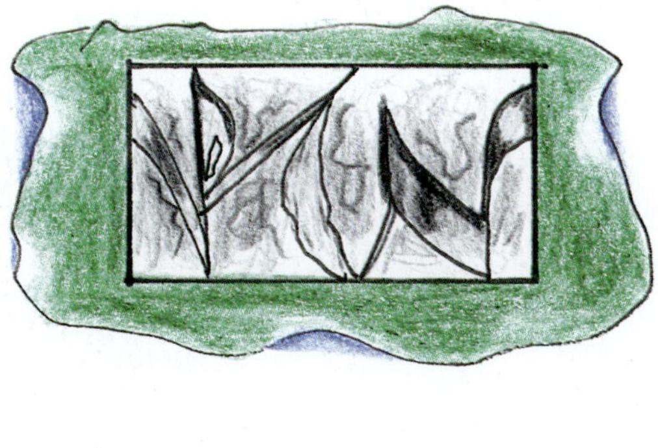

9. Once dry, with a small nib and Dr. Ph. Martin's Bleedproof White ink, write random letters all over the cover. Your letters can be upside down, sideways, backwards — whatever pleases you, and don't worry if you don't include all the letters. (You may want to write this initially in chalk pencil before using ink.) Let dry. Erase the pencil marks, then crease the folds.

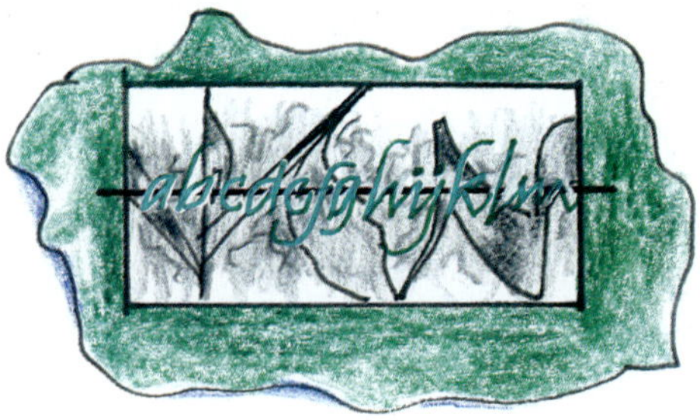

10. On the inside of your cover, measure the halfway point (3¼") and make a mark at the top and bottom. Draw a line from top to bottom. From that line mark 1⁄16" to the left and right of the middle line (top and bottom) and draw lines from top to bottom. This will be the width of the spine on your booklet (i.e., ⅛").

11. Take your ruler and line it up against the left line of your spine. With a bone folder, strongly draw it down along the ruler's edge. This will create a crease in the paper. Repeat this along the right line of your spine. You need to be able to bend these two creases back and forward to create the spine that will accommodate your folded text wove paper.

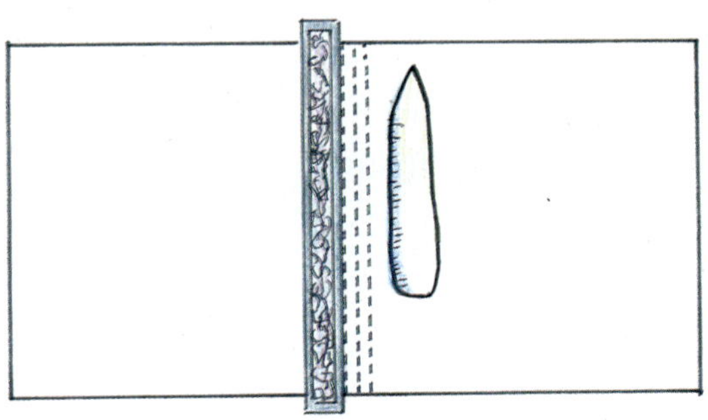

### BINDING THE BOOK:

12. There are two methods you can choose for binding your booklet: gluing or sewing. To glue the cover, first position an inch of the ribbon at the left edge of the cover and add a dot of glue to keep it in position. It will eventually be secured between the first page and the cover. Next brush white glue (or use a glue stick) on the back of the first page of your booklet interiors. Be careful not to use too much glue, otherwise you will have unwanted blobs. Carefully place the crease of your first page along the first fold line of your cover, then flatten the page using the side of your bone folder to smooth out air bubbles and wrinkles. Press the glued section between some heavy books to dry.

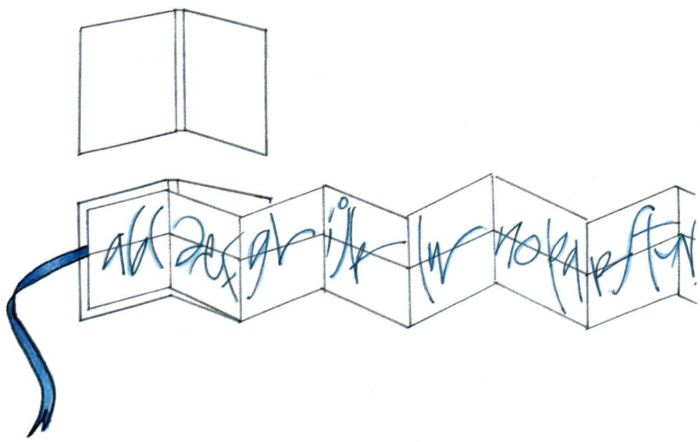

13. Once dried (an hour should be enough), fold the entire strip using your bone folder, making a sharp crease for each fold. You can use the ribbon to keep your booklet closed.

14. To sew the cover, line up the first crease of your alphabet strip along the first fold line of your cover. Position it in place and use bulldog clips to secure it as you sew. Using your needle (or an awl if you have one), pierce a hole in the middle of the crease and at equal distances above and below.

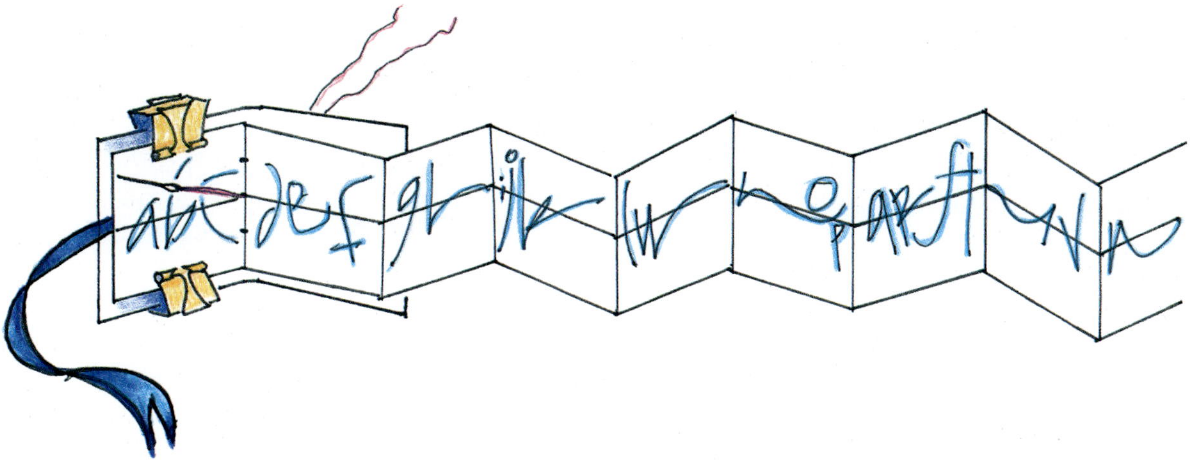

15. Thread your needle and enter the middle hole from the outside of the cover, ensuring you keep a few inches of thread on the outside. Stitch the binding as illustrated, keeping your stitches tight but making sure not to pull the thread all the way through (as you'll have to start over). Once your thread is back outside the cover through the middle hole, tie the thread and the initial tail in a double knot to secure the binding. Trim the thread and tail evenly. Your accordion book is now complete.

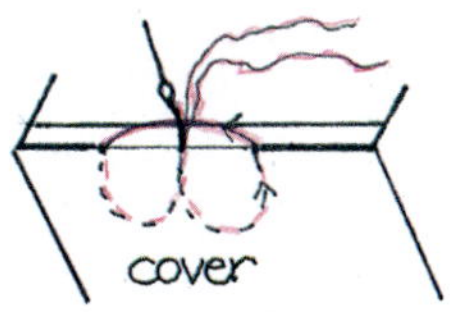


Same as technique on pages 130–131 but in reverse.

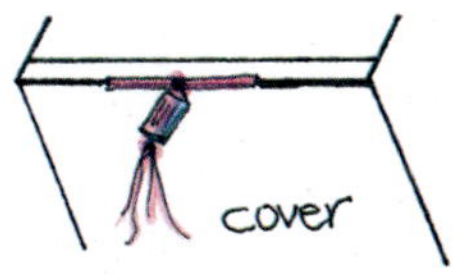


Pulled tightly with a bead attached on the outside.

**GLUED**

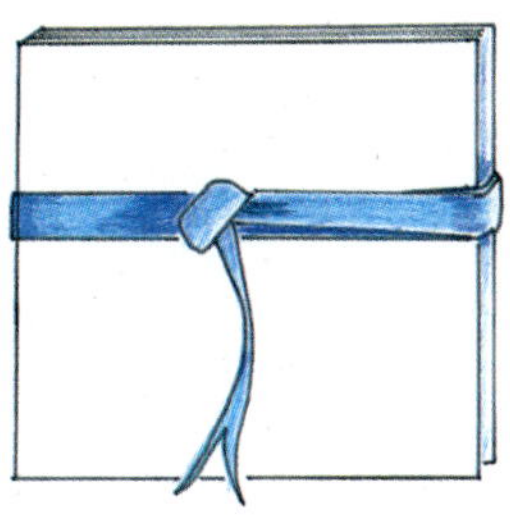

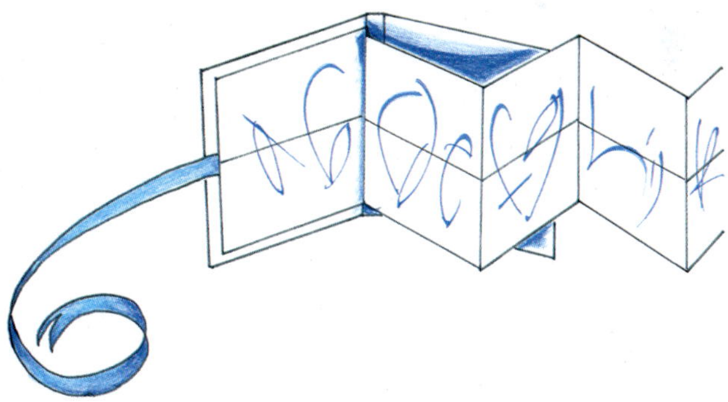

**SEWN**

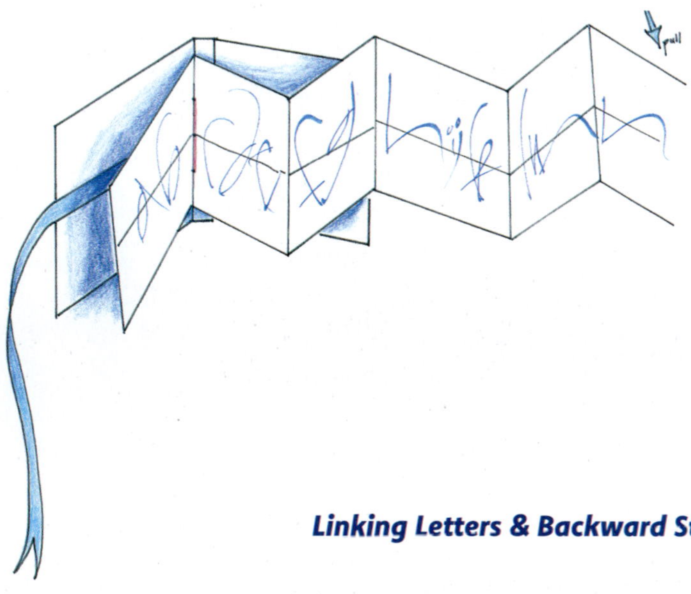


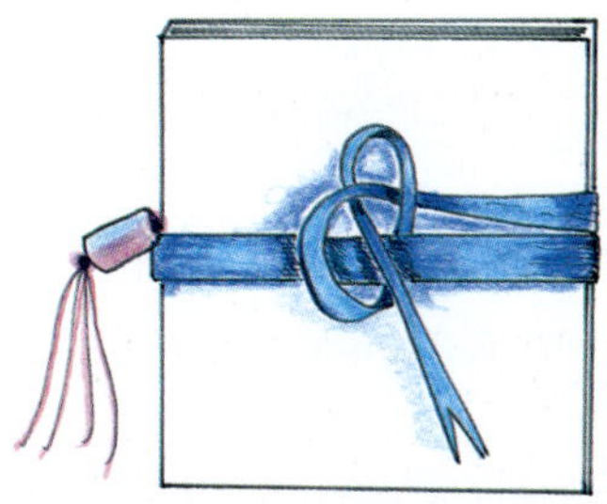

# Chapter 8

# Flying Higher with a Pointed Brush

The term "pointed brush" can be a bit confusing only in that the paintbrush often used to create these letters is commonly known as a "round brush." These brushes require an extraordinary springiness to create the desired effect. This springiness is very important.

There are so many pointed brushes available — with both natural and synthetic bristles — and the quality ranges significantly along that spectrum. To make it simple, I suggest a nylon brush that is pointy. I have tried expensive brushes that calligraphy artists have recommended, yet I find that I often prefer a nylon brush. There are some brushes that are available that have a component that can hold paint, making it as convenient as a marker but much sharper.

Let's get to know this new tool. The pointed brush is certainly a favorite of mine because of the shapes and forms you can create with it. It is also great in that it does not snag on paper. It is highly flexible, both literally and figuratively, as it can be used on a variety of surfaces that a metal nib might struggle on.

In this chapter, we will start with basic shapes and then delve right into the letters — both lowercase and capitals. You will put words together, play with and alter those letters, and then use these letters in another project.

### Speaking of Markers ...

**I will say that I love using my set of Staedtler pointed brush markers. My marker of choice is the Mars Graphic 3000 Duo. If you find another brand that suits you well for this chapter, that's great, too. The only drawback with these markers is that they run out of ink after a while and must be thrown away. But they keep their form right to the end. These markers are very good tools, nonetheless, and I have used them to produce final work published by various card companies. When they are new, they are a delight to work with and suit my quick and energetic designs. I also like working with a Pentel Arts Color Brush. It comes with a cartridge and has a nylon brush that I love to use.**

# The Feel of the Brush or Marker

I hold the pointed brush (or marker) as I would a pencil. It is not necessary to hold it this way, and other calligraphy artists (such as those in Japan and China, to mention just a few places) hold the brush delicately by the end, which offers far less control and gives a very different result. I suggest you try this technique and see what designs you can achieve. However, for our purposes, in this chapter we will hold it against the paper like a pencil. Make a few squiggles to get a feel for how the brush yields against the paper.

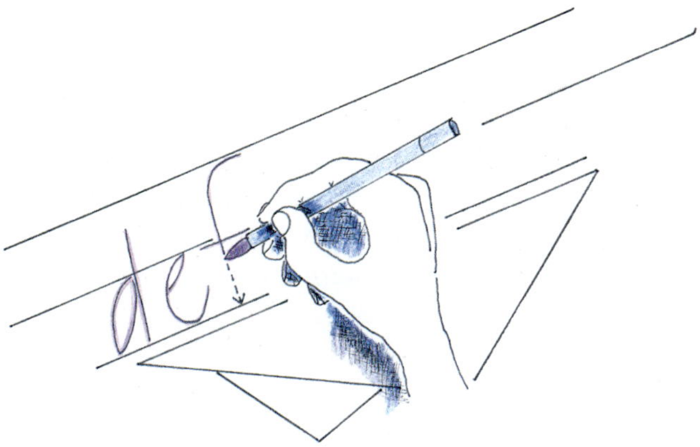

The pointed brush does not follow the rules of traditional Italic, in that there is no need to measure for your X-height and you do not need to line your paper as you did in earlier sections. Brush letter strokes are not confined to the same rules.

However, for your practice, take a blank sheet of paper and draw horizontal lines approximately 1 inch apart from the top of the page to the bottom, covering the entire page so that you have a basic guideline. Go over these lines with a black fine-liner marker so they can be seen through your practice paper (which you will lay on top of this template). With your work area ready — writing surface on a slant, a few pages under your practice sheet for a cushion and a protective sheet over your practice sheet — let's start.

Some important strokes to become familiar with are just flicks with your brush. As you practice the following four strokes, aim for even spacing as you work on training your eyes. Do a full row of each stroke.

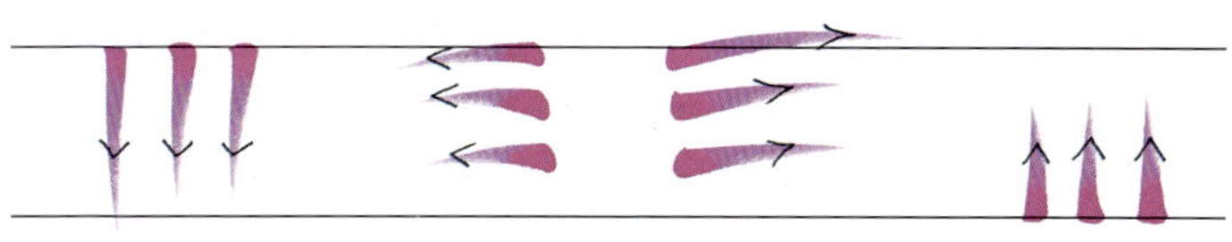

As you move forward with the pointed brush, it is important to understand that the contrast in the weight of the various strokes (the thick and thin lines) is what makes this style of calligraphy so alluring.

Next, we move on to circles. Be mindful of keeping a light hand as you make these circles, filling a full row for each example. First to the right. Then to the left. Try full circles and half circles.

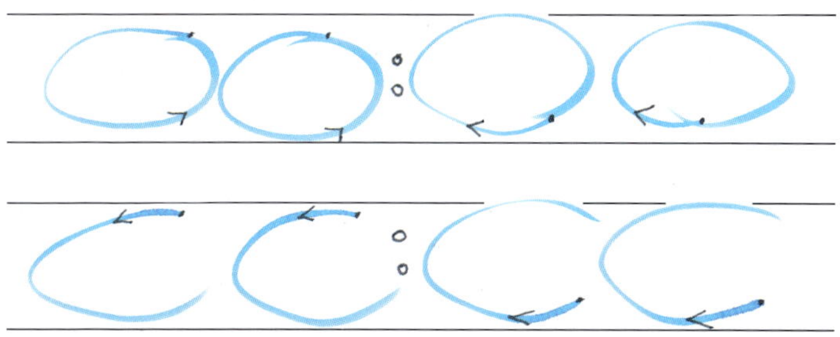

The two examples on the following page depict strong downstrokes followed by an ensuing upstroke (which is, again, more of a flick). As with flourishing, these upward flicks go up and either inward or outward. With this style of calligraphy, the upstrokes are always finer than the downstrokes, and the brush is held in a more upright position to create these upstrokes.

For the first example, start with a heavy downstroke. At the base you lift your brush so that just the tip is touching the paper and then finish with a light flick up and slightly in. Try up and slightly out, too, if you like — again making sure to lift your brush into a more upright position as you create the fine-line flick upward on the point of the brush.

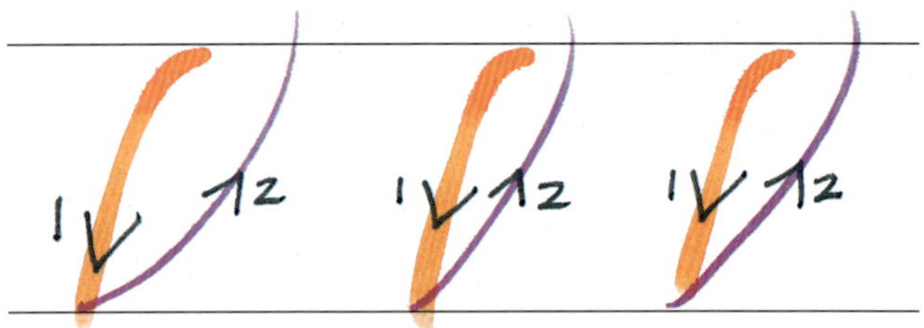

The second example illustrates a strong downstroke, followed by a light flick on the tip of the brush as you soar up and off to the right.

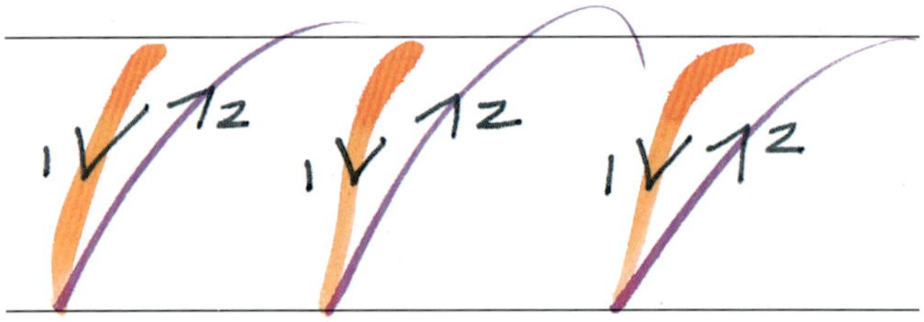

Another exercise to try is illustrated below. This consists of a strong stroke down, followed by a thin-line scoop (again, the brush is lifted to its tip before creating the fine line), then another strong downstroke. Thick, thin, thick. You are working to create contrast. The tip of your brush can touch the top of the downstroke, but it's not necessary. They can touch or not touch. The goal is contrast.

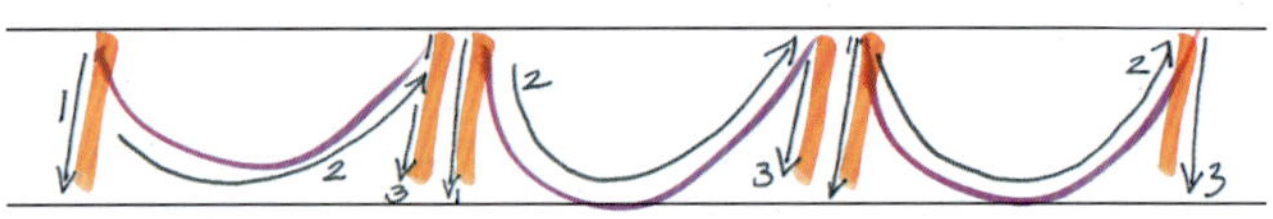

A final exercise (illustrated below) requires a strong downstroke from left to right. Then lift the brush to its tip, flick up to the left on the tip and add a final curve to the right to finish. As you practice, work on finding different endings to this curve.

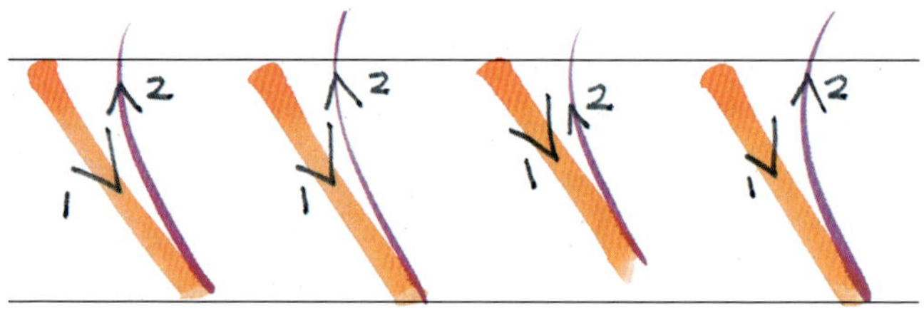

Unlike traditional Italic letters, my approach with pointed brush letters is to use as few strokes as possible to get the idea of the letter across. This differs from other calligraphy artists, and especially those who call their style "modern calligraphy." The following illustrates the difference, depicting versions of a "modern" *b* (first two images), a more traditional Italic *b* but with a pointed brush (center image), and my versions of the letter *b* with a more gestural, minimalist approach (final two images).

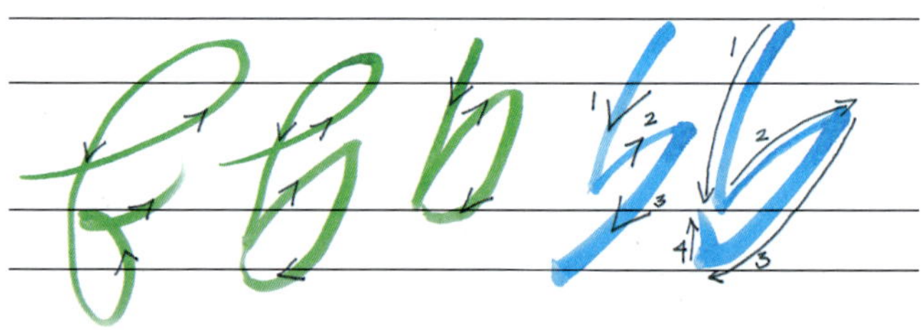

In the following pages we will explore the letter forms of the alphabet using the techniques we just learned, with an emphasis on contrasting thick and thin strokes.

# *Creating the Lowercase Alphabet with a Pointed Brush*

Our foray into the pointed brush alphabet will examine letter groups that use similar strokes. Because I use fewer strokes to create my letters when using a pointed brush, there will be more letters in certain letter family groups.

The lowercase letter *a* illustrates why some letters will have fewer strokes with a pointed brush.

For example, with a calligraphy pen, the Italic letter *a* takes four strokes. With the pointed brush, however, it takes three.

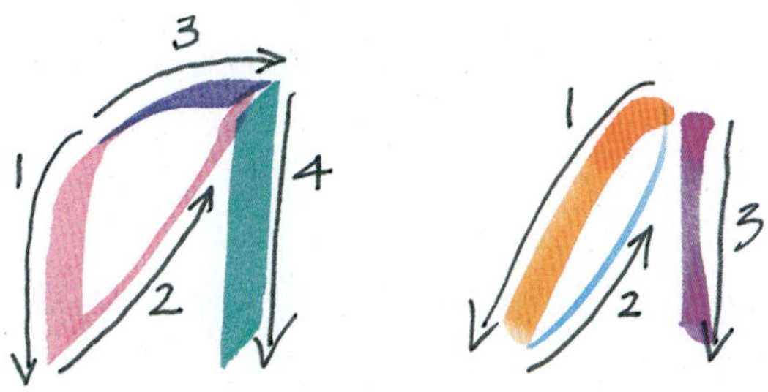

Before you begin working with these letters, take some time to line several practice pages so you will have a guideline for your calligraphy as you learn the mechanics of the pointed brush. I suggest you line your page at ½-inch, 1-inch and ½-inch intervals horizontally.

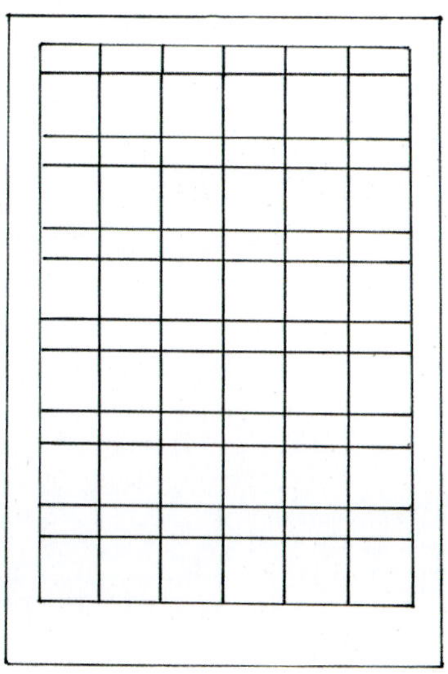

### THE VERTICAL FAMILY — I, J, L, T, F

The first group of letters is the simplest group and consists of *i*, *j*, *l*, *t* and *f*. These are very straightforward.

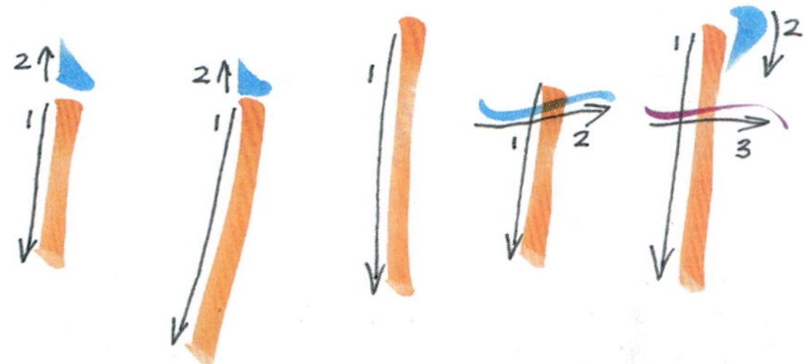

We will start with the *i*. This consists of a strong downstroke that fits between the waistline and baseline and then a small, thin flick at the top for the dot of the *i*.

The *j* starts the same as the *i*, only it extends down below the baseline and curves slightly to the left. Keep the whole downstroke strong. You can add a slight flick up at the end of the stroke if you want. Then — as with the *i* — dot the *j* with a small flick above the letter.

The next letter in this group is the *l*, which is simply a single strong downstroke that starts above the waistline and finishes at the baseline. Once again, take time to practice.

The *t* starts above the waistline and is a strong downstroke that finishes at the baseline. The crossbar is a light (thin) crossbar starting just above the waistline.

The final letter in this group is the *f*, which starts a bit to the right and comes down as a strong stroke to the baseline. You then finish it off by combining a little downstroke flick at the top of the initial downstroke (similar to what you will use to finish off the *r*), and then you add a light crossbar just above the waistline. Once again, take time to practice.

## THE DIAGONAL FAMILY — V, X, K, W, Z

The next group of letters I refer to as the diagonal letters: *v*, *x*, *k*, *w* and *z*. These letters have fewer changes in technique than some of the other letters, but there are some. Let's start with the *v*, *x* and *k*.

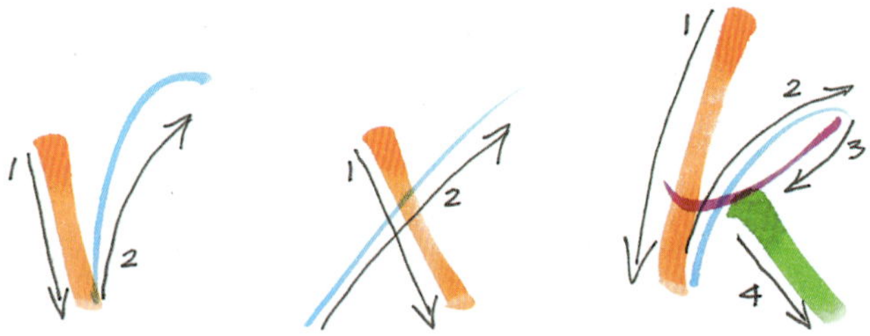


The *v* starts with a strong diagonal downstroke to the right. This is then followed by a light upward stroke to the right that curves away from the letter. The end of this stroke should rise higher than the downstroke as it tapers.

The *x* is a simple strong diagonal downstroke to the right followed by a thin, light upstroke to the right.

For the *k*, you first make a strong downstroke from the ascender line to the baseline. Then you make a light, slightly curved stroke up to the right, ensuring the stroke ends lower than the top of the initial downstroke. The third stroke is a light curving diagonal that moves from the tip of the second stroke down to the lower part of the first stroke. Finish with a strong diagonal stroke down and right, with the end dipping below the end of the initial downstroke.

The *w* can have many variations, but we will focus on one. It starts with a strong, slightly angled diagonal downstroke to the right. This is then followed by a light, thinly angled downstroke (i.e., tight to the first downstroke). Then you finish with a wide scoop that is also done with the tip of the brush as a thin line. Play with this letter, trying variations until you find one you like. (See examples at the bottom of the page.)

This brings us to the final letter ... in both senses. The *z* is a fun letter. It consists of a strong horizontal stroke to the right followed by a thin, lightly diagonal downstroke to the left that extends past the beginning point of the top stroke that is then followed by another strong stroke to the right that should parallel the top stroke but extend past it. The final stroke is a horizontal stroke that is slightly above the midpoint and starts to the left and crosses the diagonal downstroke. As you can see, this letter can be played with significantly and there are no hard and fast rules about these strokes.

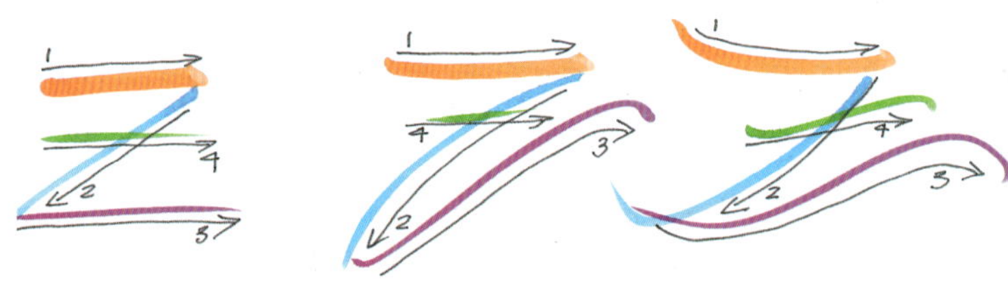

Practice lines of these letters — individually and as a group — playing with them and gaining an appreciation for the creative fun you can have with them.

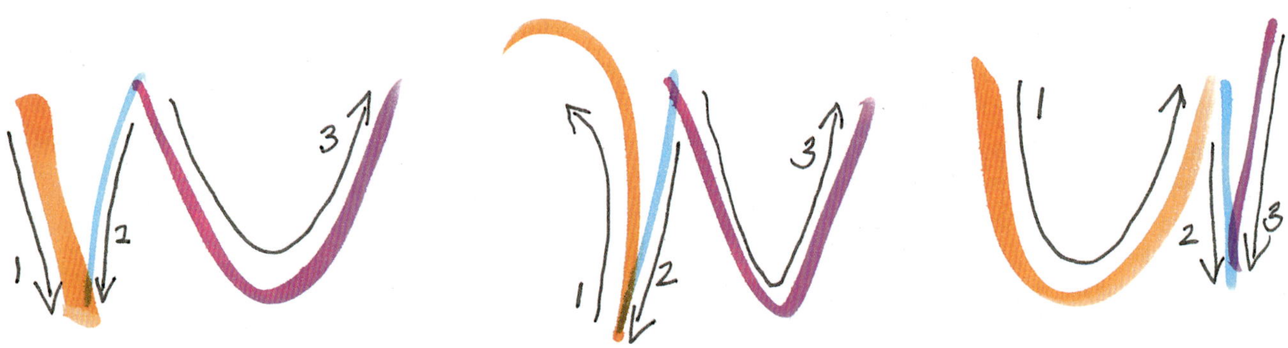

## THE "A" FAMILY — A, D, G, Q

The "a" family consists of the following letters: *a*, *d*, *g* and *q*. In traditional Italic, each of these letters would have a cap. However, using the pointed brush, I bend the downstroke ever so slightly to accommodate two strokes, thereby incorporating the cap in this stroke.

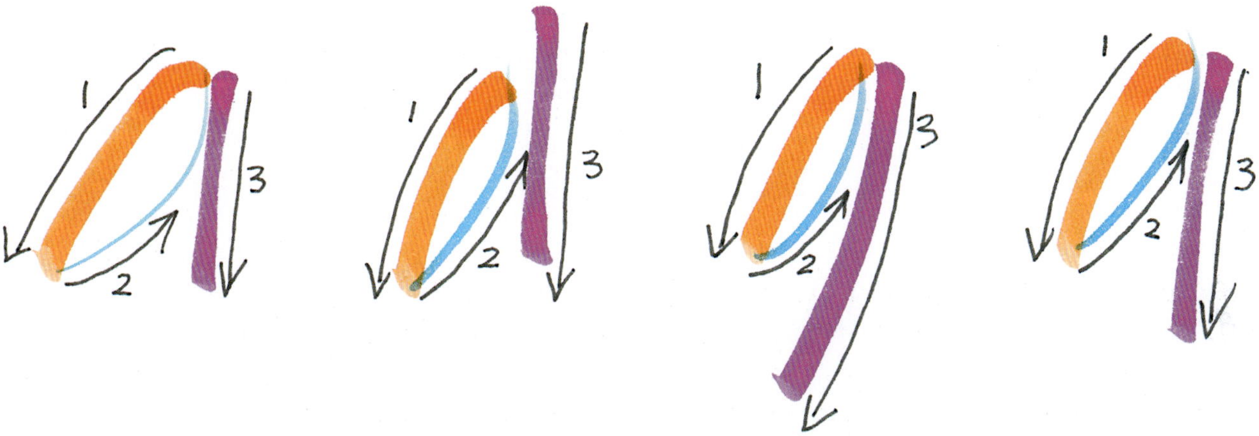


Let's start with the *a*. My first downstroke is a heavy combination that includes the cap (stroke 3 with the pen). The second stroke is a light stroke (flick) upward and in with the brush adjusted to a more upright position so that you are using only the tip. The last stroke is another heavy downstroke.

Create a row of the letter *a* in order to get a feel for the difference between that strong downstroke and the lighter upstroke, which is more akin to a light flick. As you practice, notice the spacing between each letter in the row. Work for consistency.

The remaining letters in this family (i.e., *d*, *g* and *q*) are similar to the *a*, with the cap included in the first downstroke. Note that letters that have a tail, such as the *g*, do not require an extra stroke. I simply direct the downstroke to incorporate the tail. If after viewing your downstroke you feel there is not enough of a tail, you can always add a small flick to create the desired effect.

Complete one or two rows for each of the remaining letters in this family. Then practice a few rows of these letters grouped together like a word, with a space between each grouping. As you practice, notice your spacing between letters and between groups of letters.

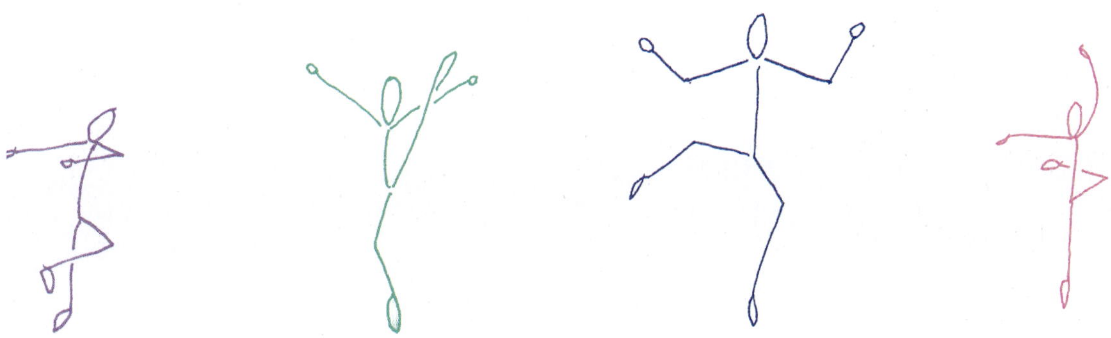

## THE "B" FAMILY — B, P, R

The "b" family of letters consists of *b*, *p* and *r*. This group of letters starts with a strong downstroke, followed by a light flick up and outward with the tip of the brush and a final strong stroke down aiming to close the space. You can see this in each of these letters.

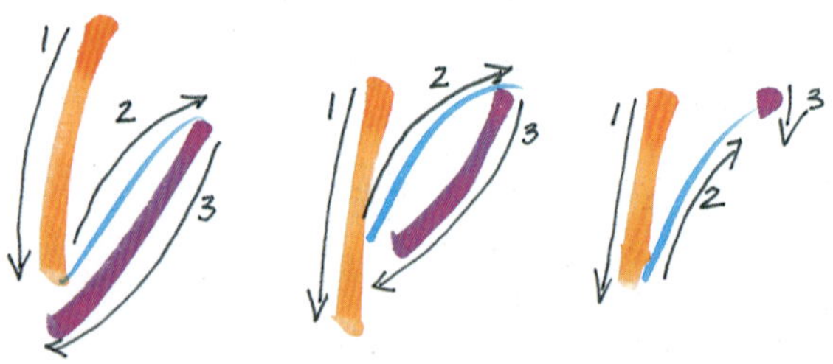

Let's take *b* as an example: a heavy, light, heavy contrast, with the last stroke aimed to close off the letter. In the case of the letter *b*, the final stroke must come down further than the end of the first stroke. It is important to note that with the pointed brush each letter may vary from one another. It is not as controlled as with the pen, allowing for more freedom of expression.

After you have practiced a few lines of the *b* you will begin to feel more comfortable and familiar with its mechanics, which are similar to those used for *p* and *r*.

The *p* begins with a strong downstroke followed by a light flick up that curves outward. It is then finished by a second strong angular downstroke with the aim (as with the *b*) to close the space out. I emphasize angularity with respect to this last downstroke, as you want to avoid looping letters with this particular style.

The *r* is relatively simple. It consists of one strong downstroke, a light upward stroke that proceeds higher than the top of the downstroke as it curves out to the right, and a downstroke flick at the end to anchor the letter. This downstroke should have a slight curve to the left.

After you have practiced a few lines of the letters in this family, letter a few more lines of the letters grouped together with space between each group. Notice your spacing.

## THE "H" FAMILY — H, M, N, U, Y

Comprised of *h*, *m*, *n*, *u* and *y*, this group of letters follows the thick, thin, thick pattern. You start with a strong downstroke. Then you make a light upstroke with the tip of the brush. Then another strong downstroke.

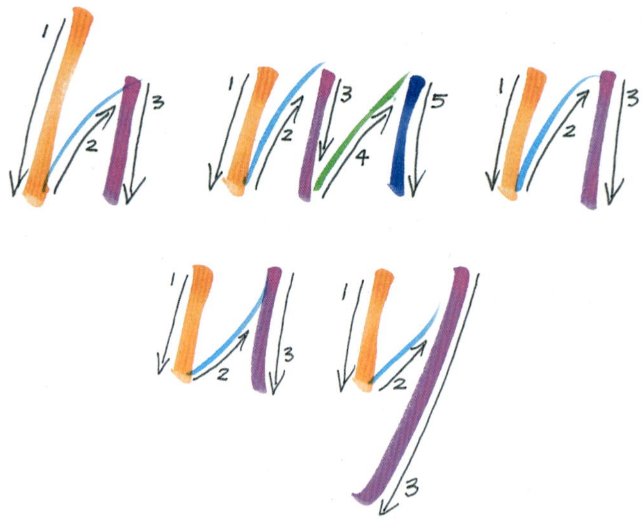

The upstrokes for the *h*, *m* and *n* letters curve ever so slightly as they arc up to the point where you will begin the ensuing downstroke.

The upstroke for the *u* and *y* curve slightly in a scoop (i.e., opposite to the upstrokes in the other letters in this family). The final downstroke for the *y* can either aim ever so slightly to the left or simply finish straight down. There is not a right or wrong with this and your design will dictate. As with the other letters, practice lines of each letter and of the letters grouped together.

## OVAL LETTERS — O, C, E

This group of letters is comprised of *o*, *c* and *e*. Each of these letters starts out the same. Using the side of the brush — held like a pencil — create the beginning of the oval with a thick, rounded downstroke. As you reach the bottom, come up onto the tip of the brush and continue to complete the oval form, as dictated by the letter.

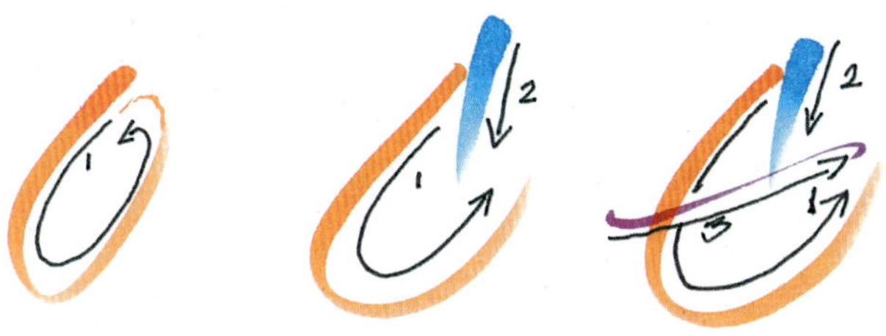


For the *o*, you will use only one oval stroke. The final fine line tip does not need to meet up with the top of the beginning of the stroke. It is fine to leave a small gap.

The first stroke of the *c* should end with the thin upstroke. The end of this part of the stroke can end at various heights as you play with this letter. The letter is then finished with a small downward flick to the left at the top of the *c*.

The *e* follows the same form as the *c* but is finished differently. After you have created the partial oval form and added the flick at the top (as you did with the *c*), you complete the letter with a final thin stroke from left to right that crosses the main trunk of the letter as well as the small downward flick, extending past the end of the letter.

As with the prior groups of letters, practice several lines of each, ending with a few lines of the letters grouped together. As you become more confident with the mechanics you will doubtless explore variations of these strokes. The pointed brush really is a fun tool to play with!

## AND NOW THE "S"

The *s* is handled separately as it is a bit more of an anomaly. It has similar features to other letters, but it is also different from most other letters in that it is written with only one stroke.

It starts out as an angled heavy stroke down to the left. When this stroke reaches the point of the curve, it moves from left to right like a crossbar, extending the line past the top of the *s*, before once again angling back to the left with a downstroke. This letter is bottom heavy, and it takes practice to soften the sharp edges where the crossbar meets the downstroke portion of the letter. Your hand will eventually adjust to the technique as you work with the brush.

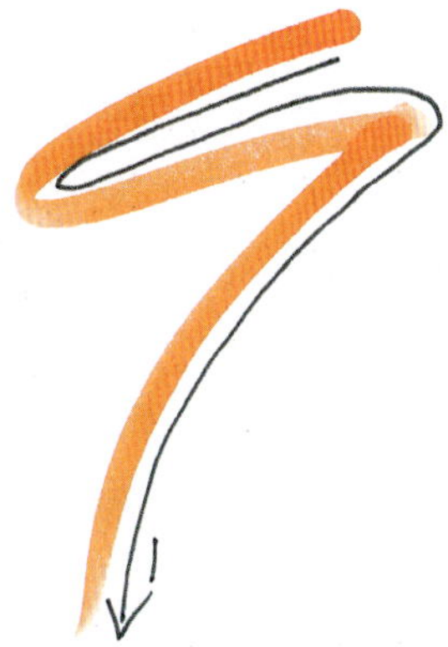


It is a letter that invites experimentation as the more abstract variations below illustrate:

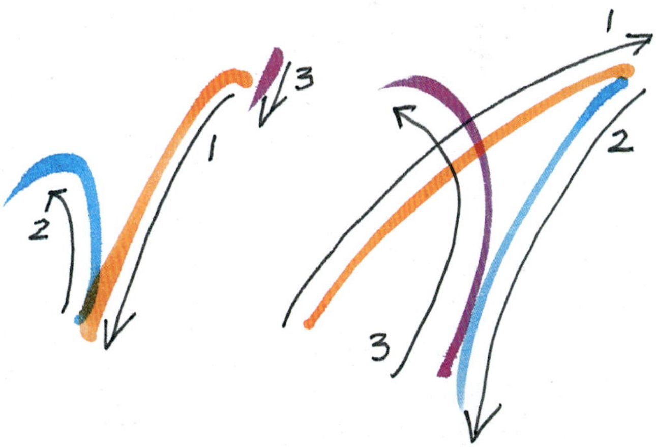


This *s* is shaped more like a cursive *s*.

# Pointed Brush Samplers

The following pages include samplers illustrating the entire alphabet with ductus using the pointed brush (both lowercase and uppercase) as well as punctuation, the ampersand and numbers (see page 158). These will be helpful references as you work with this new tool.

## LOWERCASE POINTED BRUSH ALPHABET

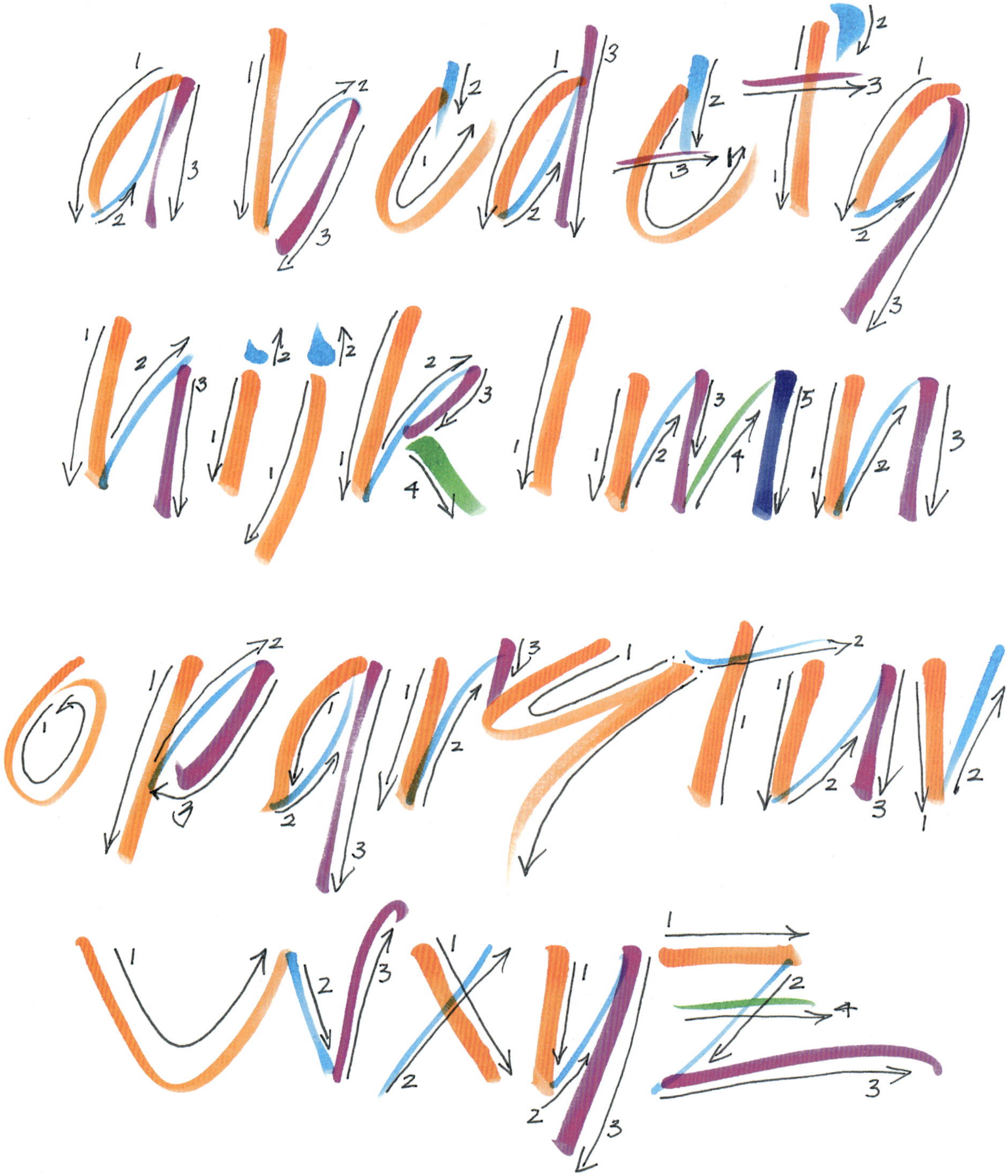

## UPPERCASE POINTED BRUSH ALPHABET

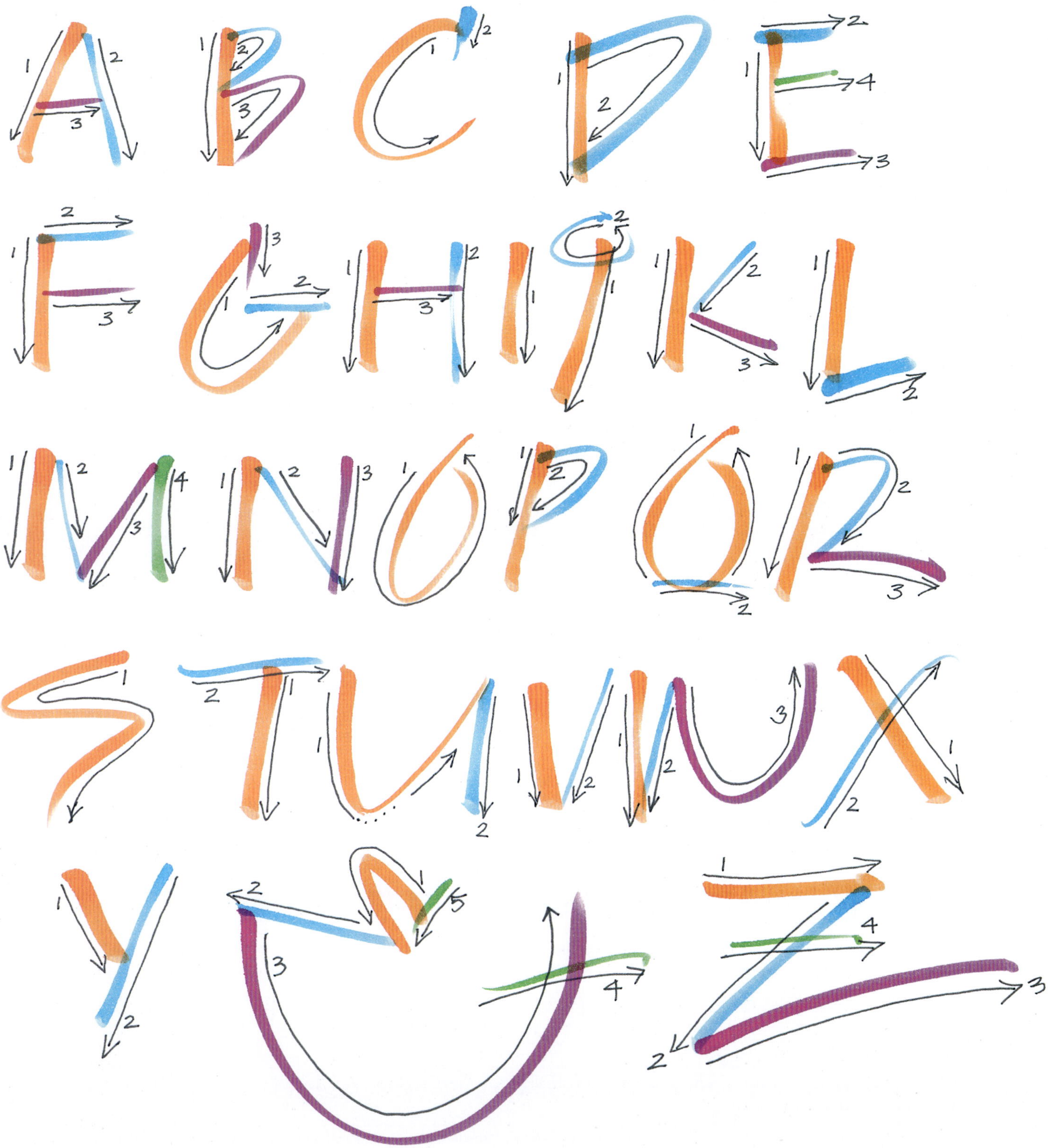

## POINTED BRUSH PUNCTUATION AND NUMBERS

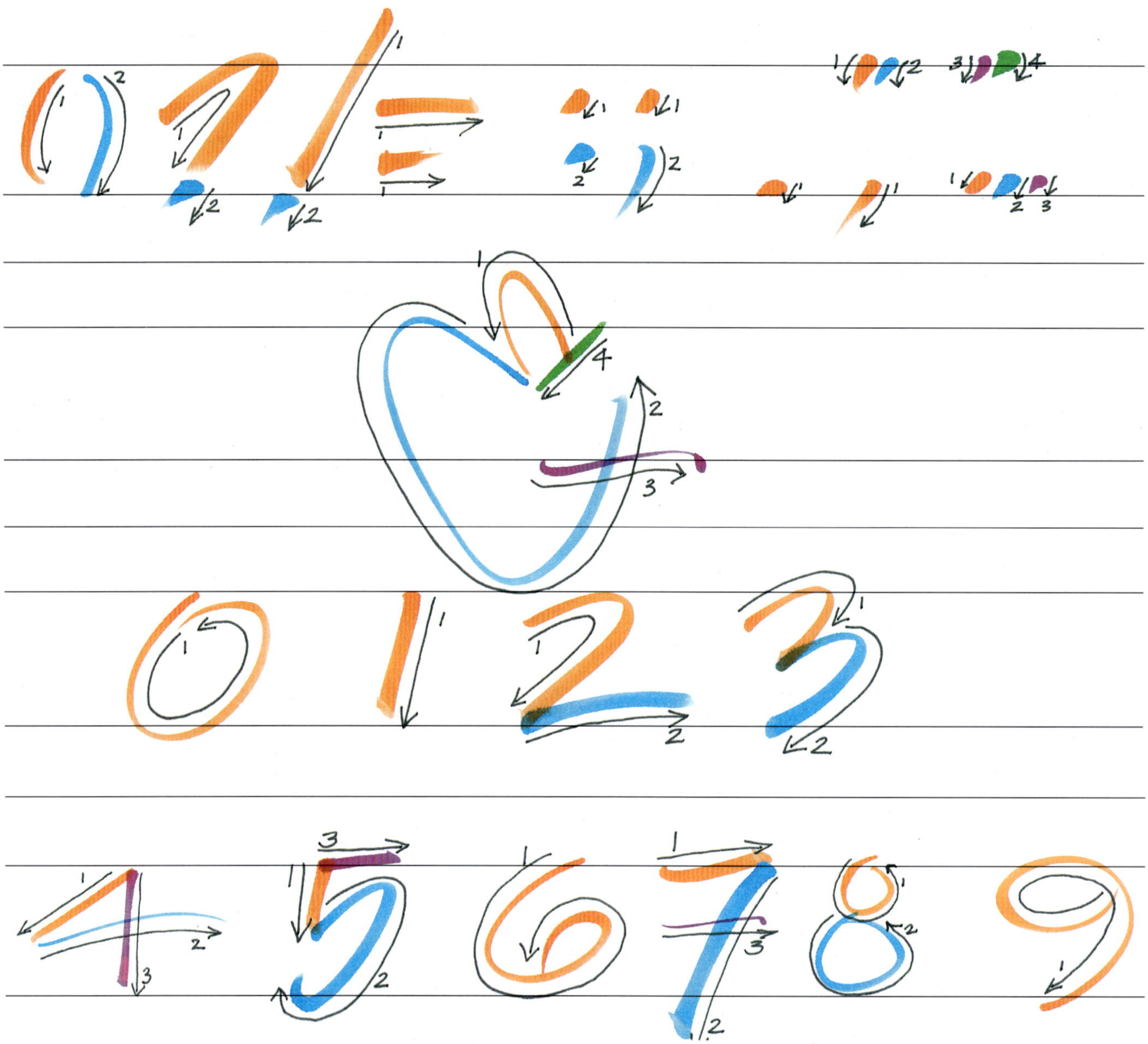

### A Reminder About Ductus and Fluidity

As in Chapter 2, when developing a more fluid ductus was discussed, the same note applies to the use of the pointed brush. The depiction of the ductus in the preceding alphabet samplers and family groups does not capture the full freedom one attains when using the pointed brush. By switching colors to depict each stroke, the momentum and flight of the pointed brush strokes was compromised. This was a conscious choice to depict the strokes that comprise each letter. The ensuing examples show the use of the pointed brush in full flight, where rigid stops have not been applied and a much more fluid and free letter form is the result.

# Using the Pointed Brush with Freedom

Like in Chapter 7, when we explored how you could alter your letter forms using your nib through various linking techniques, the letter forms created using the pointed brush can also be varied considerably, moving toward more abstract forms.

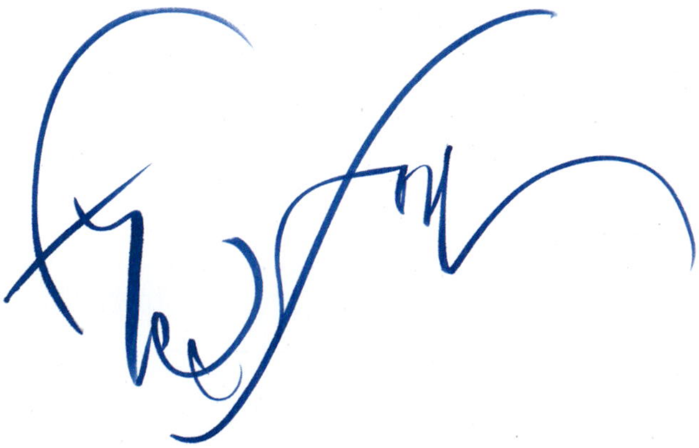

To letter in this way, it is critical to become comfortable with using your pointed brush with more freedom. The following exercises will start you along this path.

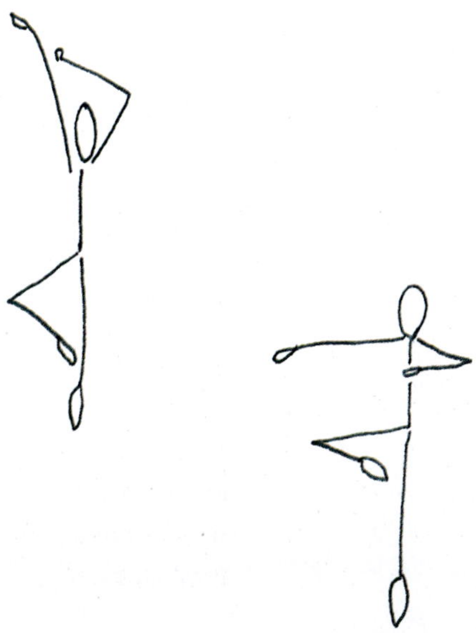

## EXERCISE ONE

### WHAT YOU'LL NEED:

- **Pencil and eraser**
- **Ruler**
- **Black fine-liner marker**
- **Practice sheet (and access to a photocopier)**
- **Pointed brush markers (I use Staedtler Mars Graphic 3000 Duo brush markers)**

Using a practice sheet, create margins and lines in pencil as depicted in the illustration below. Outline the lines with a black fine-liner and erase your pencil lines. Then make five photocopies of this template.

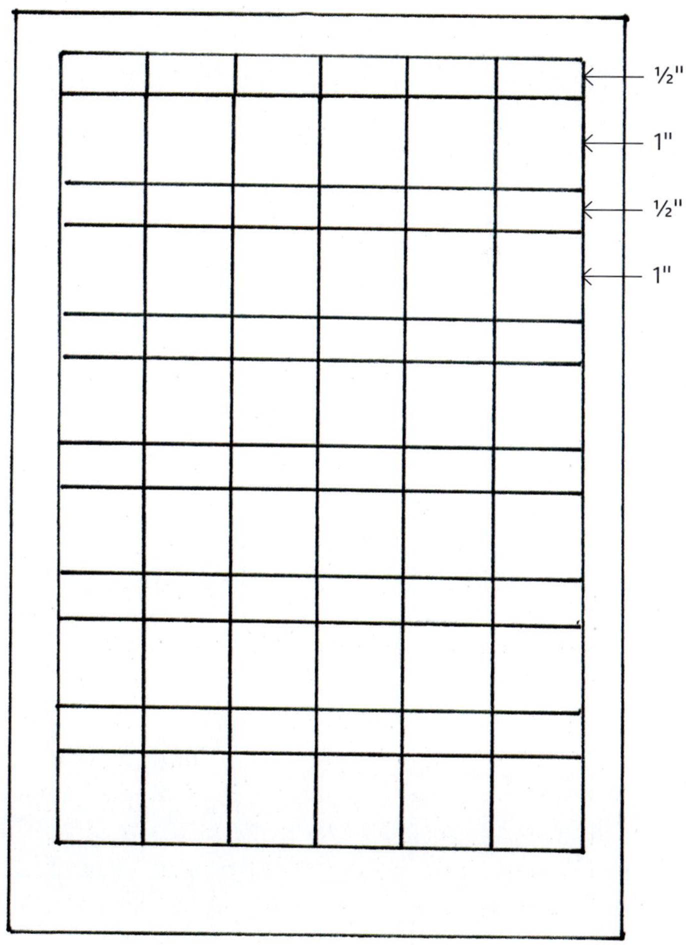

Your template should allow for six rows of letters and six variations of each letter (i.e., six columns). In pencil, starting with the letter *a*, create six different versions of this letter in the first 1-inch row. Note that the ½-inch spaces above and below this row allow for strokes to soar out of bounds (up and down). Think about how you can alter the letter forms as you move across the page, working to incorporate fluidity as you push the boundaries while still retaining a degree of recognizability.

Then proceed to the letter *b* in the next 1-inch row. Once you have finished the first page you can proceed to the next page. Continue starting in pencil as you work your way through the alphabet. If you like, you can stop after penciling each page and letter it with your pointed brush marker. The Staedtler Mars Graphic 3000 Duo brush marker works very well on practice paper.

Now that you have six variations of each letter of the alphabet, you can proceed to Exercise Two.

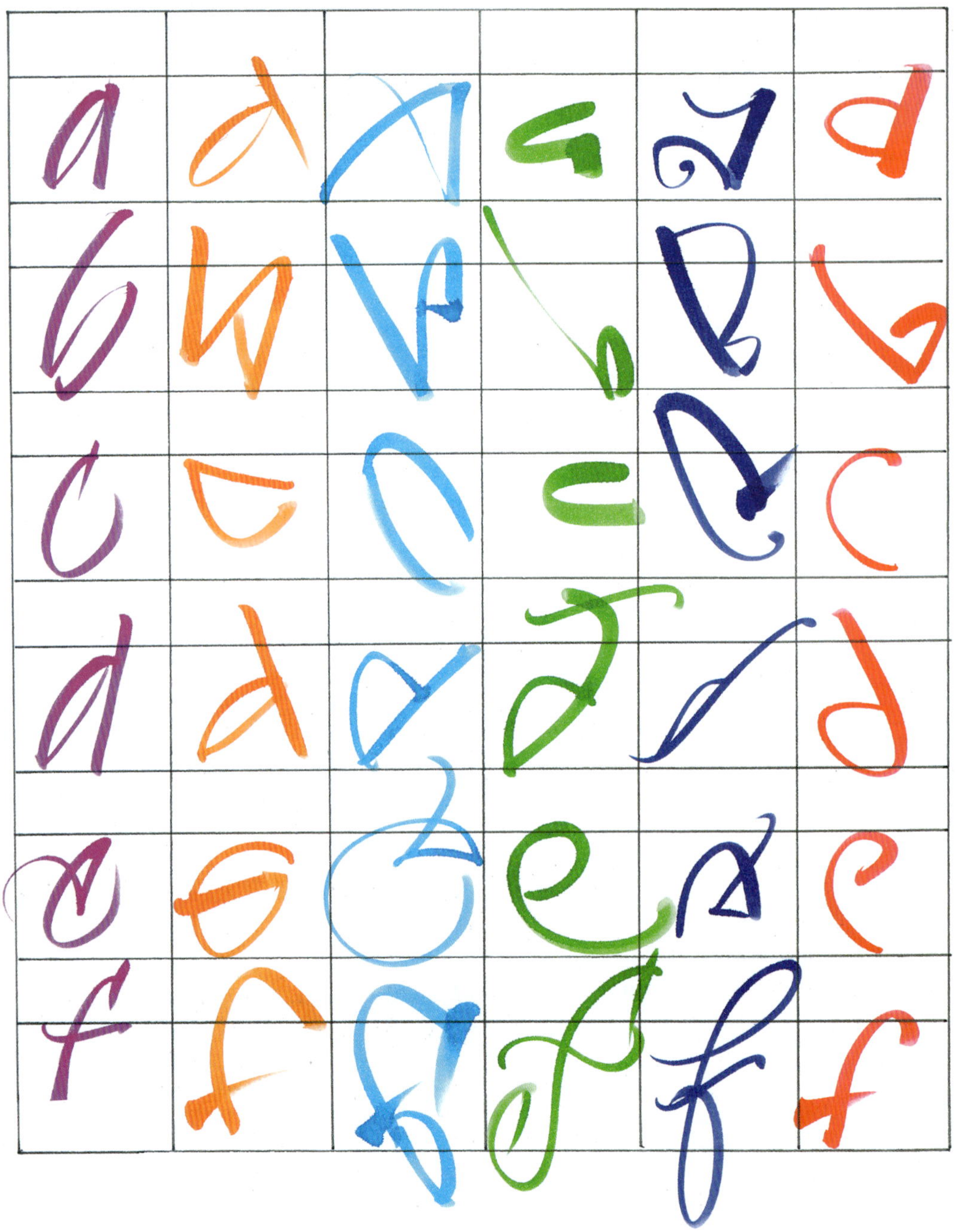

## EXERCISE TWO

For this exercise you will be using the same tools and supplies as the previous exercise.

Take a sheet of practice paper (6 inches by 8 inches will do) and create the following template.

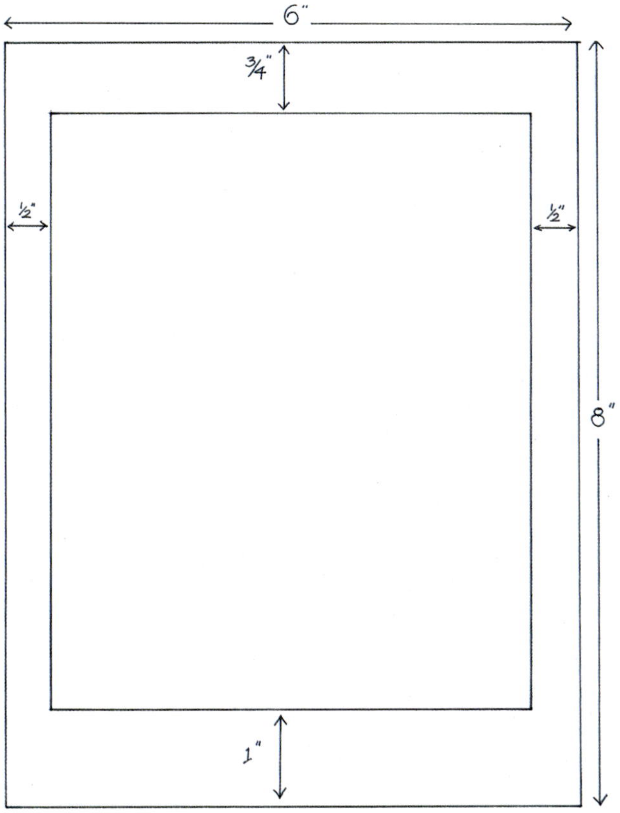


Once you have your template, make 26 copies of it, one template for each letter in the alphabet. These templates will be used for your rough drafts.

Take your first template and, while referring to your chart created in Exercise One, write the letter *a* with your pencil in as many creative ways you can think of (i.e., at least 6). Then proceed to the next letter on the next template, again in pencil. Once you have completed the entire alphabet and are satisfied with your letter forms, layout and spacing, it is time to proceed to letter them with your pointed brush marker. I strongly suggest that you practice a few on a spare sheet of paper because writing with the pointed brush is different than writing with pencil, and a few practice letters will help you get comfortable with the change.

Once you feel warmed up and ready to go, start with an easy letter — or your favorite letter. Or you can simply start with the letter *a* then proceed through the alphabet. Whatever works best for you! As with the example shown below — in this case I chose the letter *m* — push the boundaries, working to make each letter a bit (or a lot) different to the extent that it is recognizable as that letter, but barely. Your goal is a minimum of 6 to 10 variations of each letter with an eye to variety and flow.

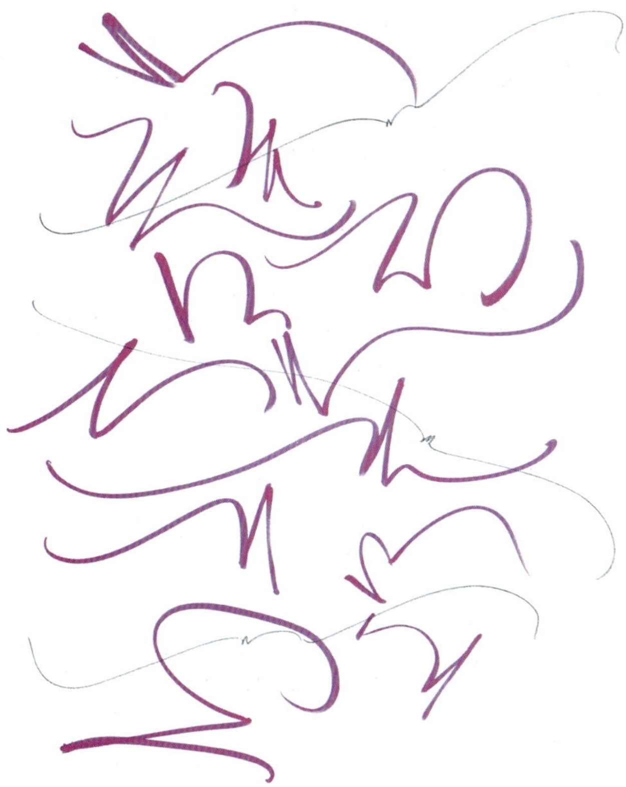

Now that you have lettered the entire alphabet and learned how to alter the letter forms more creatively, you can move on to the final project in Chapter 8.

# Project: Pointed Brush Portfolio

This project will expand on what you did in Exercise Two, resulting in a beautiful collection for you to refer to when creating pointed brush letters. It may take a few days to complete, so be sure to stay patient and enjoy the process.

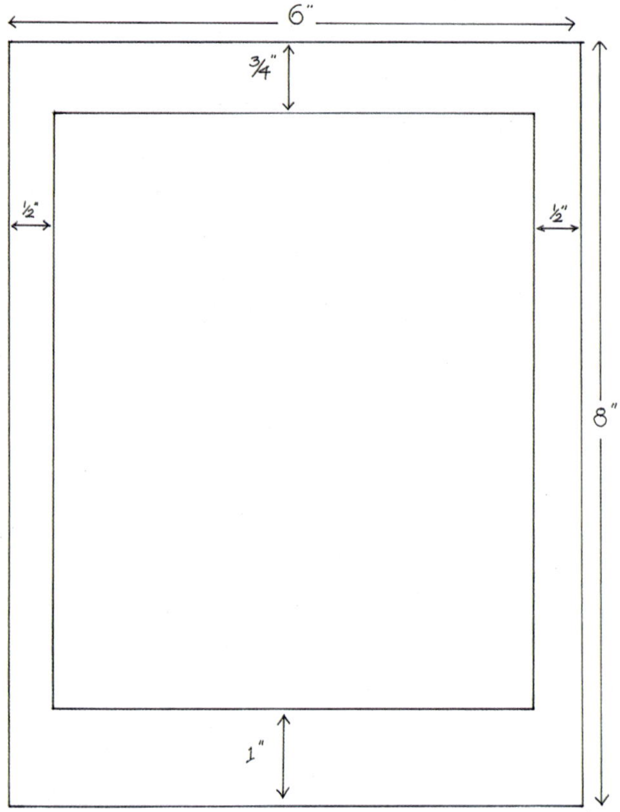


WHAT YOU'LL NEED:

- **Your practice sheets from Exercise Two (see page 161)**
- **26 sheets of 6" x 8" 140-lb. cold- or hot-pressed watercolor paper**
- **Pencil, chalk pencil and eraser**
- **Ruler**
- **Synthetic pointed brushes (different sizes), or pointed brush markers**
- **Several different color inks and/or gouache**
- **8" x 15" sheet of Arches Text Wove paper**
- **Dr. Ph. Martin's Bleedproof White ink or white gouache**
- **Ribbon**

FOR THE BOOKLET INTERIORS:

1. Once you have completed Exercise Two and have 26 lettered practice pages, study each of them carefully. Pencil in comments about what you like, which letters you love and what specifically you like about them, as well as what you like about how the letters are laid out on the page.

2. Next, take your 6" x 8" sheets of watercolor paper and lightly pencil in margins on each page (½" for left and right; 1" for the bottom; ¾" for the top). You now have 26 pages ready to create your letters on — one for each letter of the alphabet.

3. While referring to your sheets from Exercise Two, pencil in several variations of the letter *a* on one sheet of watercolor paper. You will repeat this process with each letter on the ensuing sheets, resulting in 26 pages of letters. Your letter variations can include capitals. The key is to focus on the letter's form and how you can alter it, pushing the boundaries. These penciled letters will serve as loose guidelines as well as help you to place them on the page with enough space to keep the letters distinct. Make any final adjustments to your letters and layout before you move to the next step, creating them with your marker or pointed brush.

4. With a pointed brush and ink/gouache (or your brush marker) in hand, proceed to make your final letters. You can change the colors as you move to a different letter, but I recommend that you stick to one color per letter for the sake of maintaining your momentum. I recommend practicing with your brush on scrap watercolor paper before beginning to letter on your 6" x 8" sheets. Be sure to start where you are comfortable, and as you finish each page set it aside to dry thoroughly. This applies even if you are using a marker, as the ink in the marker also needs time to dry. Once completely dry, erase the chalk pencil lines. Take your time as you complete your pages — as mentioned above, this project assumes more than one day to complete.

## If You're Short on Watercolor Paper ...

**If you find yourself short on watercolor paper, you can do the same exercise on 13 6" x 8" sheets. Simply letter on both front and back sides of the page (making sure to let each side dry completely before starting the next letter in the alphabet). But for the best results, I recommend creating 26 pages.**

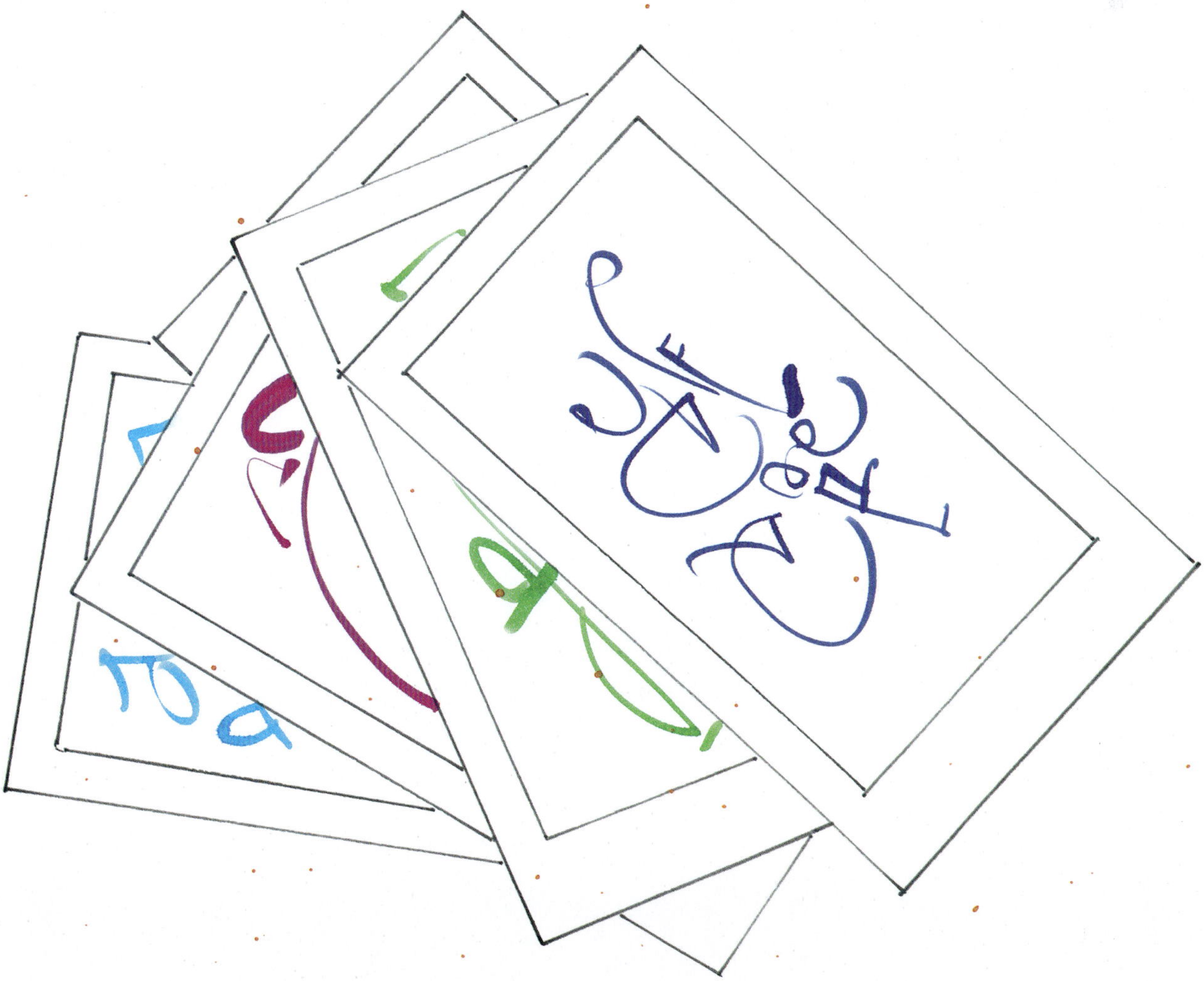

### FOR THE COVER:

While you are working on your pages you can also work on your portfolio's cover as your pages dry. Or you can leave this to the end, after you have lettered all your pages.

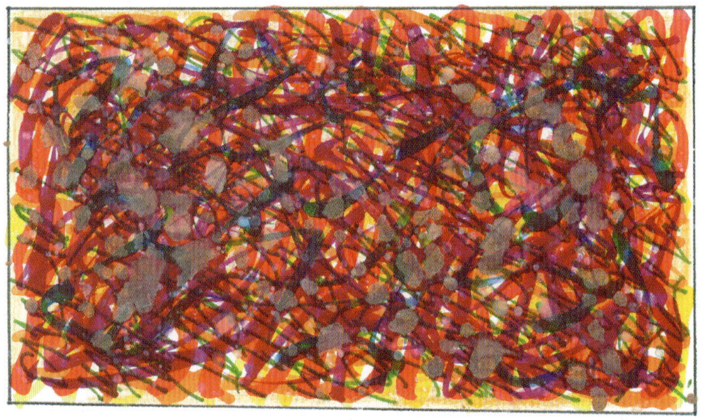

5. Take a piece of Arches Text Wove paper and cut it so that you have a sheet that is 8" x 15". Decorate this sheet with any and every sort of pointed brush letters you can imagine. Use different-sized brushes and different-color inks and gouache. Fill spots with walnut ink or other colors of your choice. Let your preferences and imagination dictate. Then let the cover dry completely.

6. Once dry, use Dr. Ph. Martin's Bleedproof White ink (or white gouache) and a smaller brush with shorter bristles to simply splatter white flecks on the cover to add some additional interest. Alternatively, you can also write letters randomly over the entire cover. Set aside and let dry thoroughly.

7. Once both the cover and interior pages are dry, simply wrap the cover around the pages and tie the bundle with a contrasting or matching ribbon.

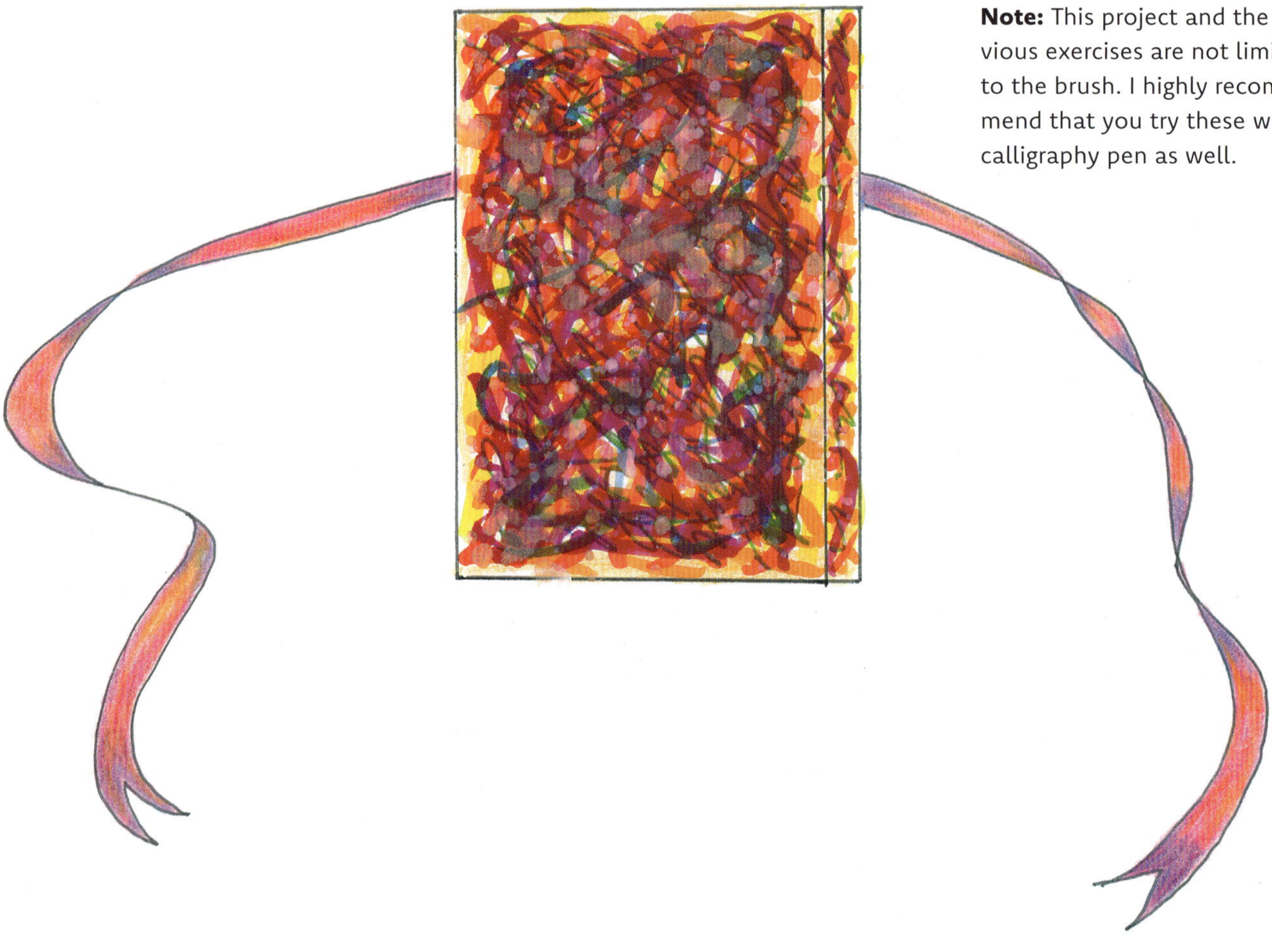

**Note:** This project and the previous exercises are not limited to the brush. I highly recommend that you try these with a calligraphy pen as well.

# Chapter 9

# Go Wild with Italic

**When I am in a workshop learning something new and pushing outside my comfort zone, I don't like to be told to "just be creative" or "you can do anything." Creativity and ambition come to the one who is well versed, not just learning. I also dislike it when an instructor says, "the possibilities are endless." I think, no, they aren't. Being told "the world is your oyster" is not true if you don't have the means to open that oyster!**

I like to be given as much instruction as possible. Only then can I learn the technique and feel comfortable enough to experiment. Then when I have experimented, seen and understood all that was instructed, I will go home to the privacy of my studio to create.

It is for this reason that throughout this book, I have given you specific words to practice, designs for you to try and colors for you to use. However, not everyone is like me, and if you are the type that prefers a different color (or ink or paint) than what I suggest and have a burning desire for a different word or quote, please go ahead. Just glean what you can from my instructions and then dance away to your own music.

In this chapter I am sharing what I have found for myself: the thrill of flight and movement!

The structures of the letter forms are not changed simply to be different, but rather so that the letters can leap and soar. If the end result is that a word can be read, that may be a happy accident. The structures are altered to the point where they can be understood but not obviously so — and perhaps not at all as we move into the abstract. There are various levels to which you will find enjoyment in this process. We do, inevitably, all fly at different altitudes.

I am guided in life by a few wonderful quotes, which are spread over these two pages:

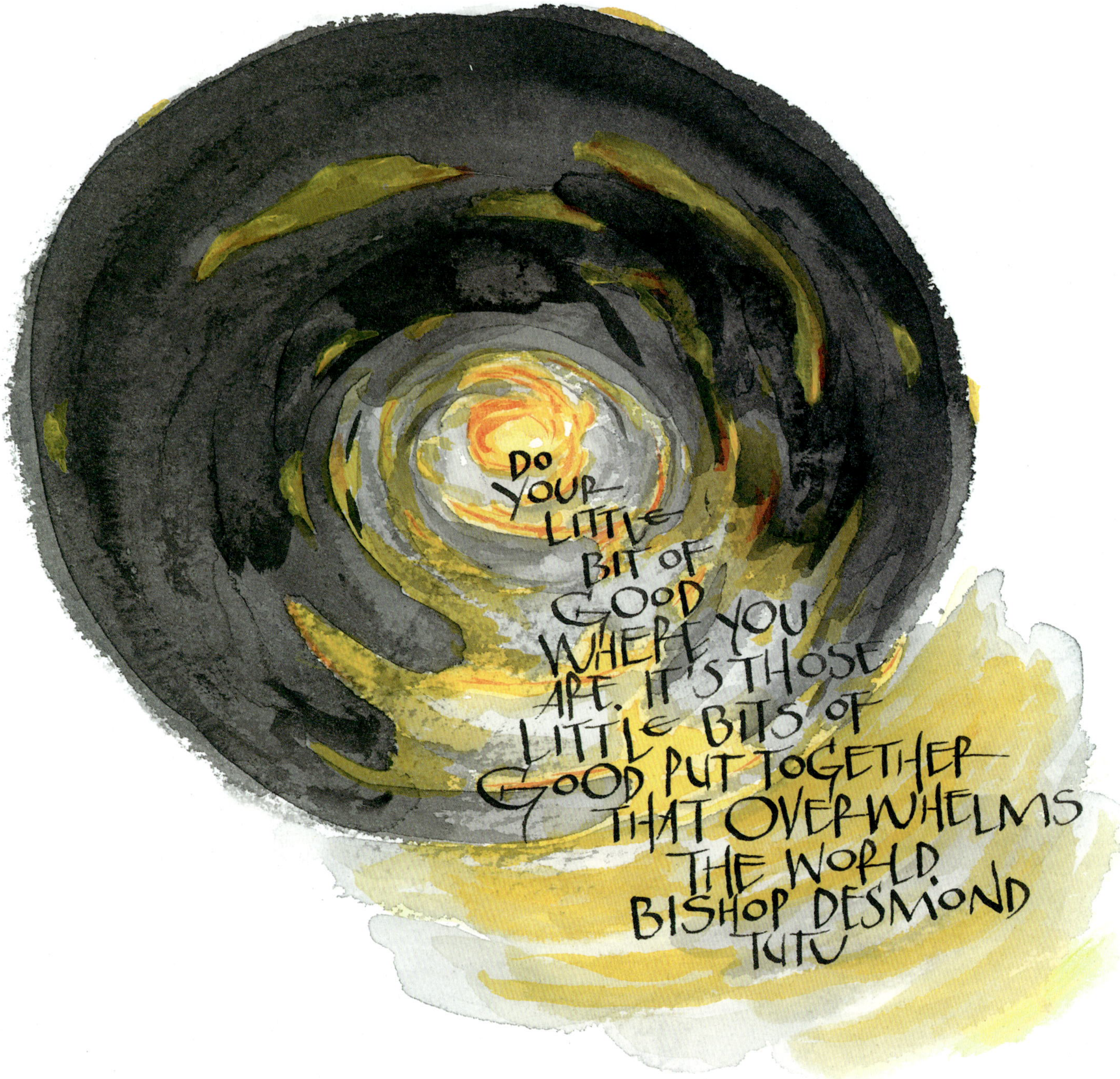

I express my art and heart through card design. I have been doing this since I was 15. Whether it is one word or many, a traditional style or abstract, monochromatic or colorful, ordered or chaotic, calligraphy is the heartbeat behind my art. A motto I have tried to live by is "don't give away anything that you don't love." This is as difficult as it is imperative.

In the ensuing pages I share with you some of my designs from the past years, reviewing the ideas that inspired the layout and discussing the techniques I used. We will then go through a step-by-step exercise to create your own piece, combining the various techniques and tools you have learned throughout this book.

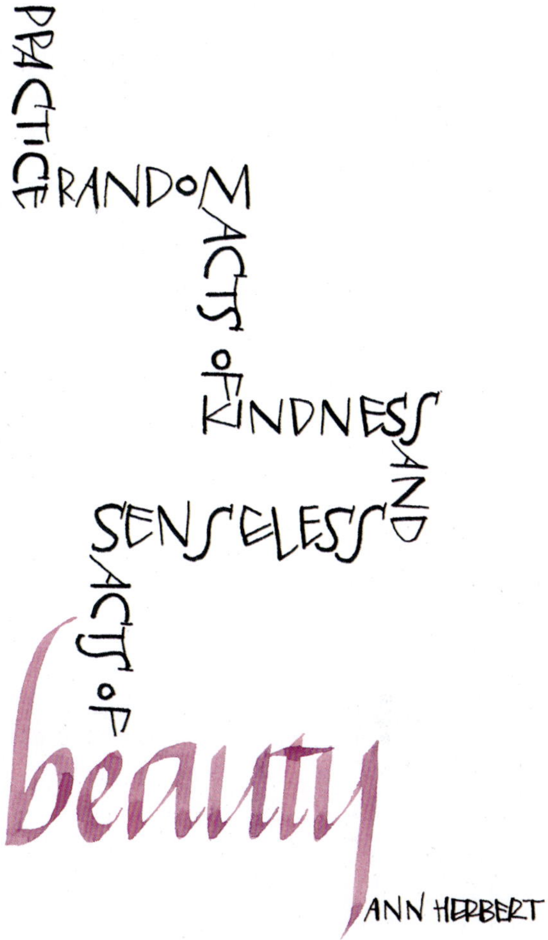


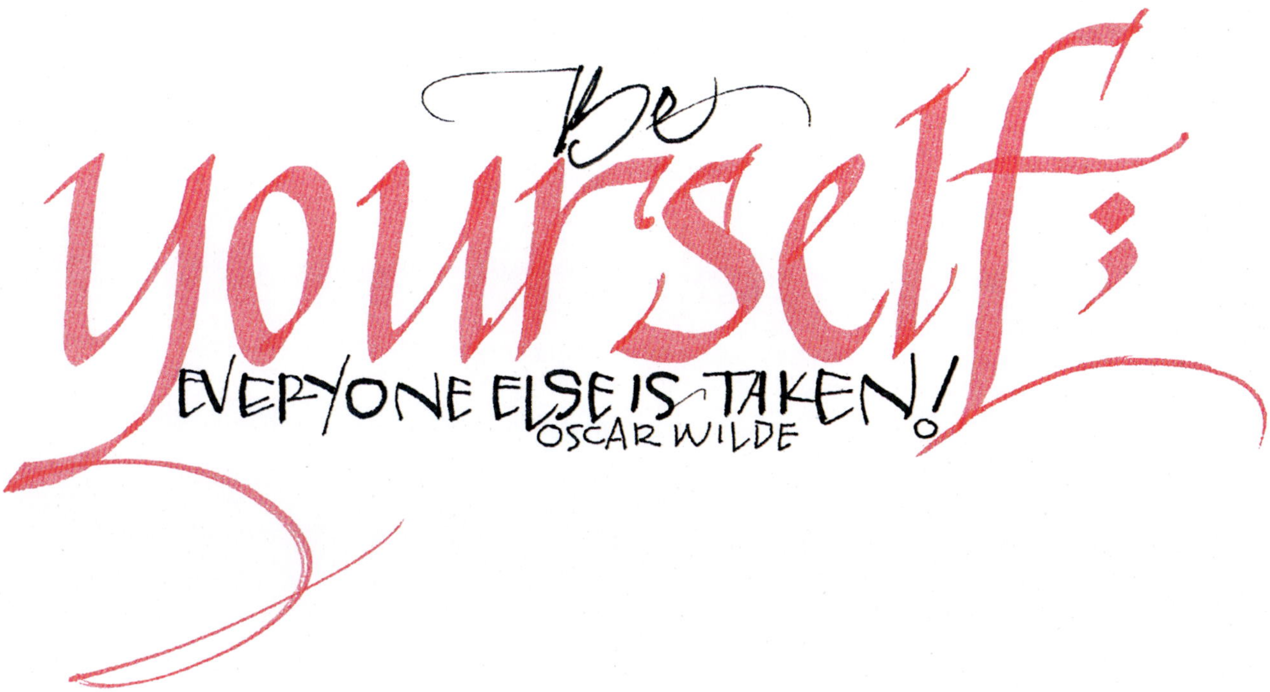

## "DANCING" WITH "FRIENDS"

These first examples illustrate that what you create does not need to be complex, and that you can create wonderful images that embody simplicity.

Images A ("Dancing") and B ("Friends") were created using a black calligraphic marker (brand new to ensure crispness) on white card-stock. The spaces were then filled in with gold gouache.

With "Dancing" my intent was to express the movement of dance, capturing the leaps, extension and freedom that dance embodies. The *d* and *c* soar; the *n* and *g* stretch — creating length/extension — and the remaining letters capture the tight movements that generate the energy to leap, soar and extend as the dancer flies across the stage. The gold gouache adds a simple yet elegant touch of color to complete the piece.

With "Friends" the intention was simply to have fun with the letters, connecting them together with playful joins — which is a very important part of friendship.

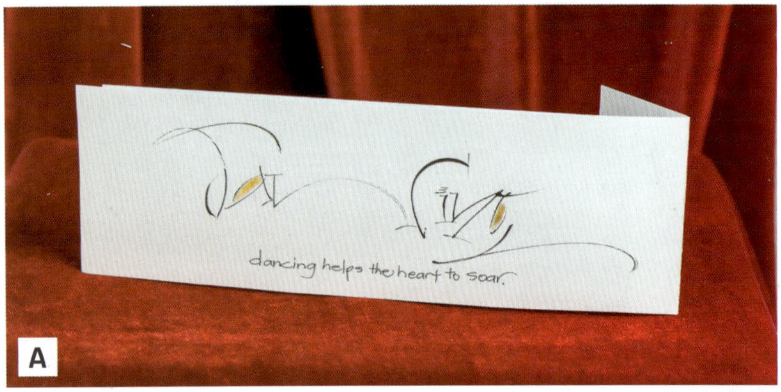

A

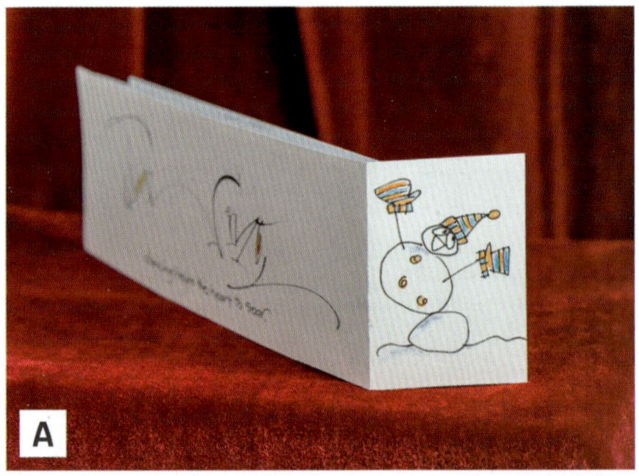
A

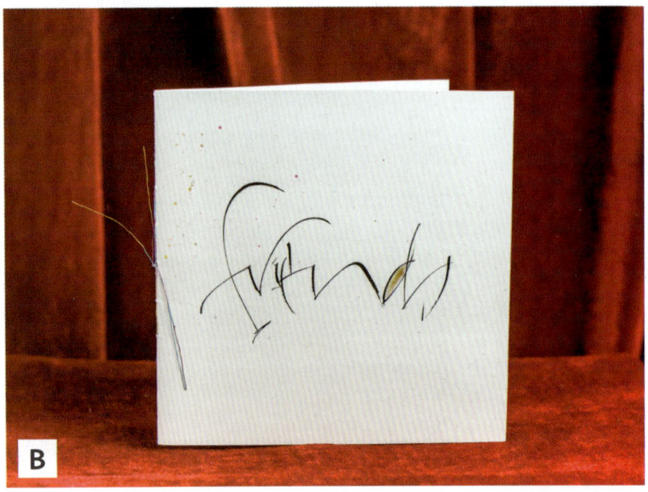
B

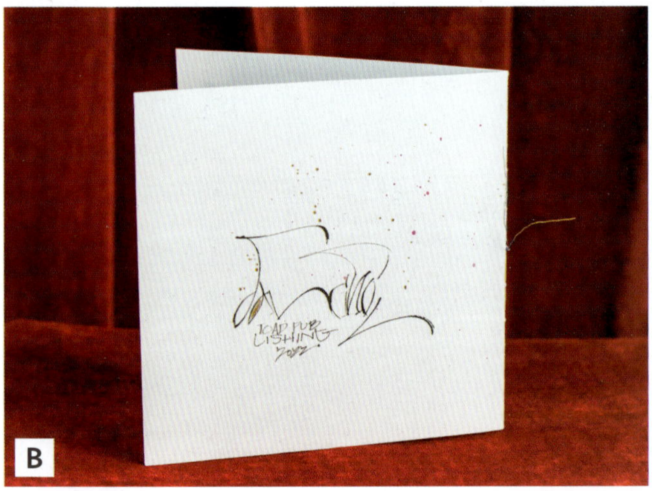
B

## “MERRY CALLIGRAPHY”

Every year my local calligraphy guild holds a year-end card exchange, with each member creating a custom card design to give to the guild members. For this particular card, I wanted to have fun and push the calligraphy — hence “Merry Calligraphy.”

I used a simple waterproof black fine-liner to letter the word “merry” across the card in a simple cursive Italic. This created my baseline. The word “Calligraphy” was then lettered multiple times, layering one word on top of the other. The first “Calligraphy” was done with a black marker. The next two were layered over it using a Speedball $3/8$-inch nib and light cobalt-turquoise gouache, followed by Dr. Ph. Martin’s Bleedproof White ink. The final “Calligraphy” was then added with a new black calligraphy marker. I chose the marker for the final layer as it was the best tool to avoid snagging on the prior layers.

The intention was to create the image of a whirling tempest, with the letters soaring upward with heightened extension. There is an epicenter that gives a sensation of explosion, with flecks of gold gouache splattered outward from it. This piece is a celebration of life, but my hope was to capture the grace and elegance of this life in the arching and soaring letters.

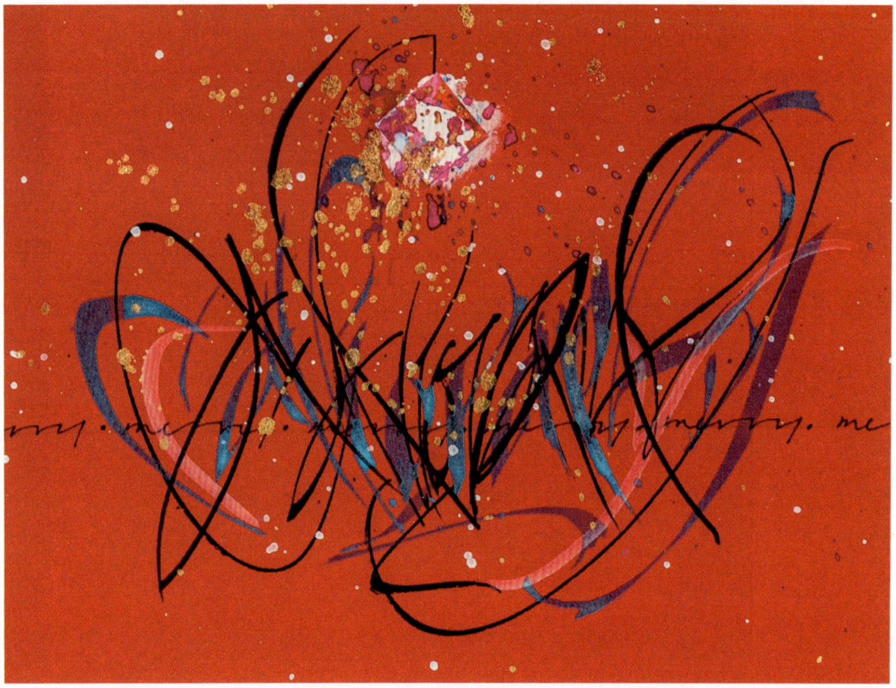

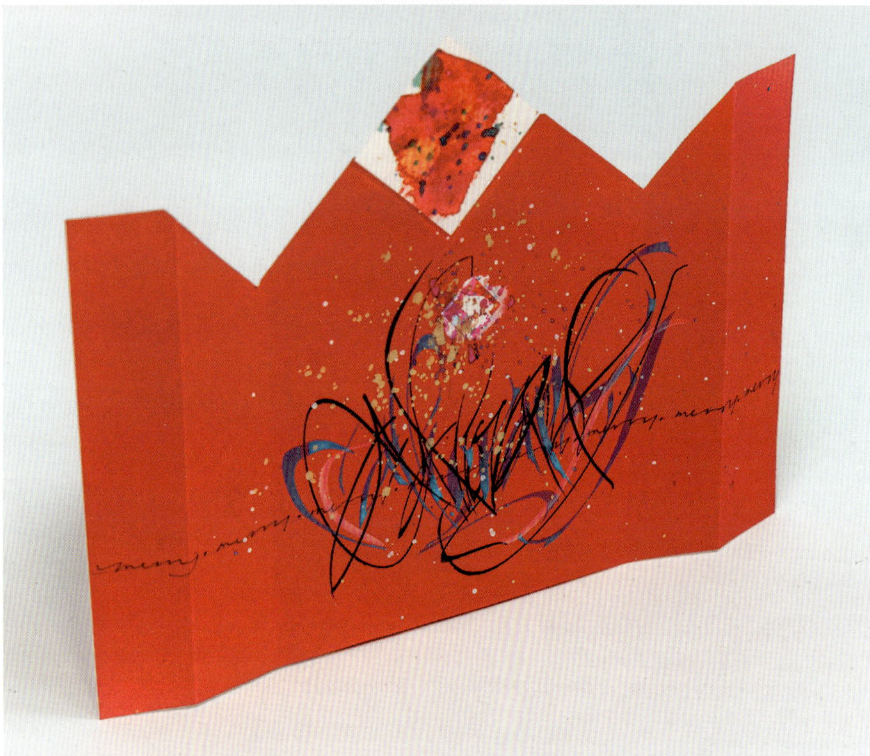

## "CHRISTMAS"

As a card designer, the year-end holiday season provides ample opportunities to make new creations. With "Christmas," I wanted to create a strong, striking image over an abstract background.

To start with, I created the background. This was done with Sumi ink and a large nib on a sheet of 140-lb. watercolor paper (you can use either hot- or cold-pressed paper for this type of work). I lettered random letters and then ran the page under cold water while manipulating the page to cause the ink to run in interesting patterns. As mentioned earlier, this is called "sink art" (learn more on page 176). Once I had the effect I wanted, I set the paper aside to dry for a bit, but not too long, as I needed the paper to be damp for the next step in the process.

Next I applied another layer of ink (I used walnut ink) to the still-wet page, filling in empty spots with random shapes and letters to add to the overall design. I then added splashes of different-color inks that bled on the wet page to create various splotches of color. In image A, I used earthy tones, like green and gold, while in image B I used pinks, purples and yellows.

Once dry, I employed a pointed brush to letter the word "Christmas" over the background using blue gouache (image A) and Dr. Ph. Martin's Bleedproof White ink (image B).

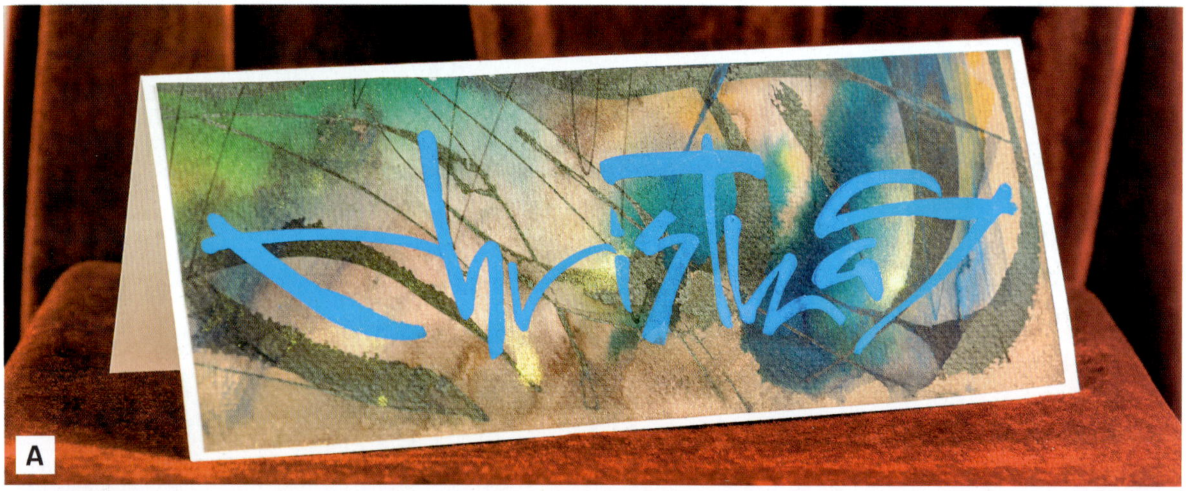


A

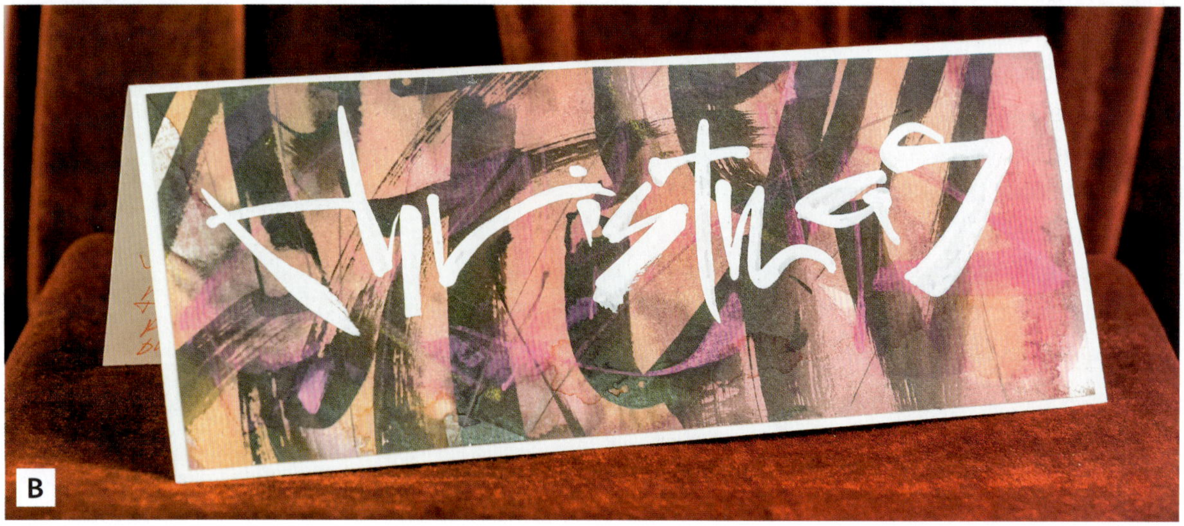


B

## "2020" AND "2022": BLACK ON WHITE/WHITE ON BLACK

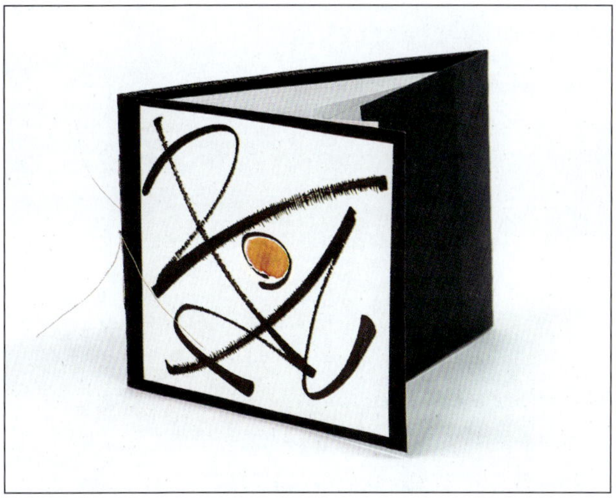

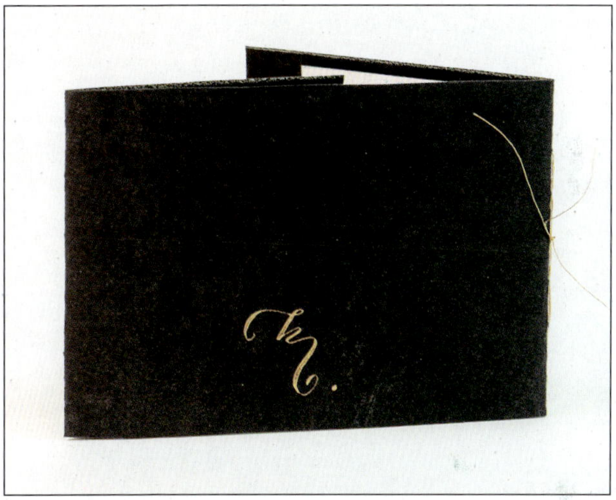

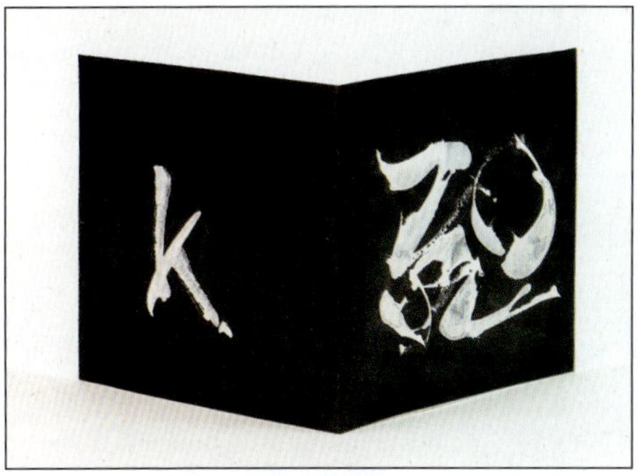

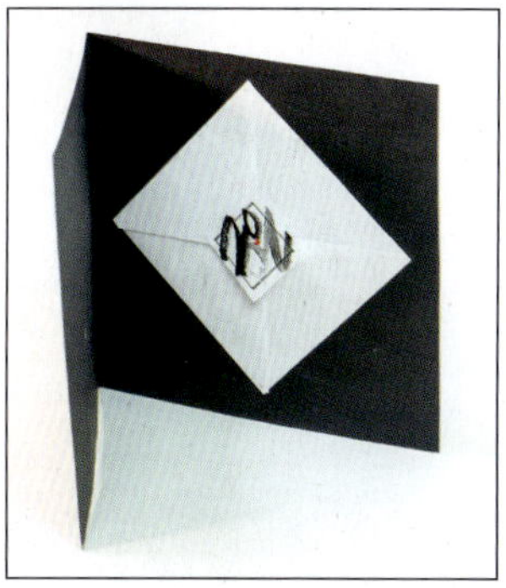

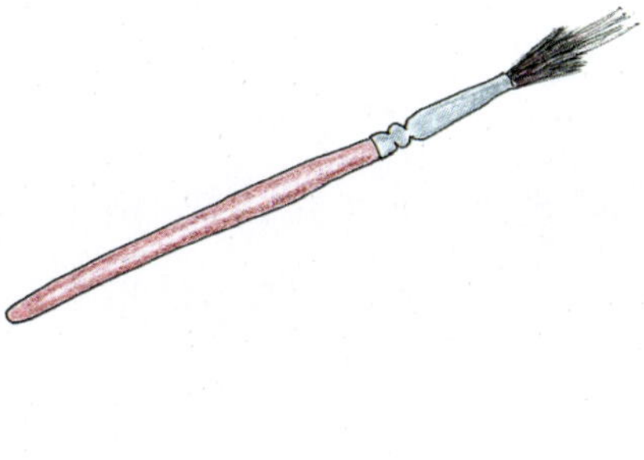

As you alter letter forms and move into the abstract, you have the opportunity to push boundaries such that forms become more difficult to decipher. It is always a challenge to find how close to the boundaries you can approach before you have gone too far. Each person will determine where that point lies.

The New Year's cards I created for 2020 and 2022 illustrate this.

For "2022" (black on white), I used a ruling pen, which is a tool that creates intriguingly ragged lines, and black Sumi ink on 140-lb. watercolor paper. The composition is of three intertwined 2's encircling a simple zero filled with gold paint. It is somewhat abstract, but for most, the numbers would become apparent fairly quickly. Especially when received in the context of a New Year's card.

"2020," however, pushes further toward the abstract edge, rendering a more dramatic and intriguing image. This piece is much harder to decipher, and it is only when you turn the image 180 degrees that you can see the full 2020. The 2 and the 0 are there, but their forms are exaggerated and certainly push the limits. Some may, in fact, be unable to see the full 2020. The image, taken as a whole, is abstract art, and the tool used to create it lends itself to such art forms: a size 4 needle point brush (it looks like a tattered squirrel's tail with a few extended hairs). I paired the brush with Dr. Ph. Martin's Bleedproof White ink on black Arches paper. The floppy nature of the brush results in highly textured, loose, unpredictable forms, and it takes patience to learn how to use it.

## ABOUT LETTER WRITING

Several years ago, I was filmed for a short spot on a CBC morning talk show. It was quite an experience as they filmed me in my dining room for a full day — simply to fill a five-minute segment on the show. The topic was on letter writing, including decorating envelopes. I love to write letters and to make them as engaging as possible. I believe a handwritten letter is a wonderful thing to send — and to receive. To make the experience as delightful as possible, I spend as much time decorating the envelope as I do actually writing the letter, turning the envelope into a work of art. This is what we focused on in the brief clip.

In the example provided, I wanted the name and address section on the front of the envelope to reflect the stamp. This was a letter to my friend Lily, a fellow calligrapher whom I highly respect. I used acrylic paint for the colorful dabs and once hardened, I lettered her name with a calligraphic marker (to avoid snags) using reasonable restraint while still allowing for some fun letter alterations I hoped she would enjoy. I wanted her name to appear like a flower reaching upward while capturing the same color as the sky in the postage stamp.

The address information (not included here for obvious reasons) was, of course, highly legible to ensure that Canada Post actually delivered the letter.

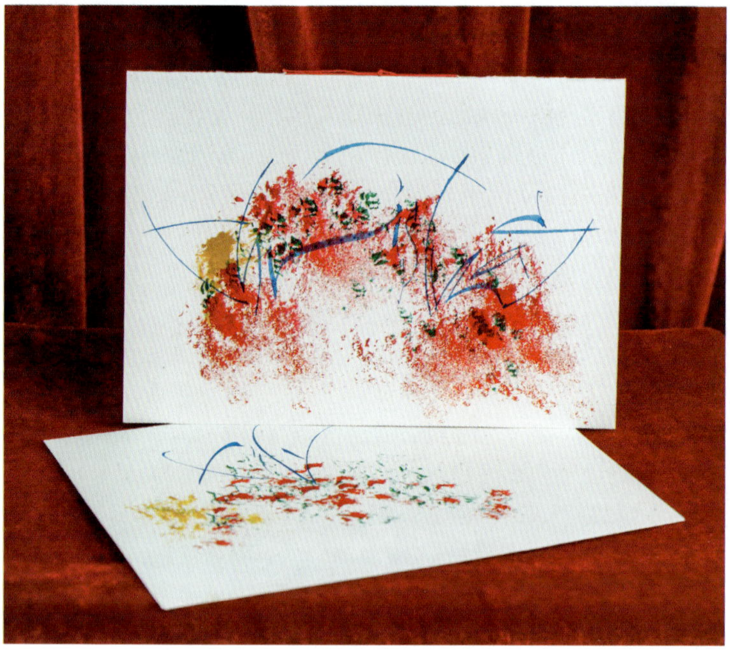

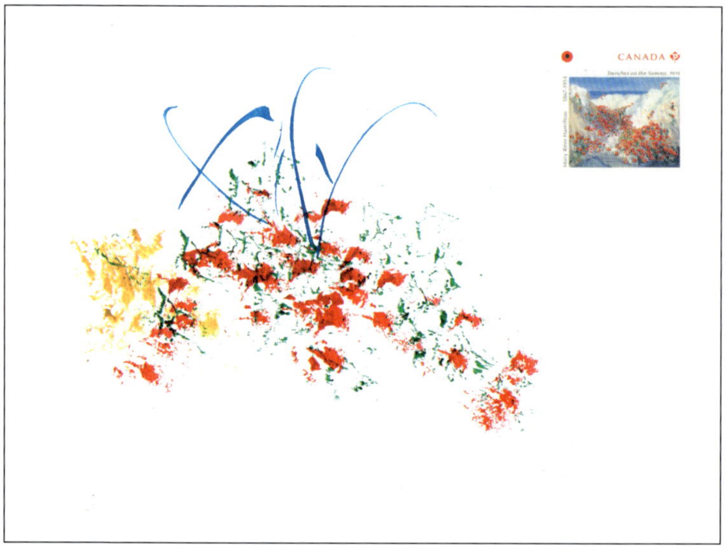

# Creating Dimension

The following exercises are intended to apply the techniques and skills you have learned to create more layered works of calligraphy art, adding increased dimension to your work.

## EXERCISE ONE

In this exercise you will letter a single word of your choice — or you can use the word *dance* if you prefer.

### WHAT YOU'LL NEED:

- **Practice sheet**
- **Pencil and eraser**
- **Three 3" x 5" sheets of 140-lb. hot-pressed watercolor paper**
- **Calligraphy pen with a metal nib (3.8 mm)**
- **Sumi ink**
- **Gouache (gold, red or a color of your preference)**

1. Choose your word. On your practice sheet, decide which of your altered letters you would like to use to express this word. If this is not easy for you, you can use my example to get a feel for this. Practice many times using a pencil first to make sure the letters flow and you are happy with the result.

2. When you are happy with your penciled letters, practice a few times more with your pen on a scrap piece of watercolor paper.

3. Now proceed to letter each of your three pieces of paper. Lightly pencil in your word as your guideline. Then with your pen and ink, write your word, not feeling obligated to trace your penciled letters but rather working freely and fluidly with the guidelines. As you finish each page, set it aside to dry completely.

4. Once your ink is dry, fill in the enclosed spaces with your chosen color of gouache.

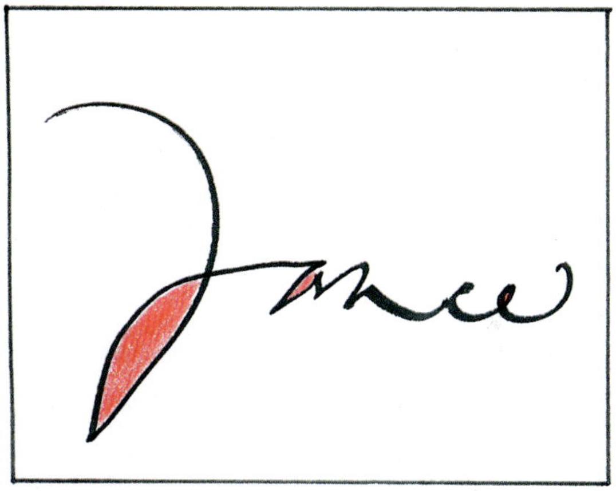

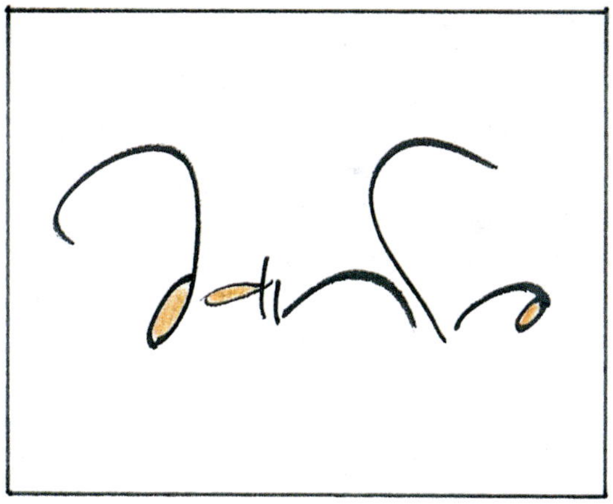

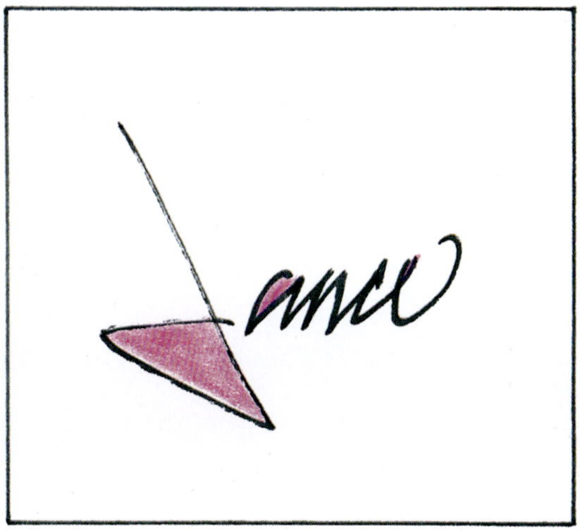

## EXERCISE TWO

In this exercise you are working on combining the sharp and rounded strokes of the word *we*, as depicted in the illustration. The downstroke, upstroke, downstroke of the *w* are pointedly sharp, whereas the strokes leading into and out of the *w* are rounded to give a feeling of lightness that leads to a sharp point at the top of the *e* before lightly curving out to finish.

### WHAT YOU'LL NEED:

- **Practice sheet**
- **Pencil and eraser**
- **One 3" x 5" sheet of 140-lb. hot-pressed watercolor paper**
- **A small, pointed brush**
- **Light colored ink (waterproof)**
- **Sumi ink**
- **Red gouache or ink**

1. On a practice sheet, pencil out the word *we*, working on the flow into, within and out of each letter to get a good feel for this movement.

2. Turn your 3" x 5" sheet 90 degrees clockwise (portrait orientation), and using your pointed brush and light-colored ink, letter the alphabet from left to right, filling the entire page. You may find it helpful to pencil in light lines every half inch or so across the page for guidelines. Focus on writing a consistent, predictable flow of letters, as this is the backdrop you will be writing over. You do not want the backdrop to pull the eye away from the central word *we*. Work to create a pattern as you write. Once finished, let the sheet dry and continue practicing the word *we* on your practice paper.

3. To complete the exercise, turn the sheet 90 degrees counterclockwise (landscape orientation) so that your background letters now run from top to bottom. (You will be writing the word *we* across these vertical letters.) You can either pencil in the word *we* on your page as a guideline to be erased later, or proceed directly with ink. Next take your pen and Sumi ink and letter the word as you have practiced it. For this exercise the *we* should stand out in stark relief from the background.

4. To finish it off, add a red dot (either with gouache or ink) in the eye of the *e*.

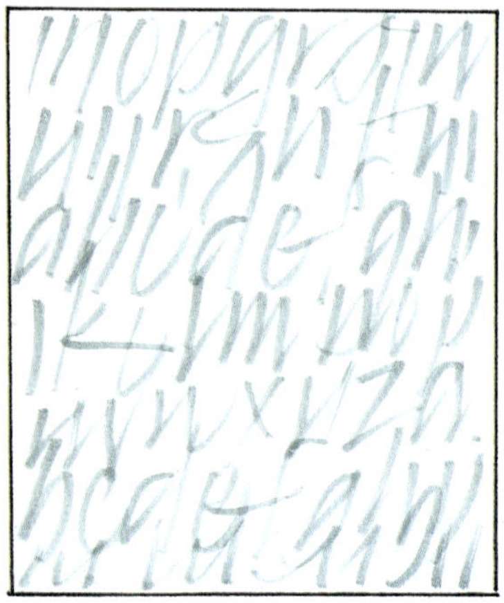

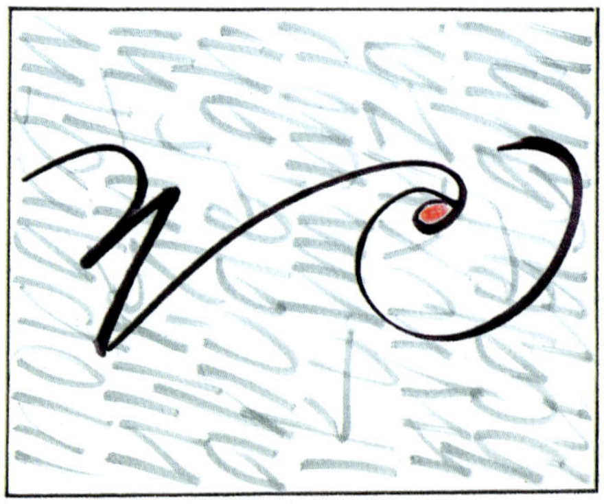

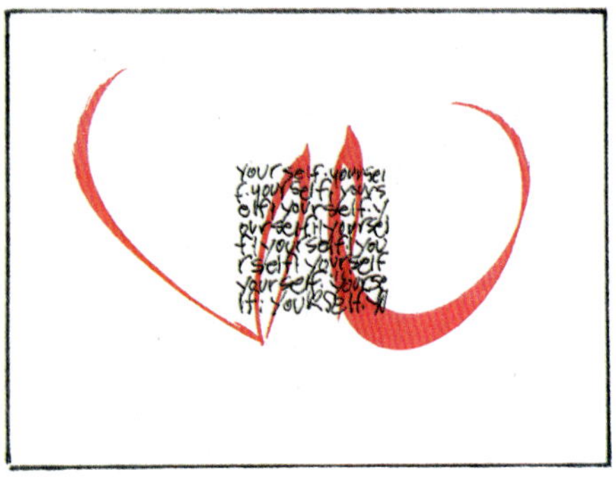

This is a variation of the exercise using the word *be* instead of *we*.

### EXERCISE THREE

Working with inks can be challenging, as factors such as climate and humidity can impact the timing for ink blending. With practice you will learn the timing for when to apply wet on wet to create the right effect. For example, if things are too wet, you will not get the wonderful blending and marbling you are hoping for. With that said, let's start.

#### WHAT YOU'LL NEED:

- **Two or three 3" x 5" sheets of 140-lb. cold-pressed watercolor paper (hot-pressed does not bleed as well)**
- **Medium or large brush**
- **Sumi ink**
- **Calligraphy pen with a small nib (2 mm)**
- **Cadmium red (or another brilliant red) ink**

1. As depicted, create a large circle with your brush using a diluted Sumi ink mixture. I suggest you work with a small jar of water and a couple of drops of Sumi ink to get the right level of dilution. Experiment on a scrap piece of paper first to make sure the circle is not too dark as you want a lighter-colored circle for this exercise. As you make the circle, fill approximately two-thirds of the sheet of paper, making sure that the circle is oriented more to the top. Do a couple of rounds with the brush to ensure that the circle has some thickness to it but is not too dense.

2. Let the circle dry a bit (just a few seconds). You want the diluted Sumi ink to still have a fair bit of moisture and if it dries too quickly you will not get the feathering effect you want when you add your concentrated inks. (This is where you might want to practice a few strokes on a separate piece of watercolor paper to work on timing.) Now take your small nib and with non-diluted Sumi ink, draw an arching line from the left border to the right border through the top third of the circle. This should cause bleeding where the concentrated stroke comes into contact with the circle. Working quickly, while your ink is still damp — and with a clean nib — place a drop of the red ink at the top right point where the line and circle intersect. This will result in more bleeding. Let it dry.

3. Try this exercise one or two more times as you get a better feel for diluting the Sumi ink and the timing for when the ink has reached the desired dampness to enhance the feathering of the ink.

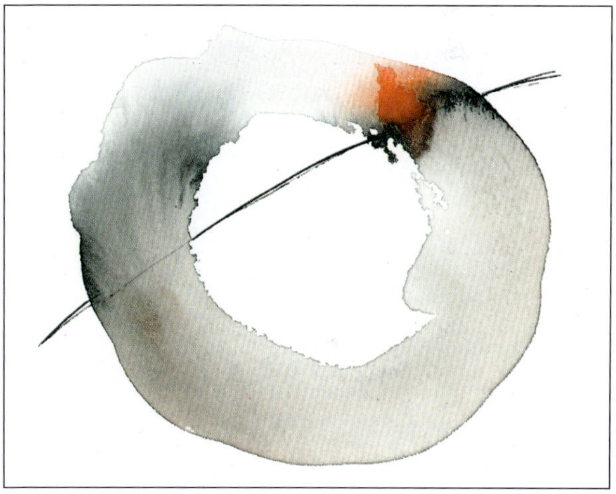

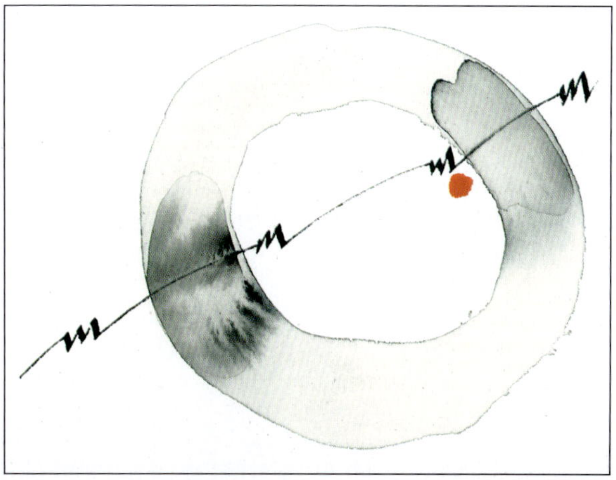

This is a variation of the exercise using letters and connecting lines (a "barbed wire" effect) instead of a single line.

## EXERCISE FOUR

In one of my designs I reviewed earlier in this chapter, I mentioned the term "sink art." With this technique, you rinse your work under running water while the ink is still wet. The water and the ink blend to create delightful and beautiful backdrops. I use Sumi ink for this process because it is not water soluble once dried. While it is still wet, there is a portion of the ink that is dry enough that it will not be washed away by water. This allows you to manipulate the ink as it dries to create beautiful backdrops for your work. This exercise focuses on adding this dimension to your calligraphic art.

### WHAT YOU'LL NEED:

- **Two or three 3" x 5" sheets of 140-lb. cold-pressed watercolor paper**
- **Medium or large round brush (such as a Chinese calligraphy brush)**
- **Sumi ink**
- **Access to a sink**
- **Calligraphy pen with a small nib (2 mm)**
- **Red or gold gouache (optional)**

1. With your brush, create a circle in Sumi ink — positioned toward the upper-right portion of your page (as depicted). Let the ink dry slightly — it must set enough that it won't wash away but be dry enough that it won't pool. Depending on the amount of ink, you will likely need to let it dry for 30 to 60 seconds.

2. Take your paper to the sink and rinse it for 2 to 3 seconds under lightly running water (like a trickle), swishing the paper around to let the water play with the ink, but not so much that it causes the ink to run off the page. Work to create a marbling effect, watching for ebbs and flows in the ink as it interacts with the water. Don't leave too much water standing on the page once you have what you are looking for. Set your page aside to let it dry completely. Note: you may not get this right the first time as it's a bit unpredictable. But don't give up.

3. Now, using a pen with a small nib, letter the word *circle* in either Sumi ink or gouache (perhaps gold or red for contrast), as depicted in the illustration. Let the paper dry completely.

4. Use the rest of your sheets to play some more with this sink art technique.

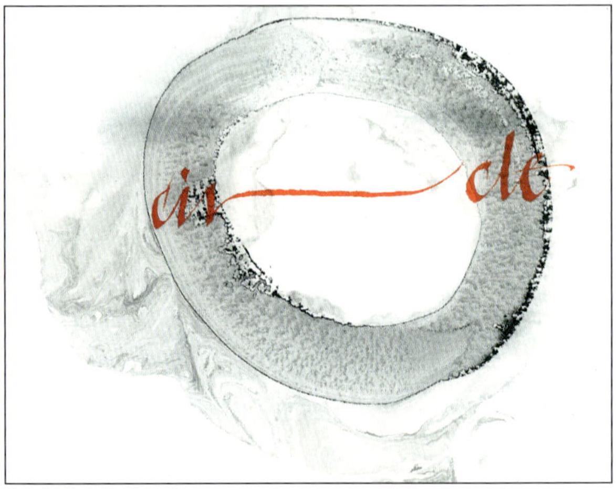

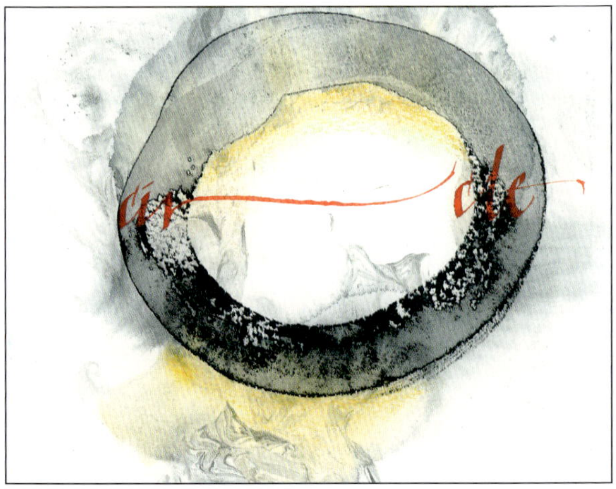

## EXERCISE FIVE

This exercise is designed to show contrast — and how simply it can be achieved.

WHAT YOU'LL NEED:

- **Two or three 3" x 5" sheets of 140-lb. cold-pressed watercolor paper**
- **Chalk pencil and eraser**
- **Small brush (which will be needed to carefully fill in the rectangle with Sumi ink)**
- **Sumi ink**
- **Ruler**
- **White gouache**
- **Calligraphy pen with a 3.8 mm nib and a 5 mm nib**
- **Cadmium red (or another brilliant red) ink**

1. Laying your paper horizontally (landscape orientation), lightly pencil in a rectangle in the upper-right portion of the paper (as depicted in the top image on the right). Taking your small brush, fill in the rectangle with Sumi ink. Let it dry.

2. Once dry, using a chalk pencil, lightly draw a sweeping line from the bottom left upward to the top right, through the black rectangle. This will serve as your baseline. Using your smaller (3.8 mm) nib, in Sumi ink write the letter *m* in a way similar to the "barbed wire" technique (see page 105) up to the left edge of the rectangle. Clean your nib, then continue on writing the *m* over the interior of the rectangle using your white gouache. Once you have squiggled through the box, complete the remainder of the squiggled *m*'s in Sumi ink with your nib (after cleaning it again thoroughly), finishing at the right edge of the paper. You can also add a bit more color for contrast, such as a dot of cadmium red, or some diamonds in red.

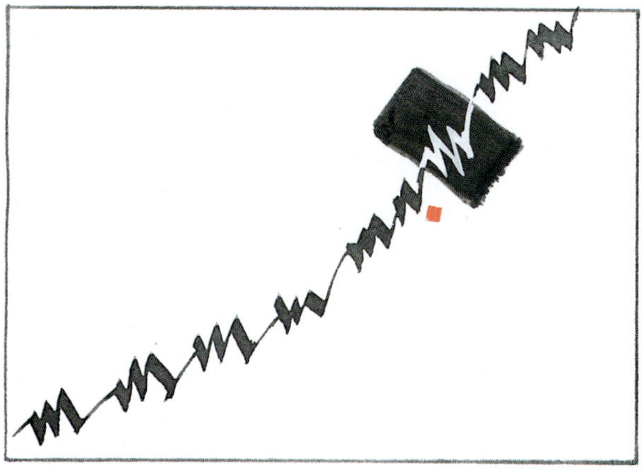

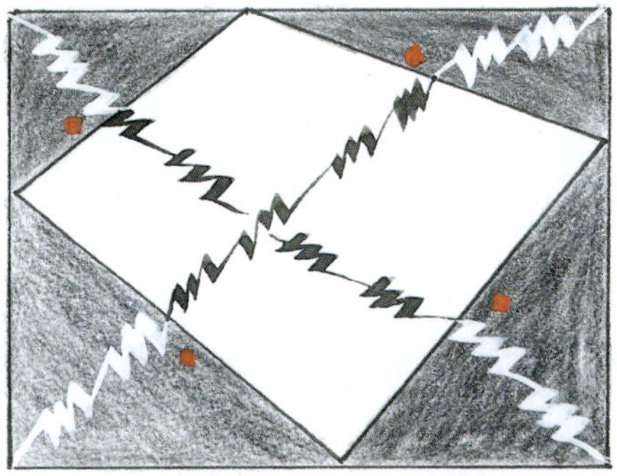

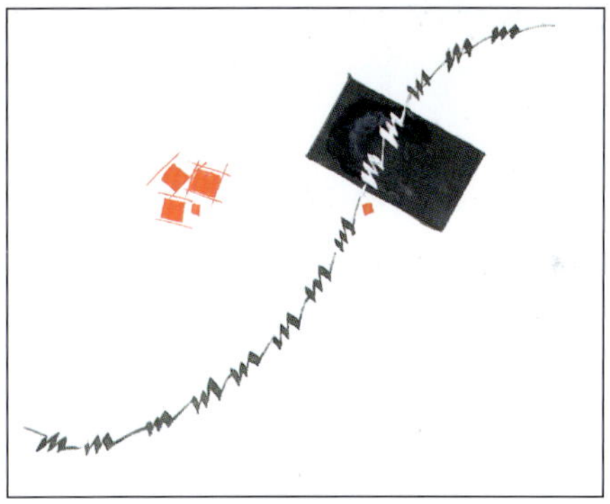

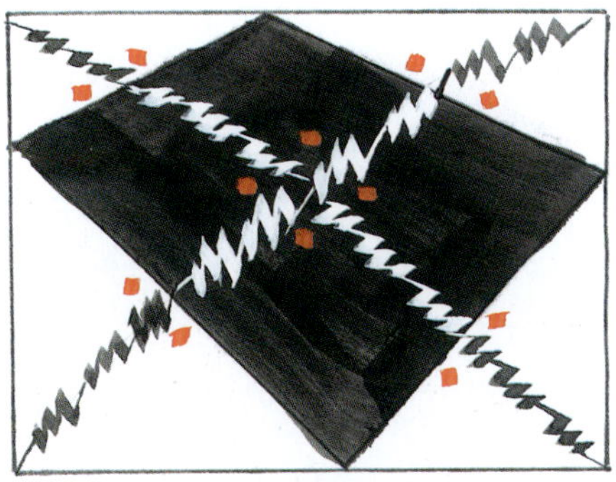

3. This exercise can then be repeated on the other 3" x 5" inch pages, playing with looser letter variations as you please.

# Different is not Enough

Though at first glance it may seem that gestural calligraphy is done randomly with speed and little thought, this is absolutely not the case. The brain and eyes are crucial in decision making, and then you trust your arm and hand to execute your decisions. Sometimes (and, with me, I would say quite often), your eye directs your hand to make a stroke, and it falls short of what your eye knew to be a good choice. So another, perhaps instantaneous, decision must be made to accommodate that shortcoming while continuing the dance without seemingly missing a beat.

As dance steps on their own are delightful and intriguing, to dance one must choreograph these steps to create a whole. Even in gestural writing you need to have an idea of where you're going — an eye for weak spots that require drama or overworked areas that need calm.

With the traditional Italic, you knew where to begin a stroke and where to end it because of the guidelines and instructions. Now your eyes become these guides, and it takes time to develop that skill and expertise. *Different* on its own is not good enough. One letter might be clever and spectacularly unique, yet it does not harmonize with a whole word. One word could be dramatic and energetic, but will it dance with a whole sentiment? If not, the result is a stagger and perhaps a fall. But this is nothing practice and repetition won't put right.

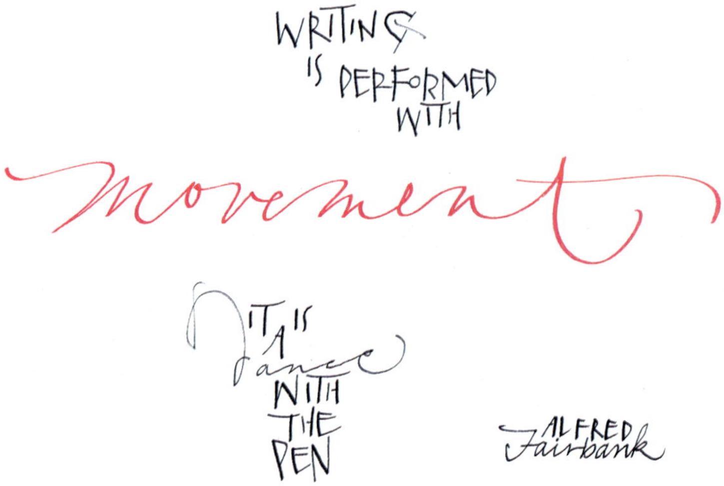


## A GESTURAL EXERCISE

This exercise is designed to help you put words together in a gestural way, allowing your eyes to guide you through this process. You will start with a few variables and work your way to larger constructs. This exercise will be done with black ink on white paper so that you can focus purely on letter forms and their placement, assessing what works and what doesn't.

You are going to letter one of my favorite quotes by Oscar Wilde: "Be yourself; everyone else is taken."

Rather than simply writing this in one single attempt, you will start with just the first two words and then gradually take on more words until you finish the entire quote in one go. This way you can see what works well together in incremental steps.

WHAT YOU'LL NEED:

- **Four practice sheets, each divided into four equal sections**
- **Pencil and eraser**
- **Pen with a 3.8 mm nib and black ink (or a calligraphy marker)**

1. Divide your four practice sheets into four equal sections. For each sheet, always start with your pencil. Then when you're satisfied with your letters, go over your pencil lines with either a small nib and ink or a calligraphy marker. Then erase your pencil lines.

2. On the first practice sheet, pencil in the first two words of the quote (*Be yourself*) in four different ways, playing with your letter forms and word placement. Once you are happy, finish your letters with ink/marker, erase your pencil lines and move on to the next page.

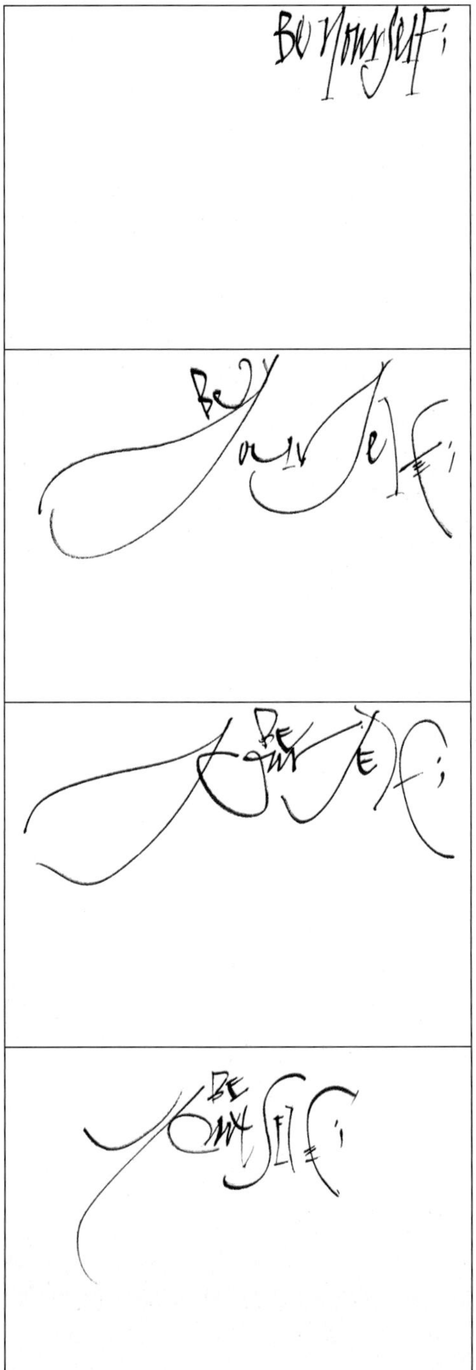

3. On the second practice sheet, letter the first four words in the quote (*Be yourself; everyone else*). Because there are more words, you will need to use smaller letters. Choose your favorite version (or favorites) from the first practice sheet and pencil it into each section, keeping in mind that you will be adding the words *everyone else* to the sentence.

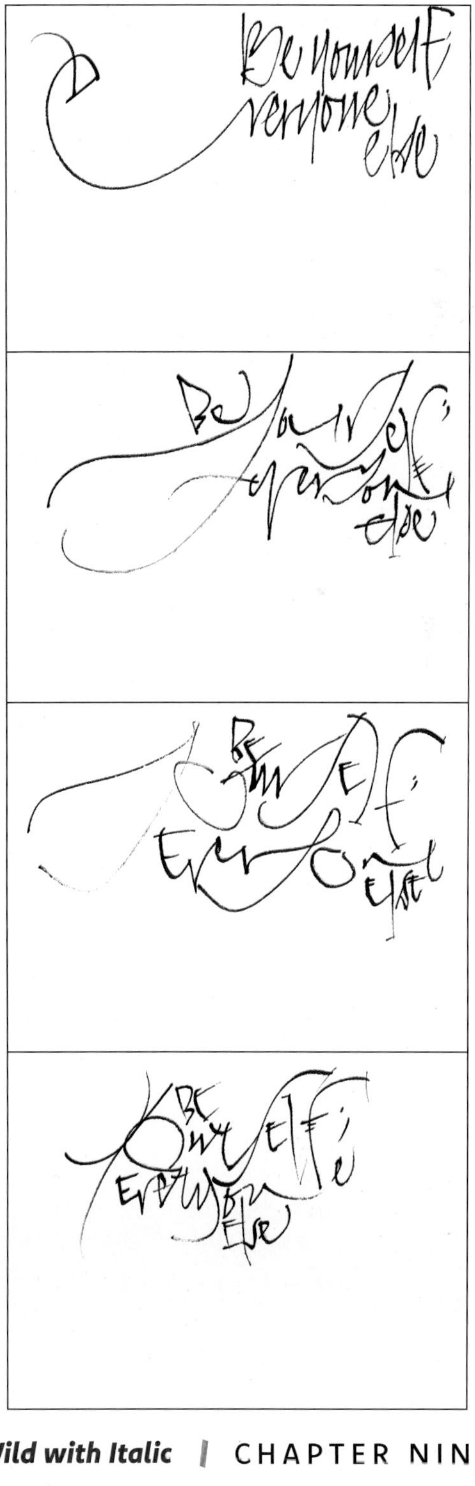

4. When you have finished this practice sheet to your satisfaction, it is time to move to the third practice sheet, where you will now be adding *is taken*. The process is the same as the prior sheet: keep an eye on how the letters and words flow and move with each other, as well as how they work with the space.

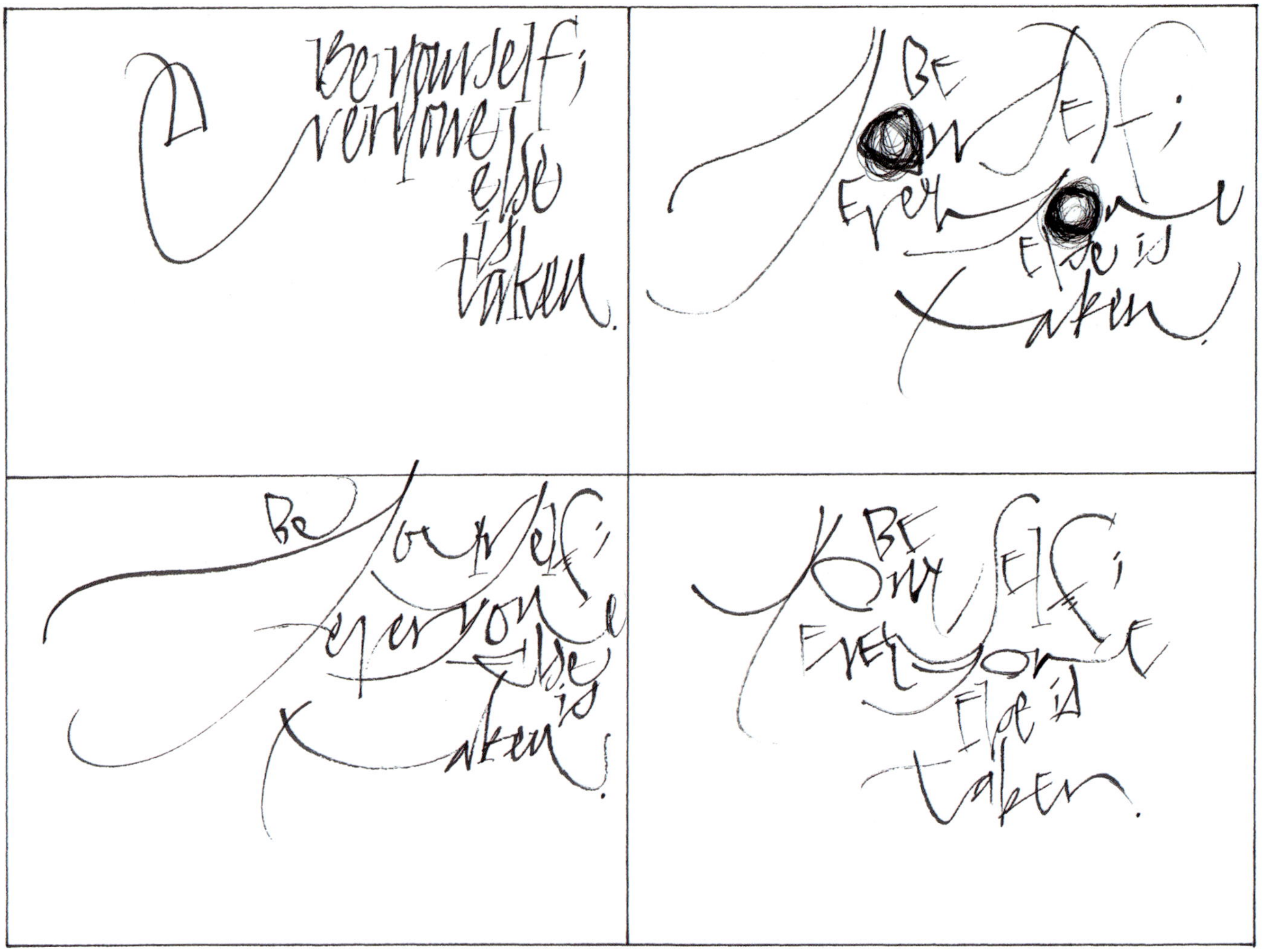

5. The final step is done on the last practice sheet. On this sheet you will write in your favorite versions of the full quote. However, you will also be adding the quote's source — *Oscar Wilde* — nearby, so it is critical to ensure that you lay out your space to accommodate this. When you have completed this exercise with ink or marker and erased your pencil lines, you will now have a template you can use for the final project in this book. And you will also have gained some significant practice on gestural calligraphy and a better understanding of layout, letter and word movement and connectivity, and how to use space more creatively.

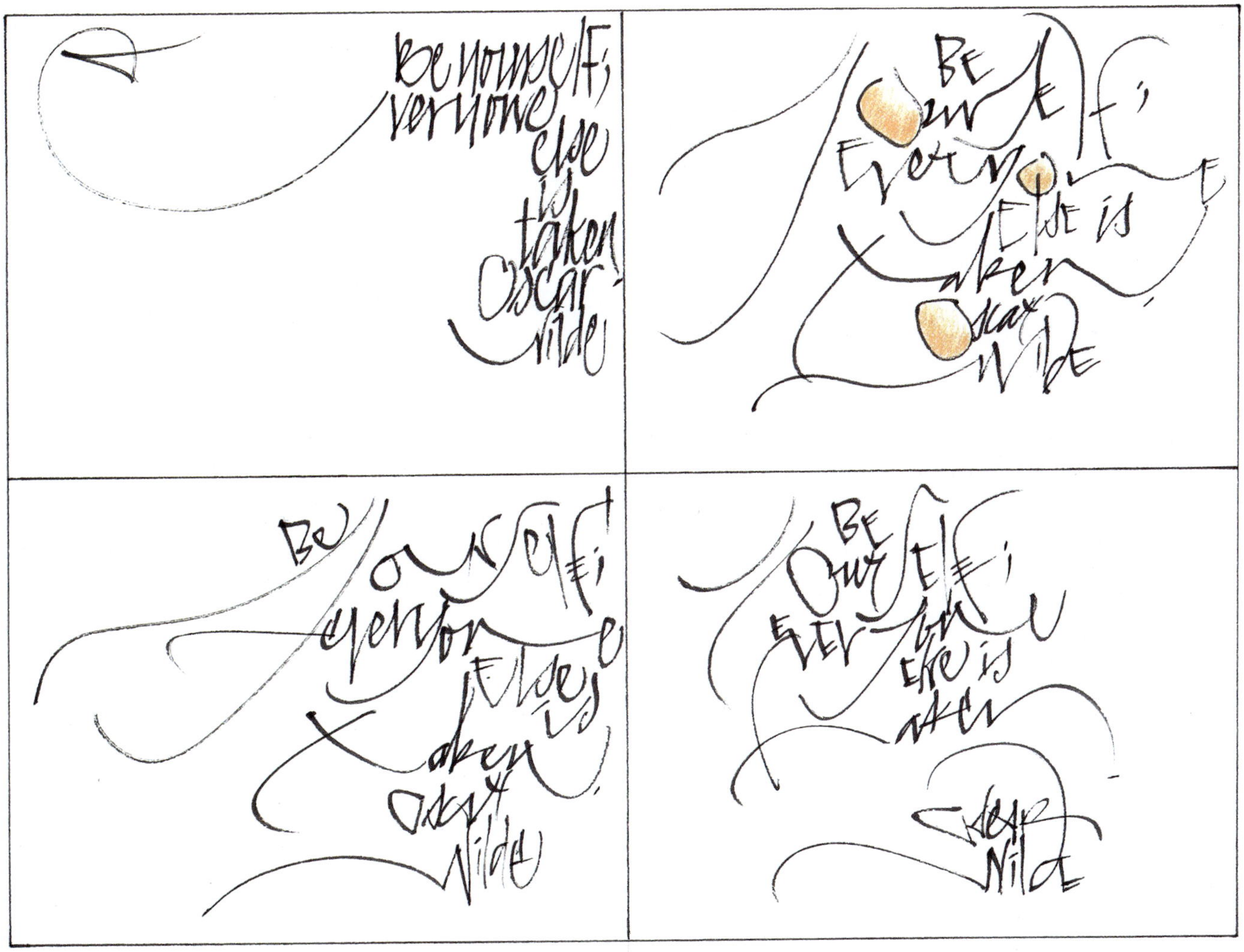

# Project: Go Wilde!

This chapter has focused on developing your eyes so you can explore your calligraphy skills in a more abstract way, incorporating techniques that will help to create deeper dimensions and layers on which you can apply your calligraphy. This is a process that takes time to develop, and this last project is intended to help you continue along this path.

WHAT YOU'LL NEED:

- **Lots of practice paper**
- **Pencil, chalk pencil and eraser**
- **Three 8" x 8" sheets of 140-lb cold-pressed watercolor paper**
- **Sumi ink**
- **Access to a sink**
- **Light table**
- **Either a light gouache or dark ink (depending on what is needed to contrast your background)**
- **A large nib (minimum 5 mm) and small nib (2 mm), or equivalently sized pointed brushes as this project will be done with both sets of tools**
- **Gold or cadmium red gouache**

1. Review the letter sampler you created in Chapter 7, which contains your favorite boundary-pushing letters (see pages 138–139). Choose your favorite *b* and *e*, as you are going to write the word *be* as depicted in the illustration. Practice with pencil first on your practice paper.

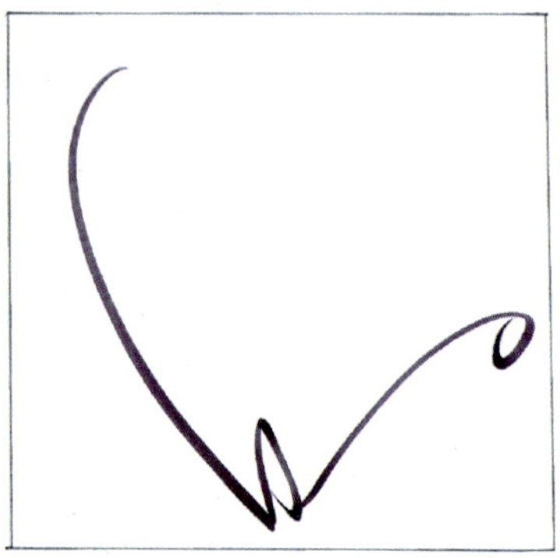

2. Once you're happy, take a scrap piece of watercolor paper and lightly pencil in your *be* as a guideline. Next practice with your large nib. Once you feel comfortable with the movement and letter forms, take one of your 8" x 8" sheets and repeat this same process — first with your pencil, then with the large nib using Sumi ink. Make sure that your *be* is large and creates an open V in the top half of the page, as depicted.

3. Let the ink dry for a minute or so, but make sure that it is still damp. It is now time for the sink bath.

4. Hold your sheet of watercolor paper under a gently running tap (trickling, really) for a couple seconds. Swirl the ink around while keeping an eye out for emerging designs. Be careful not to over-water as you do not want to wash away too much ink but rather create patterns and a marbled effect as your backdrop. This is arguably the trickiest part. As you found out in an earlier exercise, Sumi ink is waterproof, but it needs to set a bit before applying the water. If it has not set enough, much of it will wash away. If it sets too much it will not bleed and create the swirling design you seek. Once you're happy with your design, set your paper aside and let it dry completely.

5. In the V shape created by the *b* and *e*, pencil in your favorite version of the complete Oscar Wilde quote from the previous exercise with a chalk pencil. You will need to use a light table for this step. Tape your favorite template of the completed quote to the light table using your painter's tape. Then position your sink art over it so that

the quote will fit within the V of the *be* and tape it in place. When you're ready to ink your letters, keep an eye to contrast when choosing which ink you'll use for the quote. If the sink wash created a darker background, use a light gouache. If the background is light, use dark ink (I suggest Sumi ink). Using your small nib, ink your letters and set your paper aside to dry.

6. Now for a splash of color! With gold or cadmium red gouache, apply a drop where your eye tells you it would be best. Perhaps in the space of the *b* or another spot that will draw in the eye with interest.

7. Once you have completed your piece, review it critically and assess what worked and what did not. Then take your second sheet of watercolor paper and repeat the steps in the above process using your brushes as you look to improve what you have created. Experiment. Make changes that come to mind after your review.

8. Repeat the process again with your third sheet using whichever tools you prefer — brushes or pens.

The result of this project will be three somewhat similar but also distinct works of art that have helped you develop your design sense as well as honed your technical and calligraphy skills.

And now we can truly say that your possibilities are endless!

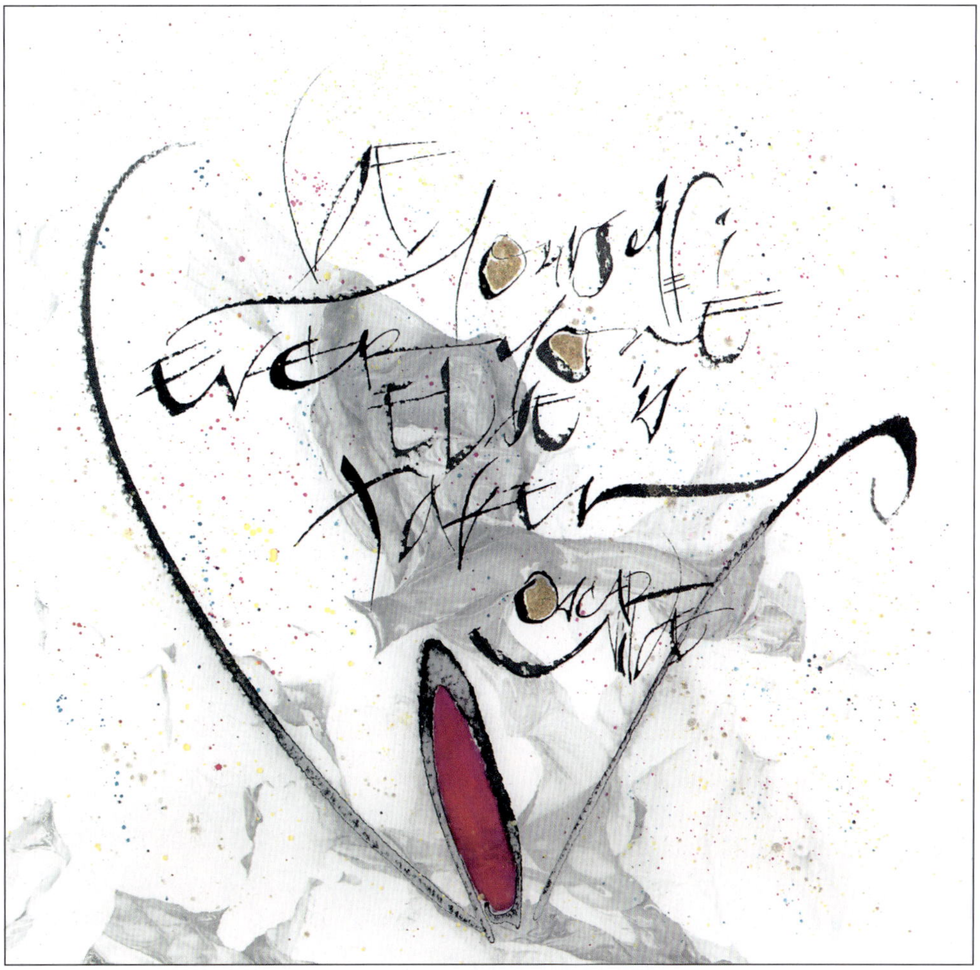

# ONE FINAL WORD

The writing of this book has been an adventure. It has helped me appreciate my chosen craft and the art I've created even more. It has pushed my own skill and art to broader levels of exploration. I am delighted to have shared this with you in the hopes that you find it helpful and encouraging as you unleash your own unique talents.

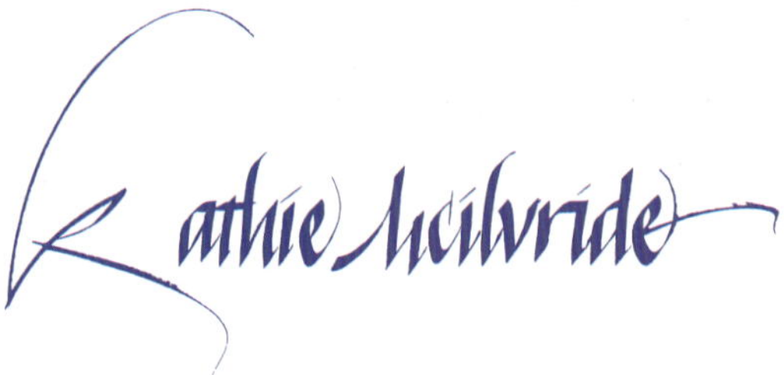

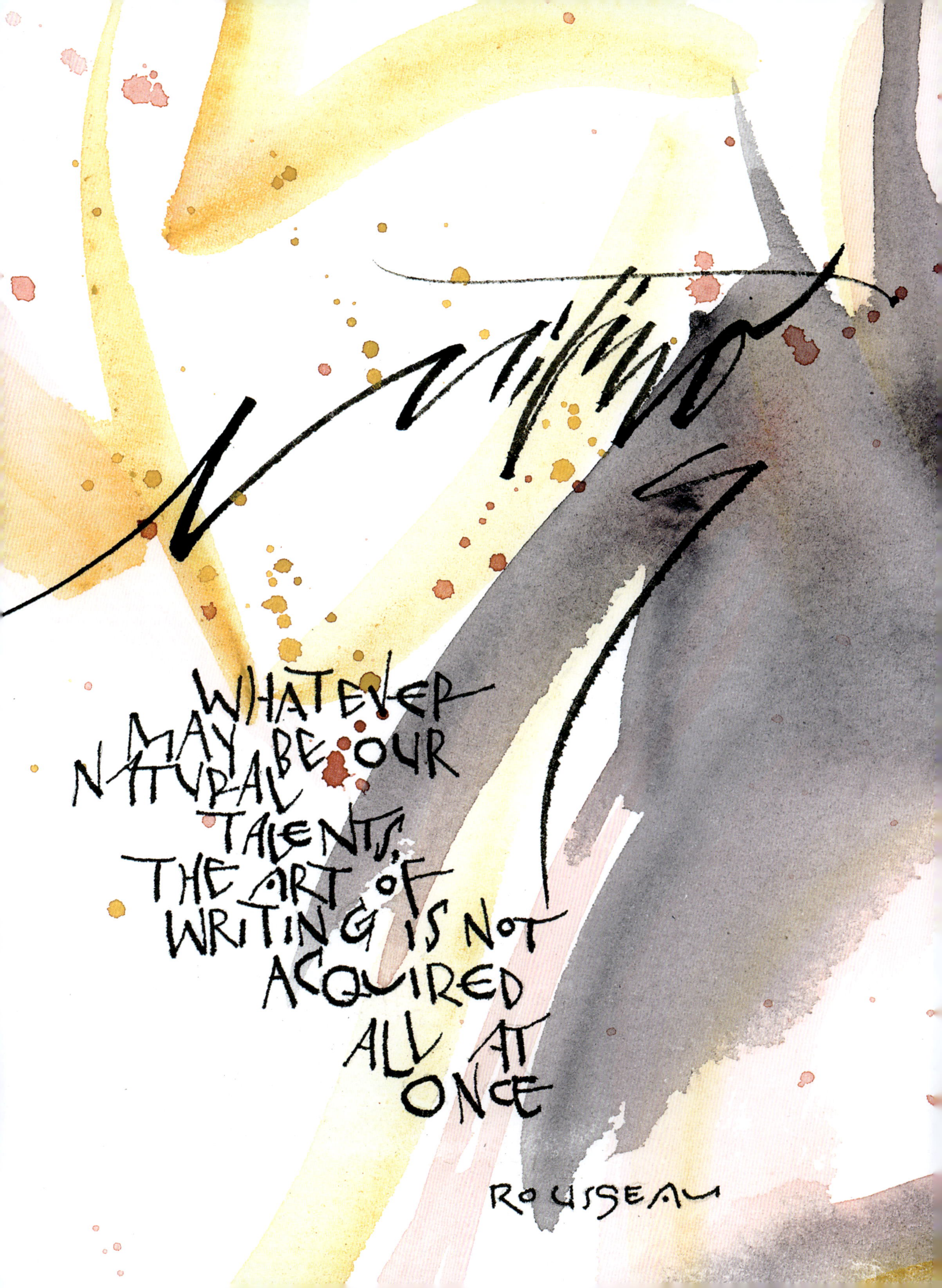
writing
WHATEVER
MAY BE OUR
NATURAL
TALENTS,
THE ART OF
WRITING IS NOT
ACQUIRED
ALL AT
ONCE
ROUSSEAU

# Glossary

**Ascender** – the top portion of a letter (the stem) that uses the space above the waistline.

**Ascender line** – the line that sits above the waistline that determines the height of the ascender.

**Baseline** – the line on which the main body of all letters sit.

**Bleeding** – the effect when ink or paint is applied to paper and instead of the line being crisp, it feathers.

**Bone folder** – a small, blunt-edged tool (pointed at one end and rounded at the other), typically made from bone or hard plastic, that is used to create a crisp crease in paper.

**Capital line** – the line that sits above the waistline and indicates the height that capital (uppercase) letters should reach.

**Cold-pressed watercolor paper** – created using cold rollers, this versatile paper has a slightly textured surface and is highly absorbent, making it useful for blending inks together (bleeding) as well as sink art. (Also see *hot-pressed watercolor paper*.)

**Descender** – the lower portion of a letter (the tail) that uses the space below the baseline.

**Ductus** – the sequence and direction of strokes that form a letter.

**Flourish** – an additional stroke that adds decoration to a letter that extends beyond the initial boundaries of the letter form.

**Gothic (script)** – also known as Black Letter, Old English and Textura, with other variants such as Bâtarde (France), this was the leading script in Europe from the 12th century to the 15th century CE, characterized by its pointy structure that reflected the architecture of the times.

**Gouache** – an opaque water-based paint that is not absorbed by paper as quickly as inks or watercolor paints. This is a good substitute to use if you find that your inks or paints are bleeding on the paper.

**Hot-pressed watercolor paper** – this is a smooth, non-textured paper that is created by rolling the paper out on a hot press. It has a low absorbency that holds color well and is good for detailed work but not good for ink blending.

**Italic (script)** – a method of writing that emerged around 1500 CE during the Italian Renaissance. This script required fewer pen lifts, utilized forward leaning letters and was less laborious than Gothic, thereby lending itself to faster writing with more elegance.

**Italic cursive** – a form of Italic that utilizes more letter joins, thereby minimizing the number of pen lifts for even faster writing. This was the precursor to modern handwriting.

**Light table** – a table or pad that contains a light. This allows you to place your work over a template to provide guidelines for your composition.

**Majuscule letters** – uppercase or capital letters.

**Minuscule letters** – lowercase letters.

**Negative space** – the empty area or background that surrounds the main focus in the art.

**Nib width (NW)** – the size of one square drawn with your pen nib. The size of the square will vary with the size of the nib, but regardless of size it is always referred to as the nib width.

**Noticing** – the word I use for the act of constantly checking your writing as you write to ensure that your spacing is consistent within and between letters, as well as between words.

**Pen angle** – this refers to the angle that the pen nib moves on the page when creating the various strokes of a letter. In traditional Italic, this angle is most commonly 45 degrees but can be adjusted upward or downward to make thinner or thicker strokes, respectively.

**Pen manipulation** – a technique wherein you lift one edge or the other of the pen nib off the page while creating strokes.

**Pen nib** – the component of the pen that contains the ink and applies it to the paper.

**Pointed brush** – a tool used for writing that utilizes a soft, pliable tipped brush as opposed to the less flexible nib.

**Positive space** – the main focus or primary object of interest in a piece of art.

**Reservoir** – the part of the nib that holds the ink. The reservoir can either be on the top or the bottom of the nib.

**Roman (script)** – developed by the Romans in the 6th century BCE, this script consisted of only capital letters and was typically painted and then chiseled.

**Script (or hand)** – refers to free-hand lettering, as opposed to non-hand lettering (such as using a typeset or a font). However, every font was created originally as a script by a calligrapher or lettering artist.

**Serif** – a short stroke that is applied at the beginning of a letter to start the ink flowing freely. It also refers to a short stroke added to complete the main stroke of a letter (i.e., a decorative stroke).

**Sink art** – a technique of rinsing a paper to which waterproof ink has been applied (such as Sumi ink). The application of gently running water before the ink has set allows for movement of the ink to create marbled backdrops to write on. This technique is used for more creative artistic pieces.

**Slope** – also known as slant, this refers to the degree that the letters should lean to the right as they flow across the page.

**Snuggle join** – the point at which two separate strokes meet, creating a right angle. This is a term of my own creation.

**Spacing** – the amount of room within letter strokes and between letters and words as well as between lines. This space should be consistent within traditional Italic.

**Template** – a piece of paper that is lined to display the baseline, waistline and lines for the ascenders, capitals, descenders and slope. The template can also depict the top, bottom and side margins. Templates are also used for design layout.

**Text wove paper** – a creamy, smooth white paper made from cotton, known for its soft texture and versatility, ideal for calligraphy (as the nib does not catch) and bookbinding. This paper is lightweight, strong and ideal if you do not want your inks to blend or bleed.

**Uncial (script)** – a short, round form of lettering that emerged from the Roman letters and was prominent from the 3rd to 8th centuries CE as it could be written on vellum or parchment and was more efficient and less costly than Roman letters.

**Vellum** – a writing surface typically made from calfskin used for manuscripts before the invention of paper. A similar writing surface was parchment, which was made from goat or sheep skin.

**Waistline** – the line that is five nib-widths above the baseline (for traditional Italic) at the top of the X-height.

**Walnut ink** – an ink made from crushed walnut hulls (alternatively it can be made with peat moss) that has a rich golden-brown color tone.

**Whisper join** – the place at which the points of two separate strokes, such as in a letter or number, meet but barely touch. This is a term of my own creation.

**X-height** – the size of the space between the baseline and the waistline. In traditional Italic this is five nib widths in height.

# Supplies

Throughout the years I have developed (through trial and error as well as advice from experienced calligraphers) a studio stocked with a wide variety of products I use with confidence knowing that I can trust them as I work and create. Many of these can be found at any well-equipped art store or ordered online from a specialty calligraphy distributor, such as John Neal Books (johnnealbooks.com) and Paper and Ink Arts (paperinkarts.com). They can also be found and ordered through Amazon and other online suppliers. These supplies are too numerous to detail, so I have provided a list of the ones I used in the writing of this book as a starting point for you as you begin your collection.

## Paper

- **Rhodia (blank white)**
- **Arches Text Wove**
- **Arches cold- and hot-pressed watercolor paper (140-lb.)**
- **BFK Rives**
- **Canson black paper**
- **Good-quality practice pad**

## Inks and Paints

- **Dr. Ph. Martin's (Tech, Watercolor, Iridescent, Bleedproof White)**
- **Moon Palace Sumi ink**
- **Walnut ink (I get the crystals to make this from John Neal Books)**
- **Golden Acrylic Paints**
- **Winsor & Newton, M. Graham & Co. and Schmincke artist-level gouache**
- **Higgins black inks**

## Pens and Nibs

- **Pilot Parallel Pens – there are eight sizes available and they can also support the left-handed calligrapher**
- **Brause, Speedball and Hiro/Tape nibs in multiple sizes**
- **EZ-A Pen – handmade by Alan Ariail (it works in a similar fashion as a Ruling Pen)**

## Pencils

- **Staedtler watercolor colored pencils**
- **Berol Prismacolor colored pencils**
- **Derwent and Stabilo CarbOthello chalk pencils**

## Brushes

- **Pentel Arts Color Brush (this is my "go-to" brush for brush lettering)**
- **Pentel Aquash Water Brush (low cost but a very good brush for brush lettering)**

The expert at anything was once a beginner

— Helen Hayes

- Grumbacher Academy large round brush (780 Round)
- Heinz Jordan Series 681 Needle Point Brush
- Stratford & York Jet brushes (small and large)
- Chinese calligraphy brush (mixed hair tip for flexibility and strength)

## Markers

- Staedtler Mars Graphic 3000 Duo pointed brush markers
- Staedtler Triplus Fineliner markers
- Kuretake Zig Memory System Calligraphy markers
- Sakura Pigma markers (Micron, Brush and Graphic)

The supplies listed here come in multiple sizes, and depending on what part of the book I was writing, paper types, sizes and weights varied, as did the sizes of my nibs, brushes, markers and fine-liners.

My studio has taken over 40 years to develop and contains supplies and materials from many other companies far beyond those used in the creation of this book. It has been a wonderful journey collecting them. It takes time to stock up, but it is a lot of fun!

# Thank-you


## Lionel

For giving me this wonderful opportunity.

## Julie

For having the patience to decipher my scribbles.

## Hartley

For cleverly solving the design puzzles my work presented.

## Lynne

For being the instigator behind this whole project and for always having my back.

## Andrew

For creating a schedule that allowed me to walk my dog and my horse daily.

## CGM

To all my dear friends in the Calligraphers' Guild of Manitoba, who I have grown to love. You have helped me develop as an artist through your regular requests for me to teach, forcing me to constantly explore and expand.

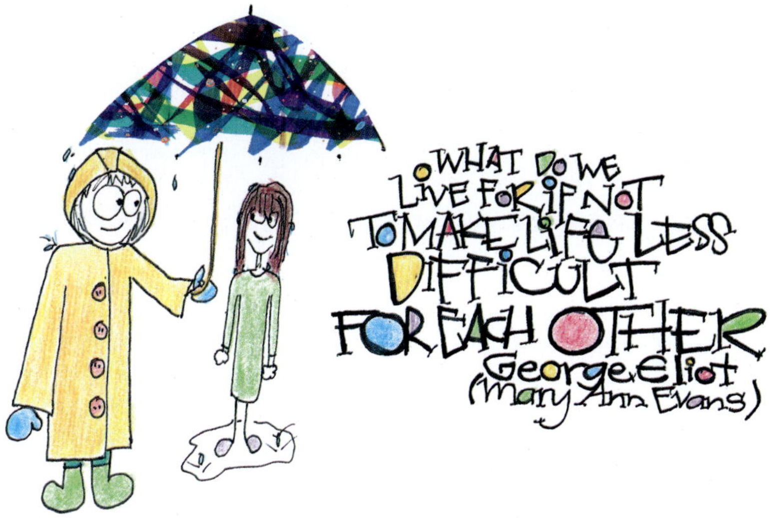


# Lauren

Who, despite her intense grief, never failed to support and encourage me every day.

# Myrtle

Who has been such a delightfully encouraging friend, when I would take my one morning off each week to go to the Glenboro Cat Rescue.

# Vanessa

For teaching me how to love.

# Charles

For teaching me how to laugh.
Love and Laughter are crucial elements of this book

# Brian

Where to begin. To my self-appointed project manager, who I only had to fire twice. For nightly martinis, supper and morning coffee, not to mention endless support and encouragement (and with some good ideas) despite my incessant whining. Who worked so hard doing everything while I worked on this book, even to the point of stuffing his own Christmas stocking.

# ABOUT THE AUTHOR

**Kathie McIlvride** has a passion for dance that transformed into a love of calligraphy. The passion for rhythm and movement evolved into a lifetime of study, discovery and play with lettering. Creating card designs and workshops in order to share this playful delight is a favorite endeavor. Kathie now works out of her century-old stone farmhouse studio in rural Manitoba, dividing her time between horses, gardens and art.

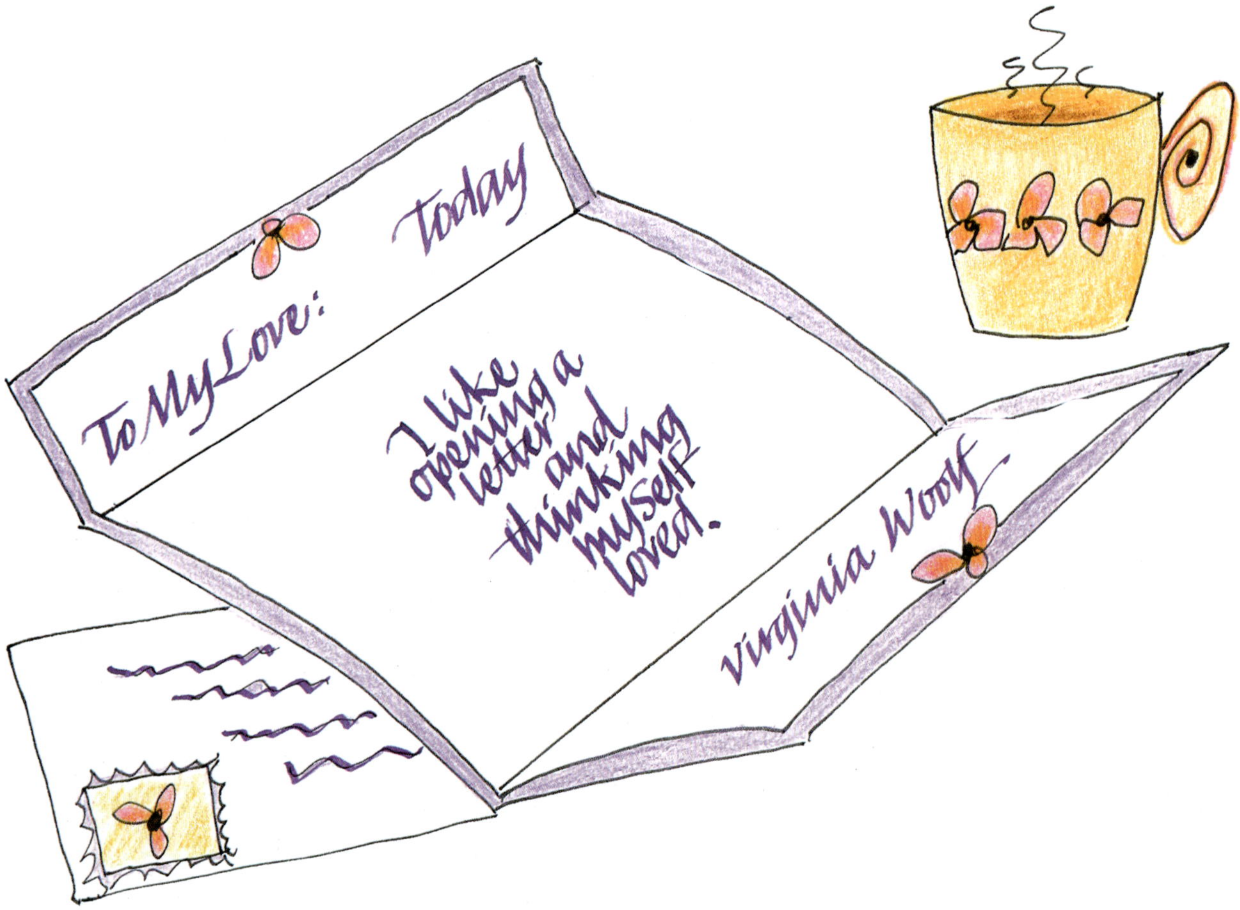